Genocide: A Thematic Approach

Genocide: A Thematic Approach

Thomas Earl Porter and John Cox

ANTHEM PRESS

Anthem Press
An imprint of Wimbledon Publishing Company
www.anthempress.com

This edition first published in UK and USA 2026
by ANTHEM PRESS
75–76 Blackfriars Road, London SE1 8HA, UK
or PO Box 9779, London SW19 7ZG, UK
and
244 Madison Ave #116, New York, NY 10016, USA

First published in the UK and USA by Anthem Press in 2025

© 2026 Thomas Earl Porter and John Cox

The author asserts the moral right to be identified as the author of this work.

All rights reserved. Without limiting the rights under copyright reserved above, no part of this publication may be reproduced, stored or introduced into a retrieval system, or transmitted, in any form or by any means (electronic, mechanical, photocopying, recording or otherwise), without the prior written permission of both the copyright owner and the above publisher of this book.

British Library Cataloguing-in-Publication Data
A catalogue record for this book is available from the British Library.

Library of Congress Cataloging-in-Publication Data: 2024949541
A catalog record for this book has been requested.

ISBN-13: 978-1-83999-839-3 (Pbk)
ISBN-10: 1-83999-839-3 (Pbk)

Cover credit: Creative Commons

This title is also available as an eBook.

CONTENTS

Preface		vii
Acknowledgments		ix
Foreword		xi
Introduction		1
Chapter One	What *Should* Be the Definition of Genocide?	13
Chapter Two	"Ethnic Cleansing" Is Genocide, Too	39
Chapter Three	Racism and Genocide	71
Chapter Four	Sexual Violence as Genocide	103
Chapter Five	Genocides of Political Groups	123
Chapter Six	Genocides of Social Groups	151
Chapter Seven	Empire and State-Building Through Genocide	179
Conclusion		203
Bibliography		219
Index		231

PREFACE

Education either functions as an instrument which is used to facilitate the integration of the younger generation into the logic of the present system and bring about conformity or it becomes the practice of freedom, the means by which men and women deal critically and creatively with reality and discover how to participate in the transformation of their world.
—Richard Schaull, Preface to Paolo Freire's *Pedagogy of the Oppressed*

ACKNOWLEDGMENTS

Thomas Earl Porter would like to take this opportunity to express his gratitude for the institutional support that permitted him reassigned time to work on this book. In particular, the North Carolina Agricultural & Technical State University Reassigned Time for Faculty Committee that evaluated the book proposal and forwarded a positive recommendation to the Provost. He is deeply indebted to all who made this work possible.

John Cox thanks his colleagues at the International Network of Genocide Scholars (INoGS) and the International Association of Genocide Scholars (IAGS) who provided helpful feedback at recent conferences. He is also grateful to his UNCC colleagues for the support and feedback, in particular, Emek Ergun, Ella Fratantuono, Oscar de la Torre, and Caitlin Schroering.

Both authors also wish to acknowledge the patience and forbearance of their respective wives—Kumbirai Khosa and Louise Clark—during the time it took to complete this book. Finally, we would be remiss if we did not thank the acquisitions and editing team at Anthem Press. We especially want to thank Jebaslin Hephzibah for her guidance, support, and encouragement throughout the interminably long process it took to bring this book to the light of day.

FOREWORD

How much genocidal behavior are you willing to accept in your society? How much do you accept already without realizing it? What should you do about it?

I am thinking about these questions after reading *Genocide: A Thematic Approach*, which weaves together so many cases of genocide into a coherent story that it is impossible for me not to have these thoughts. In this book, Professors Thomas Earl Porter and John Cox help us see the connections between the Nazis' race wars and Native American genocides, and the links to these cases with genocides against Muslim peoples in the Russian empire, the genocide of the Rohingya people in Rakhine state in Myanmar, and the complexities of the ongoing conflict in Palestine. In each, we learn why these histories matter, as the authors remind us of the lived consequences of these genocides that persist for generations.

Reading this book has also made me think about the parallel histories of the United States and the Russian Empire (and then the Soviet Union, and now the Russian Federation), which are often taught to students in the United States as if they were contrasting histories. When reading this book, it is impossible *not* to notice the similar colonial histories of both states and the genocidal aspects of both societies' experience of nation-building. The book brings anti-Black and anti-Native American genocides in the United States in the nineteenth and twentieth centuries into focus and looks at how these histories continue to have consequences today, underpinning complicated histories of conflict. We learn that this is not unlike the long histories of genocides in Russia committed against Chechen, Ingush, Circassian, and Tatar peoples. In both the United States and Russian (and Soviet) societies, the groups that benefited from these genocidal conflicts did not, and do not, think of the oppression and violence as genocide, or even as conflict.

Porter and Cox help us realize, therefore, that each genocide is more than just an occasional horrific episode in world history. Genocide is quite common, often committed in the name of progress, civilization, society-building, or state-building. This is how, many times, across history, and in our world today, people come to believe that oppression and death can be a good thing, something life-affirming. If you read between the lines, you can see that Porter and Cox are also showing us just how often genocide has been committed in the name of peace, security, and justice.

For example, almost a quarter-century ago, Putin justified the Russian war in Chechnya by citing US President Clinton's invasion of Haiti as a precedent. As US presidents justified US wars in Iraq and Libya as necessary to prevent genocide, so too did Putin use "genocide prevention" as an excuse to invade Ukraine in 2014 and 2022. In all these wars, the head of state for imperial belligerents (i.e., presidents Bush, Clinton, Bush, and Obama in the

United States and Putin in the Russian Federation) have positioned their countries as the *victims* in these conflicts and then framed their side's imperial wars as necessary for preventing mass atrocity crimes and genocide in the countries their armies invaded.

This is a book that does not attempt to hide behind a story of good guys versus bad guys, and it forces us to think critically about our values and our commitments. I think this is important because, if we want to make peace and prevent war and genocide, then it does us no good to think about the world simply in terms of "good" guys and "bad" guys (Feierstein, 2011). We have to understand why powerful states go to war, why so many citizens of those states support their leaders, why so many people in societies think that violence is necessary for peace and, most importantly, why so many people who don't support violence have such a hard time convincing their neighbors and leaders *not* to kill. This book can help us get there.

—Douglas Irvin-Erickson
Washington, DC

INTRODUCTION

The more we are able to understand how different societies have transformed their neighbors and fellow citizens from people into objects, the more we know of the specific circumstances that led to each episode of mass torture and mass murder, the better we will understand the darker side of our own human nature.
—Anne Applebaum, 2004

Why This Book?

The lessons of the Holocaust taught to schoolchildren all over the globe as a cautionary tale of the evil that human beings are capable of perpetrating on other human beings, are generally well known. Most students who register for a course on genocide assume that it will focus primarily on the violence visited upon Jews by the Nazis. The Holocaust is often the only genocide with which they are familiar. Many of them have read Elie Wiesel's moving and eloquent book *Night* in high school. Some others might be dimly aware of another genocide somewhere in Africa, perhaps from the movie *Hotel Rwanda*. The oft-repeated warning of these "lessons" is that we must "never again" allow such appalling atrocities to take place. Yet, following the defeat of the murderous Nazi regime, the five remaining decades of the twentieth century the world saw numerous other genocides perpetrated.

In Asia, we witnessed a deliberate famine in Mao's China that killed 30–50 million peasants, the slaughter of half a million Indonesian communists by their own government, which then invaded East Timor and killed hundreds of thousands there, and the Khmer Rouge's horrific genocide of their own—as well as other groups—in Cambodia. In Europe, there was the Serbian genocide in the Balkans and, finally, in Africa, one of the worst genocides in history—Rwanda. Sad to say, even this depressing list is far from complete. Since the beginning of the new millennium, genocides have continued to occur. We have seen still more millions of deaths caused by state-sponsored killings around the globe. A genocide of Africans by paramilitaries in league with the government of Sudan in its Darfur region, the murder of Yazidi (an ethno-religious minority in parts of the Middle East) males and the sexual enslavement of Yazidi women by the so-called Islamic State, or ISIS, have all taken place in the last two decades. Then, there are also the ongoing cases of the assault by the Burmese junta on the Rohingya people through a brutal program of "ethnic cleansing" in Myanmar, the genocide of the Uyghurs in China, and the possible genocides of Ukrainians by Russians and Palestinians by Israelis. It should be evident to all that genocide is a real and ongoing problem for humankind.

Like most people, you probably think of the Holocaust when you hear the word "genocide" and equate it with the Nazis' mass murder of a specific group of people—Jews—with the goal being the extermination of that victimized group. Raphael Lemkin, the Polish-Jewish legal scholar who invented the word "genocide" and first used it in his essential book *Axis Rule in Occupied Europe: Laws of Occupation, Analysis of Government Proposals for Redress* (published in 1944), considered mass killing to be just one of many types of an organized, multi-faceted campaign against a "nation" or "ethnic group" with the goal of the "destruction of [the] essential foundations of the life" of those groups. This "coordinated plan of different actions" was a process designed to "annihilate" a people (Lemkin 2008, 79), leaving no energies for a cultural or national life. Ultimately, it would lead to the tragic loss of that people's unique culture to the world, as "Our whole cultural heritage is a product of the contributions of all peoples" (Lemkin 1945, 42). Indeed, perpetrators do almost inevitably resort to mass violence, or at least the threat of violence. This violence is usually rooted in conflicts such as war, revolution, and counter-revolution, and it always involves the killing of unarmed and defenseless civilians. But to kill *a people*, you do not necessarily have to kill *people*, you need only destroy the social connections and cultural bonds that make them a people. This destruction of culture is precisely what is happening to the Uyghurs.

In Xinjiang province, China, hundreds of thousands of Uyghurs, a predominantly Muslim, ethnic Turkic people in a nation that is 91 percent Han Chinese, are currently imprisoned in concentration camps where they are tortured or forced to labor while supposedly being reeducated. They are forbidden to speak their language, while many Uyghur women have had forcible abortions performed on them, been sterilized, or been forced to use mandatory birth control. In addition, many thousands of Uyghur children have been torn from their parents and placed into so-called boarding schools where they are subjected to Chinese indoctrination. All this is clearly part of an effort to destroy their culture and therefore the essence of the Uyghurs as a people.

Although all of the methods of violence described in the 1948 United Nations' (UN)—the world organization that emerged from the ruins of World War II and is charged with maintaining peace and security and fostering international cooperation to solve economic, social, cultural or humanitarian problems—Convention on the Prevention and Punishment of the Crime of Genocide (hereafter simply the 1948 Convention) have been perpetrated by the Chinese government on the Uyghurs, it was not until the last full day of the first Trump presidency in early 2021 that the United States formally declared this repression a genocide. In 2022, the United States implemented the Uyghur Forced Labor Prevention Act, which forbids the importation of goods made in Xinjiang province. Many scholars and journalists continue to qualify their assessment of the atrocities committed against the Uyghurs by affixing the adjective "cultural" to "genocide," as if the absence of mass killing lessens the destructive impact of the Chinese government's policies on that people. Still others refer to the concept of "ethnocide" as if that too is somehow a different phenomenon altogether from genocide, even though Lemkin used the term as a synonym for his new word (Figure I.1).

As of 2022, the United States joined a half dozen other nations in declaring the forced expulsion of the Rohingya people from their homes in Myanmar to be a genocide as well.

Figure I.1 The plight of the Uyghurs has aroused worldwide attention and condemnation, 2022. Uyghur detainees listening to speeches in a camp in Lop County, Xinjiang, 2017. https://en.wikipedia.org/wiki/File:Xinjiang_Re-education_Camp_Lop_County.jpg

Myanmar is the name used there since 1989 by the military leadership for the country formerly known as Burma; that renaming is a contested issue and the US government continues to refer to the country as Burma. Names and terms carry significant meaning. Many observers continue to refer to the Burmese military campaign of murder, rape, and terror as an "ethnic cleansing." We will cover this murderous attack more fully later in the chapter devoted to ethnic cleansing as genocide. We mention it here only to underscore our belief that the use of terms such as "ethnic cleansing" and "cultural" genocide or "ethnocide" wrongly uses the type of violence employed or the death toll exacted by the actors as a yardstick to measure and thus differentiate between what are simply different *methods* of genocide.

Also on March 4, 2022, the United Nations' Human Rights Council established the Independent International Commission of Inquiry on Ukraine with an initial one-year mandate. The Commission's charge was to "investigate all alleged violations and abuses of human rights and violations of international humanitarian law, and related crimes resulting from the Russian Federation's aggression against Ukraine […] and to make recommendations, in particular on accountability measures, all with a view to ending impunity and ensuring accountability" (press release from the Office of the High Commissioner, UN Human Rights Council). The Human Rights Council resolution condemned Russia's unprovoked attack on Ukraine a week earlier and the war crimes and human rights violations committed by its troops while demanding Russia's immediate withdrawal from Ukraine on a vote of 32 in favor, 2 against, and 13 abstentions. This was an important step by the international community as this vote, unlike those proposed in the Security Council, the United Nations' body with the primary responsibility for maintaining world peace and security, was not subject to a veto by any of the Permanent Five (P-5) members. The United Nations Security Council (UNSC) is made up of 15 members, five of which—the United States, Russia, China, Britain, and France, are permanent, and ten are elected for two-year terms from the General Assembly of all the other nations' permanent representatives—can unilaterally veto any resolution put forward.

The Commission released its report one year later, on March 16, 2023. The report cited incidents of murder, rape, and torture of civilians but the authors said there was no direct proof of genocidal intent—although the matter warranted further investigation. The head of the investigation team, Erik Mose, stated that the commission had "not found that there has been a genocide within Ukraine. This said, we are following all kinds of evidence within this area, and we have noted that there are some aspects which may raise questions with respect to that crime [genocide]. For instance, certain utterances in Russian media which are targeting groups." The Commission did state that the illegal transfer of children from Ukraine by Russian authorities constituted "a war crime" (*Euronews*, "Latest News Bulletin, Morning," March 16, 2023). The very next day, March 17, 2023, the International Criminal Court (ICC)—a permanent tribunal established by the UN to investigate and prosecute individuals charged with the crime of genocide, crimes against humanity, war crimes, and the crime of aggression—issued an arrest warrant for the Russian President Vladimir Putin for that crime. The Court also issued an arrest warrant for the person in charge of this nefarious operation, Maria Lvova-Belova, the so-called Presidential Commissioner for Children's Rights in the Russian Federation. It is highly likely that Putin will also be charged with the intentional targeting of civilian infrastructure without military purpose—another war crime under the Geneva Conventions. But since Russia withdrew its signature on the Rome Statute that established the ICC and the Court does not try suspects *in absentia*, it is also highly unlikely that Putin will ever stand trial.

There is also no doubt that Vladimir Putin unleashed this war in Ukraine and therefore is also guilty of the crime of aggression. Russia's invasion of Ukraine has also led to the rape of untold numbers of women, while men, both civilian and prisoners of war, have been tortured and killed. In addition, thousands of Ukrainians have died due to the indiscriminate, and often deliberate, shelling, and bombing of civilian areas and infrastructure. These are all war crimes. The Russians have illegally annexed four different regions of Ukraine—Donetsk, Luhansk, Kherson, and Zaporozhe—and deliberately set out to make them Russian. The Ukrainians who have remained in these Russian-controlled areas of their country must carry Russian Federation passports, in itself a violation of the UN's 1948 Universal Declaration of Human Rights—adopted the very next day after the adoption of the UN's Genocide Convention—that states "no one shall arbitrarily be deprived of their nationality." The occupiers have removed all Ukrainian-language books from schools and libraries and destroyed Ukrainian cultural monuments and artifacts. Ukrainian language street signs have been replaced by Russian ones. After three years of war, several million Ukrainians have crossed the border into Russia. Many did so voluntarily in hopes of transiting through that country to Europe; however, between one and one and a half million were forcibly relocated to

Russia—in itself, another war crime under the 1949 Geneva Convention that is also included as part of the Rome Statute that set up the International Criminal Court.

The arrest warrants issued against Putin and his accomplices are for violating the universally agreed upon prohibition of the forced transfer of populations during war. At least a quarter million of these forcibly relocated Ukrainians were children. The Russian government has transferred many hundreds, if not thousands, of these children to live with Russian families or in state orphanages. In addition, thousands of other children have been taken from their parents in occupied Ukraine—according to the Russians this is supposedly for their safety, as there is, after all, a war there—and sent to special camps. There they are indoctrinated with pro-Russian propaganda and often detained indefinitely. In the April 13, 2023, online edition of the Russian news-reporting agency *TASS*, Russian officials acknowledged the transfer of 2,161 alleged orphans to Russia from Russian occupied territories in Ukraine while the Ukrainians claim the number is over 19,000, as of February 2024. Even those allowed to remain with their families in the illegally annexed regions of Ukraine will still be educated in the official history of Russia and in the Russian language. The plan is for all these children to be stripped of their Ukrainian identity—an identity Putin denies even exists—and instead become Russians. This also constitutes genocide under Article III of the 1948 Convention, "forcibly transferring children of the group to another group." On April 27, 2023, the Parliamentary Assembly of the Council of Europe declared that the deportation and forcible transfers of Ukrainian children to Russia was in fact genocide (Figure I.2).

Figure I.2 Many Russians, within Russia and those living elsewhere, oppose the invasion and war in Ukraine. March 2022 antiwar demonstration. https://commons.wikimedia.org/wiki/File:02022_1234_Russian_diaspora_protests_against_war_in_Ukraine.jpg

Moreover, as Erik Mose of the Human Rights Council Independent Commission noted above, the architects of these crimes have spoken openly about their genocidal intentions. In an article entitled "What Should Russia do with Ukraine?" published on April 3, 2022 in the state-controlled newspaper *RIA Novosti*, Kremlin propagandist Timofei Sergeitsev called for the extermination of a large part of the Ukrainian population with the remainder needing to be re-educated to be "de-Nazified." Russian soldiers have been hunting down specific Ukrainians by name—government officials, journalists, religious leaders, etc. in their campaign to supposedly de-Nazify the country. The duration of this process, according to Sergeitsev, "can in no way be less than one generation, which must be born, grow up, and reach maturity under the conditions of de-Nazification." Sergeitsev has since been charged by the Ukrainian judiciary under Article III (c) of the Genocide Convention with direct and public incitement to commit genocide. Perversely, the Russians have claimed that the Ukrainians themselves have committed genocide in the Donbas region upon its Russian-speaking persons—though many people in this area are ethnic Ukrainians who speak Russian. In 2022, the International Court of Justice ruled in favor of Ukraine to refute these unfounded Russian allegations of genocide against ethnic Russians in the Donbas. The question, however, remains, do all these heinous atrocities perpetrated by the Russians on the Ukrainian people since their invasion of that country in February 2022 rise to the level of genocide, supposedly the "crime of crimes?"

There is also the ongoing crisis in Palestine to consider. Much of the world is outraged at the disproportionate response of Prime Minister Benjamin Netanyahu's government to the barbaric, inexcusable, and indeed "genocidal" attack by *Hamas* on Israelis on October 7, 2023; the Israelis have responded by indiscriminately bombing the Gaza Strip, where *Hamas* militants hold sway. Tens of thousands of Palestinians, at least 20,000 of them children and 46,000 total, have perished as we complete this Introduction in December 2024. When the Israeli Defenses Forces (IDF) began their sweep of the territory they forced more than a million Palestinians to leave their homes—out of a population of 2.3 million. They have attacked schools, hospitals, mosques, and dwellings using the excuse that *Hamas* militants are congregating there in order to use civilians as human shields to continue their attacks on Israelis. This is a war crime on the part of *Hamas*: however, the indiscriminate bombings of civilians in Gaza constitute grave war crimes, as do the forcible dislocation of that population, the interdiction of supplies of food and medicine, and the deliberate destruction of civilian infrastructure that can only lead to more misery and death. Not only are these war crimes, it is plausibly also genocide. And leading Israeli politicians and officials have not been shy in expressing genocidal sentiments and declaring that all Gazans are the enemy. "It's an entire nation out there that is responsible. This rhetoric about civilians not aware, not involved, it's absolutely not true" declared Israeli President Isaac Herzog in October 2023. A few days earlier, Minister of Defense Yoav Gallant stated, "I have ordered a complete siege on the Gaza Strip. There will be no electricity, no food, no fuel, everything is closed [...] We are fighting human animals and we are acting accordingly" (Cox 2024). These are representative of many dozens of other such statements by top officials since the assault on Gaza began.

On December 29, 2023, South Africa filed a complaint with the International Court of Justice charging the Israeli government with genocide, the failure to prevent genocide, and incitement to commit genocide. South Africa asserts that the acts "by Israel are genocidal in character, as they are committed with the requisite specific intent [...] to destroy Palestinians in Gaza as a part of the broader Palestinian national, racial, and ethnical group" (*The Guardian*, January 4, 2024). On January 26, 2024, the Court ruled that although it could not prejudge the merits of the complaint made by South Africa at this time, the case is in fact a "plausible" one and will be further investigated and eventually adjudicated. The ICJ did, however, issue an order for Israel to "take all measures in its power including the rescinding of relevant orders, of restrictions and/or of prohibitions to prevent [...]" the possibility of genocide (January 26, 2024, Order, Application of the Convention of the Prevention and Punishment of the Crime of Genocide in the Gaza Strip, South Africa v. Israel). This Order, as with any order from the ICJ, is legally binding on *all* member states of the United Nations but can only be enforced through action by the UN Security Council. The Court stopped short of ordering, as South Africa had requested, an immediate cease-fire. As a signatory to the 1948 Convention Israel is already required to prevent the very acts being committed by the IDF in Gaza such as killing members of the group, causing serious bodily or mental harm to members of the group, deliberately inflicting conditions of life calculated to bring about its physical destruction in whole or in part, and so on. But by calling on Israel to *prevent* the possibility of genocide, the Court also implied that genocide *was* possible, especially considering the incendiary remarks made by Israeli officials. Israel must ensure that its forces do not commit any acts that fall within the scope of the Convention and immediately allow humanitarian aid to be distributed to the Palestinians. The Court expects the Israeli government to submit a detailed report on the measures they have taken to comply with this order. But with full backing of the world's only superpower, the United States, it is likely that Israel will disregard the ICC and continue to act with impunity.

In the three-quarters of a century since the founding of the state of Israel and the initial attack on Israelis by the forces of the Arab League in 1948 that was meant to forestall the establishment of the state of Israel, Arabs and Israelis have fought five different wars—1956, 1967, 1973, 1982, and 2006—that have cost hundreds of thousands of lives and embittered people on both sides. The continued illegal seizure of lands and property in the West Bank by Israeli "settlers"—in violation of international law and with the support of the Israeli government—has only made this situation more difficult to resolve. Israel certainly has the right of self-defense, but the same question posed about Russia in Ukraine can be asked here as well; are their military operations in Gaza a case of genocide? And if not, aren't the war crimes and crimes against humanity in both cases sufficiently heinous to warrant international condemnation and the prosecution of those involved in the planning and execution of these attacks? If these instances of the slaughter of innocent people are "only" war crimes or crimes against humanity, why is there such a hierarchy of misery and suffering in International Humanitarian Law?

We will therefore begin the first chapter by assessing just what constitutes genocide in the legal sense before we move on to a consideration of what the definition of genocide *should* be. There is, in fact, a legal distinction between "genocide" and war crimes and crimes against humanity. The high legal bar of "intent" to "destroy" the collectivity "as such"—and only national, ethnical, racial and religious ones at that—on the part of the perpetrators must be met before we can call them genocidists. You will see how this legal requirement has been called into question by both scholars and jurists who hold that "sustained, purposeful actions"—inferences from facts easily discernible at first glance—should be sufficient to hold genocidists to account. It is this legal precept of "intent"—the mental element that coincides with the actions of the genocidists on the ground—in the 1948 Convention that supposedly differentiates genocide, the "crime of crimes," from "only" war crimes or crimes against humanity that, as we will see are the same types of cruel actions directed against many different groups with the aim to be rid of them altogether one way or another. To be sure, we will examine some instances of atrocious war crimes in order to juxtapose them with case studies of genocide where the "intent" *was* in fact to destroy the collectivity "as such" in one way or another as required by the 1948 Convention.

We will also examine many of the genocides that have been committed throughout the past century and a half of world history to put them into thematic and structural contexts to explain better *why* they happened. This book, in exploring the themes of Racism, Sexual Violence, Ethnic Cleansing, Genocides of Political, and then, Social Groups, and Empire and State Building through Genocide, makes no claim to be a comprehensive study of the topic. It will become evident to the reader that, as a type of conflict, genocide embodies many forms and employs many different methods of violence. The case studies discussed in the various chapters are representative of those types, but they usually illustrate more than one aspect of the phenomenon. Most of them could reasonably be included in two, three, or even four of the chapters in which we explore the methods of targeted group violence that all had as their end goal the forcible destruction of that group.

For example, Stalin's deliberate starvation of millions of peasants—Ukrainian, Russian, Kazakh—is included in the chapter on "Genocides of Social Groups" because the regime's goal was at least partly, if not mostly, the destruction of the peasantry—a social class—as an independent collectivity in the Soviet Union. The prior wholesale murder of Ukrainian writers, poets, religious leaders, and the like, however, fits better in the chapter on "Genocides of Political Groups" where we also discuss Stalin's other murders of political opponents such as the "Great Purge" of the late 1930s. We argue still further, as did Raphael Lemkin, that there was another sinister reason behind Stalin's collectivization campaign and his murders of Ukrainian intellectuals and priests—the destruction of the very soul of the Ukrainian people. These efforts were supposedly justified by pseudo-Marxist rhetoric that we will briefly examine in order to understand the ostensible rationale behind these actions—not that motive matters one bit as far as the victims are concerned. Stalin's use of these different methods of violence—executions, exile into inhospitable regions, and the deliberate use of mass starvation—were part of a deliberate process that stretched back well before the 1917 Bolshevik Revolution.

Here, we see history as a prologue, with Putin continuing a long-standing Russian national project to destroy Ukrainian identity. Stalin's other genocides, such as the wholesale removal of entire peoples from their ancestral lands and exile to Siberia and Central Asia, will be addressed in Chapter Two.

Adolf Hitler also had an ideology, really more a collection of irrational grievances and racial and biological obsessions, which helped motivate his military conquests and subsequent genocide against Jews, Sinti and Roma, Slavs, and others in an effort to remake all of Eastern Europe demographically. This campaign just as easily could also been put in several different chapters. Motivated by a racist pseudo-biological ideology, Hitler and his underlings attempted to use what some scholars would call "ethnic cleansing"—albeit in an extreme form—to create a colonial empire in the western part of Russia. We see him putting this racist ideology into effect in the colonizing effort to create *Lebensraum* ("living space") for Germany. We will look at the method employed by the Nazis in the East and compare it to the American expansion to the West—America's so-called "Manifest Destiny"—in the nineteenth century. Therefore, we placed what Raphael Lemkin considered a genocide not only against Jews but also the Sinti and Roma ("gypsies") and Slavs in Chapter Two. Hitler's better-known genocidal attempt to exterminate European Jewry entirely is included in the chapter on racism, despite the obvious fact that Jews are not a racial group—though they were to the Nazis.

In the case of the Serb assault on Bosnian Muslims (1992–95), the intentional, genocidal rape of Muslim women was one of the methods—besides the massacre of Muslim men and boys at Srebrenica—employed to destroy that collectivity and this horrific episode is included in the chapter on "Sexual Violence," but the effort to build a "Greater Serbia" itself we discuss in more detail in Chapter Seven. While specific motives in and of themselves are not important—what *is* important is that a group is being destroyed—the methods used often overlap. For example, in East Pakistan (now Bangladesh) in 1971, West Pakistan attempted to murder all the members of a political group, the separatist Awami League, who had just won an election. But they also tried to destroy the Bengali ethnic group, despite being fellow Muslims, through a campaign of mass rape while simultaneously "ethnically cleansing" the region of 10 million members of the Hindu religious group. We have decided to discuss this entire effort to destroy the essential foundations of life for all of these human groups as designated by the genocidists in Chapter Five because that category of human beings is unprotected in the 1948 Convention and has been used to give cover to genocidists claiming they are "only" defending their state from civil war, armed rebellion, or domestic unrest (Figure I.3).

As we will see, this same rationale was also deliberately employed by other countries to justify their failure to intervene to prevent genocide—for example, as an excuse for inaction during the worst phases of the Rwandan genocide. While the study of these individual episodes of organized violence against specific groups is essential for an understanding of this subject, it is only through a comparative approach that we will be able to distinguish not just what is specific and distinctive in each historical case study, but more importantly what is common and inherent to all of them. This, then, would be genocide. Sadly, the commonalities all involve a deliberate decision to use violence

Figure I.3 In 2013, mass protests erupted demanding justice for the criminals responsible for the 1971 genocide. https://commons.wikimedia.org/wiki/File:Shahbag_Projonmo_Square_Uprising_Demanding_Death_Penalty_of_the_War_Criminals_of_1971_in_Bangladesh_07.jpg

to inflict suffering on civilians to remove them from a specific territory, usually under the cover of a conventional or civil war disguised as the suppression of domestic unrest. Targeted violence upon a selected victim group to destroy that collectivity is part of each of the examples of genocide we will examine.

Like most of you, we would agree that genocide, a form of conflict that usually occurs during war, is any attempt to kill defenseless individuals based on their perceived membership in *any* group that has been specifically identified by the perpetrators for destruction. This, of course, also describes war. War and genocide have many things in common, such as identifying an enemy, drawing up and implementing a plan of attack, and carrying out the plan to destroy an enemy. Lemkin believed genocide was different (and worse) than war. He wrote that war had formerly been "directed against sovereigns and armies" but what he was describing in *Axis Rule* was a war "against subjects and civilians" (Lemkin 2008, 80). Modern warfare, however, does unfortunately often involve both the intended and unintended killing of civilians. The large-scale bombings of civilian populations and infrastructure that took place during World War II, for example, were designed to defeat an enemy in war. The bombings in World War II were deliberately directed against civilians to demoralize them and shorten the war—a strategic decision. The killing stopped when the enemy surrendered, demonstrating that there was no intent to destroy them "as such." Such targeted and systematic attacks on civilians are now specifically prohibited as war crimes.

The point here is that, although civilians were targeted for destruction, it was part of a campaign of violence directed against another state and not against the civilian population that made up that state, although many of them paid a terrible price. Of course, war, such as the bloody one waged by the United States against Japan in the Pacific during World War II, can also become "racialized." Scholarly opinions differ on whether or not the atomic bombings, in particular, but also the 1945 fire bombings of Tokyo (and dozens of other Japanese cities) and Dresden and Hamburg, Germany, were justified. Most experts contend they were *not*. The question, however, remains. Is it just mass killing of the type that also occurs in warfare that is the hallmark of a genocide? The mass murder of any social group other than the four delineated in the 1948 Genocide Convention (racial, national, ethnical, or religious) is not considered genocide under international law. As we will discuss in detail, the Convention actually *precludes* categorizing much mass violence as genocide—though, of course, such violence is often still contrary to international law as a war crime or crime against humanity. But what, in fact, constitutes "mass" killing? Does there even need to be killing at all, to warrant the designation of genocide? The popular understanding of the word's definition undoubtedly is limited to the indiscriminate mass killing of a specific racial, religious, ethnic, or national human group. This mirrors the legal one adopted in 1948. The definition of the word "genocide," however, has been the subject of scholarly debate ever since it first appeared in print in Lemkin's book.

We will argue that *any* violence directed against *any* group in an attempt to destroy its social and cultural cohesion and therefore its ability to maintain itself *as* a group is genocide. The British sociologist Martin Shaw points out that the use of the word "group," however, necessarily categorizes victims by their collective experience at the hands of perpetrators who regard these populations as actually being such. He makes the excellent point that categories typically thought of in terms of identity, such as race, ethnicity, and even nation are today "either completely discredited as a social category" or now understood as being "socially and culturally constructed" (Shaw 2015, 20). Shaw, however, agrees with those scholars (such as the historian Chalk and the sociologist Jonassohn (1990), who helped pioneer genocide studies) who maintain that even if the targeted population group does not recognize itself as belonging to whatever category their persecutors consign them to, they are still attacked based upon the perpetrators' idea that this group objectively exists.

There is, certainly, also the problem of categorizing people as "victims" in any group based upon the collective violence that has been inflicted upon them by others. Agreeing wholeheartedly with Shaw that victim groups "assert *their* understandings of groups to which they belong, and their versions of identity, rather than simply accepting their attackers' classifications" (Shaw 2015, 3), genocide is still the attempt to destroy any recognized group *as defined by the perpetrator*. After all, we each have complex, evolving, overlapping self-identities; it is how the perpetrators define or identify their victims that determines their actions. Shaw makes another excellent point about word choice in that the actors in a genocide should not be, as they usually are, referred to as "perpetrators" because it is imprecise and is a term used to describe *any* sort of criminal act. For example, someone who commits murder is indeed a "perpetrator" but is usually called by the more precise word "murderer" and thus differentiated from, say, a bank robber. Because genocide is a specific crime he suggests instead the use of the word "genocidists," which was the term Lemkin used and that will be used in this book (Shaw 2015, 146).

Many of our colleagues in Genocide Studies use the term *genocidaires*, which is simply the French-language term for the same thing.

We turn now to a more in-depth study of the concept of "genocide," its origins, meanings, and usefulness in describing the horrific events that have taken place and continue to take place in our world today despite that oft-repeated mantra of "never again." While some might think the use of the word genocide to describe so many—but not all—of the vicious assaults carried out by one people against another renders the idea meaningless, we agree instead with Shaw that the widespread applicability of Lemkin's original understanding of the concept is precisely what makes the study of the subject even *more* important. Students need to see genocide as being more than just an occasional horrific episode in world history—the Holocaust, Rwanda—implemented by exceptionally bad actors. Targeted violence has been unleashed on many different peoples many different times throughout history in the name of progress, civilization, or state-building.

This knowledge can guide you as you consider why the 1948 UN Convention that gave us the legal definition of the word provided us with one so flawed and inadequate, and get you thinking about what should, in fact, be considered genocide, and how the world should respond when it occurs. You will then get beyond the simplistic reduction of history to an analysis of geopolitical power struggles between the forces of "good" and "evil" that presents the Genocide Convention as the outcome of the triumph of humanitarian ideals over that type of evil. Students should look at this document with clear eyes and understand that to accept the standard Western narrative of World War II—that "good" had triumphed over "evil"—bestows a wholly undeserved sainthood upon the Western democracies (all of whom had committed barbarous crimes in the colonial world, setting precedents for Hitler). The continued struggle between "good" and "evil" during the Cold War between the United States and its allies and the Soviet Union and their allies occasioned the rationalization for still more genocides in East Pakistan, Indonesia, Guatemala, and elsewhere. Students need to think critically about what they have learned in high school where state-mandated and prescribed lesson plans reinforce these simplistic versions of history.

This book will give you, the student, needed context to understand not only the reasons *why* such state-sponsored violence occurred in the past but why it continues to be such a reoccurring problem in the contemporary world. Today's students, tomorrow's leaders, will know how and why the understanding of genocide has changed so dramatically over the years, and more important, what this means in the context of the world in which you live. This book, written for you, should prove useful for a broad range of General Education courses that deal with ethnic violence and human rights. It may well serve also as an introductory text to upper-division courses that deal with those subjects. This approach will also be helpful for the new field of Peace and Conflict Studies as in the conclusion we will look at the deliberately crafted structural impediments to the prevention and punishment of genocide and contribute some ideas to overcome them. In the pages that follow, the use of a thematic approach instead of the usual chronological narrative should help you come to understand not only the dimensions and enormity of what is, as Samantha Power put it, "a problem from hell," but that it is a *reoccurring* one that, unfortunately, has been left for you to solve.

Chapter One

WHAT *SHOULD* BE THE DEFINITION OF GENOCIDE?

As soon as I could read, I started to devour books on the persecution of religious, racial, or other minority groups. I was fascinated by the frequency of such cases, by the great suffering inflicted on the victims and the hopelessness of their fate, and by the impossibility of repairing the damage to life and culture.
—Raphael Lemkin, 1959

Raphael Lemkin and the Origins of the Word "Genocide"

While writing his book *Axis Rule in Occupied Europe: Laws of Occupation, Analysis of Government, Proposals for Redress* during World War II, Raphael Lemkin took the Greek word *genos* (race or kin) and combined it with the Latin *cide* (the act of killing) to create the word *genocide*, meaning literally "to kill a people." The book was published in 1944, and people could be forgiven for assuming he coined the term specifically to describe Hitler's "Final Solution" of the so-called Jewish Question. Lemkin, a Polish Jew, barely escaped death at the hands of the invading German army in the early weeks of World War II but the rest of his family members were not so fortunate. It was not his own personal tragedy, however, that had moved him to address this topic. It was not even the unprecedented horror the Nazis perpetrated against Europe's Jews (and others) that he would chronicle in the pages of his important book. Lemkin had, in fact, begun thinking about this "crime of crimes" over a decade earlier.

Lemkin was, of course, well aware that one could look back into history and find many examples of genocide that had occurred in every part of the world from the beginning of time. Biblical examples abound, and almost everyone has at least heard of the persecution of Christians by Nero and other Roman leaders, grisly crimes committed during the Crusades a thousand years later, Genghis Khan's murderous conquests in Asia, and other pre-modern examples of genocide long before the term existed. A precocious and apparently unusual child, Lemkin also had read about the "persecution of religious, racial or other minority groups" (Lemkin 2013, 1–2). It was the Turkish genocide of Armenians, which began in 1915 during World War I, however, that convinced him to begin his campaign for an international law prohibiting such atrocities as "general dangers" to humanity. A quarter-century later, in August 1939, only a few days before he began his murderous assault on much of Europe, Hitler had cynically asked, "Who, after all, today speaks of the annihilation of the Armenians?" Lemkin certainly did, as he posed the question "When is the killing of a million a lesser crime than the killing of a single individual?" This new kind of conflict called for an international law and court to punish genocidists. Lemkin was aware of the repeated massacres of Armenians in the 1890s during the reign of Sultan Abdul Hamid II, with victims numbering in the hundreds of thousands, and a similar massacre in 1909, and he came to see the Turkish onslaught of Armenians in 1915 as but the final phase of a deliberate, long-term process of genocide. Some scholars have separated the massacres from the genocide by claiming these mass murders of defenseless people—the ones in the mid-1890s were carried out on the Sultan Abdul Hamid II's orders, the 1909 massacres by the new government that would soon organize the genocide—only had the aim of discouraging the development of Armenian nationalism by terrorizing them.

Lemkin had also become familiar with European and European-descended peoples' colonization practices, as well as the recent deliberate attempts at the extermination of the Herero and the exploitation of the Congolese. He realized these onslaughts were becoming ever more murderous in the modern age and he hoped to convince the League of Nations (the predecessor to today's United Nations) that acts such as "massacres, pogroms, actions undertaken to ruin the economic existence of the members of the collectivity, etc." and other "sorts of brutalities" were methods employed to wage "a campaign of extermination directed against the collectivity in which the victim is a member." This would result in "the premeditated destruction of national, racial, religious and social collectivities" (quoted in Shaw 2015, 15). Lemkin described the crime of premeditated destruction as "barbarity," and said it was a "general danger" to the entire international community. Another "general danger" was what would then be lost through what he called "vandalism." By this, he meant the "destruction of works of art and culture, being the expression of the particular genius of those collectivities" (ibid.). Later, these two international crimes were merged into his concept of "genocide"—the forcible destruction of a collectivity with the subsequent loss of its unique culture forever.

Lemkin therefore understood that there had been many wars of conquest and annihilation "in ancient times and in the Middle Ages," and said his new word described but "an old practice in its modern development." What was new was that the Nazis were waging war "not merely against states and their armies but against peoples" (Lemkin 2008, 88). The Nazis' deliberate, multifaceted campaign of destruction—political, social, cultural, economic, biological, physical, religious, and moral—would result in untold deaths not only among Europe's Jews, but also among the Slavic peoples of Poland and the Soviet Union, the Sinti and Roma (often called "Gypsies," a term that is now outdated and offensive), and others. Moreover, this colonial campaign would result in the obliteration of the social unity and cohesion that held them together as distinct peoples. While writing *Axis Rule* then, Lemkin was aghast not only at the mass murder of defenseless civilians by the Nazis but at the realization that "their cultures would be lost forever" (Lemkin 2013). Not only would untold millions of defenseless human beings die, but the entire world would also be impoverished as a result of the loss of that people's contributions to the human story, as "human life, treasures of art, and historical archives […] cannot be restored" (Lemkin 2008, 95).

This concern for the potential loss of specific, unique human cultures is central to understanding Lemkin's concept of genocide. It was not simply mass killing with the aim of conquering an enemy "but rather the calculated destruction of a group's ability to maintain its identity and its collective existence" (Cox 2017, 4). For Lemkin, the eradication and annihilation of a collectivity's cultural heritage represented the final destruction of a people, regardless of the number of survivors. As both the British sociologist Martin Shaw (2015) and the American historian Douglas Irvin-Erickson (2017) point out, Lemkin saw genocide as a deliberate *process* that was not necessarily a single, quick, murderous attack. Irvin-Erickson also notes Lemkin's earlier conception of both barbarism and vandalism were not part of any such process, and that these crimes were linked to the wars and invasions of the past. Nazi occupation policies in Poland and the USSR, however, seemed to be an entirely new phenomenon, a deliberate and systematic process combining modern ideas of racism and nationalism that called for colonial campaigns deliberately aimed at the "destruction of certain social groups by other social groups" (Irvin-Erickson 2017, 83) with the intent being to destroy the enemy to obliterate its cultural heritage. Lemkin also believed that "genocide is a gradual process and may begin with political disenfranchisement, economic displacement, cultural undermining and control, the destruction of leadership, the breakup of families, and the prevention of propagation. Each of these methods is a more or less effective means of destroying a group. Actual physical destruction is the last and most effective phase of genocide" (Lemkin, 2008, 79) (Figure 1.1).

Figure 1.1 Women's Division of the Hebrew Immigrant Society presents "Scroll of Honor" to Raphael Lemkin, c. 1951. https://digitalcollections.nypl.org/items/94e0b066-324d-ae4f-e040-e00a18067dd8.

There is always a process involved in genocide: first, identifying the alien "other," then isolating them through policies of discrimination, oppression, and persecution, and ultimately either removing them from the territory by any means necessary or forcing them to adopt the oppressor's way of life. Whether or not individuals survived was irrelevant. Genocidists killed individuals because they were members of a targeted group, and the goal was the destruction of the group itself. Lemkin therefore saw genocide as being a deliberate process on the part of genocidists designed to destroy another specific process—that is, the process of a people's cultural development. He recognized that all cultures interacted with others and thereby changed and evolved over time. He also realized that cultures were often assimilated entirely. This process, however, was the result of the interaction of ideas, values, and beliefs between different cultures and could only enrich the human experience. What Lemkin described as genocide "was forced cultural destruction, or forced cultural assimilation" (Irvin-Erickson in Graziosi and Sysyn, 2022, 155). Genocide, then, not only prevented the further development of a particular group's culture but also simultaneously precluded the possibility of that unique culture from interacting with other cultures and this loss would leave the world's cultural heritage poorer and less diverse.

Students often think of genocide in connection with the Nazis' transportation of Jews to ghettoes and then eventually to extermination camps. Auschwitz and the other extermination camps stand out in the popular imagination as being symbolic of the Nazis' genocide of the Jews. Yet, the Germans had already killed over a million Jews and buried them in mass graves in Poland and Soviet Russia before the so-called Final Solution was decided upon in late 1941 and finalized at the Wannsee Conference on January 20, 1942. Only the Nazis' failure to conquer the Soviet Union had led to their decision to murder them all. But here too, a process was at work. Raul Hilberg, the preeminent scholar of the Holocaust, demonstrated quite convincingly in his groundbreaking work *The Destruction of the European Jews* that the Holocaust unfolded in stages that cumulatively radicalized into the Final Solution (Hilberg 2003, 49; the book was first published in 1961). Students are not generally exposed to this longer process marked first by the identification of the Jews as being racially alien to the German people, then to their exclusion from the social, economic, and political life of Germany, and then their expulsion from that country altogether and then finally marked for extermination.

Prior to the unexpectedly stiff resistance the German army encountered in Russia, Hitler and his henchmen would have been content simply to expel the Jews from Europe altogether. Therefore, what some scholars now incorrectly label ethnic cleansing would have also constituted genocide for Lemkin. He was, for example, aware of Stalin's proposal to exile all of the Soviet Union's Jews to the inhospitable Far East, a region set aside for them as a national homeland. Lemkin knew that there they would be but "a handful of displaced people, cut off from their roots," sent, as Irvin-Erickson noted, to "a homeland concocted to destroy them as Jews but leave them alive" (Irvin-Erickson 2017, 78). As discussed in the Introduction, the current Chinese campaign of herding the Turkic-Muslim Uyghurs of Xinjiang Province into concentration camps to be—euphemistically—"re-educated" is the same kind of attempt to stamp out an entire culture and thus their identity as a people and should then also be considered a genocide. The Chinese authorities are not only erasing the cultural and social ties of the Uyghurs but also destroying their hereditary genetic ties through forcible abortions, the sterilizations of Uyghur women and the removal of their children from their homes. In August 2022, the United Nations Human Rights Commissioner Michelle Bachelet issued a comprehensive report that said these actions "may" rise to the level of crimes against humanity. The Chinese government continues to insist that it is fighting so-called terrorism on the part of Uyghur nationalists and simply trying to help develop the economy in Xinjiang. Many genocide scholars insist that mass killing is necessary for an understanding of the concept, and what is happening to the Uyghurs even as you read these words is at most "cultural" genocide as if that was somehow distinct from genocide when, in Lemkin's view of the concept, it is simply a different method of genocide and is in fact its end goal.

Lemkin defined genocide as "a coordinated plan of different actions aiming at the destruction of the essential foundations of life of national groups, with the aim of annihilating the groups themselves" (Lemkin 2008, 79). It was his preoccupation with the danger posed by genocide to the world's mosaic of cultural heritages that led him, while completing *Axis Rule*, to refine his category of potential victims from his original definition of "barbarism" which included assaults on "national, racial, religious and social collectivities" to being attacks concentrated on "national groups." Douglas Irvin-Erickson notes that although Lemkin fully understood that those human groups had frequently been victims of genocide before the advent of the nation-state, he "intended genocide to signify the destruction of nations, not as a group of individual people but as a human group [...] a 'family of mind [...]'" (Irvin-Erickson 2017, 85). This is not necessarily a narrowing down of victim "groups" as the world's foremost scholar on genocide and international law, William Schabas (2000) writes, since by "nation" or "national group," Lemkin did *not* necessarily mean the citizens of a state who resided within defined geographical borders. Instead, a nation, or more specifically a "people" was composed of individuals who shared a common understanding that they were members of a particular group that asserted its cultural uniqueness through "shared languages, arts, mythologies, folklores, collective histories, traditions, religions, and even shared ancestry or a shared geographical location" (Irvin-Erickson 2017, 66). What was important was that people believed that these things mattered. African Americans, for example, are a "family of mind" that consider themselves a "people," as do Jews scattered throughout the world, regardless of their nationality. Lemkin considered many different kinds of groups that possessed this kind of social and cultural cohesion to be nations, that people could simultaneously be part of several different "nations," and that the destruction of any of these groups constituted genocide.

While many students—and some academics—associate genocide and the use of words such as "destruction" and "annihilation" with mass murder, William Schabas thinks otherwise. He correctly notes that Lemkin had concluded that genocide could be accomplished by "acts aimed at destroying the culture and livelihood of the [national] group" (Schabas 2000, 25). The Holocaust—the Nazi genocide of the

Jews—has, however, become the standard by which genocides are measured. Many people do not know that in his writings on the Nazi genocide, Lemkin referred not only to the ongoing mass murder of the Jews but also to the assaults on the "national foundations" of other non-German or "non-Aryan" peoples such as the Slavs—Poles, Russians and Ukrainians, Czechs, and so on. Peoples that the Nazis believed were also "Aryan" such as the Dutch or Scandinavians would not be exterminated entirely like the Jews or drastically reduced in numbers like the Slavs, but they too would be "Germanized."

Lemkin recognized that there were many episodes through the centuries that closely resembled his concept of genocide. For these wars in antiquity, the intent was generally simply to defeat and destroy an enemy, there was no coordinated, deliberate process employed to destroy them as a people. Lemkin wrote *Axis Rule* in light of the Nazis' declared intent to reorder the political map of Europe according to racial–biological constructs; ultimately, this would lead to the destruction of many national groups and their cultural heritages. Hitler had singled out the vast spaces of Russia for expansion as early as 1923 when he wrote *Mein Kampf* ("My Struggle") while in prison. In the Soviet Union, the racist and genocidal nature of this conflict can be seen in the plans for annihilation outlined in the "General Plan for the East" drawn up by Heinrich Himmler, the head of the SS, before the invasion of the USSR. Ominously, it called for the "removal" of 80 million people from Russia to allow for its colonization. As a rather grotesque gift, Himmler planned to present the document to Hitler upon the occasion of the final defeat of the Soviet Union, which they both mistakenly believed was imminent. Under this plan, Germany's supposed need for *Lebensraum* (living space) would turn all of Russia into a colony to furnish raw materials and slave labor for the Third Reich. This sinister plan, thwarted by Germany's defeat, nonetheless took the lives of more than 15 million Soviet civilians and another 10 million Red Army soldiers during the conflict. Of the latter, at least one-third were prisoners of war (POWs) who died in captivity. All told, approximately 27 million Soviets died in the struggle against fascism. It is simply not possible to explain this incredible death toll as being merely the fate of victims of war. This was a struggle for territorial conquest and the elimination of millions of supposedly inferior Slavs and Jews; German colonists would afterward move in and put their cultural stamp on the landscape. This was a genocidal war of colonization, a "*Rassenkampf*" or "race war," where one social group, or its leadership, sought to destroy another social group.

Lemkin hoped that his concept would be applied not only to the explicitly colonial aspects of Hitler's war but more broadly to the settler colonialism and racist, nationalistic imperialism of European and European-descended powers. As he wrote in *Axis Rule*, "Genocide has two phases: one, destruction of the national pattern of the oppressed group; the other the imposition of the national pattern of the oppressor." For Lemkin, genocide did "not necessarily mean the immediate destruction of a nation" but was the result of the imposition of the oppressor's national pattern "upon the oppressed population that is allowed to remain, or upon the territory alone, after removal of the population and colonization of the area by the oppressor's own nationals"

(Lemkin 2008, 79). This tenet clearly ties Lemkin's definition to European imperialism and its disastrous impact on indigenous peoples. Hitler's plans were essentially colonial in nature as he intended to depopulate broad regions of territory in Eastern Europe by any means necessary and then send in German farmers to take their place, leaving some Slavs to labor for their new masters while Jews were destined for complete elimination. These, then, according to Lemkin, were both examples of genocide.

International Military Tribunal at Nuremberg

In the fall of 1941, just months after the German invasion of the Soviet Union, the American President Franklin Roosevelt, the British Prime Minister Winston Churchill, and the Soviet leader Joseph Stalin—known as the "Big Three"—all condemned the Nazis for the war crimes they were perpetrating upon the peoples of Eastern Europe. Churchill (who had his own grim history of colonial atrocities, dating back nearly a half-century) stated that "the punishment of these crimes must now be included among the major aims of the war" (quoted in Ginsburgs 1996, 25). After learning about the monstrous criminal acts by the Nazis, most of us would assume that there was always a plan in place to put their leaders on trial after the war. Many of your high school history textbooks claim that the Americans played the leading role in bringing high-ranking Nazis to justice. This oft-repeated narrative is inaccurate. Initially, both the United States and Great Britain had agreed simply to execute thousands of Nazis upon their capture while many more thousands were to be sent into exile. Germany itself would be de-industrialized and turned into a giant potato farm.

The Soviets repeatedly denounced the Nazi leadership for being part of a criminal conspiracy and called for them to be brought before an international tribunal upon the conclusion of the war. It was not, however, until after the *Waffen SS* (the Nazi paramilitary force) massacre of American POWs during the Battle of the Bulge in the winter of 1944 that US President Roosevelt decided that an international war crimes trial might indeed be appropriate. In February 1945, Roosevelt brought up the idea at the Yalta Conference of the "Big Three," but Churchill continued to insist that the Allies stick to the original plan and simply execute the top Nazi political and military leaders. As late as April 1945, just a week before Hitler's suicide and two weeks before Germany's unconditional surrender, Churchill continued with his efforts to undo this decision. He wrote Harry S. Truman, who became the US president upon Roosevelt's death on April 12, and again made the argument that "execution without trial is the preferable course" (quoted in Taylor 1992, 31). Ultimately, however, after years of Soviet prodding, the Allies agreed to the establishment of an International Military Tribunal (IMT) to try the Nazi leadership for its crimes.

It is also still widely believed that the purpose of the Nuremberg Trial was primarily to bring the Nazis to justice for their genocide of Europe's Jews. This was not the case. After the defeat of Nazi Germany in 1945, the Allies met in June of that year in London to finalize the plans for the trial of the Nazi leadership. Lemkin intended for his concept of genocide to be applied not only to the Nazi assault on Europe's Jews but also to their policies in other German-occupied regions used to rule most of the occupied peoples of Europe, which also targeted Poles, Russians, Sinti and Roma ("Gypsies"), and others. Lemkin hoped that this could also prevent future attacks on the ways of life and cultural traditions of any other human groups (Irvin-Erickson 2017, 2). Because there was no law against genocide in place—Churchill had called the Nazi actions against the Jews "a crime without a name"—no leading Nazis were convicted of that specific, heinous crime at the famous Nuremberg trial of 1945–46. The legal principle of "no crime without a law" prevented their being charged with such as did another legal principle—the prohibition of charging defendants with a crime under a law instituted retroactively. They were charged instead with Crimes against Peace (planning, initiating, and waging wars of aggression in violation of international treaties and agreements), Crimes against Humanity (exterminations, deportations, forced labor, and so on), War Crimes (violations of the laws of war), as well as "a common plan or conspiracy to commit" the acts listed in these counts.

Lemkin's new word was, however, included in the indictment under War Crimes. The Nazi leadership was charged with "deliberate and systematic genocide, viz., the extermination of racial and national groups, against the civilian populations of certain occupied territories in order to destroy particular races and classes of people and national, racial or religious groups, particularly Jews, Poles, and Gypsies and others." Significantly, the British prosecutor, Sir Hartley Shawcross understood that the "Genocide was not restricted to extermination of the Jewish people or of the gypsies. It was applied in different forms in Yugoslavia, to the non-German inhabitants of Alsace-Lorraine, to the people of the Low Countries and of Norway" (quoted in Schabas 2000, 36–38). In his closing statement at the trial, Shawcross made extensive use of Lemkin's concept. He noted that although the methods of destruction were "varied from nation to nation, from people to people," and that in the final analysis all of Hitler's policies had a common aim: to remove non-Germans from the lands they occupied and colonize those lands with Germans. This policy went "beyond mere Germanization" and the Nazis intended to effect the "imposition of the German cultural pattern upon other peoples" (quoted in Stiller 1992, 108).

Although none of the leading Nazis were convicted of the specific crime of genocide at the main trial due to the legal principle of "no crime without a law," some were at the subsequent trials of members of the SS *Einsatzgruppen*—"Special Forces" assigned to mobile killing units—and officials involved in the technical and logistical preparations for the Holocaust (Earl 1992, 327; Stiller 1992, 106). It was these proceedings that "helped transform genocide from Lemkin's broad conception into a concept that was understood as a specific crime against a specific group of people and led to the Nazi attempt to exterminate the Jews as being "the prototype for the crime of genocide" (Irvin-Erickson 2017, 144). The convictions at Nuremberg, however, did not take into account the Nazi crimes against its Jewish citizens and other minorities within Germany's borders before the outbreak of the World War II that began in Europe with Hitler's invasion of Poland on the first day of September 1939. The need for an international prohibition against genocide during both times of war *and* peace was now obvious to many observers.

United Nations Convention on the Prevention and Punishment of Genocide

At the very first session of the General Assembly of the United Nations in 1945, delegates from India, Cuba, and Panama, at Lemkin's urging, put forward a resolution to make genocide a specific international crime whether in time of war or peace. As Schabas notes, "this reaction to the Nuremberg IMT's judgement" led not only to the Genocide Convention itself but also to its separate, legally defined status apart from the "Crimes against Humanity" with which the Nazis had been charged (Schabas 2007). At the 55th plenary meeting on December 11, 1946 Resolution 96 (I), *The Crime of Genocide*, written by Lemkin himself, was passed. The first sentence states that "Genocide is the denial of the right of existence of entire human groups […] and results in great losses to humanity in the form of cultural and other contributions represented by these human groups" (United Nations General Assembly, "The Crime of Genocide," 1946. https://digitallibrary.un.org/record/209873?ln=en&v=pdf.)

Here Lemkin again emphasizes the loss of "cultural and other contributions represented by these groups" in his concept of genocide. It was this end result, the destruction of a culture that was genocide. This reflected his thinking in *Axis Rule*; however, as we will see below, political self-interest and the self-serving agendas of the Great Powers resulted in a quite different definition, leaving out some human groups and entirely removing the emphasis on culture that was central to Lemkin. But for now, it was agreed that several legal scholars, including Lemkin, would "undertake the necessary studies, with a view to drawing up a draft convention on the crime of genocide" to submit the law for consideration at "the next regular session of the General Assembly" (quoted in Schabas 2009, 37).

The first Secretary-General of the United Nations, Norwegian lawyer, and politician Trygve Lie, thought that the legal definition of genocide should be separated from the Nuremberg charges of "crimes against humanity" and not be similar to other acts of inhumanity "[…] which logically are and should be distinct" (quoted in Schabas 2009, 37). Many other delegates, however, saw genocide as being but one of the variety of crimes subsumed under the heading of "crimes against humanity." This concern was only one of many major points of contention fought over during the next two years about the specifics of the proposed international law against genocide. Other aspects debated fiercely by the delegates included what mechanisms should be in place to prevent and punish transgressors, whether to incorporate both physical attacks and cultural impoverishment, and—most contentious of all—how to categorize the groups to be protected under the law. In UN Resolution 96 (I), drawn up by Lemkin and then unanimously passed by the General Assembly on December 11, 1946, specific groups—racial, religious, and political—were indeed delineated. But genocide was broadly defined as the "denial of the right of existence of entire human groups" and after "racial, religious, political" Lemkin added "and other groups" to those that had been "destroyed, entirely or in part" (UN Resolution 96 (I) The Crime of Genocide).

Lemkin and two other legal scholars set to work on the first (Secretariat) draft which was then sent on to the Economic and Social Committee. As the United Nations (UN) is quite fond of acronyms, this committee is known as ECOSOC. The committee appointed another *ad hoc* (a Latin phrase meaning "for this") Committee on Genocide to continue drafting the resolution. The original definitions put forward in both the Secretariat draft and the *ad hoc* Committee draft specified that the destruction of culture was part and parcel of the concept of genocide. But in this second draft, "cultural" genocide was separated entirely from "physical" genocide at the insistence of the United States and France. Sent from there on to the General Assembly, the proposal was sent to the Sixth (Legal Committee) for final review where any mention of cultural genocide was altogether eliminated, again at the insistence of the United States, Great Britain, France, the Netherlands, and others. For their part, the Soviet Union insisted that "political groups" be removed from the proposal. As Christopher Powell writes, "The wording of the Convention was shaped by the desire of its framers not to criminalize their own behavior" (Powell, 2011, 532).

It is important for students to know that the United States, the Soviet Union, and the colonial powers Britain, France, and the Netherlands, all took part in efforts to undermine the Genocide Convention at the UN. Recent scholarship has shown the Allied victors pursued their own agendas in a successful effort to avoid accountability for their actions—and, if possible, still use it to attack their geopolitical opponents. The final text of the UN Genocide Convention was a political compromise—a document that all the victorious powers could agree upon. Stalin personally went line by line to ensure his mass murder of political opponents and "economic" groups in the Soviet Union, as well as his deportations of entire peoples to Siberia and the Soviet Far East, would not lead to charges of genocide. The colonial powers such as Britain and France were adamant that their exploitative policies that had so damaged peoples around the globe would also not come under the legal definition of genocide. For their part, the Americans wanted to ensure that no element of the Genocide Convention could be construed "in such a way as to cause us difficulties with cases such as lynching" (quoted in Weiss-Wendt in Graziosi and Sysyn, 2022, 30). The Americans, like the longer-standing colonial powers, also did not want the treatment of indigenous peoples or the destruction of their cultures to be included in the legal definition (Figure 1.2).

Stalin, who had personally approved the execution of hundreds of thousands of his political opponents, was especially keen on excluding political groups from the Convention, while the United States, not surprisingly, sought to keep language about "political groups" in as a cudgel with which to bash the Soviets. Lemkin quickly realized that the inclusion of political groups in the legal definition might imperil the final passage of the Convention. While the Soviets eventually dropped their objection to including political groups in the final version of the definition, Lemkin feared some Latin American states might still vote against any mention of political groups, as the execution of defeated opponents in places like Brazil was simply one of the hazards of political life there. One of the delegates, opining that revolutions were common in South America, complained "if this treaty includes political groups, the loser of the revolution can claim before the world that the winner violated the genocide pact and must be punished" (quoted in ibid., 98). The British also feared that the inclusion of political groups in the definition might pose a problem for states engaged in suppressing what

WHAT *SHOULD* BE THE DEFINITION OF GENOCIDE?

Figure 1.2 Robert Jackson, a U.S. Supreme Court justice and chief American prosecutor at the Nuremberg Trials, delivers his opening speech at the trial of Nazi war criminals, in 1946. https://commons.wikimedia.org/wiki/File:Prosecutor_Robert_Jackson_at_Nuremberg_Trials.jpg

they considered terrorist or subversive groups in their colonial possessions. Lemkin, desperate to ensure passage of a law against genocide, abandoned the previous position he had long held as outlined in his writings, and argued that political groups should *not* be included. The next to last draft had read that genocide should be "any of the following deliberate acts committed with the intent to destroy a national, racial, religious, or political group [...]." Political groups were now dropped so that the final draft read "any of the following acts committed with intent to destroy, in whole or in part, a national, ethnical, racial, or religious group, as such."

Lemkin originally defined genocide as a colonial crime "of destroying the national patterns of the oppressed and imposing the national patterns of the oppressors," but Britain and France did not want anything included that could call into question their colonial policies—a position the United States was willing to support given its own history of Native American oppression. The Soviets, however, wholeheartedly supported the inclusion of cultural genocide—despite their own murderous assaults on many different ethnic groups—as it would be a convenient stick with which to bash the "imperialists." Lemkin also often used the term "cultural" genocide or "ethnocide" to describe the destruction of a people's culture, and consequently the destruction of that particular human group. He did not see it as an altogether different type of genocide. Jeffrey Bachman, in his insightful discussion of the negotiations over the framework of the Convention, demonstrates that the idea of cultural genocide was in fact at the very core of Lemkin's conception of genocide. While working with the two other experts on the working draft for the convention on genocide, Lemkin had insisted that cultural genocide "was the most important part of the Convention," (quoted in Bachman, ed. 2019, 47). Lemkin believed attacks on a group's "spirit and moral unity" endangered that group's very existence and the loss of any culture is "as disastrous for civilization as was physical destruction of nations" (Lippman 1985, 11).

Although cultural genocide was included in the first two drafts of the resolution, ultimately it was removed at the insistence of the colonial powers (and specifically the United States, given its treatment of Native Americans) for the reasons we have already discussed. This arbitrarily—and wrongly—separated cultural genocide from physical genocide out of political considerations. In the end, Lemkin recognized that on this issue too "the wind was not blowing in my direction" and thought that this sticking point could also "endanger the passage of the convention [...] so with a heavy heart I decided not to press for it" (Lemkin 2013, 173). The Convention, then, reflected the agendas of the principal victors in the war. Students should know also that Lemkin's ideas were most strongly supported at the UN by member states that were former colonies—namely Egypt, India, Pakistan, China, and the Philippines. Lemkin wrote that the delegates from African nations, "on whom genocide was practiced" were in fact the most favorably inclined toward passing a law against genocide (quoted in Irvin-Erickson 2017, 152). Women within many of the delegations and in nongovernmental organizations also played a hugely important role; while most accounts understandably highlight Lemkin's indefatigable efforts to bring an international law against genocide to fruition, Lemkin went so far as to state that without the efforts of these women, there would have been no genocide convention.

Students need to know this history so they can begin to think critically about what international law really is about, and whose interests it serves. The purpose of this book is to get you to think about the many identity-based conflicts ongoing today in the world as a consequence of intolerance and the demonization of this or that group, as well as possible ways to overcome these human fallibilities. The final version of the document agreed upon by the UN General Assembly—after much rancorous debate and threats by the Great Powers to withhold their support over this or that issue—the UN "Convention on the Prevention and Punishment of the Crime of Genocide," was but a half-hearted step toward that goal. The Great Powers wanted to prevent any possibility of the Convention being applied to them, so the Holocaust was held up as the archetype or model of what a genocide should look like. The Convention, which was adopted on December 9, 1948, although it did incorporate some of Lemkin's thinking, it also, as we will see below and especially in the Conclusion to the book, was cleverly designed to protect the political interests of the Great Powers.

Articles I, II, and III read as follows:

Article I

> The Contracting Parties confirm that genocide, whether committed in time of peace or in time of war, is a crime under international law, which they undertake to prevent and to punish.

Article II

In the present Convention, genocide means any of the following acts committed with intent to destroy, in whole or in part, a national, ethnical, racial, or religious group, as such:

(a) Killing members of the group;
(b) Causing serious bodily or mental harm to members of the group;
(c) Deliberately inflicting on the group conditions of life calculated to bring about its physical destruction in whole or in part;
(d) Imposing measures intended to prevent births within the group;
(e) Forcibly transferring children of the group to another group.

Article III
The following acts shall be punishable:

(a) Genocide;
(b) Conspiracy to commit genocide;
(c) Direct and public incitement to commit genocide;
(d) Attempt to commit genocide;
(e) Complicity in genocide.

Article I's acknowledgment that genocide could be committed "in time of peace or in time of war" addressed the concerns of those delegates that understood genocide was a crime that could be committed at any time. In Article II, the linkage between war and genocide was further weakened as the four protected groups can also be attacked "in whole or in part" and, tellingly, "as such" which means with "the aim of destroying a group *in itself*, rather than group destruction as a means of defeating a state in war" (Shaw 2015, 40). Of course, as Shaw has also written, most genocides do occur during some kind of conflict, be it civil or international war. But the Nazi actions taken against German Jews from 1933 to 1939—that is, before the war, and before the "Final Solution" or mass extermination had begun—were in fact genocidal. As we know, Lemkin argued that genocide was a *process* rather than a *type* of violence. Lemkin reserved "his strongest moral condemnation for genocides committed through terror, torture and death" but genocide "did not necessarily require physical violence [...] genocide could be committed without killing a single individual" (Irvin-Erickson in Graziosi and Sysyn, 2022, 154). When Lemkin wrote about killing, he described it as but one of many techniques of genocide; although in reality genocides will usually involve mass killing. More importantly, for Lemkin, when genocide involved killing, the killing was not *in and of itself* the genocide. As a type of conflict, "genocide almost always develops out of some kind of violent conflict or as part of a process of demographic or political reordering" and "thus it should be viewed as part of those processes, rather than as a completely separate phenomenon" (Cox 2017, 11). It must be recognized, however, that genocide usually involves considerable physical violence and the killing of defenseless civilian populations, who will always resist "ethnic cleansing," mass repression, and cultural genocide.

Still, this marked a departure from Nuremberg because the defendants at the IMT trials had been tried only for crimes perpetrated during the war itself. There was, of course, ample evidence offered of the Nazis' criminal policies toward Germany's Jews from 1933 until the outbreak of the war in 1939, but the principle of state sovereignty prevented prosecution. The Chief US Prosecutor at Nuremberg, Robert Jackson, had argued that the "extermination of Jews and destruction of the rights of minorities" had only become an international concern because it "was part of a plan for making an illegal war." He claimed that it had always been the policy of the US Government not to interfere in the internal affairs of another country—despite repeated interventions in Latin America and elsewhere since at least 1898—and that other countries also had no right to interfere with US domestic policies. This international legal principle, which has been in effect since the end of the Thirty Years' War in Europe (1618–48) and its conclusion with the signing of the Treaty of Westphalia, remains a powerful impediment to the correction of human rights abuses to this day. Jackson later said the quiet part out loud, so to speak, when he repeated his questionable assertion that the US did not interfere in the affairs of other countries because we too "have some regrettable circumstances at times in our own country in which minorities are unfairly treated."

The history of racial discrimination and violence in the United States was, in the words of the Norwegian historian Anton Weiss-Wendt, "the single most important factor that prevented the United States from promptly ratifying the Genocide Convention" (Weiss-Wendt 2017, 9). In 1951, the United States *was* accused of genocide by African Americans of the Civil Rights Congress in a lengthy petition presented to the United Nations entitled *We Charge Genocide*. It was the fear of precisely this possibility that the United States—as well as the European colonial powers like France and England—insisted the Nazis' prosecution for atrocities be linked to their conspiracy to commit aggressive war as this precluded officials from these victorious powers from being charged with similar crimes for their domestic or colonial policies. Later, the US invasions of Vietnam and Iraq, among others would also have fit into any definition of an unjustified, aggressive war, as would the dozens of US interventions in Central America and the Caribbean from the late 1800s onward, peaking during the first third of the twentieth century and continuing to the present day. The United States would not ratify the Convention until 1988, four decades after its adoption by the UN. The US, however, appended its own "reservations" and "understandings" of the legal meanings of the document. For example, the US insisted that any disputes it might be involved in that were to be submitted to the International Court of Justice (under Article IX of the Convention the ICJ has the right to arbitrate cases of genocide *between states* that are signatories) for adjudication would require the specific consent of the United States. In addition, if any individual US citizens were to be accused of the crime of genocide, before they could be tried the US Senate would have to agree to a treaty entered into for that specific purpose. In effect, these caveats preclude the possibility of the charges of genocide ever being preferred against the US or its agents (UN Treaty Series vol. 78, 277).

The Debate about the Convention's Many Flaws

The limitations of the final version of the Genocide Convention adopted in 1948 as to which human groups to protect—and from what kind of assault—were beholden to both politics and to a rigid understanding of what genocide ought to look like based on the Holocaust as a template. The exclusion of political—as well as social—groups from the definition, along with the emphasis on the physical or biological destruction of the four protected groups with no mention of cultural genocide, have since been identified by many scholars and legal experts as being among the most critical flaws of the Convention. We have already seen that the major powers were glad to write their own genocides out of the Convention's definition. By holding up the Holocaust as the prime example of genocide, they were able to avoid embracing the essence of Lemkin's idea: the goal of intentional group destruction, with the destruction of a people's culture being the outcome of the crime. Some aspects of Lemkin's thought, however, do indeed appear in the Convention. For example, killing is not the only means of destruction, and the idea of destroying a people can be inferred from the prohibitions on imposing measures intended to prevent births within the group or the forcible transfer of children of the group to another group.

There are many other problems inherent in the Convention's final definition that have provoked debate over the three-quarters of a century since its adoption. We have also already briefly touched on why the caveat "as such" was included, but the word "intent" quickly takes us into the realm of law, and often into narrow legalistic interpretations lacking the nuance or perspective that could be provided by approaches deriving from the humanities or social sciences. The Convention's definition of genocide specifies that certain, specific acts must be committed by the perpetrators with the "intent to destroy, in whole or in part" one or more of the four protected types of groups for those acts to be characterized as genocidal. Intellectual approaches that are associated with the "social sciences" or "humanities"—history, anthropology, political science, philosophy, sociology, and so on—are more concerned with actions, or agency, that affect a course of events, than with an obsessive search for a proven "intent" (and rarely does a regime openly proclaim its genocidal intent). These actions are, of course, the result of motives that need to be examined to distinguish the *specifics* of a particular case study from the *generalities* of the same type of historical phenomena, but the concept of intent is a purely legal one. *Motive* is the subjective meaning of the genocidists' intentions. It is not the same as intent, not central to that legal concept, and for Lemkin was entirely irrelevant.

Lemkin did believe the "intent to destroy the group is basic to the concept of genocide" (Irvin-Erickson 2017, 129). While we do not disagree, the high legal bar of intent in the 1948 Convention means there must be a clearly enunciated goal to destroy one of the protected groups on the part of the genocidists (Lemkin said there must be a "coordinated plan" and compiled numerous decrees and laws in his *Axis Rule* to show the Nazis' intent to commit genocide). Although intent is, in fact, unquestionably present in the cases examined in this book, we contend that the *outcome* of the genocidists' *repeated actions*, and not the narrowly legal notion of intent, should define the phenomenon. Of course, the outcomes of some actions may well have been unintended, with the result still being genocidal. The real problem with the use of the word intent, as Martin Shaw perceptively noted, is that it "implies that genocide is defined by the *subjective meaning* attached to it" by the genocidists (Shaw 2015, 103) and thereby combines intent with motive. Some legal scholars such as William Schabas, however, argue that to be considered a genocide the genocidists must have a "racist or discriminatory motive, that is, a genocidal motive, taken as a whole. Where this is lacking, the crime cannot be genocide" (Schabas 2000). As we noted earlier, Lemkin was not much concerned with motive. For example, on the one hand, the Nazi genocide in Europe envisioned a complete racial–biological demographic reordering of Europe as opposed to, on the other hand, the Soviet creation of a new "Soviet man" through the cultural destruction of peoples such as the Ukrainians. What mattered to Lemkin was the *fact* that human groups were being destroyed; in both of these cases, the genocidists were destroying these groups *as* groups, and although in both cases, official pronouncements could be introduced as evidence of intent, it could also simply be inferred from the repeated actions that led to specific outcomes.

The very high legal bar of specific intent—the mental, conscious intent to commit the crime or the knowledge that one is committing that crime—requires that lawyers must prove this preplanning on the part of perpetrators to label them as genocidists and their actions as being genocide. It is also of crucial importance to understand that by "destruction" of a people, Lemkin included not only physical extermination but also subjugation, persecution, economic exploitation, and interference in procreation. Any of these things could destroy a group's ways of life and, ultimately, their traditions and culture. Where Lemkin saw that a deliberate process is necessary to carry out a genocide, however, we think that "intent to destroy the group" can be difficult to prove from the genocidists' language. Yet, a close and creative examination of language, while also examining actions, policies, and social dynamics, can help us understand—or better yet, predict—genocidal *results*.

Some experts have pointed out that genocide is, of course, an organized crime and that even in legal proceedings "intent is a logical deduction that flows from evidence of the material facts" (Schabas 2000, 222). The Convention's legalistic approach requires evidence that the genocidists intended the consequences (which must amount to "destruction," another imprecise term) that ensue from the acts committed. Long ago, the Australian historian Tony Barta questioned the Convention's emphasis on intent, noting that while many of the genocidal consequences of colonization were not intended, they nonetheless flowed quite predictably from actions taken by the settlers (Barta 1987). Intention is the general desire or plan to do something while the intent is purpose. The Convention conceptualizes intention as "intent" whereas Lemkin's understanding of intent is implicit in his assertion that there must be a "coordinated plan" with the "aim" of group annihilation. The important thing to understand is, of course, the *impact* these actions have on the targeted population group.

The UN, in the landmark trial of the Bosnian Serb general Radislav Krstic for genocide, found in 2001 that intent does not have to be explicit. We agree with the sociologist Helen Fein that although genocide "is the intent to destroy a collectivity" this "intent" can be divined by the "sustained, purposeful action" of the perpetrators, who themselves can be representatives of "the state of the victim, another state, or another collectivity" (Fein 1990, 24). We do not agree, however, with Fein's assertion that this "destruction" must entail the actual *physical* annihilation of members of the group. Another problem in the Convention's definition—besides the fact that "political" and "social" groups are altogether unprotected—is that the crucial term "group" is never clearly defined. Lemkin's idea of a group was "a family of mind," while the Convention singled out four highly specific groups, the two put forward by Lemkin in *Axis Rule* (national or ethnic) as well as those based on "race" or religion. Lemkin understood that human groups are not constituted by geographic territories or biology; yet, this is how most people understand what human groups are. But what of nonbelievers in a "religious group?" Or mixed-race children in a "racial" group? Any human group is varied and diverse. But the general belief that groups are basic and unchanging, a view that genocidists themselves most certainly agree with, is reflected in the Convention.

Another problem is the ambiguous word "destroy." Many scholars, Lemkin included, contemplate the final stage of genocide as being annihilation, but for Lemkin, this did not necessarily mean *total* elimination. The word annihilation means "the action or *process* of reducing to nothing; or of blotting out of existence" (italics ours, Oxford English Dictionary). As the American political scientist Scott Strauss (2006) has asked, however, what "in fact, does reducing to nothing mean? What counts as existence?" Even in the most devastating genocides, including the Holocaust, sizable portions of the targeted group survived, though scattered and traumatized, and having lost much of their group's cultural cohesion. Lemkin was all about *process*—genocide was the process by which one socially constructed group destroyed another socially constructed group whose culture, like all cultures, was itself in a constant process of change or evolution. Lemkin also asserted that many "different actions" could be used by the genocidists to achieve this aim. Physical extermination, or "annihilation," was but one means of doing so. For Lemkin, the thing destroyed was a people, and that was accomplished by destroying "the essential foundations of the life of national groups," meaning their social and cultural connections.

The legal definition of genocide, then, is a thoroughgoing revision of Lemkin's concept—written in light of the Holocaust, which had become the standard agreed upon by the framers of the Convention in order to avoid responsibility for their own crimes. This legal definition, unfortunately, allows for the basic misunderstanding of the phenomenon and has led to popular and simplistic beliefs about what constitutes genocide. Even academics have fallen into this trap. Steven Katz, an American philosopher, has gone so far as to assert that genocide happens "only where there is an actualized intention, however successfully carried out, to physically destroy an entire group (as such group is defined by the perpetrators)" (Katz 1994, 128). This would mean that in his view only the Holocaust (and perhaps the fate of the Nazis' Sinti and Roma victims, whom he ignores) qualify as a genocide.

This would be precisely what the framers of the 1948 Convention intended, as it excused them from being held accountable for their own crimes. Katz had the temerity to suggest that his own definition was one "that Raphael Lemkin may well have formulated a definition closer to (if not exactly like) mine had he been writing after the end of World War II [...]" (Katz 1994, 129n). Of course, Lemkin had indeed continued writing long after World War II, but this is a good example of the tendency of scholars to assert that their own definition is the one closest to what Lemkin *really* meant—as if the mountain of correspondence, proposals, book manuscripts, and so on were insufficient to discern his thinking on his own subject. Lemkin well understood the limitations of the Convention, but a limited and incomplete law was better than no law at all.

Many scholars have since addressed the inadequacies of both the language of the Convention's definition and its willful distortion of Lemkin's progressive, multicultural concept. While Matthew Lippman rightly argues in Lemkinian language that genocide "reflects a refusal to recognize the inalienable right of a collectivity to express its cultural identity and to contribute to the human mosaic [...]" he somehow concludes from his reading of the Convention that its "central purpose [...] is to preserve and promote pluralism in order to perpetuate the progress which historically has resulted from the clash of cultures" (Lippman 1994). As will be discussed later in the Conclusion to this book, the Convention is but a symbolic text that is simply "a registration of protest against past misdeeds [...] rather than [...] an effective instrument of their prevention or repression" (Oppenheim 1995, 751). It is indeed purely symbolic, and in Jeffrey Bachman's phrase, the political machinations of the Great Powers during the drafting process allowed them "to establish a culture of impunity for themselves [...] specifically in relation to the crime of genocide" (Bachman 2022, *passim*).

Other scholars have subsequently put forward their own reservations. One of the first to do so was the human rights legal scholar Pieter Drost in 1959. His definition was admirably much more inclusive because he identified "any human collectivity" as a possible victim group, his description of intent was, like Lemkin's, simply "deliberate destruction" but unlike Lemkin, this destruction needed to be of the physical existence of the human beings that made up the victim group, in other words, their murder. Scholars of genocide have also continued to grapple with both the concept of intent and the nature or definition of victim groups that qualify as a *genos*. Norman Naimark, a respected and prolific historian who has written on war and violence in Eastern Europe and beyond, rightly notes the limits of the 1948 legal definition. He holds that the attempt to destroy *any* social or political group, not just those enumerated in the Convention, is genocide (Naimark 2017). The South African sociologist Leo Kuper (1981) was vague both in his characterization of intent—he noted only that it had to be "explicit"—and also in his description of victim groups, saying only that they needed to be a "collectivity." Both Kuper and the Israeli psychologist Israel Charny, one of the most important figures in the field of genocide studies, however, agreed with Drost that mass killing was necessary for an event to be labeled a genocide. Charny, however, simply sidestepped the issues of victim groups and intent altogether by defining genocide as the "mass killing" of "human beings" outside of war in a condition of "essential defenselessness and helplessness of the victims" (Charny 1994, 17).

In their influential *The History and Sociology of Genocide* (1990), Kurt Jonasshon and Frank Chalk also avoided the problem of defining intent by substituting the verb "intend" while still employing the term "destroy" to describe the necessary result of the genocidists' actions. This was significant in that they moved toward the concept of perpetrator-defined victim groups, which is also central to our definition. Helen Fein, in her major work on genocide, also published in 1990 agreed with Kuper that victim groups need only be a "collectivity." Her characterization of "intent" as being demonstrated by "sustained purposeful action" is also wise, as what we *should* be looking at, in our opinion, are the *outcomes* of the genocidists' actions.

This extended debate over the definition of genocide may strike some students as somewhat pointless or as overly intellectualized. Why have scholars spent so much time and energy defining something that to most people might seem completely obvious? Isn't genocide simply the killing of a large number of defenseless people because of the race, nationality, or religion they belong to? Unfortunately, the word genocide has far too often either been cynically misused in its application or not used when it should have been. An example of its misuse might be when the US accused the Iraqi regime of being "worse than Hitler" when the Americans invaded in 1991, and again in 2003. A good example of not using the term when it was appropriate was when US diplomats were ordered to avoid the word genocide as the Rwandan Genocide was unfolding in 1994. These are examples of a fundamental tension underlying debates over the definition of genocide. Should we define genocide broadly and *inclusively* or narrowly and *exclusively*? More importantly, how can we define genocide from a humanistic, ethical perspective that combines intellectual vigor with deep historical understanding, and avoids creating "victimhood comparisons?"

As we wrote in the Introduction, words have meaning, and "genocide" is an especially powerful term. Therefore, we should be especially cautious and judicious in using it. Some scholars fear that if used too frequently we might strip the word genocide of its power. Others have asserted that perhaps we should define genocide more narrowly. Arguing about what does or does not qualify as a genocide, however, can generate an unseemly hierarchy of suffering. Many who disagree and call for a broader and more inclusive approach than that embodied by the 1948 Convention's definition argue that the concept has already lost its analytical usefulness. In the most extensive analysis of the UN Genocide Convention, Anton Weiss-Wendt explicitly challenges us to think outside the box of the legal definition precisely because of the political considerations and scheming that produced the UN definition (Weiss-Wendt, 2017). Many other academics agree—including the authors of the book you are holding (or perhaps reading on a tablet or smartphone). Genocide denial can be masked by the rigid adherence to the Convention's definition crafted by diplomats and legal experts with specific agendas in mind. It must be concluded, then, that the 1948 Genocide Convention is not so much a moral and principled response to Nazi barbarism as it is a political document designed to exclude from the Convention the crimes and atrocities previously committed upon the peoples of the world by the victors of World War II.

Euphemisms for Genocide

A "euphemism" is an indirect word or expression substituted for one considered to be too harsh when referring to something unpleasant. One euphemism for genocide, ethnic cleansing, is also a relatively new word in the vocabulary of political violence. The term, first used by German officials during World War II, was not widely known until some Serbian politicians redeployed it in the 1980s to complain about the expulsion of some Serbs in the region of Kosovo (part of Serbia, which was then part of Yugoslavia). When warfare erupted in much of Yugoslavia in 1991 and 1992 (see Chapter Seven) "ethnic cleansing" became widely used by journalists and others to explain mass expulsions of Muslims from various regions, in particular the "cleansing" of Muslims from eastern Bosnia. While we have become accustomed to the term as it succinctly describes the crime involved—mass expulsions, with the goal of radically changing the populations of certain regions—we should never forget that it is an ugly one, invented by genocidists.

The idea of "cleansing" a body politic or geographical area of "filth" or "vermin" reaches well back into antiquity. In his insightful book on the subject, Andrew Bell-Fialkoff defined ethnic cleansing as "the expulsion of an 'undesirable' population from a given territory due to religious or ethnic discrimination, political, strategic or ideological considerations, or a combination of these" (Bell-Fialkoff 1996, 110). We have already determined that genocide always involves a process and that any such process typically includes identifying, isolating, and then subjugating the victim group. The forcible assimilation of the group, the forced removal of that group from its home—leading to the destruction of their cultural and/or social ties—or the physical destruction of the group—are all final acts in the genocidal process. In many of these cases, of course, physical annihilation of the victim group is not the goal. This has led some academics, again using the Holocaust as a prototype, to argue that genocide *must* involve mass killing and therefore ethnic cleansing is not genocide.

Two influential American scholars of ethnic violence who hold this view, Norman Naimark and Andrew Bell-Fialkoff, assert that there is a spectrum of ethnic cleansing with genocide being only its final, most-extreme form. On one end of this spectrum, "population transfers"—the removal of an ethnic group from a territory to *prevent* ethnic conflict, often sanctioned by the international community—is merely an attempt to remove and not to destroy. "Ethnic cleansing" operations that involve violence and the forcible removal of a group in an attempt to achieve some kind of ethno-territorial homogeneity—although serious crimes against humanity, are also not genocides for these academics as again, there is no intent to wholly destroy a people (Bell-Fialkoff 1996; Naimark 2001). These "cleansings," however, also often include removing the targeted victim group's places of worship, libraries, museums, archives, and so on. In our view, any attempt to remove a targeted population deemed to be undesirable by the perpetrators from a certain territory, even absent large-scale murder, that involves interference with that group's cultural life is the essence of genocide—that is, group destruction as Lemkin defined it (Figure 1.3).

In 1947 we saw an agreed upon "population transfer" during the partition of India where up to a million people were killed; in 1948, the very year that the Convention was signed, there was an "ethnic cleansing" in Palestine where thousands died and up to three-quarters of a million people forcibly displaced from their lands. While this was happening, the Allies themselves watched with equanimity as countries newly freed from the Nazi yoke forcibly expelled 12–15 million Germans from Central and Eastern Europe (Douglas 2013). Hundreds of thousands of Germans died in this

WHAT *SHOULD* BE THE DEFINITION OF GENOCIDE?   33

Figure 1.3 From the 1947 "Partition": the separation of India and Pakistan, after the end of British colonial rule. The Partition brought about one of the largest-ever waves of "ethnic cleansings" and expulsions—perhaps the single largest in history. In this photo, Muslim refugees flee from India to Pakistan. https://commons.wikimedia.org/wiki/File:Refugees_en_route_to_Pakistan;.jpg

"population transfer" (Bloxham 2008). The authorities obviously intended to carry out the "destruction of the national pattern of the oppressed group" followed by the "imposition of the national pattern of the oppressor"—the essence of Lemkin's classic definition of genocide. The Western powers and the Soviet Union all "quite deliberately resisted attempts to encompass the phenomenon of ethnic cleansing within the punishable acts" in the legal definition of genocide (Schabas 2000, 196), the same as they had done with their own acts of violence perpetrated against subjugated peoples the world over. After all, as Martin Shaw wryly commented, "if forcible removal was recognized as genocidal, moral differences between victors and losers would become matters of degree" (Shaw 2015, 72). Shaw does, however, correctly make a distinction between "long-established "settler" communities" and those who "personally and knowingly benefit from the expulsion of others" (ibid., 80). Those Germans uprooted from the Sudetenland after having lived there since the second half of the thirteenth century were indeed "ethnically cleansed," in a genocidal sense as opposed to those Germans that had been resettled in the Polish territories incorporated into the Third Reich after 1939. While all genocides involve ethnic cleansing to some degree, not all ethnic cleansings are necessarily genocides.

When discussing Nazi genocide in Europe, Lemkin noted the Nazis' deliberate attacks on culture, "prohibiting or destroying cultural institutions and cultural activities" (Lemkin 1945, 81). By starting from the definition of genocide concocted by lawyers and diplomats for the 1948 Convention, many academics continue to wrongly distinguish such attacks from genocide by instead calling these events by yet another euphemism, "ethnocide," or "cultural genocide." For Kurt Jonassohn, as for some others in the field, this occurs when "the collective memory, identity or culture of a group was destroyed without the killing of its members" (Chalk & Jonassohn 1990, 21). Lemkin, as we know, intended it to be used as a synonym for genocide, not a different concept altogether. In a footnote to his description of genocide in *Axis Rule*, he said, "another term could be used for the same idea, namely *ethnocide*, consisting of the Greek word '*ethnos*'—nation—and the Latin word '*cide*'" (Lemkin 1945, 79). Some scholars have since correctly used the term ethnocide in the sense of being "largely synonymous with genocide" (Lemarchand 1998). Lemkin, then, acknowledged the term's usefulness. However, as Martin Shaw correctly points out, since ethnic groups are included as one of the protected human collectivities in the Convention's definition there is no need to use that term in place of genocide (Shaw 2015). We agree with Shaw and others and consider it simply another method of genocide. Most people, however, equate the term *ethnocide* with the concept of "cultural" genocide.

Chapter 2 is devoted to case studies of ethnic cleansing, Stalin deported, often brutally, many different minority peoples from their homelands before, during, and after World War II. We will also see later on in the chapters on "Genocides of Social Groups" and "Genocides of Political Groups," how entire socioeconomic groups, as well as political adversaries, were labeled "enemies of the people" and either killed or sent to Siberia. As the American historian Eric D. Weitz wrote, for the Soviets, these peoples were "sources of pollution, or filth as they endangered the 'health' of the social body" (Weitz 2003, 239). The Soviet "Great Purge" of political "enemies of the people" in 1937–38 used similar imagery, and these attacks on party members and others were referred to as "cleansings." Those who remained were forced to conform to Soviet attitudes, values, and ways of life. The Nazis, of course, took this idea to the extreme with the notion that the Jews of Germany—less than 1% of the total population of that country—somehow threatened the racial purity of the German people. This language about "blood-poisoning" is being repeated today in the United States by neo-fascist, authoritarian political figures such as Donald J. Trump. As we know, genocide is a process, and the Nazi genocide Lemkin wrote about started first with discriminatory laws and oppression, then economic destruction, then the expulsion of Jews from Germany—this last was most certainly ethnic cleansing. The "Final Solution"—the decision to murder all the Jews that the Nazis could round up in their empire—only came later.

We need to continue to remind readers of this book that central to Lemkin's concept of genocide is the deliberate destruction of a people's cultural essence *culminating* in the removal of that culture from the world's cultural mosaic. This is because many scholars—and particularly the general public—will continue to believe, whatever we say here, that mass murder and physical extermination are the true markers of a genocide. Scholars who believe genocide must involve a threat to the physical survival of the group, or more often mass killing, have, in the words of Martin Shaw "moved away from Lemkin's approach in ways that militate [work to prevent] against understanding" his concept (Shaw 2015, 13). Lemkin, however, was unambiguous in his discussion of what constituted genocide: "By 'genocide' we mean the destruction of a nation or an ethnic group" (Lemkin 2008, 79). In his earlier writings on "Barbarity," he had also specifically included "social collectivities." These social collectivities included any human group with a common cultural tradition. We remind you that Lemkin specifically asserted that this "destruction" of a nation or ethnic group does not need to be achieved through the mass killing of *all* the collectivity's members but can be done through the "destruction of the national pattern of the oppressed group" and "the imposition of the national pattern of the oppressor." "This imposition, in turn, may be made upon the oppressed population which is *allowed to remain or upon the territory alone, after removal of the population and the colonization by the oppressor's own nationals*" [italics ours] (ibid.).

Many powerful states, concerned that by virtue of being signatories to the Genocide Convention, they might be legally obligated to act to prevent it, are reluctant to acknowledge the obvious. We have already mentioned—and will discuss in more detail in a later chapter—the United States' initial reluctance to classify the 1994 events in Rwanda as a genocide; instead, the government acknowledged that only "genocidal acts" were being committed by the Hutu extremists. The use of the term "ethnic cleansing" is often just another strategy employed by world powers to avoid having to prevent or address genocides. If, as we have suggested, the concept of "genocide," first defined by lawyers and morally compromised diplomats, needs to be reimagined, then so too do the terms ethnic cleansing, ethnocide, and so-called "cultural" genocide. All of these terms are imprecise, and all are merely different forms of genocide. As the legal scholar Clotilde Pegorier has noted, the term "ethnic cleansing" in particular has been under attack by many social scientists not only for its imprecision but also because it can be seen as "a dangerous euphemism for genocide" (Pegorier 2013, 1). Martin Shaw agrees, calling it a "euphemistic term" and, more importantly, noting it is but "one of the methods of genocide" (Shaw 2015, 82–83). As we have discussed, Lemkin believed cultural genocide was the entire point of his concept and therefore "not a different type of genocide" (Irvin-Erickson in Bachmann, ed., 2019).

In our opinion, ethnic cleansing is indeed genocide and it properly belongs within its definition. Unlike genocide, the term ethnic cleansing is not codified into law—it is usually included as one of many "crimes against humanity" in international law. Shaw rightly points out that very many terms "such as *expulsion, deportation, forced migration* and *forced removal* indicate the precise harm caused" and that *genocide* describes "the general social destruction caused" (Shaw 2015, 68, italics in the original). Inherent to the act of ethnically cleansing a territory is the destruction of the cultural heritage of a people—its museums, libraries, art galleries, monuments, and places of worship. Lemkin believed that the destruction of these things was not in and of itself genocide unless it "menaces the existence of the social group which exists by virtue of its common culture" (Irvin-Erickson in Bachmann, ed., 2019, 32). If these actions were part of "a coordinated plan" aimed at destroying different aspects of their existence then it would be genocide. Other aspects could be, for example, the destruction of social, economic, and political institutions.

Lemkin's chief concern—while Nuremberg focused on the mass death caused by the Nazis—was, as the UN General Assembly Resolution 96 (I) described the "Crime of Genocide" in 1946, "the great losses to humanity in the form of cultural and other contributions represented by these human groups [...]." The definition used in this book will specifically identify concerted efforts by the genocidists to destroy the group's ability to maintain its social and cultural cohesion and thus, its existence as a group as being genocide. Genocidists' efforts to remove a human group from their homeland while removing any signs of their historic, collective achievements from the territory erased cannot help but destroy the group's heritage and the process of their cultural development itself. As Lemkin wrote in *Axis Rule,* the imposition of the conqueror's language, customs, and values on those who might remain as part of an effort to assimilate them also destroys the group by eliminating that group's culture. Lemkin unequivocally saw this as the murder of a people—genocide. Scholars in genocide studies often assert that *their* definition is closer to Lemkin's original meaning and therefore the true essence of Lemkin's conception of genocide. We make no such claim. But Lemkin's definition, and not the Genocide Convention, should at least be the starting point for analysis. Whether we label forced deportation as "population transfers" or ethnic cleansing, and the repression of a people's language, religion, and cultural expressions as ethnocide or "cultural" genocide, these processes all destroy a distinct human community and their way of life. These things are all genocide, too.

What then Should Be the Definition of Genocide?

Most academics agree that the definition of genocide arrived at three-quarters of a century ago, shaped by political considerations and national self-interests, was not only insufficiently inclusive but also lends itself to overly legalistic interpretations that can thwart any action to actually prevent genocides, such as the manner in which "intent" is usually understood. We have identified many problems with the legal definition, including not only what constitutes a "group" but also what does it mean "to destroy" such a group, what constitutes a "whole" or "part" of a "group" and why are only racial, national, ethnical (*sic*) and religious "groups" designated for protection? Perhaps it is best if we simply recognize the weaknesses of the 1948 definition by critiquing it, as we have here, and after acknowledging its influence and status refuse to be trapped by it. Rather than being drawn into the endless debate, we should instead try to focus on genocide as an all-too-common human experience—in Douglas Irvin-Erickson's words "the experience of being subjected to group destruction" (Irvin-Erickson in Graziosi and Sysyn, 2022, 151).

As Shaw has indicated, the starting point to study genocide should be Lemkin's thinking on the subject. Michelle Tusan concurs, saying that, "he gave us a valuable working definition" although one that "remains problematic" (Tusan in Graziosi and Sysyn, 2022, 200). She reminds us that Lemkin's definition also "came out of a historical context—the lead-up to World War II—and had its own politics" but she acknowledges that scholars today have begun "to reconcile themselves to Lemkin's concept, whether it is to reject or accept his formulation" (ibid.) After decades of research and reflection,

Martin Shaw argues that "we need a concept whose parameters are clear and logical, which makes the most sense of a range of cases" that describes "all targeted destruction of population groups" (Shaw 2015, 7). He proposes we restore Lemkin's original definition to its "central place in the understanding of genocide." We agree.

This book's definition, then, is as follows: "Genocide is the purposeful attempt to destroy any human group as defined by the genocidists. It is an effort to disrupt that group's social cohesion, thereby preventing its ability to maintain its cultural identity, and thus, its very existence as a group." This approach allows us to move away from legalese altogether and to adopt multidisciplinary methods of analysis to explore the social, political, and economic patterns of conflict—including processes of marginalization, oppression, and subjugation—that can ultimately lead to the destruction of groups.

Questions for Further Discussion

1. Discuss the differences between Raphael Lemkin's concept of genocide and the legal definition provided by the UN Genocide Convention of 1948. What considerations shaped the final definition arrived at in 1948? What was missing or different from Lemkin's concept?
2. Are the terms "ethnic cleansing," "ethnocide," and "cultural" genocide useful to distinguish between different forms of violence against groups?
3. What are the key components of the UN Genocide Convention of 1948 that are problematic for scholars and human rights activists? How could these components be improved?
4. Should the UN redefine or revise its 1948 definition of genocide? If so, in what ways?

Chapter Two

"ETHNIC CLEANSING" IS GENOCIDE, TOO

> *The military and BGP [Border Guard Police] slaughtered my son, who was five years old. When the military came, I was pregnant. The situation was very horrific. I could not get all of my children. I could not go to my son. He was killed.*
> —25-year-old Rohingya woman, US State Department Report, September 2018

"Ethnic Cleansing" in Bosnia and the Genocide of the Rohingya

As we have seen, many observers and experts continue to draw a sharp distinction between genocide and ethnic cleansing. Political scientist Andrew Bell-Fialkoff argued that genocide is marked by mass murder and therefore should "be treated as a separate category" from ethnic cleansing (Bell-Fialkoff 1996, 1), and Norman Naimark agreed that "ethnic cleansing and genocide are two different activities" (Naimark 2001, 3). However, they both acknowledge the exceptional violence and destruction that the term "ethnic cleansing" can obscure. Bell-Fialkoff admits that it "is a euphemism that hides the ugly truth" (Bell-Fialkoff 1996, 2), while Naimark concedes that ethnic cleansing itself is "shot through with violence and brutality in the most extreme form" (Naimark 2001, 193). Both historians, moreover, acknowledge the obvious—that ethnic cleansing is a crime against humanity and subject to prosecution under international law. It is in fact one form or method of group destruction, or genocide. The prosecution of crimes against humanity, however, has the virtue of not needing to meet the high legal bar of intent. As we will see in the Conclusion, this category of international crimes could—and should—be used to prosecute what are simply different variants of genocide such as ethnic cleansing, extermination, forcible pregnancy, and so on.

A UN General Assembly resolution described the Serbian assault on Bosnian Muslims following the destruction of Yugoslavia in the 1990s as ethnic cleansing, but went on to characterize that policy as being "a form of genocide" and this was then "reaffirmed in a number of subsequent resolutions" (Schabas 2000, 192). Samantha Power, who covered the Yugoslav Wars as a journalist and later served in high-ranking positions in the Obama and Biden administrations, noted in her book *A Problem from Hell* that in 1993 UN lawyers had concluded that ethnic cleansing could be considered genocide under the Convention (Power, 2002). Some jurists, such as Elihu Lauterpacht of the International Court of Justice, concurred. Ethnic cleansing is a tactic that always results in "deliberately inflicting on the group conditions of life calculated to bring about its physical destruction in whole or in part" and obviously causes "serious bodily or mental harm to members of the group." William Schabas—among the leading experts on law and genocide—agrees that this term then is but "a euphemism for genocide" (Schabas 2000, 192).

During the wars that wracked the Balkans during and after the disintegration of Yugoslavia in the 1990s, many journalists began to use this term in their writings and made the misnomer "ethnic cleansing" commonplace. Subsequently, both the International Criminal Tribunal for the Former Yugoslavia (ICTY) and the International Court of Justice (ICJ) agreed that—although the massacre of over 8,000 Muslim men and boys at Srebrenica in July 1995 was deemed to be genocide—the larger, generalized violence against Bosnians from 1992 to 1995 did not meet the Convention's definition of genocide. It was, therefore, a "crime against humanity" accomplished through the act of ethnic cleansing. In Bosnia and Herzegovina, the Serbs drove hundreds of thousands of Muslims from their homeland in the name of creating a "Greater Serbia," which will be discussed in Chapter Seven. The Serbs destroyed mosques, libraries, statues, and the like in an effort to eradicate any trace of Bosnian Muslim (or "Bosniak") culture—in other words, a strategy that Lemkin described as the essence of genocide. At least 100,000 civilians were killed, two-thirds of them Bosnian Muslims, and thousands of Muslim women were raped, some of them deliberately impregnated in a calculated attempt to destroy Muslim social connections and ethnic lineages. This was rape as genocide, which we also will examine in more detail later in Chapter Four. In our view, there is no question that the Bosnian Muslims were subjected to genocide by Serb and Bosnian Serb forces throughout the entire war of 1992–95, and it is absurd to treat the Srebrenica massacre as separate from the longer, wider genocide.

Some of the same journalists who popularized the term ethnic cleansing also depicted the violence in the Balkans as the result of "ancient hatreds" despite the fact that Serbs, Croats, and Muslims had lived together for centuries and that there were high rates of intermarriage between them. Michael Mann has suggested instead that modern, democratic state-building is responsible for many episodes of ethnic cleansing. In his analysis, the dominant *ethnos* (ethnic group in the sense of a nation or people) associates itself with the idea of the *demos* (the people as a political unit) and then views minorities as being "other"—who therefore must be removed from the body politic (Mann 2005, 3). This is a phenomenon readily apparent in the United States today among White nationalists and racists and fascists elsewhere—as we will see in Chapter Three. Ethnic violence in Bosnia, and elsewhere, certainly does sometimes have its genesis in state-and-empire building. It is usually the result of the manipulative actions of political elites to mobilize their populations in an effort not only to bring about homogeneity in their respective lands but also to solidify their own political power. Nonetheless, it was here, 30 years ago in Yugoslavia, that the term ethnic cleansing gained currency. It has since been used—inaccurately—to describe murderous political violence around the globe.

Another instance of the misuse of this term was the expulsion of 750,000 Rohingya Muslims in 2017 from Myanmar—also known as Burma—to Bangladesh by the Buddhist-dominated military leadership. The Rohingya had lived in Rakhine state—formerly known as Arakan—in the northwest of Burma for generations. The Bengali name for the region is "Rohang" and, thus, Rohingya means "inhabitant of Rohang."

Many of the Muslim inhabitants forced out of Rakhine state were descended from Bengali Muslims who had migrated there from that region both during British colonial rule and after World War II. Like the Serbs, who pointed to their persecution by the Croatian allies of the Nazis during World War II to justify their actions, the Burmese Buddhists remembered the Rohingya fighting against other Buddhists in Arakan during that same conflict. The Rohingya Muslims had allied with the British, who had promised them an independent state after the war and fought the Buddhists, who had allied themselves with the Japanese. The Rohingya chased many Buddhists out of Arakan altogether (Ibrahim 2018). After the war's end, the new Buddhist-dominated Burmese government denied citizenship to the Rohingya and the Burmese government has ever since viewed them as illegal immigrants—even excluding them from the official census. Immediately after obtaining their independence from Britain in 1948, the Burmese government instituted a repressive regime of discrimination against the Rohingya that was similar in some respects to the South African system of *apartheid* (racial "separateness," enforcing racist rule) instituted in that same year (Lee 2021). Like Blacks in South Africa before the end of White rule in 1994, the Rohingya had no freedom of movement and could not travel without official permission. They received no essential services such as education or healthcare but were obligated to serve in the military and to perform manual labor on public works projects. The United Nations General Assembly declared *apartheid* in South Africa a "crime against humanity" in 1966, and subsequently, the UN Security Council affirmed this finding in 1984. The Rohingya lived under a similarly repressive regime and it is no wonder, then, that some Rohingya joined armed militias and began a long-running insurgency in hopes of joining the northern part of Rakhine state to Bangladesh, the neighboring majority-Muslim nation that was established in 1971.

After a series of guerilla attacks by Rohingya militias, the Myanmar government launched a horrific attack on the civilian Muslim population of Rakhine state in 2017. In a report released in October 2017 by the Office of the High Commissioner for Human Rights (OHCHR), entitled *"Mission Report of the OHCHR Rapid Response Mission to Cox's Bazar, Bangladesh,"* the "systematic process" employed by the Burmese military to drive the Rohingya entirely out of the country and into Bangladesh was detailed. This was a deliberate strategy to spread fear and trauma among the community through deliberate massacres and the indiscriminate killing of anyone who resisted—more than 6,000 Rohingya were killed in the first month alone of this so-called clearance operation—a strategy that included the widespread rape of the Rohingya women.

The genocidists detained and brutally interrogated any male between the ages of 15 and 40 whom they suspected of being involved in the guerilla campaign. Many Rohingya cultural, religious, and political figures were imprisoned. To cover these crimes, the military burned down the Rohingya villages that had been emptied. Marzuki Darusman, the chair of the Independent Fact-Finding Commission Mission on Myanmar, reported in September 2018 that the security forces burned down and razed nearly 400 villages. Worse, ordinary Buddhist civilians joined in the murderous mayhem along with the Myanmar military and then looted the property of the inhabitants after they had fled in terror (press.un.org/en/2018/sc13552.doc). As a result, approximately

600,000–700,000 Rohingya poured into Bangladesh on foot and by boat, joining the several hundred thousand already there as a result of earlier communal violence. The Prime Minister of Bangladesh reported to the UN General Assembly in September 2018 that well over one million Rohingya had entered the country over the previous few years. A UN study released in 2018 estimated that at least 24,000 people had died in the violence (ibid.). Secretary General of the United Nations Antonio Guterres called this "clearance operation" a "textbook example of ethnic cleansing," (BBC News, January 23, 2020). The United Nations report, however, called the campaign of murder, rape, and terror what it truly was—genocide.

In a speech at the United States Holocaust Memorial Museum on March 21, 2022, the American Secretary of State Antony Blinken agreed that the violence directed against the Rohingya constituted genocide, saying the mass atrocities committed by the Myanmar military demonstrated the "intent to destroy Rohingya, in whole or in part." In his remarks, Secretary Blinken also drew parallels between what had happened to the Jews in Nazi Germany and what had happened to the Rohingya in Myanmar. In Myanmar, as in Germany, the groundwork was "laid far in advance, over years […], through a steady process of dehumanization and demonization." Like the Jews, who the Nazis compared to rats, and the Tutsis in Rwanda compared to cockroaches by the Hutus, the Rohingya "were compared to fleas, to thorns, to an invasive species." Similar to the German Jews and other groups targeted for genocide, the Rohingya had their rights and citizenship methodically stripped away. In 1978, the Burmese military forced the Rohingya to register with the government as aliens and embarked on a campaign of terror that led to 250,000 Rohingya fleeing to Bangladesh. In 1991, the military undertook another campaign of violence to create "A Clean and Beautiful Nation" that caused another 250,000 Rohingya to flee to Bangladesh. The Nazis had also tried to create such a nation, and even an entire continent, that was *Judenrein* (free of Jews), through a campaign of discrimination, violence, and terror. This "ethnic cleansing" of Germany ultimately led to the "Final Solution." The genocidal regime in Cambodia, the Khmer Rouge, harbored similar visions of racial "purity" as have other murderous governments. As Secretary Blinken noted, "the path is a familiar one, mirroring in so many ways the path to the Holocaust and other genocides." Although Blinken and other US officials are silent about crimes committed by their allies and clients, for example, Saudi Arabia's massive war crimes in Yemen over the last decade, Secretary Blinken was correct on this matter. The last stage of the Burmese genocide of the Rohingya began in 2017. It continues today.

Hitler's "Race War" in the East

The Nazi genocide of the Jews is well known and extensively chronicled. Less familiar is the genocide perpetrated against the Slavic peoples of Eastern Europe. Hitler's worldview was there for all to see in the lengthy, brutish manifesto he wrote in the early 1920s, *Mein Kampf*, in which he clearly enunciated his racist, Social Darwinian policies and wrote of invading Russia to achieve the necessary *Lebensraum* (living space) for future colonization by the master Aryan race. Hitler wrote, "But if we talk about new soil and territory in Europe today, we can think primarily only of Russia and its vassal border states" (Hitler 1971, 654–55). Lemkin wrote about Hitler's *Rassenkampf* (race war) in his book *Axis Rule*. Writing in 1943, he noted that whereas previously wars had largely been limited to "activities against armies and states" in "the present war [...] genocide is widely practiced by the German occupant." This war was waged "not merely against states and their armies but against peoples" (Lemkin 1945, 80–81). Lemkin saw German policy as leading to the virtual physical annihilation of Slavic peoples through many different methods, such as decreasing birthrates by separating the sexes and deporting males for forced labor elsewhere; decreasing the available food rations for the non-German population; and depriving these "undesired national groups" of "elemental necessities for preserving health and life" (Lemkin 1945, 86–88).

Taking Hitler at his word—and the true horror of Hitler and Nazism is that he meant every word of his pronouncements—we can then begin to understand why tens of millions of Soviets died in the conflict. Hitler's ravings clearly indicate that he equated "Jewishness" with "Bolshevism" [communism] as he believed that with the Communist takeover in 1917, the Russians had been contaminated by the Jews and were now inferior beings whose lives were of little value. The American historian David Crowe writes that Hitler believed that Marxism was a Jewish doctrine that "systematically planned to hand the world over to the Jews" (Crowe 2008, 94). Convinced that the Jews were the source of all Germany's misfortunes since 1914, Hitler "married his racial ideas with his foreign policy goals of *Lebensraum* in the East [...]" and any "campaign against the Jews was an essential part of the war for Aryan survival and expansion" (quoted in ibid., 103). It was not a coincidence, then, that the mass killings of Jews, which had begun in Poland in 1939, accelerated dramatically and became systematized with the invasion of the Soviet Union two years later. Hitler's war against Russia should be seen as the "struggle for territorial conquest, a clash of ideologies and the *Rassenkampf* that it undoubtedly was" (Forster 1986, 15).

We have already seen in the previous chapter how Himmler had drawn up a blueprint calling for the "removal"—one way or another—of tens of millions of Russians to make way for colonization by German settlers. It was decided at a conference of German State Secretaries in Berlin in May 1941 that providing food for the army and the civilian population of Germany had the highest priority; "as a result, millions of people will surely starve" (Hamburg Institute for Social Research, 1999, 142). The utter indifference to the fate of these civilians, born of the Nazis' racist contempt for the lives of Slavs, can be seen in the deliberate implementation of the callous "Hunger Plan" designed to seize food supplies for the German army and civilians fully aware that tens of millions of people would starve to death (Tooze 2007). The German army encircled and besieged Leningrad (both before and after the existence of the Soviet Union, the city has been known as St. Petersburg) just two months after the start of the invasion in June 1941 and cut off food supplies for 900 days. The inhabitants were forced to eat wallpaper paste scraped off the walls that had been made from potatoes, along with grass and weeds. They even boiled leather goods to make edible jelly while some resorted to cannibalism after all the zoo animals and household pets had been consumed.

Figure 2.1 Young girls assembling machine guns to help defend Leningrad during the siege, 1943. https://commons.wikimedia.org/wiki/File:Two_little_girls_assemble_submachine_guns_during_the_siege_of_Leningrad,_1943._(46089025944).jpg

Over the course of two and one-half years, approximately eight hundred thousand people were starved to death in that one city—nearly equaling the total death toll for the United States and Great Britain combined in all of World War II (Figure 2.1).

The millions who were purposely allowed to perish, if not murdered outright, point up the difference between Hitler's war in the West and the racial struggle in the East. In early 1941, the *Wehrmacht* (German army) calculated that in the opening months of the war, it would capture two to three million prisoners, including one million in the opening weeks of the campaign. On March 30, 1941, Hitler told his senior military commanders that he "wanted to see the impending war against the Soviet Union conducted not according to customary military principles, but as a war of extermination against an ideology and its adherents, whether within the Red Army or in a non-military function" (quoted in ibid., 17). Many of the men in the *Wehrmacht* saw the war as a struggle between Aryans and Jews due to the "ceaseless and ruthless propaganda of the regime against the 'Jewish-Bolshevik *Untermenschen*' [racially inferior 'sub-humans'] to which the soldiers had been exposed throughout their youth" (Crowe 2008, 197).

The population was to be mercilessly exploited, as the German army was expected to feed itself from stocks and reserves available in Russia. In contrast, orders sent to German troops fighting in France in June 1940 warned that the French should not be mistreated. In addition, any illegal acts toward the general population, such as robbery or rape, were to be punished as crimes in France. Sex offenses such as rape in France were considered to be merely "racial offenses" or "fraternization" in Soviet territory. German troops in France were supposed to pay in cash for any purchases, although these rules were not strictly enforced. German troops were also supposedly forbidden from interfering with the cultural life of the French. Punishments for plundering in Russia were far lighter than in the Western and Eastern European countries that Hitler invaded. In fact, while soldiers in France were prohibited from living off the land, pillaging by troops and the senseless slaughter of livestock was par for the course in Russia. Despite any official decrees or orders, German occupation authorities nonetheless pursued a campaign of state-sponsored larceny throughout its territories in Europe, as Gotz Aly demonstrated in his 2005 book *Hitler's Beneficiaries: Plunder, Racial War, and the Nazi Welfare State.* An exhibition entitled "The German Army and Genocide" that opened in 1995 exposed the sheer criminality of the German army's conduct in the East, with hundreds of photographs, military documents, and personal letters home from all ranks proving the collaboration between the SS and the *Wehrmacht.* In his influential and painstakingly researched *Hitler's Army: Soldiers, Nazis, and War in the Third Reich*, Omer Bartov concludes that the German army was not merely an apolitical, professional fighting force following orders in the service of their country. Instead, it was thoroughly indoctrinated and imbued with Nazi racist ideology through a carefully planned campaign of propaganda that, for many, began in grade school and was then reinforced through mandatory participation in the "Hitler Youth." This led to a highly motivated military that considered both Jews and Slavs to be subhuman.

The German treatment of Russian civilians, millions of whom were stripped of their possessions and sent to Germany to perform forced labor, was reprehensible and heinous in the extreme. Hitler's scheme calling for the colonial exploitation of Russia's land and resources fit in perfectly with his long-held conviction that the Slavic peoples were merely "redskins." From his childhood reading of romanticized accounts of the American West he concluded that the success of the United States' "Manifest Destiny" was made possible only after the settlers had "shot down the millions of redskins to a few hundred thousand" (Westermann 2016, 3). Hitler drew from this American example and believed that after defeating the Red Army millions of Germans would settle on farms in the former Soviet Union. Final victory for Germany would have resulted in the destruction of the Russian people and their historical culture—another Nazi genocide.

The Native Peoples of North America

Hitler's plan for the resettlement—or outright murder—of supposedly inferior peoples to obtain the necessary *Lebensraum* for German settlers is, of course, properly viewed with revulsion. In the popular mind, the Nazi movement and its ideology occupy the depths of human evil and the Holocaust is *the* example of inhuman cruelty. The burning hatred that leads to violence against targeted "others" is incomprehensible to most people, and they assume that this period in history was some kind of aberration, a detour so to speak from the progressive and enlightened aspects of the Western tradition. With the moral clarity and indignation that permeates all his work, the Swedish writer Sven Lindqvist debunked this tendency to see the Nazis as somehow disconnected from the larger contours of European history. They had been made into "the sole scapegoats for ideas of extermination that are actually a common European heritage" (Lindqvist 1996, 9). Raphael Lemkin had identified many instances of state-sponsored violence against religious minorities in early modern Europe that he hoped to explore for a future history of genocide. These episodes included the murder of Albigenses in France during the twelfth and thirteenth centuries, "conversos"—Jews who had converted to Christianity in the Iberian Peninsula (Spain and Portugal) in the fifteenth and sixteenth centuries—and, of course, many violent attacks on Jews throughout Europe as well. Western civilization obviously carried within it the potential for genocidal violence and this made possible other holocausts before *the* Holocaust. The idea of progress and the sense of superiority it conferred upon Europeans served to justify the appropriation of land, extraction of resources, and forcible removal of native inhabitants in the quest for profit.

Settler colonialism brought Europeans into conflict with native peoples in the New World as they sought to make over these supposedly empty lands to their benefit. The near destruction of the indigenous peoples of North America is but one example among many. The result of the Europeans' arrival was an unmitigated disaster for these native inhabitants. In the United States, for example, the US Census Bureau estimated that by 1900, after four centuries of contact, only 237,000 out of an estimated original population of five million had survived (Thornton in Haines and Steckel, eds. 2000). Most of these deaths were from diseases such as smallpox and were not necessarily intentional, but the frequent massacres, forcible relocations, and efforts to "kill the Indian, but save the man"—that is cultural genocide and forced assimilation— most certainly were. This was probably, in the words of David Stannard "the worst human holocaust the world had ever witnessed" (Stannard 1992, 146). Lemkin himself had called the treatment of Native Americans "cultural genocide par excellence […] the most effective and thorough method of destroying a culture, and of de-socializing human beings" (quoted in Decker in Moses and Stone, ed. 2008, 94). Before his early death from poverty and overwork in 1959 at age 59, Lemkin had intended to investigate in detail the genocide of the "Indians" in North America. He wanted "to prove that genocide was not an exceptional phenomenon, but that it occurs in intergroup relations with a certain regularity, like homicide takes place in relations between individuals" (quoted in Bryant 2020, 28). This, in fact, is a central thesis of the book. "Genocide" is not only a reoccurring problem but is in fact far wider a phenomenon than generally acknowledged.

This certainly was the case with settler colonialism throughout the world, where European attempts at domination invariably provoked resistance from native peoples that was then used to justify harsh settler responses that included massacres, forcible removal, deliberate starvation, and ultimately attempts at cultural eradication (Whitt and Clarke 2017). The English had already perfected this technique in the seventeenth century when they colonized Ireland in much the same manner they would America—seizing lands and forcing the natives to work for them while deporting others. This worked so well that English imperialists implemented the same techniques in their settler colonies in the New World. Of course, many scholars still resist applying the term genocide to the catastrophe inflicted upon the indigenous peoples of North America. Obviously, there was not necessarily an "intent" to destroy the group "as such," to use the language of the UN Genocide Convention of 1948, when whole villages and societies were wiped out by disease. There were very many diseases such as smallpox, cholera, scarlet fever, and typhoid for which Native Americans had no immunity. Many indigenous peoples suffered and died from pathogens without ever setting eyes on a European settler. The English, French, and Spanish all established empires in North America, yet it was the English—who would eventually become "Americans"—that so keenly lusted after land for agricultural production. It was among those colonists that an ideology of expansion and eliminationism took root.

In his influential study of America's aggressive imperial expansion, the American historian Walter Nugent shows how the idea of "unused lands" available for the taking enticed settlers to colonize successive "wests." This idea was common among all settler-colonists throughout the eighteenth, nineteenth, and twentieth centuries. For example, after the Holocaust, many European Jews influenced by the Zionist movement moved to Palestine—"a land without people for a people without land" goes an infamous and inaccurate Zionist mantra. In America, settlers first rushed into the trans-Appalachian "west" then, after the influx of white farmers had led to the forcible displacement of the native population, other White settlers pushed into the trans-Mississippi "west" and from there on to "the Far West." One of the best-known instances of the outright seizure of indigenous peoples' lands for white colonization was the Removal Act of 1830. The state of Georgia wanted to expropriate over five million acres of Cherokee land for white farmers' use—of course, enslaved Africans would be doing much of the work— and, in concert with the Federal government, offered as compensation land west of the Mississippi. Not surprisingly, the Cherokees refused to agree to leave their homeland. The Georgia legislature ignored their protestations and passed a series of laws that by 1830 resulted in the confiscation of all their land (Banner 2005). The Cherokees sued, and the lawsuit reached the United States Supreme Court. The Court found in favor of the Cherokees, asserting that as "sovereign nations" the state of Georgia could not extend its jurisdiction over Native Americans on their lands. Only the Federal government could negotiate with these independent peoples. President Jackson pushed for legislation to seize these lands illegally and in violation of the Constitution—as was pointed out by many representatives, including the well-known frontiersman Davy Crockett— and the Removal Act of 1830 barely passed in the US House of Representatives. The act resulted in the ethnic cleansing of five different peoples—the "civilized" tribes: Cherokee, Chickasaw, Choctaw, Creek, and Seminole nations. It was, of course, an astonishingly bad deal for these peoples. Promised 32 million acres in the West as well as $68 million to be paid out in annual installments, the responses were varied but the results were the same. The Choctaw reluctantly agreed and were the first to head out on what became known as the "Trail of Tears," but the resettlement process was botched and they suffered mightily from exposure, disease, and hunger before reaching their new home in "Indian Territory" (Oklahoma). Fully one quarter of the Choctaw—at least several thousand people—perished before reaching Oklahoma (Alvarez 2016). Probably twice that number of Cherokee died when they were forcibly resettled by the US Army at the end of the 1830s. This was not the "intent" of the authorities, but was the outcome nonetheless and therefore an ethnic cleansing as a method of genocide. Worse was still to come.

By the end of the American Civil War of 1861–65, most of the Native Americans east of the Mississippi had been cleared out. The victory of the Union in the Civil War gave impetus to a movement that called upon young (white) men, in the words of newspaper editor Horace Greeley, to "Go West." The Homestead Act of 1863 promised 160 acres free to anyone—including European immigrants but excluding Native Americans—who would settle on these lands and improve them. In 1860, there were 1.4 million European-Americans west of the Mississippi and 360,000 Native Americans. By the end of the nineteenth century, there were 8.5 million Americans in the "Far West" and less than a quarter million Native Americans (Kakel 2013). By then, most Americans had come to believe in their "Manifest Destiny" as the result of a campaign of propaganda that justified expansion at the expense of these supposedly savage and backward peoples in the name of progress. The term itself first appeared in an anti-Mexican editorial penned by John O'Sullivan in the July–August 1845 volume of the journal *The Democratic Review*. O'Sullivan wrote in favor of the United States annexing Texas—that it did after starting and winning the Mexican-American War. He asserted that foreign powers (meaning Mexico) were "thwarting our policy and hampering our power, limiting our greatness and checking the fulfillment of our manifest destiny to overspread the continent allotted by Providence for the free development of our yearly multiplying millions" (quoted in Westermann 2016, 20). The "millions" O'Sullivan was referring to were White Americans, not the few free Blacks and certainly not the "heathen Indians" and Mexicans still populating America's West. As Carroll P. Kakel III has perceptively noted, "Manifest Destiny was a conviction that God intended America to be under the control of the "White" Americans. It was, in many ways, an early projection of Anglo-Saxon supremacy, with a distinctly racist element to it" (Kakel 2013, 22). At the end of the nineteenth century, after the victorious conclusion of the "Indian" wars, Senator Albert J. Beveridge would again invoke God's will to advocate for the continued expansion of "His chosen [white] nation" so as "to finally lead in the regeneration of the world" (quoted in Waller 2007, 204). Many people do not know that Rudyard Kipling wrote his infamous 1899 poem "The White Man's Burden"—replete with racist references to "natives" as "half-devil, half-child"—as an exhortation for the United States to join the European powers in their "civilizing mission" as they brutally subjugated peoples around the globe.

Several treaties solemnly signed with the Plains peoples by US officials in the middle of the nineteenth century supposedly set aside vast tracts of land in perpetuity for the sole use of these peoples. The agreements stipulated that, although army forts could be built along the wagon routes to the West Coast and Southwest to protect settlers, the newly established tribal boundaries were to be respected and annual payments made as compensation for the tribes' forbearance. It was assumed that these lands were of little use to settlers. In 1868, by the Treaty of Fort Laramie, the United States recognized the sovereign right of the Sioux people to the exclusive use of the Black Hills in South Dakota. The discovery of gold in the Rocky Mountains, however, and then more gold and silver in western Montana, and still later more of these precious—at least to whites—minerals in the Black Hills of South Dakota, meant that these treaties had, of course, to be renegotiated. The miners extracted billions of dollars' worth of gold there, and worse, the new masters of that land dynamited a sacred mountain to carve four of their US presidents' faces into it and renamed it Mt. Rushmore. In 1980, the US Supreme Court ordered that the US government pay the Sioux $100 million in recompense; the Sioux have steadfastly refused to accept payment for land that was not for sale, and with interest, that sum of money due them is now over $2 billion.

White miners had flooded into these regions, and settlers soon followed. The army charged not only with protecting whites from attack by the enraged natives, but also with "protecting the Indians from the depredations and encroachment of white settlers, speculators, and traders," struggled to do either (Westermann 2016, 119). A series of skirmishes between Natives and settlers led to US Army reprisals and eventually full-scale military campaigns against the indigenous peoples, the most famous of which was "Custer's Last Stand" at the Battle of Little Bighorn in 1876. This battle, "one of the most complete disasters in American military annals," cost the lives of over 250 US soldiers and an equal number of Sioux (quoted in ibid., 134).

The lands set aside for the Native Americans, then, were generally of poor quality and considered "worthless" by White Americans—unless miners found gold. Whites violated treaties and encroached upon native lands at will. Forced onto "reservations"—concentration camps, in reality—Native Americans were subjected to wretched and lethal conditions, often not receiving promised foodstuffs because of widespread corruption as government agents enriched themselves. The reservations were rife with disease and epidemics. These factors contributed to a steady decline of the indigenous population; in 1853, US Indian Agent Thomas Fitzpatrick described the reservation system as "the legalized murder of a whole nation" (quoted in Kakel 2013, 190). Those Native Americans who refused to go to their assigned lands would be forced to do so by the army. One tactic was starvation. The coming of the railroad meant that the vast plains were now more easily reachable, and buffalo hunters slaughtered millions of the poor creatures and brought them to the point of extinction. This obviously affected the Plains native peoples greatly as the buffalo was a primary source of food, with their skins and hides providing clothes and shelter as well. As more and more settlers poured into the West, the cycle of dispossession, subjugation, and yes, extermination, continued. The buffalo hunters well knew that the end of the great herds of bison would mean the end of the natives. "Kill every buffalo you can [...] for every buffalo dead is an Indian gone" (quoted in ibid., 191). The outright murder of tens of thousands of Natives also continued. Massacres and organized campaigns of murder were carried out by the regular army but even more often by citizen militias. Territories were "cleansed" of the peoples that had lived there for centuries to make way for more White settlers. In Minnesota in 1862, Santee Sioux revolted against the land theft and the violence they had endured; volunteer militias brutally suppressed them. The surviving warriors were placed in cattle pens and 39 of them were later hanged in the largest mass execution in US history, with the others imprisoned. The remaining women and children held hostage during the revolt, were transferred to a distant fort to be imprisoned. Along the way, they "were assaulted by angry white citizens. Many were stoned and clubbed; a child was snatched from its mother's arms and beaten to death" (Churchill 1997, 226) (Figure 2.2).

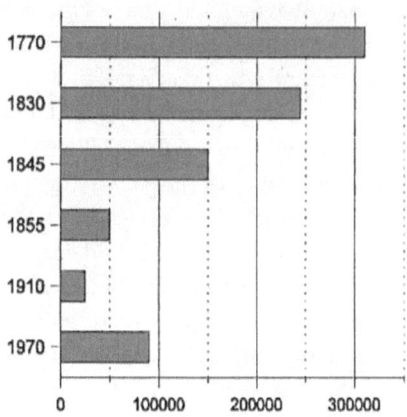

Figure 2.2 Indigenous population in the state of California. Note the rapid decline in the mid-1800s, the height of the "California Genocide" that accompanied the Gold Rush. https://commons.wikimedia.org/wiki/File:Native_California_population_graph.jpg

In Colorado and California, the earlier process of removal—akin to so-called ethnic cleansing—was replaced with outright extermination. In the former, in 1864, the territorial government formed a cavalry unit tasked with the extermination of any "hostile" Cheyenne found in Colorado. Governor John Evans declared, "Any man who kills a hostile Indian is a patriot!" In his view, *all* Native Americans were hostile and therefore he urged local citizens to join the armed militia and "pursue, kill and destroy" any they came across. The newly formed Third Regiment did just that. These murderers attacked peaceful villages and killed hundreds of women, children, and old men. They committed horrific atrocities upon the bodies of their victims (such as cutting out women's genitals and waving them on a stick or wearing them on their hats, tearing open pregnant women's bodies and removing the unborn children, and scalping the dead). The men faithfully followed the orders of their commander, Colonel John Chivington, who had promised "to kill all the Indians I come across." Chivington instructed his men to "use any means under God's heaven to kill Indians [...] kill and scalp them all, little and big" because "nits make lice" (quoted in ibid., 229). In California territory, it was perfectly acceptable—and legal—to enslave Native American children. These "indentured" unfortunates ultimately numbered more than 10,000. Wave after wave of settler militia attacks steadily drove their parents to the farthest reaches of California's mountain regions, where they starved to death. As the American historian Michael C. Bryant notes, the "pattern of genocide replayed in California much as it did throughout the North American continent: settler encroachments on Indian lands led to Indian raids on settler livestock, which invited the indiscriminate killing of Indian men, women, and children by settler militias" (Bryant 2020, 30). These massacres led to the virtual annihilation of both the Yana and Yuki peoples.

By the end of the nineteenth century, most Native Americans had been forced onto reservations by the army. If they ventured off, seeking in vain to return to their ancestral lands, they were forcibly returned. One such incident resulted in the massacre at Wounded Knee, South Dakota, on December 29, 1890. Not unlike the Serbs' murder of over 8000 Muslim men and boys in Srebrenica a century later, an acknowledged genocidal massacre that took place during a prolonged campaign of so-called ethnic cleansing, the murder of over 300 Lakota Sioux was a genocide too. Twenty US soldiers received the Medal of Honor for carrying out this atrocity. In 2022, the US House of Representatives included a requirement in the annual defense bill that these medals be revoked. The infamous "Battle" of Wounded Knee might have marked the end of the so-called Indian Wars; the genocide, however, would continue unabated.

Now that white settlements stretched from "sea to shining sea" and Native Americans were concentrated—we use the word deliberately—on reservations, the question of what to do with them arose. Should they be left to their own devices or "civilized?" In 1875, C. Augustus Haviland, the editor of a Chicago newspaper, penned an article entitled "The Indians: How to Protect Them and Ourselves." In this editorial, he discounted any possibility of making them into "civilized beings" and helpfully suggested that perhaps they ought to be placed on islands in the Great Lakes and off the coasts of Maine and California; where they would be "entirely isolated from any other race of human beings" (quoted in ibid., 76). Strangely enough, the Nazis resurrected this impractical, indeed ridiculous, idea for the resolution of its "Jewish problem" in 1940. Hitler's minions resurrected a bizarre plan that had been popular among anti-Semites for several decades—the removal of all the Jews of Europe to Madagascar, an island off the southeast coast of Africa. The plan envisioned before Germany began to lose its war against the Soviet Union was simply to ethnically cleanse Europe of its Jews, as they had already done in Germany, by exiling them beyond the Ural Mountains into Siberia—something Stalin would later consider for Russian Jews as we will see later in this chapter.

As we have been saying, there is, of course, no real difference between ethnic cleansing and genocide. They both destroy the soul and spirit of a people. Targeted violence is also always part of the process and the numbers of the dead from that process are not the yardstick by which to measure the impact of genocidal violence. The distinction between genocidal massacres and genocide is, in our view, and as opposed to that of some other scholars, one without a difference. We have already noted that, in Colorado Territory for example, and at Wounded Knee, occasional genocidal massacres *did* in fact occur. More troubling, from the repeated calls for the complete elimination of Native Americans sprinkled throughout US history—and the other genocidal massacres in US history as in Wilmington, NC, in 1898, in Tulsa, OK, in 1921, and Rosewood, FL, in 1923—we can state without doubt that the United States was a genocidal society (McWhirter, 2012).

Many whites in Australia, southern Africa, and North America simply assumed that native peoples would somehow fade away as more and more land came under settler cultivation. When this did not happen, however, they were quick to assert that the indigenous peoples should be removed altogether. We will explore the connections between settler colonialism and genocide later, in Chapter Seven. In North America, from the very first days of the new Republic, many whites called for the complete annihilation of the natives. A blood-curdling letter written to the North Carolina "Council of Safety" by three "founding fathers" of the United States just days after they signed the Declaration of Independence shows true genocidal intent. In this letter, they called for a military campaign against the Indigenes of North Carolina that "would extinguish the very race of them and scare to leave enough of existence to be a vestige in proof that a Cherokee nation once was [...]" (https://docsouth.unc.edu, accessed August 8, 2022). Also in North Carolina, that state's first governor baldly stated that a "war of extermination will continue to be waged between the races until the Indian race becomes extinct must be expected. While we cannot anticipate this result but with painful regret, the inevitable destiny of the race is beyond the power or wisdom of man to avert" (https://governors.library.ca.gov, accessed August 8, 2022).

As we will also see in the next chapter, these sentiments extended to African Americans as well. As with those formerly enslaved people, however, there were also those who, in the words of a writer for the *New York Herald*, wanted to "emancipate" them "from political disabilities [...] thus merging them into the great common nationality of United States citizens" (ibid., 30). This would necessarily require their "Christianization" and adoption of "modern [white] ways"—efforts the five "civilized" tribes had undertaken in the early part of the century to no avail. This supposedly humanitarian alternative to extinction was one in which "American Indian cultures would probably die out but Indian bloodlines would survive" (ibid., 251). As noted earlier, this was not possible for the Jews in Nazi-controlled Europe as Hitler's "Final Solution" envisioned their complete disappearance as a people from the face of the earth. The Native Americans survived (in drastically reduced numbers) but their ethnic identities—their cultural practices, beliefs, language, and so on—were often destroyed. Both case studies are, in our opinion, genocides. Subsequent US government efforts to "Kill the Indian, Save the Man" were exactly what Raphael Lemkin had in mind when writing *Axis Rule*. The deliberate intent to destroy Native American cultures and accustom them to Euro-American ways of life—accomplished through schools established both on and off the reservations by the Bureau of Indian Affairs—was a textbook example of Lemkin's meaning when he coined the word genocide. Thomas Jefferson Morgan, the Commissioner for Indian Affairs from 1889 to 1893, wrote "education should seek the disintegration of tribes, and not their segregation [...]. In short, public schools should do for them what they are so successfully doing for all other races in this country—assimilate them" (ibid., 64).

These schools, generally staffed by missionaries whose primary goal was to Christianize the "heathen Indians," also emphasized English language courses with the children forbidden to speak in their native tongues. Punished harshly if they did, the boys were also forced to cut their hair and all the children had to wear what was for them strange and uncomfortable clothing. Sexual abuse was common. Often far from home (and deliberately so), the psychological trauma these children endured is difficult to imagine. The curriculum mandated that the boys learn vocational skills and farming, while girls learn domestic skills such as cooking and sewing. The Carlisle

Indian Industrial School in Carlisle, Pennsylvania, opened in 1879, served as the model for several hundred others, and is perhaps the most well-known of the off-reservation boarding schools (many reservations also had these boarding schools). The Carlisle School is famous for having as an alumni America's greatest athlete ever—Jim Thorpe— who won gold medals in both the pentathlon and decathlon at the 1912 Olympics. Jim Thorpe (whose Sac and Fox name was *Wa-Tho-Huk*) won those two gold medals for the United States more than a decade before Native Americans were "granted" American citizenship in 1924. Olympic officials subsequently stripped him of those medals because he had accepted a small payment to play professional baseball prior to competing in the Olympics, thus violating his amateur status. The International Olympic Committee restored those medals to him more than a century after he first won them, in July 2022. Jim Thorpe was perhaps the most outstanding player in the early days of the National Football League (NFL) and also played six seasons of Major League Baseball (MLB)—three decades before Jackie Robinson became the first Black player in MLB. Thorpe continues to appear at the top of "best athletes of all time" lists, but endured discrimination, and racist condescension from sportswriters, throughout his life, which was very unhappy in his later years.

But Thorpe's life, though difficult, was probably happier than those of the other hundreds of thousands of Native American children in the United States who were stolen from their families at an early age and sent off to these boarding schools— in other words, forcibly taken from one group and transferred to another which, by any definition, including the legal one approved by the UN Convention, amounted to genocide. In 2009, President Barack Obama apologized "on behalf of the people of the United States to all Native peoples for the many instances of violence, maltreatment and neglect inflicted on Native peoples by citizens of the United States" (US Senate Joint Resolution 14, 111th Congress, First Session, April 30, 2009). On October 25, 2024, President Joe Biden specifically apologized for the unconscionable practice of separating generations of Native American children from their families for more than 150 years and sending them to boarding schools for forced assimilation. Acknowledging the horrific atrocities and injustices perpetrated against the Native peoples of North America is, of course, the morally decent thing to do, as is admitting that many of the promises made in treaties with them were subsequently broken. Honoring these promises after nearly two centuries would mean more than any fine words uttered by American presidents (Figure 2.3).

In Canada, we can see much the same process, with an intense genocidal effort lasting almost to the end of the twentieth century to eradicate the language, culture, and identity of the children of the "First Nations." As in the United States, European settlers expanded across Canada in the nineteenth century and signed a series of treaties with "First Nations" indigenous peoples that promised financial compensation in return for land. In 1876, the Parliament passed the "Indian Act" that required Native peoples to live on designated "reserves" that they were not to leave without permission. In 1920, another "Indian Act" mandated that all "First Nations" children between the ages of 7–15 attend "residential" schools closely modeled after those in

Figure 2.3 An example of cultural genocide: A young Navajo man named Tom Torlino when he entered Carlisle Indian Industrial School in 1882, and three years later. https://commons.wikimedia.org/wiki/File:Tom_Torlino_Navajo_before_and_after_circa_1882

the United States. Even if a school was located nearby, the Canadian government assigned children to schools far away from home so that their parents could not "interfere." Over 150,000 children were "educated" by religious figures in these residential schools between 1870 and 1996, with sexual abuse and neglect common. Children were, as in the United States, severely beaten for speaking their native language. One survivor recounted how "I lost my language for 40 years because they told me it was the devil's tongue. I was brainwashed" (*The Guardian*, September 2021). In May 2021, 215 bodies of children, some as young as three years old, were found buried at one of these schools in British Columbia. An estimate of 4,000 dead is now widely considered far too low and searches are underway at other schools for more bodies. The United Church of Canada, the largest Canadian Protestant denomination, apologized in 2000 for its role in running 15 residential schools. In 2008, Prime Minister Stephen Harper offered a formal apology on behalf of the Canadian government and also established a Truth and Reconciliation Commission (TRC). The Commission collected thousands of hours of testimony that revealed the extent of the mistreatment these children endured. In 2015, the TRC concluded that the system of residential schools had amounted to "cultural genocide" and in 2022, the current Prime Minister, Justin Trudeau, apologized again. In July of that same year, Pope Francis went on a "penitential pilgrimage" to Canada and apologized for the abuse that had occurred in the Catholic-run residential schools. The Pope told indigenous leaders he felt "shame and sorrow for the role that a number of Catholics, particularly those with educational responsibilities, have had in these things that have wounded you, in the abuses you suffered and in the lack of respect shown to your identity, your culture, and even your spiritual values" (CNN World Online, July 24, 2022). He also acknowledged that what had occurred was in fact genocide. Speaking with reporters on his return flight to Italy, he said "I didn't say the word [in Canada] because it didn't come to my mind, but I did describe the genocide. And I asked for forgiveness for this process which was genocide" (*The Guardian* News website, July 30, 2022). Raphael Lemkin also called it genocide. In both the United States and Canada, discrimination and racism continue to afflict these first peoples of North America. This genocide by the Euro-Americans, like other ethnic cleansings such as that of the Palestinians by the Israelis (below) or of the Armenians by the Turks (in Chapter Seven), failed because of the strength and resolve of the peoples targeted.

Russian and Soviet "Ethnic Cleansings"

The Circassians

Writing in the 1830s, the French political thinker Alexis de Tocqueville compared the historical trajectories of the United States and Russia to one another. In his famous book *Democracy in America*, he wrote: "all other nations seem to have nearly reached their natural limits [...] but these are still in the act of growth. The American struggles against the obstacles which nature opposes to him; the adversaries of the Russians are men" (Tocqueville 2003, 470; first published in 1835). The United States expanded westward, encountering "the wilderness and savage life" which they conquered by force of arms. They then attempted to "civilize" the peoples they had vanquished and brought under their control. The Russians expanded eastward and to the south, where they too encountered "alien" and "savage" peoples. In the east, they burned down villages, carried out mass executions, and enslaved women. Greedily extracting furs such as sables, minks, and ermines as tribute from these conquered peoples, the Russians held women, children, and old people as hostages unless quotas were met—something that King Leopold II of Belgium would later emulate in the "Belgian" Congo. The Russians annihilated entire tribes of native peoples—some tribes even committed mass suicide rather than submit to Russian rule. In the south, the Russians almost completely exterminated the Sunni Muslim Circassians in a military campaign that lasted for over half a century. Starting around the turn of the nineteenth century, the Russian army conducted repeated campaigns of brutality as they fought Circassian militias for control of the region. The Russians burned every Circassian village to the ground and slaughtered the villagers' livestock in an organized campaign of terror designed to force them to flee to Ottoman Turkey. Most notably, the Russians razed every mosque and erected Orthodox churches in their place.

When the Circassians resisted, the Russians responded by massacring peaceful villagers. Atrocities similar to those perpetrated upon Native Americans by the US genocidists were also common. The lands Circassians had tilled for millennia were turned over to the Kuban Cossacks (a semi-nomadic people employed by the Tsars as cavalry units) as payment for their services to the Russian army. Cossacks and regular soldiers together ethnically cleansed the Circassians from their homeland and Russian settlers and colonizers poured into the region. As one Russian general said: "We need the Circassian lands, but we don't have any need of the Circassians themselves" (Natho 2009, 357). In 1857, Dmitrii Miliutin, a Russian army general soon to become the Minister of War, argued that the Circassians should not only be "removed" from the land for settlement by Russians, but that "eliminating the Circassians was to be an end unto itself—to cleanse the land of hostile elements" (King 2008, 94). The tsar approved the idea and the decades-long Russian campaign of exceptional brutality against the Circassians culminated in the complete removal of over one million people from their native land. The only Circassians left in Russian-controlled territory had to accept "Russification" and resettlement out of the region. As the Russian General Staff later noted: "In this year of 1864 a deed has been accomplished almost without precedent in history: not one of the mountaineer inhabitants remains on their former places of residence, and measures are being taken to cleanse the region in order to prepare it for the new Russian population" (Jersild 2002, 12).

Other peoples pushed back into the Caucasus Mountains including the Chechens and Ingush. These so-called "natives" fought tenaciously against the Russian colonizers, often coming down from the mountains into the settlements below to fight against settlers and their military protectors—both the Cossacks and regular Russian army soldiers stationed in forts. As in the American West, this uneven struggle continued for decades. Again, in a fashion resembling American tactics, Russian forces advancing into the Caucasus region routinely massacred innocent civilians and burned down entire villages. Many Chechens and Ingush (who are related peoples) left Russia for the Ottoman Empire along with the Circassians in the late 1860s, but guerilla warfare continued for several more decades. After the Bolshevik Revolution of 1917, the region briefly was independent until the Soviet Union attacked and forcibly reintegrated it into the USSR as part of a northern Caucasus republic. The Soviets had great difficulties subjugating these conquered lands as fierce resistance to Russian rule continued. Finally, the Soviets had to send in the army—and the air force—to pacify the mountain peoples. They continued to rebuff subsequent efforts to modernize them through education as they persisted in their traditional ways of living. As the American historian Norman Naimark wrote, "Chechen women and girls continued to stay in their homes, with their flocks, or in the fields; Chechen men increasingly turned to the Sufi brotherhoods that provided shelter and relief from Sovietization campaigns" (Naimark 2001, 93). A full-scale rebellion broke out when the Soviets tried to collectivize their farmlands in 1932–33 and they fought against the Red Army with every weapon at their disposal. Like other peasants in the Soviet Union, they preferred to slaughter their livestock and burn their crops before they would turn them over to government officials. In 1936, the regime formed the "Chechen–Ingush Autonomous Soviet Socialist Republic," but the Chechens and Ingush continued to resist assimilation into the Soviet Union. With the coming of World War II, Stalin, the cruel Soviet leader who, despite being an ethnic Georgian embraced Russian chauvinism, would have the cover he needed to crush any non-Russian peoples he mistrusted.

World War II and Stalin's Destruction of Peoples

The Volga Germans

Tensions continued to exist between the Soviet government and the mountain peoples, but Hitler's attack on the Soviet Union in 1941 made other supposed internal enemies a higher priority than the Chechens and Ingush. The first order of business for Stalin was the deportation of the Volga Germans. Invited to settle in Russia by Catherine the Great in the eighteenth century, these people were, in fact, ethnic Germans who retained the language, culture, and beliefs of their native land while residing in their own autonomous region. Brought in by Catherine to teach Russian peasants superior methods of farming, a century later they had "had no effect whatsoever" on them and the Germans looked "with dislike and contempt upon the Russians," a feeling that was "returned by the latter with interest" (Kreindler 1986, 388). The persecution of the Germans by the Soviet state began almost immediately after the Bolshevik seizure of power in 1917, as the communists never trusted them. The Volga Germans were fiercely religious Protestants and very much attached to their farmsteads; needless to say, Soviet atheism and socialism did not agree with them. Stalin had already begun his assault on their lifestyle during collectivization, but fearful of upsetting Hitler, he largely left them alone after signing the Non-Aggression Pact with the German dictator in August 1939.

Once the war started, however, all bets were off. Fearful that they might support their ethnic kin, within two months of the German invasion the entire Volga German community was deported to "special settlements" in Siberia and Kazakhstan, with many being sent to the *Gulag* (an acronym for "Main Administration of Camps") to perform forced labor. The process was finished within three months. Absent the vicious cruelty and terrible living conditions once resettled, it would be instructive to bear in mind that the United States did exactly the same thing in World War II to citizens of Japanese ancestry living on the West Coast (Reeves, 2016). Some scholars assert that well over a million Volga Germans were resettled (Merten 2015, 168), although other experts, using the suspect 1939 Soviet census, have a total figure of less than half that number (Kreindler 1986). In any case, untold thousands perished on the way or shortly after arrival. In addition, Stalin banned all ethnic Germans from serving in the Red Army, instead drafting them into labor battalions where they were forced to work under horrific conditions. After the war, many of the survivors left the Soviet Union and returned to their homeland—Germany. Others remained in Siberia and Central Asia until the collapse of the Soviet Union when, because of their blood-relatedness as ethnic Germans, they were welcomed home to the newly unified Germany.

The Chechen–Ingush Peoples

Despite the fact that many Chechens and Ingush volunteered to serve in the fight against the Germans, Stalin suspended recruitment in the region in 1942. Many other of the region's inhabitants resisted induction into the military and, after the Germans arrived, some even collaborated but, according to one scholar, they did not do so "in any meaningful way" (Naimark 2001, 95). Stalin, however, now had the pretext he needed to relocate an entire "alien" people. The official reason given, according to archival secret police sources, was that "Many Chechens and Ingush were traitors to the homeland, changing over to the side of the fascist occupiers, joining the ranks of diversionaries and spies left behind the lines of the Red Army by the Germans. They formed armed bands at the behest of the Germans fighting against Soviet power" (ibid., 94). Another reason, according to the Russian historian Aleksandr Iakovlev, was that the regime feared the revival of Muslim sentiment in the region (Iakovlev 1995, 120–220). This would make sense, as 35 years later, the USSR invaded Afghanistan for largely the same reason—the Soviets feared Muslim fundamentalism or radicalism might spread into their own Central Asian republics. The deportation, like the others, was a massive undertaking and not accomplished without violence; anyone who resisted was promptly shot. Of the 400,000 Chechens and 90,000 Ingush (Kreindler 1986), Naimark estimates that 10,000 died in the resettlement process alone from exposure, hunger, and disease; but it was during the initial months upon arrival at the "special settlements" that the death toll really mounted. There was absolutely no provision made for this sudden influx of people and the Chechens and Ingush had no food, shelter, or medical care. In their first three years of exile, approximately 100,000 of them perished (Naimark 2001, 95–96).

For both the German and "mountain peoples" resettlement operations, desperately needed war materiel had to be diverted from the battlefront. For the Chechen–Ingush deportations 6,000 trucks and over 15,000 freight cars were required for several months—not to mention the more than 100,000 special police troops needed to transport the unlucky victims and then to guard them once they reached their destinations (Conquest 1991, 259). Stalin's determination to rid the Soviet Union of these "enemies of the people" at any cost—in the midst of a total war, the largest in history—mirrored that of Hitler. When questioned about the use of railroad cars needed on the Russian front to transport Jews to the camps, Hitler said that the prosecution of the war and the extermination of the Jews had "equal priority." We agree with the Chechen and Ingush historians who consider this a genocide, though Naimark, once again demurs, saying Stalin's goal "was to destroy the Chechen and Ingush nations without necessarily eliminating their peoples" (Naimark 2001, 98). He does acknowledge, however, that immediately after the war the Soviets renamed streets, bulldozed graveyards and monuments, and allowed no mention of the region's previous inhabitants in the history books. Even in exile, the regime forbade the use of their language and prevented them from practicing their culture. This is genocide, too.

In the nearly eight decades since their "resettlement," the so-called mountain peoples have continued to resist their dispersal and the marginalization of their culture. Many of them returned to their homeland after Stalin's death. The regime sought to prevent this, stating that even though their status as "special settlers" had been ended "this does not mean that they have the right to the return of their property confiscated during their expulsion, nor do they have the right to return to the places, from which they were expelled" (ibid., 98). As they had done for the Jews (see below), the Soviets tried to cobble together a "homeland" for these peoples in Central Asia. The Chechens and

Ingush rejected this proposal and instead traveled back to their native land in defiance of the Soviet regime. When they returned, they found Russians in their homes and violence often resulted. The Soviet government relented and reestablished the Chechen and Ingush Autonomous Republic in 1957 but the resistance continued, as did the dream of an independent homeland.

Upon the collapse of the Soviet Union in 1991, the Chechens quickly declared their independence. This sparked the First Chechen War (1994–96) under Russia's new President, Boris Yeltsin. Russian forces invaded the newly formed Republic of Ichkeria expecting a quick and easy victory. When met with determined resistance the Russians quickly resorted to their usual tactic of excessive brutality against the civilian population. Despite widespread massacres of civilians and the indiscriminate torture and murder of any male Chechens that they captured, the region devolved into a bloody patchwork of warlords and rebel fighters. By the time Vladimir Putin came into power—in 1999, and he is still in power today—the region was ungovernable. Putin once again sent in massive numbers of troops and resumed the indiscriminate bombing of cities that are still the trademarks of the Russian army, as seen later in Russia's assistance to the Syrian dictatorship in its murderous war against its own people (2011–present) and now in Ukraine, which Russia invaded in February 2022.

The Chechens fought back with terrorist acts that shocked the world. Putin promised "to wipe them out in the shithouse" and by 2005 probably 150,000 Chechens had died in what could definitely be considered a genocide. Eventually, Ramzan Kadyrov, the son of a former strongman, consolidated control over the region in 2007. Promising loyalty to Putin, this psychopath has instituted a criminal reign of terror in Chechnya that includes the subjugation of women and a genocidal campaign against LGBTQ people (Brown, in Cox, ed., 2022). He brought several thousand Chechen fighters into Ukraine—the *"Vostok"* (East) unit—in 2022 to support Russia's brutal "special operation" and for his subservience was promoted by Putin to Lieutenant General. This collaboration with Chechnya's eternal enemy, however, has provoked many Chechens into forming a new resistance movement. Volunteer Chechen forces have joined with the Ukrainians as they defend themselves from the criminal assault of the Russians. These freedom fighters have formed the Sheikh Mansur Battalion (Sheikh Mansur was an eighteenth-century Chechen warlord who fought against Russia on behalf of both the Chechens and Circassians) and have picked up where their forebears left off. Even now, they are working toward the restoration of the independent Chechen Republic of Ichkeria.

The Crimean Tatars

The Crimean Tatars were another Muslim people deported to the vast spaces of Central Asia by Stalin. Descendants of the Mongol Empire, the Tatars in the Crimean Peninsula came under Russian control in the late eighteenth century. Unlike the Caucasus, where the indigenes lived in the mountainous areas with Russians and Ukrainians in settlements below, Crimea was a more mixed society with Tatars mainly farming in the north of the peninsula, and Russians and Ukrainians throughout, especially on the seacoast. After the Soviets seized power, they established the Crimean Autonomous Republic in 1921. It only lasted until 1944 when Stalin deported the entire Tatar population, numbering approximately 200,000 people to Central Asia (Naimark 2001; Kreindler 1986). Accused of collaboration with the Germans (and, according to both Naimark and Kreindler, there is at least some truth to the charge), special police units once again surrounded villages and forced men, women, and children onto trains for "resettlement." As usual, the conditions were horrific. Thousands died of thirst and hunger on the way to Kazakhstan and there was a complete lack of sanitation and medical attention. Forbidden to return to their homeland, the Tatars faced harsh and difficult conditions in exile without any help from the state or the local inhabitants. Some Tatar historians estimate that nearly half the population perished (Naimark 2001). As with the Chechens and Ingush, the Tatar names of towns and cities were changed and monuments were destroyed. The Soviets burned Tatar books and the history of the region was rewritten to suggest the Tatars were nothing but thieves and bandits. Nonetheless, like the other deported peoples they have since returned to their homeland. Probably several hundred thousand Tatars now live in Crimea under Russian control, with another several hundred thousand still in Central Asia (and an unknown number in Turkey). Just before the illegal Russian seizure of Crimea in 2014, the Ukrainian Supreme Council recognized the Tatars as an indigenous people of the region (Ukraine has also recognized the emerging Republic of Ichkeria, asserting that the Chechens, like the Ukrainians, are a formerly colonized people). The Russians do not agree, of course, classifying them as a "national minority" and not an indigenous people (Vanguri 2016). Making up only 15% of the total population in Crimea today, the Tatars are effectively strangers in their own land.

Stalin also took advantage of the opportunity the war provided to deport other, smaller minority peoples as well. Russians and even some Ukrainians repopulated these regions once cleared—though there are reports Stalin wanted to deport the Ukrainians as well, but "there were too many of them." The Soviet secret police and special interior troops moved 200,000 Meskhetians, 130,000 Kalmyks, 70,000 Karachi, and 42,000 Balkars from their ancestral homelands to Central Asia. All told, at least 1.6 million people, most of them Muslim (except for the Christian Germans and Buddhist Kalmyks) were exiled. Robert Conquest's pioneering study concluded that half a million people died in transit or during the first few years of resettlement (Conquest 1986), the dissident Soviet historian Roy Medvedev concurs, claiming "more than five million were deported [...] and hundreds of thousands died of hunger, cold and disease" (Medvedev 1972). These Soviet ethnic cleansings, along with the one contemplated for the Jews—discussed below—were part of a calculated, racist plan to destroy these peoples "as such." Stalin knew there was virtually no chance these ethnic groups, attached to their own customs and culture and with long histories and traditions would ever become loyal "Soviet" citizens. After removing them from their land and erasing any sign of their existence there, the remnants would presumably be assimilated into the Central Asian populations and they would disappear from history altogether. They would become, in the words of the British historian Bertram Wolfe, an "unpeople" (Wolfe 1952).

Stalin and the Jews: Another Soviet Ethnic Cleansing?

Stalin gave his famous victory toast to the Russian people at a reception for Red Army commanders in the Kremlin on May 24, 1945. Of the 27 million war dead probably slightly more than half of the victims were ethnic Russians, however, Stalin raised his toast "first of all" to the Russian people "because it is the most outstanding nation of all the nations who belong to the Soviet Union" (*Pravda*, May 25, 1945). No mention was made of the contributions of the other peoples of the Soviet Union, and certainly not of the ethnic groups that Stalin had ordered uprooted from their homelands and sent to Central Asia or Siberia. As for the Jews, the Soviet press early in the war had often included specific, explicit discussions of Nazi efforts to exterminate them. On December 18, 1942, *Pravda* published the joint declaration of 12 nations "On the Hitlerite Regime's Extermination of Europe's Jewish Populations." This document noted that German forces had "brought to life Hitler's oft-repeated desire to eliminate the Jewish people of Europe." Two days later, however, in another declaration, the Soviets mentioned only the sufferings of the Russians, Ukrainians, and Byelorussians. In the Ministry of Foreign Affairs' first draft version of this declaration—with notes written in Minister of Foreign Affairs Vyacheslav Molotov's own hand—it was indignantly noted that foreign perceptions of Nazi atrocities seemed to assume that "allegedly, the requisitions, robbery, and executions were directed only against Jews" (United States Holocaust Museum RG 22.009.01.04, 24–25). This sentence, crossed out by Molotov himself, was not included in the final version.

Molotov—whose wife was Jewish—instead took pains to write about the tolerance and lack of racism in the Soviet Union and that "the younger generation of Jews [in the Soviet Union] had had absolutely no experience with antisemitism and racial chauvinism was unknown." As was customary, he quoted Lenin, the principal leader of the 1917 revolution and the first head of the Soviet state, as saying "the use of the vile prejudices of the most uncivilized strata of the population against Jews so as to encourage [...] the monstrous slaughters of peaceful Jews [...] evokes such disgust from the entire civilized world." In his usual sycophantic manner, Molotov also included not one but *two* quotes from Stalin. The Great Leader had written a note to the Red Army in which he reminded its soldiers that they were "fighting in its great liberation struggle free from feelings of racial hatred [...]" because the Soviet people had "been raised in the spirit of racial equality and respect for the rights of all people" (ibid., 39–40). In fact, antisemitism was, and remains to this day, deeply ingrained in the Russian psyche. The tsarist secret police were the authors of the notorious fake *Protocol of the Elders of Zion*, knowing it would find a receptive audience. The motto of the proto-fascist "Black Hundreds" in pre-revolutionary Russia—that has since resurfaced in recent years—was "Beat the Jews and Save Russia."

As we will discuss later, Stalin had used this ingrained antisemitism to come to power by blaming Jews for the internal party opposition to his rule. His major opponents, Kamenev, Zinoviev, and Trotsky, all had Jewish family backgrounds, though none were "Jewish" in a religious sense. Indeed, Stalin shared Hitler's view of Jews as a "race." Any concern for the fate of the Soviet Union's Jews during World War II was for propaganda purposes only. For example, in 1942, the regime allowed the establishment of the Jewish Anti-Fascist Committee (JAC). Its purpose, like the four others established at the same time (for women, young people, scientists, and Slavs) was to lobby similar foreign constituencies for support of the Soviet regime in its war against Hitler (Rubenstein and Altman 2008). Its chair was the well-known Jewish actor and head of the State Jewish Theater Solomon Mikhoels—who, as we will see, met with an untimely demise on Stalin's orders in 1948 as the prelude to the state-sponsored antisemitic campaign that nearly culminated in genocide. Mikhoels traveled widely in the West and raised millions of dollars for the Red Army from American Jews. The regime also allowed the celebrated Jewish writers Vasilii Grossman and Il'ia Ehrenburg, who were also members of the JAC, to document the suffering of Soviet Jews with an eye both toward using these materials in future war crimes trials and for fundraising. Mikhoels had already warned in a 1941 radio broadcast that the Nazis planned "the total annihilation of the Jewish people" (ibid., xxii). The JAC kept a running count of the Jewish victims of Nazi criminality and made sure these details were widely disseminated—outside of the Soviet Union. These reports so shocked the conscience of American Jews that a committee of Jewish writers, artists, and scientists—whose honorary head was Albert Einstein—suggested that a compilation of these documents be published to provide a full accounting of the magnitude of Jewish suffering at the hands of the Nazis.

When, at the end of the war, Ehrenburg and Grossman tried to publish their work, entitled *The Black Book*, Georgii Aleksandrov, the head of propaganda in the Soviet Union, forbade its publication. Aleksandrov, who was also head of the special "Extraordinary Commission" charged to "conduct an exact inventory of all the evil crimes of the Hitlerite army on the territory of the USSR," claimed that the Jewish writers implied that the destruction of the Jews was the Nazis' primary intent. He accused Ehrenburg and Grossman of making the unwarranted claim "the Germans established some kind of hierarchy in their destruction of the peoples of the Soviet Union" [...]. In his view, the investigations "of the Extraordinary State Commission convincingly demonstrate that the Hitlerites destroyed, at one and the same time Russians, Jews, Byelorussians, Ukrainians, Latvians, Lithuanians, and other peoples of the Soviet Union" (quoted in Weiner 2001, 216). He concluded that this officially sponsored effort was fatally flawed because it created the impression that the "Germans fought against the USSR for the sole purpose of destroying the Jews" (Redlich, ed. 1995, 366).

This change in policy signaled that Stalin had once again given his underlings permission to pursue openly antisemitic policies. Stalin would soon return to exploring the possibility of resettling virtually the entire Jewish population to the Soviet Far East. As People's Commissar for Nationalities in the early years of the Soviet Union, Lenin had ordered Stalin to set up autonomous regions for the many non-Russian peoples. In his early theoretical (and plagiarized) work "Marxism and the National Question" Stalin had denied that the Jews were even a nation since they "live in different parts of the globe, never seeing one another, never acting jointly either in peacetime or in war" (quoted in Vaksberg 1994, 4). In the late 1920s, Stalin and the Communist leadership set up two different organizations to "resettle" all of Russia's Jews in the Crimean peninsula. In 1926, Mikhail Kalinin, whose official title was President of the USSR, urged Russia's Jews to move there in order to establish and preserve their nationality in the Crimea, since only then "can the Jewish masses have hope or the future of their nationality" (quoted in ibid., 61). Tens of thousands of Jews poured into the Crimea and established their own farms. Ultimately, such a concentration of Jews in the region could not but have led to the creation of an autonomous region or even a Jewish Union Republic (the equivalent of a US state). Stalin, however, had other plans; he claimed that the native peoples of the region, the Crimean Tatars had not taken kindly to this influx of an "alien" people and therefore there was too great a possibility of ethnic conflict. To remedy this situation Stalin proposed to uproot the Jews yet again and send them to the Russian–Chinese border in the Far East where they would have the "chance to create their own state." Despite the Soviet propaganda about the Jewish cultural renaissance in the faraway region of Birobidzhan, by the late 1930s, Jews were being removed from the social, political, and economic life of the Soviet Union. Preparations were underway for antisemitic show trials. Having now been singled out, marked, and identified as Jewish in their Soviet internal passports, the process of concentrating them well away from their homes in European Russia could begin. This steady march to another purge came to an abrupt stop with the outbreak of the war.

In 1946, barely one year after the end of World War II, the campaign against Russian Jewry resumed. A particular target was the Jewish *intelligentsia* (a Russian word that has also passed into English usage, meaning educated elites such as scholars, writers, poets, composers, and so on). Stalin and his subordinates, infected with a virulent antisemitism, believed that untrustworthy Jews dominated the entire cultural sphere—art, literature, cinema, and so on. (Rapoport 1990). A campaign against Jewish cultural figures commenced on cue. Led by Stalin's loyal henchman Andrei Zhdanov, this so-called *Zhdanovshchina*—meaning the wicked deeds of Zhdanov, though of course he acted on orders from Stalin—would spread from the cultural sphere to medicine, science, the army, and throughout the Communist Party itself. In an eerily similar fashion to what the Nazis did in 1933 in Germany, the Party "cleansed" (the Russian word *chistka* literally means cleansing) Jews from all state bodies such as university faculties, research institutes, and the officer corps. The Soviet press attacked the Jews daily and accused them of "rootless cosmopolitanism," implying they had no allegiance to the USSR, and some were arrested and charged with trying to detach the Crimea from the USSR. By this time, however, the state of Israel had come into existence; ironically, it was the Soviet Union that would supply the Israelis with the weaponry they needed to wrest the land from its indigenous inhabitants—the Palestinians. The Soviet Constitution provided for the possibility of emigration for persons who wished to return to a "homeland." This was not even theoretically possible before the creation of the state of Israel, and of course, was no longer necessary since a "homeland" for the Jews now existed in the USSR—albeit far away in Asia.

The organized campaign to root out the supposed Jewish traitors accused of infecting all areas of Soviet life with "bourgeois" Western influences included deportation to the labor camps in Siberia and even murder. In early 1948, the great Jewish actor Solomon Mikhoels, who had labored so hard on behalf of the Soviet Union during the war, died in a car "accident," not unlike the "accidents" that seem always to befall Putin's enemies today. Zhdanov, who had spearheaded the anti-Jewish campaign, also died in 1948; and although he died of a heart attack, his death eventually served as the pretext that Stalin needed for his final purge. A nurse registered a complaint with the secret police alleging that the doctors attending Zhdanov had deliberately killed him as part of a conspiracy against the Soviet leadership, including Stalin. Stalin's daughter, Svetlana Alliluyeva, later said that her father did not believe the denunciation (Alliluyeva 1967). In 1952, the nurse's letter, taken from the secret police archives, provided the impetus for Stalin's *pogrom* (a violent attack on Jews with the intention of either killing them or expelling them) that would ethnically cleanse European Russia of its Jews. By the time the so-called "Doctor's Plot"—also referred to in Russia as the treachery of the "Vermin Doctors"— was revealed to the Soviet people tens of thousands of Jews had already been forcibly deported to Siberia, and thousands more leading Jewish intellectuals had been imprisoned or murdered (Figure 2.4).

Stalin's very own "Final Solution" continued apace. The secret police hastily built four large concentration camps in Siberia just before Stalin's death, and supposedly, a "Deportation Commission" was established. There are many personal accounts and letters that indicate the Soviet leadership drafted a "Jewish Statement" that begged Comrade Stalin personally to "protect" the Jewish people from the "understandably indignant anger prompted by the traitor-doctors [...] by dispatching them to the developing territories of the East." Rapoport reconstructed the letter from the descriptions of Jewish intellectuals who had been compelled to participate in its composition and

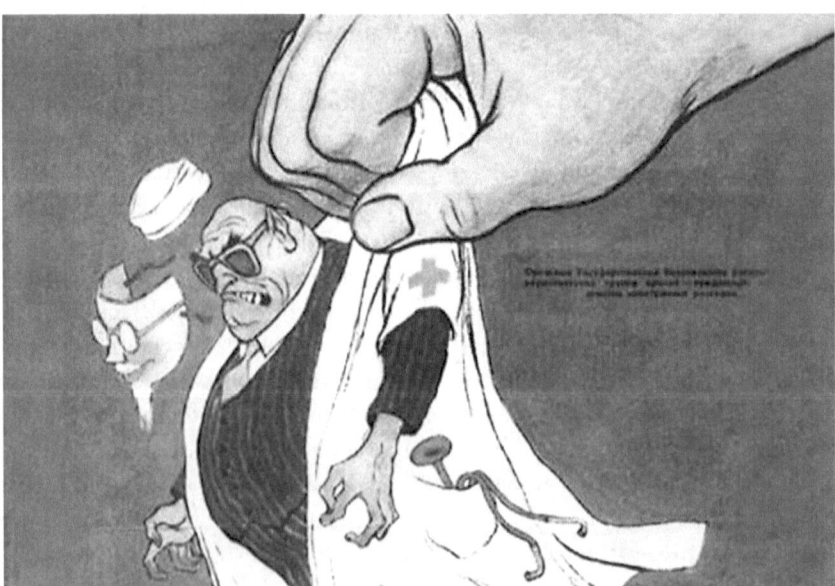

Figure 2.4 1953 cartoon from Soviet publication depicting the supposed treachery of the Jewish doctors whom Stalin accused of conspiring against the nation's leadership. Stalin's antisemitic propaganda rivaled that of the Nazis in some ways. https://commons.wikimedia.org/wiki/File:Krokodil_edition_1953.jpg

then forced to sign it to provide the necessary justification to deport the remaining Jews in European Russia to Soviet Asia. The authors also angrily denied that antisemitism even existed in Soviet Russia. Historians have not found any definitive evidence that such a deportation was imminent. In his biography of Stalin, Robert Service argued "Whether Stalin really intended the deportation of the Jews in the early 1950s remains unknown, though this is widely treated as a fact; and no conclusive proof has come to light" (Service 2006, 637).

Be that as it may, Stalin's murderous expulsions of the *kulaks* during collectivization, and the "resettlement" of Kalmyks, Chechens, Ingush, Crimean Tatars, Volga Germans, and other peoples from their homelands during the war provided all the proof the two million surviving Soviet Jews needed that they had been spared a similar fate by the dictator's sudden death in March 1953. The Jews of the Soviet Union continued to suffer discrimination and harassment for two more decades. Surviving European Jews, however, had the option of leaving Europe and going to Palestine. In 1971, the Soviet Union also finally allowed its Jews to leave. The exodus accelerated with the collapse of the Soviet Union in 1991 and continues to this day; after the beginning of the Russian-Ukrainian war in 2022, thousands more Jews left for Israel, which accepts them under its "Law of Return." Almost two million Jews have left Russia over the last half-century, more than half of them went to Israel and joined the other Jews who had already fled Europe from antisemitic terror and violence to the "Promised Land" of Palestine.

The Palestinian Nakba (Catastrophe)

The mass expulsions of Muslims by the Serbs from part of Bosnia in the 1990s, and of the Muslim Rohingya in Myanmar in recent years, both received widespread attention from the world community; nonetheless, the genocidists were successful in their endeavors. Our final case study involves yet another 800,000 Muslim people forcibly expelled from their lands by people who wanted that territory for their own ethnicity and expansionist nation—the ethnic cleansing of Palestine by the Israelis in 1947–48. This crime, according to the Israeli historian Ilan Pappe, "has been erased almost totally from the global public memory" (Pappe 2006, xiii). The *Nakba*, or catastrophe, writes Pappe "has ever since been systematically denied, and is still today not recognized as an historical fact, let alone acknowledged as a crime that needs to be confronted politically as well as morally" (ibid.). The euphemism used here by the Israelis during their military operation was the Hebrew word *tihur*, which literally translated means "cleansing" or "purification."

Martin Shaw argues that the Israeli destruction of the Arab society in Palestine was not only a "settler-colonial" genocide, but also an "extension of the exclusivist nationalism which had recently brought about extensive genocidal violence in the European war" (Shaw and Bartov 2010, 244). "Settler-colonialism"—a concept also to be discussed later in more detail in Chapter Seven, "Empire and State-Building through Genocide"—usually involves an imperial power sending its own settlers to a land for occupation and settlement. The fact that there might already be other people living on the territory was, of course, unimportant. We have already discussed the impact of settler colonialism on Native Americans in the United States and Canada and on the peoples of Eurasia and the Caucasus. There was no Jewish state in Europe, however, but Jewish nationalism did develop by the turn of the twentieth century. The emerging Zionist movement had concluded that Europeans would never accept Jews as equals and that they should instead return to their biblical "Promised Land" in the Middle East.

It is important to note that this realization dawned on many Jews decades *before* the Holocaust. Many Israelis today are descended from those Jews who migrated to the Holy Land in the late nineteenth and early twentieth centuries. And, of course, the Jewish people were not completely new to the region. Many had lived there peaceably for thousands of years with their Arab neighbors. In 1917, the British government indicated that it would support the establishment of a "national home for the Jewish people in Palestine." Many Jews left Europe and migrated to Palestine, and this movement understandably gained great momentum during the years of Nazi tyranny and genocide. As more Jews moved into the region by the 1930s, the Palestinians, who had also lived there for centuries and constituted the large majority, understandably felt threatened. Conflict was not inevitable, but leaders on both sides refused to coexist and eventually resorted to violence. The ideology of Zionism, although specifically Jewish nationalism, was similar to other European nationalisms in that it privileged its own over the "other." Zionists consequently sought to create a pure ethnic space by removing Arab peoples from Palestine. Like other European settler-colonialisms, it justified seizing territory from its inhabitants in order to develop "empty lands"—"a land without a people for a people without land" is still an oft-heard slogan, suggesting that the Arabs who had populated Palestine for thousands of years were invisible.

According to Daud Abdullah, Zionism, "like other strands of European colonialism [...] considered any territory 'empty' and available if its people had not achieved national independence and statehood" (Abdullah in Bachman, ed. 2019, 229). This was, as we noted earlier, an exercise in both settler-colonialism *and* nation-building. The European colonialist mentality is apparent in the writings of the founder of Zionism, Theodor Herzl. He wrote that in establishing the Jewish state the Israelis could constitute "part of the wall of defense against Asia; we would serve as an outpost of civilization against barbarism" (ibid., 2019, 240). Zionist thinkers had also long held that a "Jewish" state should not contain any Arabs. While the Nazis were murdering his fellow Jews in Europe, Yosef Weitz wrote "it must be clear that there is no room for both peoples in this country [...] there is no other way but to transfer the Arabs from here to the neighboring countries; to transfer all of them; not one village, not one tribe should be left" (Rodinson 1973, 40). Even before the new United Nations presented its plan for a partition of Palestine into a Jewish state and a Palestinian one, Jewish paramilitary forces had expelled over a quarter million Arabs from their lands, burning their villages and seizing their livestock (Morris 1987, 179). Once the UN revealed the final map for the "equal" division of Palestine between Jews and Arabs—and it most definitely was not "equal"—the Arab League (a coalition of Arab states) rejected it outright. As Rashid Khalidi put it, "the native people of Palestine, like the native people of every other country in the Arab world, Asia, Africa, America and Europe, refused to divide the land with a settler community" (Khalidi 1997, 15).

The conflict worsened markedly soon after the UN published its plan for partition, and guerilla fighting and terrorism brought misery to both sides. When the Israelis declared independence on May 14, 1948, the Arab League attacked. This First Arab–Israeli War ended with the victory of Israeli forces and the complete demographic transformation of Palestine. At least 700,000 and possibly more than 800,000 refugees fled the region (Morris 2004, 602–04). Benny Morris estimates that the Israelis purposefully destroyed between 400 and 500 villages and towns. Later, they would be rebuilt, repopulated with Jewish settlers, and then given Hebrew names. Moshe Dayan, an Israeli military commander who later became foreign minister, bragged that "You do not even know the names of these Arab villages, and I do not blame you because geography books no longer exist." Those Palestinians who remain in Israel today constitute 20 percent of Israel's population, but their children learn the history their oppressors want them to learn, and the use of the Arabic language is severely restricted. All road signs are only in Hebrew. These colonizing tactics are prime examples of Lemkin's classic definition of genocide. There is no doubt that for those Palestinians the "national pattern of the oppressed group" has been replaced with the "national pattern of the oppressor." Millions of Palestinians have fled into neighboring countries while those remaining behind are still today stateless and with more than two million penned up in the Gaza Strip in what has been called "the biggest prison on earth" (Pappe 2017). Jewish settlers have also encroached upon what by international law is Palestinian land in the occupied West Bank of the Jordan River; there the settlers live under Israeli law while Palestinians are subject to military rule, a two-tier system of law that resembles *apartheid*, Jim Crow segregation, or the colonizers' classic avoidance of local legal jurisdiction through the principle of "extraterritoriality."

In October 2023, after the horrific, unjustified attack by the terrorist group *Hamas* (the Islamist group governing the Gaza Strip) on Israeli concert-goers and residents of *kibbutzim* (Jewish farming communities) on the border of the Gaza Strip and Israel, the Israelis responded with the immoral, unlawful tactic of collective punishment of civilians from a specific ethnic group by cutting off the 2.3 million inhabitants of the Gaza Strip from food, fuel, and water. This is against the 1948 Genocide Convention as it is "deliberately inflicting conditions of life calculated to bring about [...] physical destruction," at least "in part." Worse, the bombing campaign by the Israeli Defense Force (IDF) did not discriminate between the *Hamas* terrorists and Palestinian civilians. In fact, at a press conference in front of international correspondents, the President of Israel, Yitzhak Herzog, made the outrageous assertion that "It is an entire nation that is responsible." The Israeli onslaught has resulted in the deaths of tens of thousands of innocents, mostly women, children, and old people (as of this writing at the end of 2024 at least 46,000 Palestinians have died). Over a million Palestinians in North Gaza were ordered to leave their homes and cram into South Gaza when the Israeli army began its assault. Subsequently, these unfortunates were forced to move *en masse* again when the IDF continued its advance into South Gaza, then displaced yet again and again. In the West Bank, armed Israeli "settlers" moved out of their illegal settlements and once again expelled Palestinians from their homes with the assistance of reserve military units. Many then moved into the homes of the former Palestinian residents.

All of this is reminiscent of the horrors of the first *Nakba*. Calling Palestinians "human animals," some Israeli cabinet members have called for their "resettlement" in Egypt, Jordan, Saudi Arabia, Chile, and even the Congo in Central Africa! It has long been believed that the founding of a Palestinian state, as envisioned by the original UN partition plan, was the only way out of this terrible situation. This "two-state solution" was preempted by the Arab attack on Israel and the subsequent war in 1948 and is difficult to envision today, given the dismemberment of the Palestinian West Bank by Israeli settlements, which has accelerated dramatically in recent years. In the 1990s, the short-lived hopes for peace in the Middle East based on a two-state solution ended with the assassination of Israeli Prime Minister Yitzhak Rabin in 1995, two years after the signing of the Oslo Accord between Israeli and Palestinian leaders—an imperfect agreement, but one that held out some promise of a better future. So while the dream of a two-state solution becomes more elusive as Israel tightens its control of the West Bank while destroying Gaza in the lopsided "war" that began in October 2023, as of September 2025, 157 of the 193 United Nations members states have formally recognized Palestine as a sovereign nation. The United States continues to be the most significant impediment to Palestinian statehood. Again, not easy to imagine at this moment, given the vastly uneven power dynamics between the Palestinians and Israel.

In December 2022, the United Nations General Assembly voted to petition the ICJ (also known as the World Court) to weigh in on Israel's "occupation, settlement and annexation [...] of Palestine." The World Court issued its opinion in July 2024 and found that Israel's "annexation and [...] assertion of permanent control over the occupied Palestinian territory and continued frustration of the right of the Palestinian people to self-determination, violates fundamental principles of international law and renders Israel's presence in the occupied Palestinian territory unlawful" (*The Guardian*, July 18, 2024). The World Court ordered Israel to cease building new settlements in Palestinian territory and even demanded "the evacuation of all settlers from existing settlements" as rapidly as possible and to allow "all Palestinians displaced during the occupation [since 1967] to return to their original place of residence" (ibid.). The World Court also ordered that restitution, including the return of all land, immovable property, and other assets seized since the start of Israel's occupation in 1967, be made where possible.

In response to the World Court's ruling, Israeli Prime Minister Benjamin Netanyahu asserted that "The Jewish people are not occupiers in their own land [...]" and that "the legality of Israeli settlements in all parts of our homeland cannot be disputed" (ibid.). In January 2024, Netanyahu had already declared that Israel would never accept the creation of a Palestinian state. As "never" is a very long time, however, the Palestinians will continue to advocate for their own state and to commemorate the *Nakba* every 15 May, the day after Israeli Independence Day. Since 2011, Israel has criminalized this marking of *Nakba* Day. The Israelis, for whom the unjustified *Hamas* attack on October 7, 2023, has been compared to the *Al-Qaeda* attack on America on September 11, 2001, will undoubtedly and deservedly mark that day henceforth. These remembrances, however meaningful and justified, can also be used by political actors to manipulate emotions and pit one human group against another to realize their own goals of state-building or of enhancing the existing power of that state. We will examine this aspect of genocide more fully in Chapter Seven.

Conclusion

In *Axis Rule*, Raphael Lemkin described genocide as the destruction of the essential foundations of the life of national groups—though, as we have demonstrated, by this he meant more than simply what the Convention considers those to be in a world of socially constructed nation-states. Lemkin also identified the various genocidal methods that could lead to the "disintegration of political and social institutions, of culture, language, national feelings, religion and the economic existence of national groups" (Lemkin 2008, 79). He made clear that the distinctions between cultural, economic, physical, and biological forms of genocide were without a difference as they were all but different *techniques* of genocide. Any of these various methods of attack would ultimately result in the "destruction of the personal security, liberty, health, dignity, and even the lives of the individuals belonging to such groups" (ibid.). We have seen how some scholars have a puzzling tendency to differentiate between genocides either by the expressed intent of the genocidists or the number of group members physically eliminated. This tendency to "rank" genocides is also apparent when they are "qualified" by the use of the adjective "cultural." Scholars such as Lawrence Davidson have defined cultural genocide as the "purposeful destructive targeting of out-group cultures so as to destroy or weaken them in the process of conquest or domination" (Davidson 2012, 1–2). Kevin Chamberlain has added that this "destruction of a people's cultural heritage amounts to the destruction of a people's memory, its collective consciousness and identity. In other words it is ethnic cleansing by another name" (quoted in Abdullah, Bachmann, ed. 2019, 228).

As we have demonstrated in this chapter, both "ethnic cleansing" and "cultural genocide," are simply genocidal methods or processes. These methods of genocide rip apart the social and cultural bindings of a group and lead to the destruction of those characteristics that make a people unique and distinct. Norman Naimark has acknowledged—despite adhering to the theory that there is a distinction between ethnic cleansing and genocide—that in cases where "forced deportation is not genocidal in its intent, it is often genocidal in its effects" (Naimark 2001, 3–4). As we have said, it is precisely the *outcomes* we should be using to define actions and not the emphasis on intent, a legal precept that, in any case—thanks to rulings by international tribunals—can now sometimes simply be inferred from actions on the ground. Therefore, the case studies in this chapter were—and are—even by the UN definition, genocides, too. More importantly, they are precisely what Raphael Lemkin had in mind when he coined the term "genocide," meaning the "murder of a people."

Omer Bartov believes that applying Lemkin's idea or the UN legal definition to the different historical cases that many scholars categorize as ethnic cleansings serves only to make the concept of genocide itself "almost meaningless." We disagree, and instead concur with Martin Shaw, who argues that if the concept "can be shown to have wider applicability than previously thought [...] it becomes *more* meaningful" (Shaw and

Bartov 2010; 246–47). There are settler genocides still ongoing today. In August 2022, the last member of an uncontacted tribe in the Amazon jungle died. Cattle ranchers have murdered all the other members of his tribe so that they can clear the land for their livestock. These uncontacted peoples, referred to as "indigenous peoples in voluntary isolation," number somewhere around 10,000, but their population is fast dwindling as their ecosystem is destroyed in the name of development—logging operations, farming, and cattle ranching—especially in Brazil. Those who are not able to retreat further into the jungle are simply murdered. The same scenario that played out with the indigenous peoples of North America is being repeated as you read this book. There might not be excessive body counts among the victim groups but the end result is the same: the genocidists destroy the targeted group's social and cultural cohesiveness—genocide.

Questions for Further Discussion

1. Compare and contrast Hitler's *Rassenkampf* to America's "Manifest Destiny." To what extent are these two case studies similar? Is it accurate to label Native American reservations as "concentration camps?"
2. Would the Colorado Territory murder and "ethnic cleansing" of Native Americans in the nineteenth century be a genocide according to the United Nations Convention of 1948?
3. Each of these case studies can be classified by the various motivations of the genocidists such as colonization, ethnic state-building, suppression of possible resistance to imperial rule, or profit. Do these motivations matter, considering the outcomes?
4. What links all of the case studies in this chapter together? Beyond the obvious—that is, the chapter's theme, ethnic cleansing.

Chapter Three

RACISM AND GENOCIDE

The problem of the Twentieth Century is the problem of the color line.
—W. E. B. DuBois, 1903

Racism is Inherently Genocidal

The previous chapter described genocidal ideas and practices that had much in common; in particular, a new ideological force that would be an indispensable component of modern genocide—racism. Racial obsessions and racism developed over the last five centuries and by the early 1800s had completely taken hold in Western thought, gripping the popular imagination and invading virtually all areas of intellectual and cultural life. And as Martin Luther King, Jr. would declare many decades later:

> In the final analysis, racism is evil because its ultimate logic is genocide [...] If one says that I am not good enough to live next door to him, if one says that I am not good enough to eat at a lunch counter, to have a good, decent job or to go to school with him, merely because of my race, he is saying, consciously or unconsciously, that I do not deserve to exist (King 1967).

Dr. King concluded this section of the speech with words that have not lost their accuracy, despite whatever progress we have made over the last two or three generations: "We must honestly see and admit that racism is still deeply rooted all over America. It's still deeply rooted in the North, and it's still deeply rooted in the South."

Racism has never been a monopoly of the United States, though. It was invented in Europe and brought to the Americas by the colonizers and settlers. While most civilizations had long regarded "infidels" and other outsiders with disdain, it was only in the last five hundred or so years that our current concepts of race evolved. As David Roediger, one of the foremost experts on the subject, phrased it: "Race is a human-invented, shorthand term used to describe and categorize people into various social groups based on characteristics like skin color, physical features, and genetic heredity. Race, while not a valid biological concept, is a real social construction that gives or denies benefits and privileges" (Roediger 2014). Terms that translate as "race" in various languages had, until the fifteenth or sixteenth century (or later) in many parts of the world, usually meant something like "type" or "group." But as European colonizers or adventurers increasingly came into contact with people of darker skin colors, they developed new and much more malignant ideas about "race." For most Europeans, "race" came to mean something unchanging and genetic. Indeed, the fifteenth-century Spanish concept of *Limpieza de sangre* (an ugly term, like all racist terms: "cleanliness of the blood" or "blood purity") helped pave the way for these ideas.

European racism reached its apex, or nadir, during the 1800s and into the next century. Crudely labeled "Caucasian, Mongolian, Ethiopian, American, and Malay" by Europeans circa 1800, "races" came to be defined in ever-more elaborate, preposterous ways. We will drop the quotation marks for the remainder of the chapter but want our readers to understand that race is completely fictitious and invented. By the end of the 1800s, Europeans and North Americans had carved the human race into many dozens of races, often with creative and absurd distinctions. There was supposedly a southern Italian race, for example, that was separate from the northern Italian race (!). And Italians, Irish, Hungarians and Poles, and other eastern Europeans, among others, were not considered "white" in the United States until well into the twentieth century (Roediger 2018). In the United States today, in a desperate attempt to preserve white privilege, many racists are willing to include Hispanics as "white" while still arguing about whether or not Jews are white.

Racial notions and obsessions were sometimes driven by forces of progress and modernization. As noted by historian David Crowe, "the Enlightenment helped create a new atmosphere of tolerance that saw some Jews gain civil and political rights" (Crowe 2008, 43). Yet the preceding Scientific Revolution as well as the Enlightenment—intellectual and secularizing movements of the 1600s and 1700s—promoted a quest to classify everything in nature, which contributed to the compulsion to classify human beings by race. Another paradox is that the highly laudable anti-slavery abolitionist movement of the early 1800s had the unintended consequence of inducing defenders of slavery to formulate new arguments, which invariably rested upon skin color or race. And it must be said that the large majority of white abolitionists were imbued with racist and paternalistic attitudes. The radical abolitionist John Brown (1800–59), who led a revolt in Virginia (now West Virginia) in 1859, was among the few white folks who could be found, on either side of the Atlantic, who believed in the equality of all peoples. (It should be remembered that enslaved peoples, and free Black people in the United States and Britain, helped lead the abolition movements against slavery; abolitionism is sometimes wrongly depicted as a white Christian movement.)

Racism is a crucial element of modern genocide not simply by dehumanizing future victims, but by dividing the human race into rigid categories with supposedly fixed, unchanging characteristics. Thus, unlike in previous centuries, with the advent of racial thinking to be a Jew or an African was supposedly to *always* possess certain presumed, negative traits, and to be incapable of acquiring the "civilized" ways of the colonizers. Something that we want all readers of this book, and all our students, to understand: Paleontologists, anthropologists, historians, and other scholars have debunked not only these notions of racial hierarchies but also the idea that there is any basis whatsoever for the belief that the human race is composed of distinct, separate races. From a 1998 statement of the American Anthropological Association: "Human populations are not unambiguous, clearly demarcated, biologically distinct groups. Evidence from the analysis of genetics (e.g., DNA) indicates that most physical variation, about 94%, lies *within* so-called racial groups. Conventional geographic 'racial' groupings differ from one another only in about 6% of their genes. This means that there is greater variation within 'racial' groups than between them" (AAA 1998). It might sound like a nice, liberal platitude to state "we are all one race, the *human race*"—but it happens to be true.

Social Darwinism emerged from this swamp of European racism, applying Charles Darwin's theories on natural selection to so-called races. Darwin analyzed genetic variation and competition in nature, while Social Darwinist thinkers saw competition among races as the driving force in history. It was not Darwin but Herbert Spencer, a leader of this new movement, who coined the phrase "survival of the fittest." Social Darwinism lent an even more lethal edge to racism: Competition among races is the driving force in history, its adherents argued, and thus humanity actually benefited from the inevitable disappearance of supposedly inferior peoples. Some American and European statesmen developed a nostalgic way of referring to the "vanishing races," as if the causes of their disappearances were mysterious (Brantlinger 2003). But such subtlety was usually not necessary: It was perfectly acceptable in polite elite circles to speak openly about the eradication of "inferior" peoples. Referring to the "savage races" in 1867, one prominent British writer and theologian intoned, "They are without a past and without a future, doomed [...] to a rapid, an entire, and, perhaps for the highest destinies of mankind, an inevitable extinction." They pass through the world "learning nothing, inventing nothing, improving nothing," and their disappearance will leave "no trace of their existence" beyond their physical remains. In his infamous manifesto *Mein Kampf*, Adolf Hitler stated that "the victory of the best race" is "the precondition of all human progress"—and he was simply articulating the viewpoint of most educated white Europeans.

In 1919, as Britain was combating a revolt by the Kurdish people in northern Iraq, future Prime Minister Winston Churchill declared, "I do not understand the squeamishness about the use of gas [...] I am strongly in favour of using poisoned gas against uncivilised tribes." European racism was expressed not only in such murderous proclamations but in the paternalistic and narcissistic attitude set forth in Rudyard Kipling's 1899 poem "The White Man's Burden"—that the colonized peoples were not only "half-devil," but "half-child" in need of the presumably benevolent, selfless assistance of the "civilizers."

Centralized states, and ideologies of nationalism, arose during this same era in much of Europe, and nations came to be defined in racial terms—that is, in the view of many Europeans, a nation comprised members of a single "race," with common cultural and linguistic traditions, rather than peoples of varying ethnicities or religions who were united in citizenship and legal equality. Thus, racism often lent individual nationalisms a militaristic and exclusive character. And it was hardly coincidental that racism flourished during the era that European nations were engaged in the imperialist land-grab now known as the "scramble for Africa," as we discuss further in Chapter Seven. From the 1860s until World War I, the leading European powers competed for land and resources on the African continent. While Europe enjoyed a century of relative continental peace with but the brief wars of German unification, including the Franco-Prussian, from 1815 to 1914, European powers extended their control from 35 to 85 percent of Africa's territory. Racism was not the only motivating factor, but it certainly fueled and justified the seizure of huge tracts of land in Africa, with deadly consequences. As one scholar observed, racism "provide[d] ideological legitimation for a vast project of conquest and genocide" (Traverso 2003, 63).

However, it was not only racial philosophies or mentalities that arose during this period of the "New Imperialism." European colonizers implemented murderous and even genocidal practices that foreshadowed the horrors of the twentieth century. The gravest crimes of the "New Imperialism" occurred under the Belgian administration of King Leopold II, who took control of the Congo in the 1870s, established an administration called the "Congo Free State" in 1885, and governed the huge territory as his personal property until 1908. In pursuit of ivory and rubber, as well as the status of a major colonial power, Leopold's authorities, complemented by a motley collection of adventurers, inflicted hideous violence upon the Congolese people. The monarch himself never set foot on the African continent. As we will read in Chapter Seven, as many as 10–11 million Congolese ultimately perished under Leopold's rule—which exceeded in magnitude, but not in calculated cruelty and exploitation, the tactics of French, British, Portuguese, German, Italian, and other European colonizers elsewhere on the continent. The Congolese catastrophe, which calls out for much greater attention, was little known to the public or even to historians—outside central Africa—before the publication of a 1998 book (Adam Hochschild's award-winning *King Leopold's Ghost*), and remains, in comparison to the Holocaust and other comparable calamities, virtually unknown today.

Also obscure in the pages of history are the deaths of tens of millions of Indians, Brazilians, and Chinese from famine under British rule (or resulting from British economic policy) in the late nineteenth century. These deaths resulted from the economic distortions and exploitation of colonialism, exacerbated by "El Niño" weather patterns. India experienced few famines before British rule but endured many severe ones in the last quarter of the nineteenth century. British administrators—guided by the ultra-free-market economic philosophy of the time—were, with rare exceptions, miserly in their efforts to alleviate starvation during the worst disasters. In one case, the British official presumably responsible for relief efforts declared: "The doctrine that in time of famine the poor are entitled to demand relief would probably lead to the doctrine that they are entitled to such relief at all times." Another official, Sir Richard Temple, required starving Indians to travel to camps for work on railroad and canal projects, whereupon he offered a meager diet of barely 1,000 calories per day for heavy labor. This age of imperialism of the late nineteenth and early twentieth centuries claimed at least 50 million victims in India, China, and Brazil alone (Davis 2000). Without deeply held racist doctrines, such brutal indifference to human life would not have been possible.

It was also during this time that the leading imperial powers developed lethal new technologies and often experimented upon their colonial subjects. Aerial bombing and other technologies led to heavily one-sided encounters, such as the Battle of Omdurman in Sudan in 1898, in which 48 British troops were killed while more than 10,000 Sudanese perished. "Like other colonial powers," noted Sven Lindqvist in a scathing critique of racism and imperialism, "the British had already been bombing restless natives in their territories for several years" by World War I. "It began with the Pathans on India's northwestern border in 1915 [...] The British bombed revolutionaries in Egypt and the rebellious Sultan of Darfur in 1916. The 1917, bombers put down an uprising" on India's border with Afghanistan, and in 1920 "Enzeli [aka Anzali, a large port city] in Iran was bombed in an attempt to create a British puppet state" (Lindqvist 2003, 42–43).

Genocide often accompanied or resulted from European colonialism, especially once the colonizers determined that they wanted the land, rather than the forced labor, of local populations. The commanding German officer responsible for the Herero and Nama Genocide of 1904–08, General von Trotha, wrote to fellow officers: "The exercise of violence with crass terrorism and with cruelty is my policy. I annihilate the rebellious tribes with streams of blood [...]. Only on this seed can something new emerge that will remain" (Schaller and Zimmerer 2008). After the genocide, von Trotha wrote a public statement in a South-West African newspaper proclaiming that, while in earlier stages of colonization, the Europeans needed the labor of the natives, "later they must disappear" to make room for European settlers and in accord with the "law of the survival of the fittest" (Schaller and Zimmerer 2008). In a war that is less well known than the Herero Genocide, the Germans were simultaneously suppressing the Maji-Maji Revolt in East Africa, in the process killing more than 200,000 people and employing tactics that would later be part of Western counter-insurgency strategies during the Cold War: destroying villages and crops and otherwise attempting to eliminate the rebels' supposed bases of support. Again, Chapter Seven investigates European colonialism and imperialism at much greater length.

Australia's "Stolen Generations"

The previous chapter included a lengthy passage about the genocide of Indigenous peoples in the United States and Canada. Those genocides included egregious forms of cultural genocide, as discussed in the last chapter—in particular, the kidnapping (which is an accurate term to describe it) of tens of thousands of Indian children who were then interned in so-called boarding schools, where they were stripped of their language and culture and often subjected to physical and sexual abuse.

The term "Stolen Generations" refers to the Aboriginal and Torres Strait Islander children who were forcibly removed from their families by Australian federal and state government agencies and church missions under acts of their respective parliaments. These practices spanned from approximately 1905 to 1967, though in some areas, the practice continued into the 1970s. The policy of assimilation that underpinned these removals aimed to integrate Aboriginal children into white society by severing their ties to their families, culture, and identity. The rationale behind the forced removal of these children was rooted in a paternalistic and racist ideology that deemed Aboriginal culture and way of life as inferior. Policymakers believed that the best way to "save" Aboriginal children was to remove them from their cultural environment and assimilate them into the dominant white society. This often involved placing children in institutions or with non-Indigenous foster families, where they were prohibited from speaking their native languages or practicing their cultural traditions (Powell 2011).

The impact of these policies on the Aboriginal and Torres Strait Islander communities has been devastating. Children were taken from their parents, often without consent and sometimes by force. They were placed in environments where they experienced neglect, abuse, and cultural dislocation. The trauma of separation from their families and communities left lasting psychological scars, leading to intergenerational trauma that continues to affect Indigenous communities today. The "Stolen Generations policy" was often justified under the guise of child protection, yet it had catastrophic consequences for those who were taken. Many children lost all connection to their cultural heritage, their language, and their identity. They were often subjected to harsh living conditions, and many suffered physical, emotional, and sexual abuse. The policies not only disrupted individual lives but also undermined the social and cultural fabric of entire communities.

In recent decades, there has been a growing recognition of the injustices suffered by the Stolen Generations. The landmark "Bringing Them Home" report, published in 1997, was a result of a national inquiry into the separation of Aboriginal and Torres Strait Islander children from their families. The report documented the experiences of the Stolen Generations and made numerous recommendations for addressing the legacy of these policies, including calls for reparations and formal apologies from the government (Jones 2024, 145–46). In 2008, then-Prime Minister Kevin Rudd delivered a formal apology to the "Stolen Generations" on behalf of the Australian government. This apology was a step toward acknowledging the wrongs of the past and beginning the process of healing and reconciliation (ibid., 644). However, it hardly resolved the historical injustices; survivors and their descendants continue to struggle with the effects of trauma and dislocation.

The American Model of Racist Violence and Terrorism

Raphael Lemkin observed that while racism "reached its peak in those modern totalitarian nations which evolved ideas of racial unity and destiny"—that is, Nazi Germany and a handful of other fascist or Stalinist states—its "deepest roots have been cast in the non-totalitarian culture of North America" (Lemkin 2014, 38). And by "North America," he seemed to be referring specifically to the United States, though he was well aware of Canada's history of racism against its Indigenous or "First Nations" peoples. Racism and deeply racist practices proliferated (and continue to do so) throughout the United States, but it was the "Jim Crow" South that it was especially egregious and codified into a vast system of laws as well as social mores (Fredrickson 2003). Jim Crow was a system of racial segregation and discrimination that enforced the separation of African Americans from whites in virtually every aspect of life. It was established in the late nineteenth century after the Reconstruction era (which followed the Civil War and lasted from 1865 to 1877) and persisted well into the 1960s, shaping the social, political, and economic landscape of the South.

The system of Jim Crow—which took its name from a stereotyped minstrel character of the earlier 1800s—consisted of:

Segregation Laws: Jim Crow laws mandated the segregation of public facilities, including schools, transportation, restaurants, theaters, parks, and restrooms. These laws required separate facilities for African Americans and whites, often designating inferior facilities for African Americans.

Voting Restrictions: Jim Crow laws also included measures aimed at disenfranchising African Americans, such as poll taxes, literacy tests, and "grandfather clauses," whereby you could not vote unless your grandfather had voted. It is often said that "women gained the right to vote in 1920," with the passage of the Nineteenth Amendment; but it should be known that *Black* women (and men) could very rarely exercise their right to vote, in much of the country, until the mid-1960s.

Economic Discrimination: African Americans faced significant economic discrimination under Jim Crow, with limited access to education, employment opportunities, and fair wages. They were often relegated to low-paying jobs with little opportunity for advancement.

Social Segregation: Beyond legal segregation, Jim Crow enforced strict social codes that dictated separate spaces for African Americans and whites in social settings. Interracial marriage was prohibited, and there were social norms that enforced racial hierarchy and superiority.

Violence and Intimidation: The Jim Crow system was upheld through violence, intimidation, and the threat of vigilante justice by groups like the Ku Klux Klan. African Americans who challenged segregation or attempted to assert their rights faced harassment, lynching, and other forms of violence. According to the most comprehensive study of lynching—extra-legal murders, often by hanging or burning—at least 4,400 people, mostly Black men (but also some Italians, Mexicans, and other immigrants, especially Chinese, as well as labor organizers) were lynched between 1877 and 1950 (EJI 2018). Here we must pause to once again remind the reader that *killing* people is not the only way to kill *a people*. The American model closely followed Lemkin's assertion that genocide could be accomplished through a broad spectrum of acts—political, social, cultural, economic, biological, physical, religious, and moral—that "ranged from repression and marginalization to acts of oppression and sometimes (but not always) violence [...]" acts that today "we would call 'structural violence' or 'cultural' violence" (Irvin-Erickson 2022, 150). No wonder then, that the United States (and South Africa) did not want the Convention applied to government-sanctioned segregation—not to mention lynching.

While legal segregation officially ended with the Civil Rights Movement (usually dated 1955–68) Jim Crow's legacy continues to influence American society. The words of Martin Luther King, Jr., quoted at the beginning of this chapter, are still true more than 50 years later: "We must honestly see and admit that racism is still deeply rooted all over America. It's still deeply rooted in the North, and it's still deeply rooted in the South."

The United States underwent a brief "racial reckoning" after the horrifying public lynching, by police officers, of George Floyd in Minnesota in May 2020, which sparked a summer of protests. But this momentum dissipated before much genuine progress was made.

Genocidal Massacres in Wilmington and Tulsa

Racism in the United States was—and is—manifested not only in legal discrimination and social attitudes but also often in violence. Sometimes, extreme violence. The authors of this book have both lived and taught in North Carolina for many years and can attest that there is little if any knowledge, among our fellow Carolinians, about a horrifying event that took place in our state in 1898. On November 10, 1898—almost precisely, to the hour, 40 years before *Kristallnacht* in Germany, which heralded the onset of the Holocaust—a racist mob descended on the Black community of Wilmington, on the east coast of North Carolina, and conducted a rampage that led to many dozens of deaths (probably about 200) and the destruction of the city's Black community. Notably, they began by burning down the *Daily Record*, one of the very few African-American daily newspapers in the country at that time (Figure 3.1).

While it had the appearance of a spontaneous outbreak of violence—and is still erroneously termed a "race riot"—it was actually a meticulously planned *coup* (overthrow of a government) orchestrated by white supremacists seeking to oust a biracial government and consolidate white dominance in the region. It was organized and led by such figures as future governor Charles Aycock and long-time US Senator Ben Tillman. (This book's authors both live in Greensboro, NC, where until very recently a major freeway and many other sites, including a school, were named after Aycock. Greensboro is also, however, the site of the famous 1960 Woolworth's sit-in launched by four North Carolina A&T State University students, where one of the authors of this book has taught for more than 30 years).

Figure 3.1 The African-American newspaper, the *Daily Record*, was among the first targets of the genocidal mob in Wilmington, NC in November 1898. https://commons.wikimedia.org/wiki/File:Wilmington_vigilantes.tif

Following the Civil War and Reconstruction, which was formally ended by 1877 throughout the region, Southern states implemented laws and practices aimed at maintaining white supremacy and disenfranchising African Americans. Despite these efforts, a biracial coalition known as the Fusionists emerged in North Carolina, advocating for progressive reforms and challenging the existing power structure. In Wilmington, Fusionist leaders, including Black politician Alexander Manly, gained influence and support, posing a direct threat to the white elite's grip on power. The local Democratic Party harbored deep-seated resentment toward the Fusion movement and its challenge to white supremacy. As in other periods of history, the specter of an alliance between working-class white and Black folks was deeply troubling to the elites. In the lead-up to the 1898 election, Democratic leaders, including former Confederate soldiers and members of a white supremacist group, the Red Shirts, launched a campaign of fearmongering and racist propaganda. They stoked white resentment by spreading false rumors of Black men assaulting white women—a common theme over the decades, and the pretext for many lynchings—and warned of the "Negro domination" that would result from Fusionist rule. (A brief historical note: During the long years of Jim Crow racism and segregation and racism, the Democrats—in the South—were the more overtly racist of the two major parties, while the Republicans were associated with their first president, Abraham Lincoln. It was only in the 1960s and 1970s, during the tenure of President Richard Nixon and afterward, that the Republicans became more openly associated with racism than the Democrats.)

On November 8, 1898, amid widespread voter intimidation and fraud, the Democratic Party won a landslide victory in North Carolina, including in Wilmington. Buoyed by their electoral success, white supremacists in the city began plotting to overthrow the still legal Fusionist government by force. Two days later, on November 10, a mob of armed white men, including members of the Democratic Party, the Red Shirts, and the Ku Klux Klan, descended upon Wilmington with the intent to terrorize and subjugate the African-American population. The violence that ensued was swift and brutal. Black-owned businesses were looted and destroyed, homes were ransacked, and African-American residents were assaulted and murdered in the streets. The newly elected Democrat mayor, Alfred Moore Waddell, who had previously lost his bid for Congress to a Fusionist candidate, played a central role in the coup. He led the white mob in seizing control of the city, forcing the Fusionist mayor and other elected officials to resign at gunpoint. In a calculated act of defiance, Alexander Manly, whose newspaper had been a target of white supremacist ire, fled Wilmington to avoid being lynched (Zucchino 2020).

This genocidal massacre resulted in the deaths of an estimated 200 to 300 African Americans, the forced exile of many others, and the overthrow of the duly elected biracial government. In the aftermath of the riot, white supremacists solidified their hold on power in North Carolina, implementing laws and policies that disenfranchised Black voters, segregated public spaces, and perpetuated further racial discrimination and violence. The 1898 massacre and *coup* represented a violent backlash to progress, a recurring theme in race relations in this country. The historian Timothy Tyson wrote, "At the end of the 19th century, Wilmington was a symbol of black hope."

"Thanks to its busy port, the black majority city was North Carolina's largest and most important municipality [...] Blacks owned 10 of the city's 11 eating houses and 20 of its 22 barbershops. The black male literacy rate was higher than that of whites" (Tyson 2006, 1).

Wilmington was far from the only site of racist pogroms and massacres. The summer of 1919 is referred to as "Red Summer" due to bloody massacres from Washington, DC up to Chicago, down to Elaine, Arkansas, Texas, Arizona, and elsewhere. (It is always important to remember: Racism and racist violence were never a Southern monopoly.) Two years after the bloodshed of 1919, one of America's most notorious pogroms took place, in Tulsa, Oklahoma. The Tulsa Race Massacre of 1921 was one of the most devastating episodes of racial violence in American history. It occurred in Tulsa, Oklahoma, over the course of two days, May 31 and June 1, 1921. The horrors occurred in the Greenwood District, a prosperous African-American neighborhood also known as "Black Wall Street." Greenwood was a thriving African-American community in Tulsa, characterized by its bustling businesses, vibrant culture, and relative economic prosperity. Despite segregation and racial discrimination elsewhere, Greenwood flourished, becoming a symbol of Black success and self-sufficiency. In a pattern we have witnessed for many decades and that we have already commented upon, but that bears repeating: Black success provoked hostility and violence. (The election of Barack Obama in 2008 is a recent example; his election elicited widespread panic and racist hysteria among many white people and led to the creation of new movements, heavily tinged by racism, such as the Tea Party and now the so-called Freedom Caucus.)

On May 30, 1921, a young African-American man named Dick Rowland was accused of assaulting a white woman, Sarah Page, in an elevator. What actually happened remains unclear, but Rowland was arrested the following day, sparking tensions between the Black and white communities (Ellsworth 2021). Rumors of the alleged assault spread rapidly, stoking hysteria among the white population. Sensationalized accounts in local newspapers further fueled the flames of racial hysteria. As tensions escalated, a white mob gathered outside the courthouse where Rowland was being held, demanding that he be handed over and executed.

The next evening, the situation spiraled out of control. Armed white mobs descended on Greenwood looting, burning, and destroying homes, businesses, and churches. The violence was indiscriminate and brutal, with reports of shootings, arson, and other acts of extreme violence, including an aerial bombing, against African Americans. Predictably, local law enforcement and government officials failed to protect the residents of Greenwood. In some cases they were complicit in the violence, deputizing white citizens and even participating in the destruction. By the morning of June 1, much of Greenwood lay in ruins, with thousands of African-American residents left homeless and destitute. The exact death toll remains unknown, as official records were incomplete and many victims were never accounted for. Estimates range from dozens to hundreds of people killed, with thousands more injured and displaced. In the aftermath of the massacre, there was a concerted effort to suppress and downplay the events. Local authorities and media outlets minimized the scale of the violence, and survivors were often silenced or intimidated into silence. The massacre was largely omitted from history books and public discourse for decades—or when it was mentioned, even up to today, is characterized as a "race riot," implying that Black folks, as well as whites, were running amok and killing one another.

In June 2024 a dismal, outrageous coda to the Tulsa massacre occurred. There were still two survivors remaining, 109-year-old Lessie Benningfield Randle and 110-year-old Viola Fletcher. With the assistance of a legal team, they brought suit against the State of Oklahoma and on June 12, 2024, after a final brief and appeal, the state's Supreme Court rejected it. Their reasoning? "Lawyers representing the defendants argued that the two survivors lacked standing to sue and that in 1921 when the massacre occurred, governmental agencies involved were shielded from liability by sovereign immunity." The previous year it had been dismissed on procedural grounds. "I would like to see justice," Ms. Randle said from her Tulsa residence in a November 2023 interview. "It's past time. I would like to see this all cleared up and we go down the right road. But I do not know if I will ever see that" (Burch 2024). In January 2025, the US Department of Justice (DoJ) released a report on the massacre. "The Tulsa Race Massacre stands out as a civil rights crime unique in its magnitude, barbarity, racist hostility and its utter annihilation of a thriving Black community," a DoJ spokesperson said in a statement after the report's release. "In 1921, white Tulsans murdered hundreds of residents of Greenwood, burned their homes and churches, looted their belongings and locked the survivors in internment camps." After more than a century no one could be held criminally responsible, she added, "but the historical reckoning for the massacre continues." This reckoning has indeed come to pass. In June 2025, 104 years after the massacre, Monroe Nichols, Tulsa's first African-American mayor, approved a $105 million dollar reparations package.

In the view of the authors, African Americans are due massive reparations. Justice can never truly be fully achieved after centuries of genocidal violence, slavery followed by Jim Crow, then followed by innumerable forms of exploitation and oppression ever since, and barely mitigated by the gains achieved by the Black freedom struggle over the decades. Gains that are always imperiled and often being overturned, for example by recent Supreme Court decisions on voting rights. But an attempt at partial justice would include reparations. And it is not as if there are no precedents for reparations—a term that seems to terrify so many Americans. As journalist Wesley Lowery pointed out in a 2024 article, the federal government paid $25,000 to the families of Italian immigrants lynched in New Orleans in 1891. Lowery also pointed out that President Harry Truman, in 1946, signed a bill creating a "claims commission" that paid roughly $1.3 billion to Indigenous tribes for the violence and land theft they had suffered; after 40 years of delay, the US government eventually paid reparations for the imprisonment of 120,000 Japanese-Americans (yes, Japanese-*Americans*) during World War II. Our earlier section on Wilmington and Tulsa did not have space for the dozens of other anti-Black massacres of that era. Another one occurred in Rosewood, Florida, in 1923; survivors later received $150,000 payments "and their descendants were given access to a scholarship fund; and $10 million was paid to the hundreds of Black men unwillingly included in a Tuskegee study on the effects of untreated syphilis" between 1932 and 1972 (Lowery 2024). Germany has paid huge reparations to Holocaust survivors and their descendants. We ask our readers to calmly and compassionately consider the arguments in favor of reparations that have been advanced by many, including Wesley Lowery and Ta-Nahisi Coates, whose persuasive articles can be found in the bibliography.

Racism and German Nazism

Racism was taken to its fullest and most murderous expression by the German Nazis. To the Nazis, the Jews were a "race"—and idea that, like all their ideas, was unoriginal. Racial antisemitism was invented in the late 1800s, throughout Europe and America. The Jews were not a religious or ethnic or social group, but now deemed to be a "race"—which meant that conversion to Christianity did not offer an escape from persecution, as it had in previous centuries. Central to Nazi racism was the notion of Aryan supremacy, a warped belief in the superiority of the so-called Aryan race, which Hitler and his followers considered to be biologically and culturally superior to all others. (But again, the term "Aryan" was widely employed on both sides of the Atlantic over the half-century before Hitler took power.) The Nazis' supremacist ideology served as the foundation for the regime's policies of racial discrimination, exclusion, and ultimately, extermination. Jews, Romani people, Slavs, disabled individuals, and others deemed undesirable were targeted for persecution, segregation, and ultimately, annihilation.

The next few pages will offer an overview of the Holocaust, which was a product not simply of German history, but of Western history. The Nazis invented little, if anything, either in the realm of ideology or in colonial practice—although they took certain trends in Western history to their most deadly extremes.

Anti-Jewish Prejudice in History

Prejudice and discrimination have plagued the Jewish people throughout much of their history. The origins of this unreasoning hatred can be traced to at least 3,000 years ago. Persecution flared into violent repression during the first century CE when the Roman authorities crushed a Jewish rebellion (66–70 CE) and destroyed the Second Temple. In that same century a new faith, eventually known as Christianity, split off from Judaism and began to develop its own scriptures and theology. Based upon some dubious accounts of Jesus's trial and execution in the New Testament—accounts that biblical scholars and historians have shown to be wildly inaccurate in their depiction of a weak and compassionate Pontius Pilate being ordered about by Jewish priests—Christian theology blamed the Jews collectively for the death of Jesus. Matthew 27:25 in the New Testament was often invoked; after Pilate "washes his hands," the Jewish crowd supposedly declares "His blood shall be on us and on our children." Christian teaching further stigmatized the Jews for failing to accept the divinity of Christ. The fact that Jesus was born, lived, and died a Jew would be forgotten in coming centuries.

In Christian Europe throughout the Middle Ages, religious and cultural antisemitism persisted and was the basis for additional forms of discrimination. Jews were usually barred from owning land and from military service and, in a classic example of a self-fulfilling prophecy, these restrictions served to create or validate certain stereotypes—for example, that Jews were cowardly and devious and incapable of honest work or agricultural labor, preferring parasitical financial dealings (which they had been pushed into!). By the late twelfth century fantastical allegations were invented, most notably the infamous "blood libel" myth, which alleged that Jews abducted and murdered Christian children in order to use their blood in religious rituals. Such myths intensified the anti-Jewish sentiments that were embedded in Christian theology and popular culture and sometimes provoked murderous pogroms. ("Pogrom" refers to a violent mob attack, usually organized by governing elites, but with popular participation. The term has usually been associated with anti-Jewish attacks and massacres, but as you have seen earlier in this chapter, it is also an appropriate term to characterize massacres such as those in Wilmington, NC, and Tulsa, OK).

In looking at the history of anti-Jewish violence we see a pattern in place that has continued to the present day: Periods of social crisis and instability, especially when combined with religious zealotry, have proven to be especially dangerous for Jews. The First Crusade (1096–99) provides an example of the perils of Jews of Christian zeal. In 1096, Crusader forces attacked the Jewish populations of some German-speaking communities (in modern-day western Germany); as many as 4,000 Jews died in these massacres. A severe social crisis, the Black Death (1347–51) was another pivotal moment. Jews were scapegoated and accused of causing or spreading the bubonic plague, as we now know it, leading to numerous massacres. This practice of blaming or scapegoating Jews for social or economic problems is a long-standing, recurring tradition that would reappear in pre-Nazi Germany. In Europe's Early Modern period, generally dated from c. 1450 to the late 1700s, antisemitism continued to evolve alongside religious upheavals and socio-economic changes. The Protestant Reformation, which began in 1521, introduced new theological justifications for antisemitism, with Martin Luther's writings containing virulent antisemitism, accusing Jews of usury and of rejecting Christianity.

Additionally, the Spanish Inquisition and the expulsion of Jews from Spain in 1492 forced many Sephardic Jews into exile or conversion, contributing to widespread anti-Jewish sentiments across Europe. And as mentioned near the beginning of this chapter, Spain also invented the concept of *Limpieza de sangre* around this time, a big step toward the biological-racial depiction of Jews that would sweep all of Europe four centuries later. The Portuguese Inquisition further intensified persecution, demonstrating how religious intolerance fueled anti-Jewish bigotry and hysteria during this period. Economic competition also played a significant role. Jews were often involved in money lending and finance, roles prohibited for Christians under Catholic doctrine. This economic activity made Jews vulnerable to resentment and accusations of exploitation, reinforcing negative stereotypes about their supposed greed and financial cunning.

We have already seen that the eighteenth-century "Enlightenment" was a mixed blessing: democratizing and secularizing, yet simultaneously contributing to racial categories and beliefs. Similarly, this period was paradoxical for European (and American) Jews. While these secularizing trends began to weaken the theological hold of anti-Judaism, it was rejuvenated and given a more lethal potential by the racial ideologies that dominated European thought during the 1800s. While Jews had previously been viewed as a religious or ethnic group, they now came to be seen by many Europeans as a "race." Therefore, the negative qualities that had been falsely associated with Jewry were now depicted as genetic, and therefore immutable and unchanging.

This "racializing" of antisemitism would later have lethal consequences: during times of persecution and pogroms, a Jew could no longer convert to escape his or her fate—an emotionally difficult option, but an option nonetheless for previous generations. By the turn of the twentieth-century-modern and pre-modern forms of Judeophobia converged and were given new force by racism and other anxieties stirred by the rapid and, to some, unnerving political and cultural trends of that era. By the end of the nineteenth century, modern antisemitism, while adopting and perpetuating many stereotypes and motifs from earlier centuries, had become a political force in much of Europe, and in its racial rather than religious incarnation, it differed in character from anti-Jewish prejudice of the late Middle Ages and Early Modern period.

Preconditions for the Holocaust: World War I and Its Aftermath

World War I erupted in late July 1914 and quickly became the most destructive, lethal war in human history—to that point. The "Great War" as it was called (as there was not yet a second world war) claimed the lives of roughly eight million troops and a similar number of civilians: 16–17 million total. New technologies were employed to devastating effect—chemical warfare, aerial bombardments (though quite primitive, compared to the next world war), deadlier forms of artillery and tank warfare; and the final stages of the war and its aftermath were accompanied by the Spanish flu pandemic, spread in part by the movements and then repatriation of troops. Incredibly, the flu claimed more victims than the war itself. And in its wake, WWI not only left behind a ruined continent, but also created angry, traumatized, and disillusioned populations, for all this destruction seemed meaningless. Few people were happy with the war's conclusion, and the cynicism, foolishness, and hypocrisy of world leaders were revealed, inducing many millions of people to look for new political movements.

In Germany, revolutionary uprisings brought down the German "Second Empire" (or *Reich*) and sent the emperor, Kaiser Wilhelm II, into exile in November 1918. A democratic government led by the moderate Social-Democratic Party (SPD) took power. Before the armistice that officially concluded WWI had even been signed, a myth began to circulate that purportedly explained the cause of Germany's capitulation. The brave, selfless, and undefeated soldiers at the front had supposedly been betrayed—"stabbed in the back"—by pacifists and socialists as well as by domestic politicians who, far from the front, supposedly conceded the war (Evans 2020, 47–83). The stab-in-the-back myth converged and drew sustenance from antisemitism—for, in the imaginations of Germany's growing number of right-wing nationalists, "the Jew" lurked behind the treacherous forces of liberalism and socialism. The resort to such a "Big Lie" to mobilize and galvanize support has since been effectively utilized by Donald J. Trump, who still claims to have actually won the 2020 election but to have been the victim of massive fraud, an outlandish but poisonous assertion.

Adolf Hitler and the Birth of the Nazi Party

It is evident from his writings that by September 1919 at the latest Adolf Hitler—who was born in 1889 in Austria and grew up there, and fought in the German army during the war—had become convinced that "the Jew" was the chief evil in Western society, and this belief was the cornerstone of a consistent but irrational worldview. Hitler saw race and racial conflict as history's principal driving force. His oratory and writings from the early 1920s were filled with the language of biological and racial determinism, and with an antisemitism that was expressed in uncompromising, lurid tones. "With diabolic joy in his face, the black-haired Jewish youth lurks in ambush for the unsuspecting girl whom he defiles with his blood," he wrote in his turgid, long-winded, racist manifesto *Mein Kampf* (Hitler 1971, 448). He wrote this dreadful tome while serving a thirteen-month prison sentence, in comfortable conditions, after launching an attempted *coup*, known as the "Beer Hall Putsch," in Munich in November 1923. "All great cultures of the past perished only because the originally creative race died off through blood-poisoning" he continued, and so on and so forth *ad nauseam* for many hundreds of pages (ibid.). This type of language is also being used in the United States today. Hitler also viewed Jews as an invading force. They were not merely a nuisance, but an existential threat, largely because of their connection to Marxist subversion in his imagination. We note that other genocidists have also depicted their victims as "invaders" or "foreigners," regardless of how long they had lived there: such was the case during the genocides in Rwanda and elsewhere, while in other cases (e.g., the Armenian and Bosnian genocide) the victims were accused of conspiring with outside forces.

In his inelegant prose, Hitler argued that Marxism and Bolshevism were merely Jewish creations—a weapon to "enslave and rule the peoples with a brutal fist" (ibid., 449). If Germany did not defeat the "Jewish menace," Germany and Western Civilization itself would instead be defeated. Of Hitler's adherence to such delusional, hateful beliefs there is no question. He continued to rail against the Jews into the final hours of his life when he even claimed that British and American military forces were "the troops of Jewry" (Friedländer 2008, 659). In late 1919, Hitler discovered a group in Munich that would serve as the instrument for the "regeneration" of his adopted homeland—the German Workers' Party. Quickly asserting himself as leader of the tiny group, Hitler renamed the party the "National Socialist German Workers' Party." (NSDAP; "Nazi," an abbreviation of the German for "National Socialist," soon became the party's informal designation.) Throughout the 1920s, the Nazis were but one of many small right-wing groups in a chaotic political landscape. It was only from about 1928 onward that they distinguished themselves as the largest and most dangerous of the multitude of far-right organizations, in part through the efforts of the master propagandist, the odious Joseph Goebbels. As the Nazis gained votes in the elections, industrialists and other businessmen began to take them seriously—they had previously dismissed the Nazis as uncouth riff-raff—and corporate Germany saw that they could use the Nazis to terrorize and eventually crush Germany's strong labor and leftist movements (Figure 3.2).

The Nazi party won more votes than any other party, 37 percent, in the July 1932 elections, which like the multitude of hastily called elections of the early 1930s failed to resolve the deepening political crisis. In this election as well as the subsequent 6 November vote, half the electorate voted for either the Nazis or the Communists, while the centrist parties were pushed to the margins. Petrified by left-wing revolution and lacking options or imagination, traditional conservative elites like Franz von Papen, one of three short-term chancellors as the government sank into near-chaos in

Figure 3.2 "The Eternal Jew": Poster for a 1937–38 antisemitic exhibit staged by the Nazis. This repellent poster depicts "the Jew" as both a capitalist profiteer (note the coins in his right hand) and a Bolshevik (the Communist hammer and sickle under his left arm). https://commons.wikimedia.org/wiki/File:Der_ewige_Jude_postcard.jpg

the early 1930s, persuaded the 85-year-old President Hindenburg to offer Hitler the chancellorship—which Hindenburg did on January 30, 1933.

The conservatives mistakenly thought they could control the "drummer boy," as they sometimes contemptuously called him. They were not the only ones who failed to anticipate the ruthlessness and determination with which Hitler would consolidate power. The powerful working-class parties—the Social Democrats (SPD) and the Communist Party (KPD)—also failed to perceive the danger and spent more time denouncing one another than attempting to unite to combat the Nazi threat.

The Nazis' first targets were not German Jews *per se*, but political opponents, particularly members of the large Social-Democratic and Communist movements, many of whom were Jewish. Four weeks after Hitler's appointment, in the early hours of February 27, 1933, the Reichstag (parliament) building was partially burned down. Historians believed for years that the arson was the work of a lone, wayward Dutch radical, but newer evidence suggests that the Nazis may have set the fire. In either case, the fire was convenient for the Nazi leadership, which immediately seized upon it as a pretext to solidify power, decrying the arson as the work of "communists" bent on taking power and unleashing a reign of terror on real and imagined enemies. On March 23, the Reichstag passed the Enabling Law, allowing Hitler to essentially rule by decree. By the end of Hitler's first year, tens of thousands of KPD members were under arrest, many of them subjected to the ghastly symbol of Nazism that would later define its rule throughout Europe: the concentration camp.

Stages in Anti-Jewish Persecution

In 1933 the German-Jewish population totaled about a mere 510,000, less than one percent of the country's total population. Approximately 80,000 German Jews had fought in Great War and 12,000 had died in service—evidence of Jewish patriotism that made little impact on public opinion, which grew steadily more racist during the 1930s. The Nazis initiated their rule with the ruthless suppression of left-wing organizations, and they also wasted little time clamping down on the Jewish population, who in the Nazi worldview were responsible for virtually all the ills of society. "The adjective *jüdisch* [Jewish] [...] was attached to every phenomenon of the modern world objectionable to the Nazis," wrote historian Alon Confino, "and then some. Jews were responsible for bolshevism, communism, Marxism" as well as "capitalism, conservatism, pacifism [...] materialism, atheism." The Jews were also responsible for those features of the Weimar Republic that were so abhorrent to the Nazis: its "cabaret and club scene, as well as sexual freedom, psychoanalysis, feminism, homosexuality [...] modernist, atonal, and jazz music" and avant-garde art and film (Confino 2014, 107).

During the first six years of the Third Reich, the Nazis steadily increased the legal persecution and social ostracizing of the German Jews. The Nazis' first overt attack upon the Jewish population was the declaration of April 1, 1933, boycott of Jewish-owned businesses. Within another week the new regime began its legal assault on the Jews, issuing the "Law for the Restoration of the Professional Civil Service" on April 7, which forced Jewish and other "politically unreliable" employees out of government jobs—including positions in law and education. The 1935 "Nuremberg Laws" went further in institutionalizing Nazi racial ideology as the basis for citizenship and political rights. Section 1 banned marriage between Jews and "Aryan" Germans, an important step in isolating the Jews and bringing about their "social death," as some historians have described it, which would make it easier for German gentiles to harden their hearts or ignore the worsening plight of their Jewish neighbors.

The Nazis systematically implemented their racist ideology through a combination of legal frameworks, propaganda, and state-sponsored violence. The Nuremberg

Laws of 1935 stripped Jews of their citizenship and legal rights, institutionalizing discrimination and paving the way for further atrocities. Propaganda, including films, posters, and speeches, demonized minority groups, dehumanizing them and justifying their persecution in the eyes of the German populace. State institutions, including the SS and Gestapo, ruthlessly enforced racial policies, rounding up individuals deemed "inferior" and sending them to concentration camps, where they faced forced labor, starvation, and extermination in gas chambers.

Our students and readers should know that the US Holocaust Memorial Museum provides the best online encyclopedia—or encyclopedia of any sort—for Nazism and the Holocaust. To quote from their entry on Nazi racism: "The Nazis tried to use science to prove their racial theories. They recruited doctors and other scientists to help them. These officials tried to categorize people into races. They measured and described people's physical features, like noses, skulls, eyes, and hair" (USHMM 2022). Yet "these attempts at categorization failed to prove Nazi racial theories. In fact, their efforts revealed that human beings could not be scientifically categorized into races. Humankind is simply too naturally diverse. However, this reality did not stop the Nazis" (ibid.)

The *Kristallnacht* (Crystal Night, or Night of Broken Glass) pogrom of November 9–10, 1938, heralded a violent new stage in anti-Jewish persecutions. Using as a pretext the murder of a Nazi diplomat by a German-Jewish teenager in Paris, Goebbels and other Nazi leaders unleashed a wave of violence throughout the Greater Reich (Germany and Austria). By the morning of 10 November, at least one hundred Jews had been murdered, hundreds of synagogues as well as Jewish-owned businesses had been vandalized or destroyed, and some 26,000 Jewish men were arrested and dragged off to concentration camps. Significantly, these were the first German Jews to be arrested simply for being Jewish. The Nazi regime placed the responsibility for the destruction upon the Jews themselves. It assessed the Jewish community about $100 million for the damage and another $400 million for the murder of the Nazi diplomat. By this time, antisemitic persecution enjoyed greater public support. The widespread indifference and even opposition to the anti-Jewish boycott of April 1933 had evolved, after several years of propaganda and social separation, into grudging or outright approval of antisemitic persecution.

World War II

The Nazi regime had tormented its Jewish citizens for six years, but it was the war (1939–45) that led directly to the wholesale mass murder of European Jewry. As the Third Reich expanded into Poland and eventually the Soviet Union—countries with much larger Jewish populations than Germany itself—Nazi policy radicalized, and collaborationist or ultra-right governments and movements in Europe also targeted Jews for extermination, sometimes with little encouragement from Berlin.

On September 1, 1939, a week after signing a "Non-Aggression Pact" with the Soviet Union, Germany invaded Poland, initiating World War II. In his mind, the war against Poland was both a war for territory or *Lebensraum* ("living space," a long-cherished goal of certain German elites predating Hitler)—presumably needed for a greater Germany that would encompass ethnic Germans throughout the region—and a racial war against the "dreadful [racial] material," as he viewed the Poles (Crowe 2008, 159). His chief of staff explained that it was "the intention of the Führer to destroy and exterminate the Polish people" (Snyder 2010, 121). See Chapter Two for more on the Nazis' fanatical anti-Slav bigotry. In the first days of the invasion, special German units, the *Einsatzgruppen*, were unleashed upon Poland's defenseless civilians, both Jews and non-Jews. Augmented by other units, five *Einsatzgruppen* composed of roughly 4,200 men murdered 50,000 Poles, mostly non-Jews, by the end of 1939 (Crowe 2008, 160). These special units would later play a prominent and indispensable role in the murder of Soviet Jews, after the subsequent invasion of that country. At this stage, the Nazi leaders considered various options for how to deal with the millions of Jews who had fallen into their hands. Tens of thousands of Polish Jews were killed or died of conditions imposed upon them by the occupiers, but the Nazis had not yet decided upon systematic mass murder as their answer to the "Jewish Question." They considered some plans that may appear to be fantastical—such as deporting mass numbers of Jews to the island of Madagascar, off Africa's southeast coast. As a transitional measure, while debates continued at different levels of the German administration, the Germans instituted a policy of ghettoization. Beginning in late 1939, German forces squeezed Jews into sealed-off quarters of numerous cities. They later extended this policy into other corners of occupied Europe, but the largest ghettos remained in Poland until their occupants were deported en masse to killing centers (often called "death camps") later in the war.

Operation Barbarossa and the "Final Solution"

There should have never been any doubt that Nazi Germany, driven by its quest for *Lebensraum* and the imperative of destroying "Judeo-Bolshevism," would attack the USSR when it perceived the time was right. By the summer of 1940, Hitler routinely bellowed to his colleagues that the Soviet Union must be "utterly destroyed" and its occupants, like the Poles, reduced to "a people of leaderless slave laborers" (Gellately 2003, 259). On March 30, 1941, Hitler instructed his generals that the war would be one of "extermination" (a *Vernichtungskrieg*).

Early on June 22, 1941, three million German soldiers, backed by thousands of tanks and airplanes and 600,000 troops from other countries, stormed across the USSR's western border in Operation Barbarossa. The German invasion heralded a new stage in the mass murder of Jews, Slavs, and others, and led directly to the systematic, centralized genocide that would later be designated the Holocaust. In the first few weeks after the invasion, German policy evolved from mass murder of Communist and Jewish men to a much broader targeting of all Jews—including women, children, and the elderly. This genocidal policy predated and led to the decision for a "Final Solution to the Jewish Problem" later in the year.

In the summer and fall of 1941, after its initial military successes, the Nazi empire found itself ruling over several million more Jews, in addition to those in the General Government. At this point, the Nazi leadership moved quickly toward the decision for a genocidal "final solution" (their term) to the so-called Jewish question. Decisions were now being shaped by a climate of euphoria over the initial successes in the Soviet campaign, tinged with anxiety over what to do with the millions of Jews in German-occupied lands, whose numbers dwarfed those of the Jewish population within Germany. This anxiety would deepen later in the fall as the German advance into Russia slowed and was halted outside Moscow in early November. After two years, localized mass murder, driven by racial and demographic schemes and the brutality intrinsic to them, evolved into systematic genocide. Once the decision for an exterminatory "final solution" was made and conveyed, by late October 1941, administrators like Hans Frank adapted with alacrity. "Gentleman, I must ask you to rid yourselves of all feeling of pity," Frank announced to subordinates in Krakow in December. "We must annihilate the Jews wherever we find them" (Mazower 2008, 376–77).

In the fall of 1941, the Nazis began constructing killing centers, all located in German-occupied Poland, designed specifically for the mass murder of Jews. Chelmno and Belzec, which began operating in December 1941 and March 1942, respectively, were the first. Chelmno was also the first to use gas. 150,000 people were killed in this fashion—Russians, Poles, and Romany as well as Jews, who were the principal target and the large majority of victims at Chelmno and the other five killing centers. The Germans had opened a camp at Auschwitz, outside the town of Oświęcim, Poland, in 1940, and in October 1941, the Germans began a large-scale expansion, adding a second camp, Birkenau, which included gas chambers and crematoria. The Auschwitz-Birkenau complex eventually included dozens of subcamps and labor camps and took on the character of a monstrous city unto itself, where more than one million Jews—as well as scores of thousands of Poles, Russians, Romany, and others—were murdered. Treblinka consumed the second-largest number of lives, approximately 800,000.

Jewish Resistance

Jews did not always "go like sheep to the slaughter," to invoke a phrase that was often heard in the first years after the war. Like Hitler's other targets, Jews devised varied strategies for resistance and survival. In the most spectacular and visible examples, Jewish people—usually young, and including both men and women—fought the Nazis with arms in hand. Much more often, they found less visible or spectacular ways to resist, organizing hundreds of clandestine religious schools (*yeshivot*) in Poland; arranging secret libraries and archives throughout the ghetto system; raising money to support prisoners' families; and producing and distributing prohibited literature. All these activities deprived their tormentors of one of their goals: to dehumanize the Jews and destroy their culture and heritage.

The Warsaw Ghetto Uprising of April–May 1943 was perhaps the most direct, dramatic, and "successful" resistance effort. An underground resistance movement had taken form in 1942, and after a brief revolt in January 1943, they launched a full-scale uprising on April 19, 1943, as the Germans moved in to liquidate the ghetto (that is, deport the remaining Jews to the Treblinka death camp and close the ghetto). Military victory was impossible, as the rebels knew, but they managed to tie down the German forces for nearly a month and kill several dozen (Figure 3.3).

Figure 3.3 Jews being rounded up for deportation to the Treblinka killing center after the crushing of the Warsaw Ghetto Uprising. https://commons.wikimedia.org/wiki/File:Stroop_Report_-_Warsaw_Ghetto_Uprising_06.jpg

Despite anti-Jewish hostility among many other anti-Nazi fighters, an estimated 20,000 to 30,000 Jews fought in Soviet-led partisan groups, and perhaps one-sixth of the fighters of the French *Maquis* guerrilla fighters were Jewish, although Jews constituted less than one percent of the country's population (Ainsztein 1974, 394–95). Even in the most debilitating circumstances imaginable—in the extermination centers—there were several notable examples of organized resistance. In 1943, Jewish prisoners organized armed revolts in Sobibor and Treblinka; the following year, the underground organization in Auschwitz blew up a crematorium. In other ways as well, Hitler's Jewish victims found ways and means to maintain their dignity and humanity in the face of the Nazi onslaught. "Resistance" entailed much more than armed struggle, and any discussion of Jewish responses should also consider such concepts (which were often not clearly distinct from one another) as defiance, nonconformity, resilience, and various survival mechanisms, including simply a refusal to submit—that is, to attempt to continue civilized life under uncivilized conditions.

The Nazis' Non-Jewish Victims

The Nazis' racial fanaticism and grandiose schemes to re-order Europe claimed other victims in addition to the Jews. First among them were ethnic Slavs—Russians and other Soviet peoples, as well as Poles—who had the misfortune not only to be viewed as *Untermenschen* (sub-humans), to use the Nazis' terminology but also to inhabit territory that was coveted by the German leadership. Roma and Sinti peoples, popularly known at the time as "Gypsies"—a term that should now be discarded forever, though until recently it was still used by non-Romany scholars—also suffered grievously at the hands of the Nazis. Ultimately, somewhere between 200,000 and one million were killed in the *Porrajmos* (Devouring), as it is known today by Roma. Estimates for Roma victims vary widely because of the fact that pre-World War II census figures are far less reliable than for most other European populations. Further, "Roma did not and do not today generally operate as a single, monolithic entity," genocide specialist Mark Levene argues, "so much as a mosaic or network of diverse, dispersed, if ethnically and culturally related, peoples" (Levene, 2014, 136).

From the early 1930s, Nazi policies increasingly marginalized and persecuted these communities. The Nuremberg Laws of 1935, which institutionalized racial discrimination, categorized Roma and Sinti alongside Jews as "racially inferior" and deprived them of basic rights such as marriage and citizenship. And this, despite the fact that Roma and Sinti had served in the German military and were often fully assimilated. During World War II, the persecution evolved into genocide—which is exactly what it was, although some Holocaust historians mistakenly argue otherwise, out of a misguided "victimhood competition." Roma and Sinti were rounded up and interned in concentration camps across Nazi-occupied Europe. One of the most infamous of these camps was Auschwitz-Birkenau, where an estimated 23,000 Roma and Sinti died as a result of starvation, disease, forced labor, and systematic extermination in gas chambers in Auschwitz-Birkenau (Sierra 2024). The centuries-old oppression of Roma and Sinti continued until the end of the war, with survivors facing continued discrimination and marginalization in the post-war period. Unlike Jewish survivors, many Roma and Sinti did not receive recognition or reparations for their suffering until decades later. The historical neglect of their plight has contributed to ongoing challenges in acknowledging and commemorating their experiences.

Chapter Two included a lengthy section on the Nazis' anti-Slav racism and its genocidal consequences. Here, we now wish to inform our readers of racist policies and crimes perpetrated against other groups, specifically Roma and Sinti peoples; peoples deemed to have disabilities; and Afro-Germans. As in all areas of its ideology (political philosophy) and practices, the Nazis did not have to invent anything. They borrowed from the garbage heap of Western civilization and imperialism, taking some ideas and practices to unprecedented lengths. Eugenics is an example of this. In the spirit of Social Darwinism, which applied Darwin's theory of a struggle for survival to human interactions, proponents of eugenics sought to perfect their own "race." These movements attempted to trace the "transmission of social traits, especially undesirable ones, and undertook to classify individuals, groups, and nations on a scale of human worth," as historian Henry Friedlander wrote in an important book on eugenics and T4, and then "proposed biological solutions to social problems and lobbied for their implementation" (Friedlander 1997, 4–5). This movement focused its attention on the supposedly feeble-minded ("idiots" or "imbeciles" in the parlance of the time), asserting that low intelligence led to immorality as well as crime.

This was not a fringe movement: It had considerable support among the American populace and educated elites, and legislatures in more than half of the states of the country were swayed to enact sterilization laws, beginning with Indiana in 1907. In 1927, the US Supreme Court upheld a Virginia law ordering the compulsory sterilization by state institutions of handicapped patients diagnosed with "hereditary form[s] of insanity or imbecility." Writing for the unanimous majority, Justice Oliver Wendell Holmes declared that American society should "prevent those who are manifestly unfit from continuing their kind [...] Three generations of imbeciles are enough." Holmes did not stop there: The nation must sterilize those who "sap the strength of the State" in order to "prevent our being swamped with incompetence [...] It is better for all the world," he continued without embarrassment or fear of censure, "if instead of waiting to execute degenerate offspring for crime, or to let them starve for their imbecility, society can prevent those who are manifestly unfit from continuing their kind" (Cohen 2016, 2).

Inspired in part by these American precedents, Hitler's government enacted the "Law for the Prevention of Hereditarily Diseased Offspring" in July 1933. This was the legal basis for the compulsory sterilization over the next 12 years of roughly 400,000 Germans who were deemed by special medical boards to possess "genetic disorders," a list that included "feeblemindedness" or "mental deficiency," "manic depression," "genetic blindness," and "chronic alcoholism" (Crowe 2008, 117–21). But far worse was to come: A program of mass murder known as Aktion T4, named after the street (*Tiergartenstrasse*) and address from whence it was organized, began in 1939 and was a significant step toward the genocide of six million Jews. Individuals deemed to be *Lebensunwertes Lebens* (lives unworthy of life)—and accused in Nazi propaganda of being a "burden" to the German public—were singled out for extermination. German bureaucrats and doctors willingly lent themselves to this grisly and horrifying program—"if not me, someone else would do it, and I need this job"—which ultimately claimed the lives of at least 250,000 Germans (few of whom were Jewish). T4 experimented in methods that would very soon be used against Russian and Polish political prisoners and POWs, and much more widely against Jews, once the Holocaust was fully underway. It should be known that few of the criminals ever paid any price. Like many Nazi murderers, they kept their jobs in post-war West Germany (and, even more often in East Germany). One such person, a Dr. Hermann Pfannmüller—who carried out his "work" in an especially gleeful, shameless, and jovial fashion, it was later reported—murdered at least 3,000 "patients." He was tried in Munich, West Germany, in 1951 and sentenced to only one to five years in prison. Others were treated even more kindly in post-war Germany (ibid., 153).

Afro-Germans and the So-Called *Rheinland Bastarde*

This ugly term—"Rhineland bastards"—referred to people of mixed African and German descent, primarily the offspring of French African occupation troops stationed in the Rhineland region of western Germany after World War I. The presence of African occupation troops in the Rhineland following World War I led to the birth of children of mixed racial heritage. These children, viewed as symbols of perceived "racial degradation" and a threat to the purity of the Aryan race, became targets of Nazi persecution. (The authors would like to place quotation marks around every ridiculous and repulsive term employed by the Nazis, but for stylistic reasons decline too; but never take seriously a word like "Aryan.") The Nazi regime propagated the notion of racial superiority and advocated for the preservation of its supposed master race while demonizing individuals of mixed race as "racial pollutants" or "bastards" (Crowe 2008, 133).

The persecution of the so-called Rhineland bastards took various forms, including legal discrimination, social ostracism, and forced sterilization. Nazi racial laws, such as the Nuremberg Laws of 1935, classified individuals with any degree of Jewish or non-Aryan ancestry as inferior and subjected them to systematic discrimination and persecution. "Rhineland bastards" faced exclusion from certain professions, educational institutions, and public services, as well as harassment and violence from Nazi sympathizers. Additionally, the Nazi regime implemented coercive measures to prevent the reproduction of individuals deemed racially inferior. Forced sterilization laws were enacted as part of the regime's eugenics program, targeting not only individuals with disabilities but also those considered racially impure, including Afro-Germans.

As in many other aspects of Nazi persecution and racism, the Nazis simply expanded upon beliefs and practices that already existed, while taking them much further. "Racism was a part of Black people's everyday lives in Weimar Germany"—the democratic republic of 1919–1933 that preceded the Nazi dictatorship. "White German women who married Black men were often ostracized, making it difficult for them to find work as well" (USHMM 2022). But conditions worsened considerably, and quickly, once the Nazis took power, declaring an ethnic German *Volksgemeinschaft* ("people's community") that most certainly did not include the small number of Afro-Germans. The "Law for the Restoration of the Professional Civil Service," passed in April 1933, just two months into Hitler's dictatorship, removed people of "non-Aryan descent" from the German civil service.

Nazi racist ideology poisoned all aspects of life in Germany. "Many Germans embraced this ideology and openly discriminated against Black people on their own initiative [...] Some Black people remember life in Nazi Germany as a time in which strangers spat on them and called them racial slurs with impunity" (USHMM 2022). Afro-Germans would eventually be forcibly sterilized—a policy that had actually been proposed *before* the Nazis came to power, in 1927 (Crowe 2008, 133). And the term "Rhineland bastards" was also used during that time, by non-Nazis as well as by hardcore racists and fascists. "During World War II, Nazi policies against Black people became more extreme," reports the US Holocaust Memorial Museum. "This occurred in the context of the broader radicalization of Nazi policies against supposed racial and political enemies. Because of laws and policies that sharpened discrimination and racism in Germany, many Black people ended up imprisoned in workhouses, prisons, hospitals, psychiatric facilities, and concentration camps" (USHMM 2022).

The End of the "Thousand-Year Reich"

Hitler's regime—which he had promised would last one thousand years—collapsed ignominiously in March and April 1945, its final days marked by recriminations and back-stabbing within the leadership and vast misery among the German populace.

Göring, Himmler, Goebbels, and other Nazi chiefs such as Martin Bormann—men who had once ruled much of Europe—descended into petty infighting, scrabbling for power where little still existed. The Führer—once master of at least half of Europe—spent his last ten days at the center of a surreal drama in a sprawling bunker under the streets of Berlin. The day after marrying his mistress, Eva Braun, in a bizarre and dismal ceremony, he and his new wife committed suicide. Hitler's long-time loyal accomplice and henchman Joseph Goebbels and his wife followed suit the next day, but only after poisoning their six children. The Allied victory prevented Hitler from achieving his goal of a "*Judenfrei*" (Jew-free) Europe, but the Nazis had killed two-thirds of the continent's Jewish people, largely eradicating centuries of tradition and culture that had contributed mightily to European culture, science, and literature—most of all, perhaps, in Germany.

We Charge Genocide

On the morning of December 17, 1951, Paul Robeson and a handful of other activists and intellectuals walked into the halls of the United Nations and presented, to the UN Secretariat, a book-length petition accusing the United States of committing genocide against its African-descended citizens. (We will describe it as a "petition," which is how it is always labeled, but it should be known that it is actually a 238-page book, in its current format). On that same day, William Patterson delivered the same document, *We Charge Genocide: The Crime of Government Against the Negro People* to a UN gathering in Paris.

Paul Robeson's name—as well as Patterson's—should be known to all Americans. He was one of the most accomplished artists and activists of the last century. Born in 1898, Robeson first came to prominence as an All-American athlete at Rutgers in the late 1910s. He was a great professional football player for a brief period before an unspoken color barrier was established; along with another African American, Fritz Pollard, he starred with the Akron Pros, who won the inaugural NFL championship in 1920, the year before Robeson joined them. Over the subsequent decades, he established himself as a great singer (please look him up on YouTube!) and actor, as well as an orator and activist. Like other authors and signers of the *We Charge* petition, he suffered greatly during this period of unhinged anticommunism of the 1950s known as McCarthyism, for its loudest proponent, Wisconsin Senator Joseph McCarthy. As you will see later in this chapter in Guatemala, "communists" were spotted (and misidentified) everywhere, and the Civil Rights Movement and even Martin Luther King, Jr. were routinely denounced as "communists." The practice of labeling one's political opponents seeking to attain social justice as "Marxists" and "communists" continues to galvanize the opponents of freedom and true democracy to this very day.

We Charge Genocide is a landmark document in the history of civil-rights activism, a powerful indictment of racial violence and discrimination in the United States. Written by the Civil Rights Congress and presented to the United Nations in 1951, it lays bare the systemic oppression and violence experienced by African Americans, making a compelling case that these injustices constitute genocide under international law. It should also be recognized that this was among the very first documents, and the Civil Rights Congress was among the very first organizations, to really take the UN Convention seriously, study it closely, and act upon it (Jones 2024, 53–54).

As we have seen, African Americans faced pervasive racial discrimination, segregation, and violence across the United States. Lynchings, police brutality, and institutionalized racism were rampant, denying African Americans their basic human rights and dignity. Against this backdrop, *We Charge Genocide* was a bold and uncompromising condemnation of racial oppression, drawing attention to the urgent need for change. *We Charge Genocide* argues that the systematic violence and discrimination faced by African Americans constitute genocide as defined by the 1948 Genocide Convention. Much of the document consists of a detailed accounting of instances of racial violence, including lynchings, police killings, and mob attacks, arguing that these atrocities were part of a deliberate campaign to destroy the African-American community. By framing racial injustice as genocide, the authors sought to elevate the urgency of addressing systemic racism and holding perpetrators accountable under international law. *We Charge Genocide* was far ahead of its time in many ways, including by appealing to the UN and the international community, as Malcolm X and other Black activists of the 1960s and 1970s would do. *We Charge Genocide* also highlights the complicity of the US government in perpetuating racial violence and discrimination. It accuses federal, state, and local authorities of failing to protect African Americans from violence, of actively participating in discriminatory practices, and of obstructing efforts to achieve racial equality. By exposing the government's role in perpetuating genocide, the document challenges the myth of American exceptionalism and innocence and calls for immediate, radical reform.

Raphael Lemkin had deeply conflicted feelings about *We Charge Genocide*. He is often depicted as being hostile to the petition, but it was more complicated than that, as best analyzed by Douglas Irvin-Erickson in his essential 2017 book on Lemkin, which we have already cited more than a few times. By the time of the December 1948 UN Genocide Convention—which, after passage by that body still had to be adopted by individual states, a process the Lemkin labored over for the remainder of his life, writing hundreds of letters to officials of dozens of countries—the Cold War had set in. (More on this below, in the section on Guatemala.) Conservative US politicians opposed the Convention, believing it would infringe on America's ability to wage its foreign policy without international interference, and perhaps aware that the United States itself had committed genocide. It was not until 1988 that the US Senate adopted the Convention, and still today, as we write this book in 2024, the US government is deeply suspicious of any international body or set of laws that could place the United States under scrutiny.

Desperate to win support from the United States, Lemkin compromised some of his principles by appealing to conservative lawmakers on the basis of anticommunism. "Lemkin's goal," writes Douglas Irvin-Erickson, "was to show the most conservative of US politicians that his law," the Genocide Convention, "could be an essential element for them to use to combat communism" (Irvin-Erickson 2017, 205). Lemkin, still not fully familiar with US politics, perceived (correctly) that "the political establishment" associated the emerging Civil Rights Movement, and any form of Black activism, with "communism"—as always, loosely and imprecisely defined (ibid., 206). And indeed, the Civil Rights Congress was led by some members of the Communist Party USA, further alienating Lemkin from *We Charge Genocide*. But during this contentious period he willfully (and wrongly) asserted that African Americans being lynched were murdered as individuals and not as members of a targeted human group. Chapter Five provides another example of his willingness to abandon his principles or points of view in the name of political expediency. While some may say that Lemkin might have viewed the use of "genocide" in the context of African-American experiences as overly broad or as diluting of his term's original intent, his emphasis on coercive actions leading to the destruction of a human group's social cohesion clearly identifies the United States as a pre-genocidal society. And, as we saw earlier in Chapter Two, he believed that US Government policies concerning Native Americans were plainly genocidal.

Hastening to curry favor with anticommunist migrants or their political representatives from parts of Eastern Europe that were oppressed by the Soviet Union (from the Baltic republics of Estonia, Lithuania, and Latvia, as well as Poland and elsewhere), Lemkin denounced *We Charge Genocide* in an editorial with the *New York Times* that went so far as to argue that "the negro population" was improving in its material conditions and "prosperity" (ibid., 207). Eleanor Roosevelt made the same argument. Conditions for Black folks did eventually improve to some degree—due to the Civil Rights Movement—but this was certainly not evident in 1951. It is a tragedy that he alienated some powerful potential allies in his quest to appease racist political elites, in an attempt to win support for the Convention that sometimes became misguided. His own social and national background, also, may have prevented him from grasping the centrality of race and racism to the history of the United States. Yet, in his defense, he reconsidered some of his views in his last years (he died not long after, in 1959). He acknowledged this, and offered somewhat of an apology, in his memoir (Lemkin 2013, 100). Toward the end of his life, Lemkin delivered passionate condemnations of racist American laws and policies, such as the virulently racist Chinese Exclusion Act of 1882 and the internment of 115,000 Japanese-Americans during World War II, and he also denounced "genocidal" as the lynching of Black Americans (Irvin-Erickson 210). Lemkin was a hugely important and influential human being and for the most part a highly laudable person. Yet, like all of us, he was complicated, but he was capable of evolving on issues and debates such as *We Charge Genocide*.

Racism and Genocide in Guatemala

The Cold War—the competition between the United States and the USSR for influence around the world for four and a half decades following 1945—never led to a "hot war" between the two nuclear superpowers but was not "cold" or peaceful for most of the peoples of the globe. It served as a cover or justification for the world's superpowers to install, finance, or at least condone murderous regimes in their respective spheres of influence, with the Americans being somewhat more successful and far-reaching. In the small Central American nation of Guatemala, the US administration, alarmed by the moderate land reforms of a left-leaning government, overthrew the democratic state in 1954 and installed a military dictatorship that murdered hundreds of thousands of real and perceived opponents over the next four decades. This dictatorship's violence reached a grisly crescendo under Generals Lucas Garcia and Rios Montt between 1981 and 1983. A pattern that was all too familiar in Central and South America as the 1970s and 1980s unfolded: Facing a left-wing guerrilla movement, the military's "counter-insurgency" campaigns targeted civilian populations that supposedly provided support for the guerrillas. Guatemala's Mayan Indians—long oppressed in that country's highly stratified and racist society—suffered the brunt of this campaign, and tens of thousands of Indians were killed by government troops or allied "death squads" (Figure 3.4).

This genocide had its origins in a long history of colonialism, racial discrimination, and socio-economic inequality. Since the Spanish conquest in the early sixteenth century, the Mayan people have been marginalized, exploited, and subjected to severe human-right abuses (Grandin 2000, 16, 82). The twentieth century saw increasing political instability in Guatemala, culminating in a civil war that began in 1960. This conflict pitted leftist guerrilla groups against the Guatemalan dictatorship.

The civil war intensified during the 1970s and early 1980s, with indigenous communities, particularly the Mayans, caught in the crossfire. The government viewed the Mayan population with deep suspicion, often labeling them as sympathizers or collaborators with the guerrillas. This suspicion set the stage for a brutal campaign of repression and extermination. The most intense period of violence occurred between 1981 and 1983. General Efraín Ríos Montt seized power in a military coup in March 1982 and implemented a scorched-earth policy aimed at eradicating the insurgent

Figure 3.4 Mayan (Ixil) women fought for 30 years for justice after the genocide of the 1980s. Here, they celebrate in 2013 after former Guatemalan former dictator Rios Montt was found guilty of genocide. https://commons.wikimedia.org/wiki/File:Guatemala_4,_GHR_16_(9269372204).jpg

threat. With cavalier disregard for the lives of those affected (and often killed), Rios Montt once "joked" that he was not carrying out a scorched-earth policy, but a "scorched communist" policy. Needless to say, there were few "communists" among his victims (indeed, there was never much of a Communist presence in Guatemala).

Under Ríos Montt's command, the Guatemalan military launched widespread operations targeting Mayan villages. The government's strategy included mass killings, forced disappearances, torture, sexual violence, and the destruction of homes and crops. Villages were razed, and survivors were often forced into "model villages," which functioned as concentration camps under strict military control. The genocidal campaign was marked by its systematic nature. According to the United Nations-sponsored Historical Clarification Commission (CEH), over 200,000 people were killed or disappeared during the civil war, with more than 80% of the victims being indigenous. The CEH concluded that the Guatemalan state committed acts of genocide against the Mayan people, with the intent to destroy their culture and presence in the country (Sanford 2003).

Survivor testimonies and extensive documentation have provided a chilling account of the atrocities committed. The stories of massacre sites, such as the infamous Dos Erres massacre of December 1982, in which soldiers brutally killed over 200 villagers, including women and children, have become emblematic of the genocide. Eyewitness accounts and forensic evidence have corroborated these harrowing events, highlighting the extreme cruelty and systematic nature of the violence. By the late 1980s significant international pressure led to a peace process and, eventually, some accountability for the crimes committed. In 1996, the Guatemalan government and guerrilla forces signed the Peace Accords, officially ending the civil war. The accords included provisions for human rights, indigenous rights, and the establishment of truth commissions to investigate the atrocities. The CEH's final report in 1999 was a landmark document that detailed the extent of the violence and the state's responsibility (ibid.).

Race and Genocide in the Darfur Region of Sudan

As we have already seen in the first two chapters, the twenty-first century has brought no respite from the scourge of genocide. Sudan, in the northeast of Africa, was ruled by a genocidal dictator, Omar al-Bashir for 30 years until his overthrow in 2019. His overthrow has not alleviated the suffering of the Sudanese people; another anti-democratic military group took power. A civil war erupted in April 2023 pitting one military faction, the Rapid Support Forces (RSF), against the Sudanese Armed Forces. But the RSF is hardly a liberation army: its origins lie in the Janjaweed, a paramilitary largely responsible for the genocide described below. As we complete this book in late 2024, at least twelve million Sudanese have been displaced in 20 months of fighting and perhaps 25,000 killed, primarily Masalit and Fur peoples. The RSF is principally guilty of genocidal atrocities, while the Sudanese government also has much blood on its hands.

Twenty years earlier, beginning in 2003 in the Darfur region of western Sudan, conflict erupted between the Sudanese government and its allied militias—the Janjaweed, composed primarily of Arab nomad tribespeople—versus an assortment of rebel groups. A systematic genocide was unleashed targeting the black African population, resulting in massive loss of life and suffering. Historically marginalized within Sudan, Darfur is an ethnically diverse but impoverished region. The population includes black African groups such as the Fur, Zaghawa, and Masalit, alongside some Arab tribes. Tensions over resources such as water, exacerbated by environmental degradation and desertification, have frequently led to conflicts in recent decades, especially during the "Second Civil War," which began in 1983. At the same time, it should be known that "there was a certain amount of intermarriage among the various peoples of Darfur, including non-Arabs and Arabs," as Samuel Totten reminds us (Totten and Parsons 2013, 514). "Thus, different groups of people cohabitated as neighbors, friends, and even relatives—and not as sworn enemies" stemming from ethnic or racial divisions (ibid.). Like Rwanda and Yugoslavia, the strife in Sudan cannot be explained by "ancient tribal hatreds." However, the situation escalated dramatically in the early 2000s.

The roots of the Darfur conflict lie in a complex intersection of ethnic, economic, and political factors. Key among these was the Sudanese government's neglect of Darfur and its failure to address grievances related to political marginalization. The emergence of armed rebel groups, most notably the Sudan Liberation Army (SLA) and the Justice and Equality Movement (JEM), in 2003 marked a significant turning point (Baltrop 2011, 30–35). These groups accused the government of oppressing non-Arab populations and demanded greater autonomy and development. In response, the Sudanese government unleashed a brutal counter-insurgency campaign. The government armed and supported the Janjaweed militias, who conducted widespread attacks against the black African population. Villages were systematically destroyed, and civilians were subjected to massacres and widespread rape as well as forced displacement.

Often supported by official Sudanese government forces, Janjaweed troops engaged in scorched-earth tactics, burning villages, looting, and killing indiscriminately. The scale of the atrocities led to a massive displacement crisis, with millions of Darfuris fleeing to refugee camps in neighboring Chad or becoming internally displaced within Sudan (Prunier 2011). The international community, initially slow to respond, eventually recognized the severity of the crisis. In 2004, the United States officially labeled the situation in Darfur as a genocide. This made little if any difference to the beleaguered peoples of Darfur, who continued to suffer—in particular the Fur, Massalit, and Zaghawa peoples (Totten and Parsons 2013, 515). By 2008, it was estimated that over 300,000 people had died, either directly from violence or indirectly from disease and starvation. More than 2.5 million people were displaced, living in appalling conditions in overcrowded camps with limited access to food, clean water, and medical care (de Waal 2015).

There has been considerable debate among experts about the nature of the race and racism in Sudan. There is no doubt that the conflict has often been simplified, for Western audiences, into a simple story of "Arab supremacists" oppressing black Africans. Yet as Alex de Waal, a prominent expert on Sudan, has pointed out, "characterizing the Darfur war as 'Arabs' versus 'Africans' obscures the reality." He continued, "Darfur's Arabs are black, indigenous, African Muslims—just like Darfur's non-Arabs, who hail from the Fur, Massalit, Zaghawa and a dozen smaller tribes" (quoted in Totten and Parsons 2013, 516).

The Darfur genocide had significant legal and political repercussions. In 2009 and 2010, the International Criminal Court (ICC) issued arrest warrants for President Omar al-Bashir, accusing him of war crimes, crimes against humanity, and genocide. But as we have seen many times—up to the present (2023–24) war on Gaza—indictments carry little weight in world politics. It was only with his overthrow in 2019 that al-Bashir's crimes came to an end, and he was arrested and remains imprisoned (by his successors, which include his former accomplices).

Tragedy and genocide continue to blight Sudan and its region. After a long and often bloody struggle, South Sudan won its independence from Sudan and became the world's newest and youngest country in 2011 under the rule of the Sudan People's Liberation Army (SPLA). The SPLA based itself primarily upon the Dinka people and created a narrative and mythology that the Dinka were a "martial race" that had "'liberated' and therefore officially 'owned' the south," explains historian and political scientist Clémence Pinaud in her 2021 book *War and Genocide in South Sudan*, to date the most authoritative assessment of this conflict (Pinaud 2021, 58–59). Pinaud argues that the SPLA has fostered "a form of racism—extreme ethnic group entitlement—with genocidal potential" (ibid., 3), a potential that has been realized during a civil war that erupted in 2013 between Dinka forces loyal to the president, SPLA leader Salva Kiir, and forces composed principally of the Nuer ethnicity, the second-largest group in South Sudan—forces initially led by Kiir's onetime vice president, Riek Machar, who split with Kiir after being falsely accused by him of attempting a coup in December 2013 (ibid., 145). Genocidal rape has been a hideous feature of the war and genocide against the Nuer, rape that is often committed by gangs (that is, women—as well as some men and boys—raped repeatedly by multiple perpetrators) and is often followed by murder (ibid., 177–79). Of a population of only 11 or 12 million, at least 400,000 people were killed during the 2013–18 civil war, most of them civilians, while fully one-third of the nation's population was displaced. As in Sudan to the north, sporadic fighting, genocidal ethnic cleansings, and other atrocities have not ceased in South Sudan.

Conclusion

On successive days—December 9 and 10, 1948—the UN General Assembly adopted the Genocide Convention and then the Universal Declaration of Human Rights. Following the horrors of World War II, which claimed 55 million victims (half of them from the Soviet Union) the international community wanted to prevent such massive destruction and loss of life from ever happening again. As we have noted earlier, the phrase "Never again" became somewhat of a mantra. Yet it rings hollow to many peoples around the world, who can detect considerable hypocrisy among the victors of World War II. And especially to those peoples, such as in Guatemala, Sudan, Rwanda, and Bosnia, who have been subjected to genocide in the post-WWII world, often with the complicity of the world powers. Neither of the authors is too happy when our students cite a dictionary definition of a complicated term, rather than use our assigned readings, nevertheless: Merriam-Webster defines "virtue signaling" as "the act or practice of conspicuously displaying one's awareness of and attentiveness to political issues, matters of social and racial justice, etc., especially instead of taking effective action"—and the imperialist (and Soviet) powers that emerged victorious from the war can be justly accused of this.

As noted in Chapter Two, the Swedish writer Sven Lindqvist, who authored several incisive books on European racism, debunked the tendency to see the Nazis as somehow disconnected from the broader patterns of European history. They were made into "the sole scapegoats for ideas of extermination that are actually a common European heritage" (Lindqvist 1996, 9). Aimé Césaire, a famed author and politician from the French colony of Martinique, offered a similar critique of Western hypocrisy. He argued that Nazism has its roots in the culture of colonialism and reminded his audience that before much of Europe was victimized by Nazism, "they were its accomplices [...] they tolerated" Nazi-like beliefs and practices "Nazism before it was inflicted on them [...] because, until then, it had been applied only to non-European peoples." (Césaire 1955, 36).

"The natural supremacy of the white race and its corollary, Europe's civilizing mission in Africa and Asia, the view of the world beyond Europe as a vast area to be colonized," wrote the historian Enzo Traverso, were not Nazi inventions. "The idea of colonial wars as conflicts in which the enemy was the civilian population of the countries to be conquered, rather than an army; the theory that the extinction of the inferior races was an inevitable consequence of progress: these central tenets of Nazi ideology were commonplaces of 19th-century European culture" (Traverso 2005).

The following chapter analyzes another dreadful topic—sexual violence in the context of genocide, a topic that intersects with racism. For in each of the cases that Chapter Four examines, racism was a factor, often in surprising ways that underscore the pervasiveness as well as grotesque absurdity of racial categories and racism. In the genocides that unfolded more-or-less simultaneously in Bosnia and Rwanda, it would appear to an outsider that race was not a factor. After all, it was white people killing other white people in Bosnia, while in Rwanda it was black Africans killing other black Africans. Yet in both cases, the perpetrators had been led to believe that their victims belonged to a separate race, of outsiders and enemies.

Questions for Further Discussion

1. Identify the principal factors that gave rise to racist ideas. How did slavery contribute to racism, or vice versa? And what do you think of the authors' argument about the "paradox" whereby a positive development (such as the Enlightenment) contributes to something very negative, that is, racial categories and white supremacy?
2. It is clear that racial ideas and racism lead to genocide. What are some *specific ways* in which racism and imperialism generate genocidal violence? Try to think of at least a half-dozen factors, with examples.
3. The massacres in Wilmington and Tulsa are not very well known, and rarely appear in standard US history textbooks, despite their significance. Why is this?
4. In history books these events, such as Wilmington 1898 and Tulsa 1921, are often referred to as "race riots," instead of genocidal massacres. Why is this? Do you see any parallels with changes being made today to US History texts on related topics?
5. Based on this chapter and upon your own experiences and observations: Why is it important, or even essential, that we continue to discuss and critique racism?

Chapter Four

SEXUAL VIOLENCE AS GENOCIDE

Indeed, we cannot keep telling the world in endless sentences: Don't murder members of national, racial and religious groups; don't sterilize them; don't impose abortions on them; don't steal children from them; don't compel their women to bear children for your country; and so on.
—Raphael Lemkin, letter dated August 26, 1946

"Gendercide" is Genocide, Too

Raphael Lemkin recognized that one of the ways genocidists can accomplish their aim of destroying entire human groups is through the calculated use of sexual violence. In *Axis Rule*, he provided ample documentation about Nazi policies designed to reduce the birth rates of peoples of "non-related blood" to the Germans, such as the Slavs, while increasing the birth rate of the Germanic peoples who would replace them. Lemkin wrote that the Nazis implemented a wide range of policies to ensure this depopulation of one group and its replacement with another, the "biological" ones listed in the quote above, and the "physical" ones with which people are more familiar such as deliberate starvation and mass killings. He quoted Hitler as saying, "We have developed a technique of depopulation [...] to remove millions of an inferior race that breeds like vermin" to repopulate the territory with the "superior" race (quoted in Irvin-Erickson 2017, 91). These policies included providing "subsidies to women of subjugated peoples for having illegitimate children by members of the *Wehrmacht*" (Lemkin 2008, ix). In addition, Lemkin "identified decrees and regulations separating men and women, making it illegal from approved racial groups in Northern Europe to resist the sexual demands of German soldiers, rewarding German soldiers for having illegitimate children, and laws to subsidize women in occupied countries who were forcibly impregnated" (quoted in Irvin-Erickson 2017, 154).

Women have suffered from dreadful sexual violence during wars throughout history. Since ancient times conquerors have killed the men and enslaved the women of their enemies with the ultimate result being the disappearance of those people. Lemkin recognized the Nazis' aims with their biological reordering of the demographics of Europe, and he had wanted to include forced sterilization, forced abortions, the abduction of children, and the use of rape "to compel [...] women to bear children for your country" as acts of genocide at the Nuremberg trials. Lemkin understood that the Nazis had tried to destroy peoples not only through various other methods, including mass killing but also through these biological techniques. The 1948 Genocide Convention, however, does not explicitly address sexual violence such as rape. Some of the acts delineated in the Convention that might apply include (b) Causing serious bodily or mental harm to members of the group; and (d) Imposing measures intended to prevent births within the group (this last would be the outcome if rape results in pregnancy and the woman cannot then reproduce within her group). Rape is always a heinous and criminal act and committed during an armed conflict it is also a war crime. If widespread and encouraged, or even sanctioned, it is then a crime against humanity. It is only genocidal, however, when it is used in a "massive, organized and systematic" campaign "not only as a tool of war, but also to implement a policy of impregnation in order to further the destruction of a people [...]" (Fisher 1996, 92).

After World War II, the International Military Tribunal for the Far East (the equivalent of the Nuremberg Trials in Germany) convicted Japanese soldiers of rape as a war crime. A half-century later, the International Criminal Tribunal for Rwanda ruled that the mayor of the town of Taba, Jean-Paul Akayesu, was guilty of "Genocide" and "Direct and Public Incitement to Commit Genocide, and Crimes Against Humanity (Extermination, Murder, Torture, Rape, and Other Inhumane Acts)." This established the precedent that rape and sexual violence may constitute genocide if committed with an intent to destroy a targeted group (*The Prosecutor v. Jean Paul Akayesu* 1998). Therefore, perpetrators of systematic mass rape can now be charged with genocide if the intent to destroy the group, in whole or in part, is proven. Siobhan Fisher asserts that deliberate impregnation is a crime separate from the rape itself and that it meets the 1948 Genocide Convention's definition because, as mentioned, pregnancy would prevent births within the group (Fisher 1996, 92). Forcible impregnation in and of itself, although now considered a crime against humanity—with a much lower standard of proof for "intent" than genocide—is not specifically defined as one of the methods of genocide under the Convention. According to Fisher, forcible impregnation is not outlawed as a genocidal technique—because this would be counterintuitive. Forcible impregnation doesn't destroy life, it creates it, and there is then no killing involved (ibid., 95). Of course, the community itself would be irreparably harmed and therefore these kinds of deliberate attempts to impregnate women are directed against the group itself, and not the individual—a crucial part of Lemkin's concept. Human Rights Watch has also taken the position that forcible impregnation is distinct from rape, asserting that "the forcible impregnation of women, or the intention to so impregnate them, constitutes an abuse distinct from the rape itself and should be denounced and investigated as such" (ibid., n.6).

Charges of genocide could perhaps be preferred for forcible impregnation under acts (b) and (d) of the Convention, but (d)—Imposing measures to prevent births within the group—might not be legally applicable if the woman did not become pregnant or was sexually assaulted in other ways that are now also recognized by the law as constituting rape. For all women attacked in this way, however, the genocidal intent remains. The intent to destroy the group "can be established either directly, through admissions or statements of the perpetrators, or indirectly, through circumstantial evidence" (ibid., 95). This could include statements from the genocidists, or the practice of holding women captive until they no longer could undergo a termination of the pregnancy. In addition, the obvious physical and mental trauma involved may prevent women from conceiving and bearing children of their own group later—yet another possible violation under the Convention. Finally, in some societies, women subjected to such atrocious and inhumane treatment are no longer "marriageable" afterward. With this outcome, regardless of whether these women were or were not impregnated "it is rape to drive a wedge through a community, to shatter a society, to destroy a people. It is rape as genocide" (MacKinnon 1994, 12). Helen Fein agrees that this "interdiction of the biological and social reproduction of group members" could be genocide if the intent is "to destroy the group in the long term" (Fein 1999, 44).

Mass rape without the intent or outcome of the destruction of a specific group then, although still a horrific violation of human dignity, is not genocide. Committed during time of war, as it usually is, makes it a serious war crime. If "part of a widespread or systematic attack against any civilian population in furtherance of a State or organizational policy," where the perpetrator was aware of this wider context, every single rape would then also be a crime against humanity (Report of the International Law Commission 2017, 9). Like genocide, crimes against humanity can be committed in times of war or peace. Unlike genocide, which is legally defined and proscribed by the Convention on the Prevention and Punishment of the Crime of Genocide—as are War Crimes through the Geneva Conventions and Additional Protocols—crimes against humanity are not codified into a single treaty of international law. There is, however, a broad consensus on the types of criminal acts included in this category; the United Nations has recognized 11 different acts as being crimes against humanity. These include murder, extermination, enslavement, forcible transfer of population, imprisonment, torture, rape—including sexual slavery, enforced prostitution, forced pregnancy, enforced sterilization, or any other form of sexual violence of comparable gravity— persecution against any identifiable group or collectivity, enforced disappearance of persons, apartheid and any other inhumane acts of a similar character. All of these are crimes that "deeply shock the conscience of humanity" (ibid.).

We have argued that mass killing or persecution alone is insufficient to warrant the use of the term "genocide." It must also be recognized that very many atrocities are as bad or worse for the victims than those deemed "genocidal," history is replete with instances of mass killing and inhuman exploitation that fall short of what is the uniquely irreparable and sinister crime of genocide. The Atlantic slave trade is perhaps the most egregious example of a crime against humanity in history, but it was not genocidal against Africans per se—though for those enslaved and then held in bondage along with their descendants it most certainly was, as was the colonial rule of Europeans beginning in the late nineteenth century. The atrocious World War II Japanese policy of forcing hundreds of thousands of women into sexually accommodating its soldiers throughout occupied Asia is another example of a horrific crime against humanity— but in and of itself it was not genocide. The same holds true for the first two case studies of this chapter, the sanctioned—or at least tolerated—mass rape of Chinese women by Japanese soldiers, and the frenzied, undisciplined sexual assault of German women by Red Army troops. These atrocities took place during World War II, and in the German case extended months after the conclusion of hostilities. All these dreadful episodes of human suffering and degradation cry out for acknowledgment and the remembrance of its victims. These cases were both heinous war crimes and crimes against humanity, but they were not genocides. To legally be genocidal the intent or the outcome of these episodes of mass rape must be the destruction of a specific group—though, of course, not necessarily its complete annihilation. The intent or outcome of group destruction through the forced pregnancy of any identifiable group of women, however, should be included under the definition of the crime of genocide. As we will discuss in the Conclusion, the broader inclusivity of victim groups and a lower standard of proof for the category of Crimes against Humanity make this category preferable for the prosecution of genocidists.

Some scholars have also substituted the term "gendercide" to analyze "gender specific traumas" or "gendered harms" (Randall 2015; Warren 1985; Jones 2004). The deliberate policy of rape and forcible impregnation pursued in East Pakistan—now Bangladesh—by the Pakistani army against Bengali women in 1971, by Bosnian Serbs in Bosnia against Muslim women in 1992–95, and by Hutus against Tutsi women in 1994, are all textbook cases of gendered violence with the intent to commit genocide. There is no need to invent a new term or parse out the particular violence done to a specific gender when the intent or outcome is to destroy the group as a whole. As you now know, Lemkin did not see genocide as a single act or event but a process composed of different methods and techniques. The word Lemkin coined some 80 years ago to describe this phenomenon—genocide—will suffice. The problem with the term is not the term itself, but the limitations of the Convention. There are, to be sure, other examples of what some have called "gender-selective" mass killing such as the massacre by Serbs of more than 8000 Muslim men and boys at and around Srebrenica in 1995. Tens of thousands of other Bosnian Muslim civilians also died at the hands of Serbs but only in that particular instance did the International Criminal Tribunal for the former Yugoslavia (ICTY) find genocide had been committed as all the men of that town were murdered and the women and children completely removed from the area. In all of these cases listed above, however, the intent was to destroy the collectivity—either entirely or in a specific region. That constitutes genocide carried out through specific, gendered techniques.

Of course, men are also sexually assaulted in wartime. In a series of ghastly wars in the Democratic Republic of Congo over the last quarter-century, men have been the victims of at least 10% of the rapes employed widely by all sides. Men were often subjected to large-scale rape in Bosnia and Croatia during the 1992–95 war. Since antiquity, forms of sexual violence against males have included, besides rape, enforced sterilization, enforced nudity, being forced to rape others (including family members), enforced masturbation, and other acts of sexual violence (Sivakumaran 2007). Berina Zutic Razic, a Sarajevo-based legal advisor for TRIAL International, a non-governmental organization that works with judges, prosecutors, and support staff to make them more sensitive to the concerns and apprehensions of wartime sexual violence victims, noted that the stigmatization of victims comes from prejudices that are deeply rooted in society in general. For example, rapes of males are rarely reported, and "in many cases of sexual violence against men, judicial officials decline to classify these crimes as rape."

In addition to the well-documented, widespread, and systematic rape of civilian Ukrainian women by Russian soldiers in Putin's "Special Military Operation," there are also many reports of the rape of male Ukrainian prisoners of war, and even more horrific if possible, there are verified instances of the castration of some prisoners by their captors. These are, of course, all heinous war crimes. A charge of genocide would be appropriate if the intent—or outcome—of the rapes perpetrated against the women of Ukraine is their deliberate, forcible impregnation with the intent of destroying the group's ability to maintain itself. In the case of the men, however, genocide is neither the intent nor even a possible outcome of these depraved violations of human dignity. There are, however, other cases of gendered group destruction such as that of sexual minorities that may qualify. The Nazi persecutions of LGTBQ peoples, gay men in particular—tens of thousands were arrested, and ultimately, 10,000–15,000 perished in the camps—was not an attempt to destroy an entire gender, of course, but an attempt to destroy a particular social group, that is, gay men. And those men, once arrested, who promised not to engage in homosexual activity were often released as they were still considered "racially valuable." Women were not even included in the law against homosexuality because they too were still racially valuable according to Nazi ideology and therefore able to produce "Aryan" children (Figure 4.1).

It is also possible, however, that the repeated, systematic, anti-gay purges by the Chechen regime under the strongman Ramzan Kadyrov would qualify as genocide under our definition (Brown in Cox, *et al.* ed. 2021). Gay men in Chechnya, a small Russian republic, are arrested and tortured to reveal their cohorts. They have often

Figure 4.1 London, 2018: Protesting the criminalization of LGBTQ peoples in several countries in the British Commonwealth, in particular Uganda in East Africa. The woman on the left holds a sign calling out Ugandan President Yoweri Museveni for his harsh persecution of queer and trans Ugandans. https://commons.wikimedia.org/wiki/File:I_AM_A_PROUD_LESBIAN_(41535434182).jpg

been killed by the regime, whose leader Kadyrov is closely allied to Russian President Vladimir Putin, or released to have their families murder them as "honor killings." This kind of homophobia is deeply ingrained in many societies of varying religious traditions. Except for some African countries such as Uganda, Tanzania, and as of March 2024 predominantly Christian Ghana, however, most societies that have criminalized consensual homosexual behavior are those whose legal systems are derived from Sharia law (Islamic law presumably based on the Muslim holy book Qu'ran, and the teaching and actions of the Prophet Muhammed, as recorded in the *hadith*. In reality, there is great diversity among the world's 1.7 billion Muslims, and widely differing interpretations and applications of Sharia).

In majority-Muslim Chechnya the number of murdered gay men is quite small, at least when compared with the death toll in Nazi Germany, but the singling out of this specific human group for removal from society and the impossibility of escape if caught makes this a possible case of genocide. The same is true in majority-Christian Uganda, where homosexual activity is criminalized and punished with imprisonment—sometimes for life—and on occasion even with the death penalty. In Tanzania homosexual activity between men is punishable by imprisonment from 30 years to life; as in Nazi Germany, however, there is no mention of lesbians in the penal code. In Brunei, Iran, Saudi Arabia, Yemen, Sudan, and parts of Nigeria and Somalia the death penalty can be imposed for homosexual activity. In Nigeria, gay marriage, same-sex relationships, and membership in gay rights organizations are banned. Homosexual activity is punishable by up to 14 years in prison. Another human group that is under attack throughout the world is that of transgender women. "Transphobia" is the almost visceral fear and hatred of those "contravening traditional gender norms, as well as norms regarding cisgender, heterosexual male behavior, and so on" (Brown in Cox, 185). According to a *Forbes* newsletter of November 13, 2023, over 300 transgender women were murdered throughout the world in but a single year, with their bodies often horribly mutilated. Genocidists try to destroy the identity of any victim group, and by denying transgender women their identities these murders should be seen as genocidal. As Haley Marie Brown writes, "if we do not recognize the impact of transphobic violence on the lives of transgender women, we ourselves risk becoming perpetrators through inaction" (ibid., 190).

The violence directed at the erasure of transgender women, then, is indeed genocide. It is a human group, a collectivity in and of itself. Sexual violence directed against gay men (or women, as often happens in South Africa) can also be considered genocidal. The case studies we will examine below will address violence against heteronormative women—women who are assigned female at birth and have congruence with their gender identity and the sex assigned to them at birth. We do not draw these kinds of distinctions lightly, and most certainly do not mean to minimize the suffering and horrific brutalities any victims of arbitrary persecution have endured, but in order to prevent genocide we must not only know it when we see it, but we also have to know what it is not. As we have stressed repeatedly, it is the deliberate destruction of any human group, including that of transgender women. Distinctions drawn between the harms inflicted upon heteronormative men and women, like those drawn between other kinds of groups, obscure the fact that what is usually being threatened is the social existence of the entire collectivity. Martin Shaw has called for an end to such "terminological madness." "Gendercide," or even more specific terms such as "gynocide" for the murder of women, or, as one important scholar has suggested "androcide" for the gender-specific murder of men, as well as the murder of transgender women—before someone employs the term "transgendercide"—is genocide, too.

Japan: From Isolation to Imperialist Power

Commodore Matthew Perry led a flotilla of US Navy ships into Tokyo Bay in 1853 to force Japan to open itself up to foreign trade after centuries of isolation. This "gunboat diplomacy" intimidated the Japanese, who, forced to accept a series of unequal treaties with the Western imperialist powers, quickly realized they would need Western technology to safeguard themselves from encroachment on their territory and the plundering of their wealth. State-sponsored programs of industrial development, implemented as a calculated policy of "defensive modernization," would require the importation of Western ideas and techniques. The Japanese learned this lesson quickly. In less than a quarter-century, the Japanese sent their own modern gunboats to Korea to force its government to sign a treaty of commerce—much as the Americans had done to them.

By the early twentieth century, the country was fully industrialized and producing munitions and industrial goods, as well as textiles. Japan, however, had limited natural resources and they were forced to import most of the raw materials they needed. To obtain these Japan itself became an imperialist power, embarking on their own empire-building quest that led to Pearl Harbor, and ultimately to the unprecedented carnage of Hiroshima and Nagasaki, where civilians were made to pay for the crimes of their rulers. Japan undertook a series of conquests that established it as the foremost military power in the region. Joining in with the other imperialist powers from the West in carving up China in 1894–1995, Japan seized Manchuria in that country's northeast. In 1904, Japan launched a sneak attack on the major Russian naval base at Port Arthur in Manchuria and, after obliterating that fleet, subsequently sank yet another fleet in one battle without the loss of a single warship. The emerging Japanese Empire also defeated Russian land forces in Korea and forced the tsar (the Russian monarch) to accept terms. Many colonized peoples celebrated Japan's victory over Russia as an Asian country had defeated a European one.

Japan now had its own colonial empire as they controlled Manchuria, Korea, and Taiwan. The Japanese occupation of these lands—especially in Korea—was harsh. In that nation, the Japanese forced Koreans to adopt Japanese names and follow Japanese religious practices. Books written in Korean were banned. This attempt to erase Korean identity was genocide, too. Fighting alongside the British, French, Russians, and Americans in World War I against the Germans, Austro-Hungarians, and Ottoman Turks, Japan emerged from that conflict with control over several other islands and territories in the Pacific but was dissatisfied with those spoils. Japan was now a Great Power, but still dependent on the West for natural resources—especially oil. Japan seized the rest of Manchuria in 1931, and in July 1937 launched a full-scale invasion of the rest of China. While Americans tend to date the start of World War II from the attack on Pearl Harbor in 1941 and the Europeans two years earlier in 1939 when Hitler and Stalin invaded Poland, the attack on China marked the true beginning of that global conflict. The American oil embargo imposed on Japan in the summer of 1941 convinced the Japanese Empire that the West wanted to prevent Japan from taking its rightful place as a powerful, industrialized, and modern nation and it was resolved to attack Pearl Harbor to prevent American interference in the Japanese militarists' creation of a "Greater East Asia Co-Prosperity Sphere." To accomplish this, Japan launched military operations across the whole of Southeast Asia, supposedly to create an "Asia for the Asians." In truth, their occupation and treatment of the peoples they invaded and brutalized was even worse—and in some cases far worse—than that of the European colonialists. The Japanese invasion of the rest of China in 1937, like those of Hitler in Europe and Mussolini in Africa, marked new campaigns of imperial conquest by "so-called 'have not' nations, to secure their national survival and express their national identity by conquering additional imperial zones of their own" as had the British and French before them (Overy 2022, xiii).

The Rape of Nanking (Nanjing)

The horrific atrocities and crimes Japan's military forces committed during World War II have not received as much attention in the history books as those perpetrated by the Germans. The unbridled barbarism the Nazis unleashed upon Europe that resulted in the deaths of tens of millions of people stands as perhaps the worst example of human cruelty in history. Some historians, such as Iris Chang, contend that Japanese troops also murdered up to 19 million Chinese in their own quest for empire (Chang 2011, 217). More reliable estimates put that number at six–ten million dead total in Asia during the period 1937–45, with at least half being Chinese. Like many Germans, the Japanese elites had a sense of racial superiority and justified their seizure of other countries as being necessary for a great power to maintain itself. They despised the Chinese despite the fact China's civilization was—and is—the longest continuous one in human history and Japan itself had been heavily influenced by its religion and culture. It took Japanese forces six months of hard fighting to reach the capital of Nanking. The leader of the Chinese Nationalist forces, Chiang Kai-Shek, abandoned the city along with his government advisors and ministers. He ordered the army to stand and fight, but by this time the soldiers were exhausted and it was obvious to everyone that the city would fall quickly. Some Americans and Europeans who had remained in the city, led by the German businessman and Nazi party member John Rabe, set up a neutral area—the Nanking Safety Zone—where anyone within its limits would be safe from the Japanese. Ultimately up to a quarter of a million Chinese civilians would be saved by this Nazi, leading one scholar to dub him "the Oskar Schindler of China" (Chang 2011, 109). At least that many Chinese, however, were killed after Japanese troops took control of the city.

Japanese troops had waited outside the city's massive wall—the world's longest circular wall, constructed in the fourteenth century—for the Chinese to surrender.

SEXUAL VIOLENCE AS GENOCIDE 111

After a brief fight, the Chinese army was ordered to withdraw, leaving the 200,000 civilians and those soldiers who remained behind at the mercy of the Japanese soldiers. The Japanese army moved into the city on December 13, 1937. The commanding general, Matsui Iwane, had previously retired from his army career but had volunteered to serve again once Japan went to war. He realized after but one week in Nanking that his troops were out of control, raping Chinese women at will and then usually killing them, executing anyone they suspected of being a soldier, and in general terrorizing the entire population. He issued orders forbidding the mistreatment of the Chinese. They were not obeyed. Matsui, who suffered from chronic tuberculosis and was forced to return to Japan to convalesce, only later learned of the full horror and extent of the atrocities. He said to a trusted aide, "My men have done something very wrong, and extremely regrettable" (quoted in ibid., 52). Replaced by Emperor Hirohito's uncle, Prince Asaka, for the next six weeks, the soldiers of Imperial Japan ran amok with virtually no interference from their officers and committed the most heinous and atrocious war crimes imaginable (Figure 4.2).

In Nanking the Japanese soldiers raped women of any age; and were especially eager to find *hia gu niang*—young girls. They raped women in the streets, in full view of passers-by. They raped them in front of their families. They raped 10-year-old girls and 80-year-old women. Those who resisted the soldiers were simply killed. Even if they submitted, the soldiers still often killed them—usually in gruesome ways that we will not describe here. Many girls were taken back to their barracks and raped repeatedly before they too were killed. For amusement, the Japanese soldiers sometimes forced fathers to

Figure 4.2 A memorial to the victims of the "Rape of Nanking" at one of the sites of the atrocities. https://commons.wikimedia.org/wiki/File:Nanjing_Massacre_Memorial_(10151598764).jpg

rape their daughters, sons their mothers, and brothers their sisters. According to Iris Chang—author of *The Rape of Nanking*, the most authoritative and well-researched book on the subject—many Chinese women were impregnated by their rapists. This subject is so sensitive, though, that it has never been adequately studied. Chang wrote that to her knowledge, not a single Chinese woman has ever come forward to admit their child was a product of rape. After birth, many mothers choked to death or drowned their children; uncounted pregnant Chinese women took their own lives by throwing themselves into the Yangtze River.

Japanese forces also rounded up any males between the ages of 15 and 50 who might have been in the army. These prisoners were butchered in horrific ways such as being burned alive, buried up to their shoulders to be torn apart by hungry dogs, or by simply being lined up along the banks of the Yangtze River and machine-gunned. Perhaps the most barbaric method was beheading, which some turned into a "contest" that was widely publicized in newspapers for the folks back home in Japan—complete with photographs. The post-war International Military Tribunal for the Far East estimated the number of deaths in Nanking at over 250,000. Matsui returned to Nanking for two days in February 1938, where he condemned the actions of his troops and laid the blame for their undisciplined outrages at the feet of the officers in charge—including the emperor's uncle. Matsui, immediately recalled to Japan for this unheard-of attack on the honor of Japanese officers—and especially a member of the royal family—went back into retirement. Still more atrocities were in store for the Chinese people under Japanese occupation.

After the United States entered the war and bombed Japan in the famous raid led by Colonel James Doolittle, the surviving aircrews landed their planes in China. Enraged, the Japanese forces massacred tens of thousands more Chinese civilians; thousands more died after being deliberately exposed to the plague by infected fleas spread over major metropolitan areas by Japanese aviators. Still others were subjected to inhuman medical experiments similar to those conducted by the Nazis on Jews in the death camps. Millions would also perish from starvation and disease. There was no "Final Solution" for the Chinese envisioned by the Japanese warlords but specific regions were targeted and then destroyed with all of its inhabitants massacred. This, most certainly, was genocide, even if the sexual violence perpetrated upon the Chinese and other Asian women by the Japanese was not.

Prince Asaka was never brought to justice, however, as General Douglas MacArthur granted immunity to the entire Imperial family. The International Military Tribunal for the Far East held General Matsui responsible for the Rape of Nanking and executed him in 1948. Thirty years later the ashes of Matsui and six other war criminals executed by the Allies were placed in the Yasukuni Shrine, where important Japanese government officials often visit and pay their respects, infuriating peoples across all of Asia, but especially in China. Japan has still not fully accepted responsibility for its war of imperial aggression and criminal conduct. Unlike the Germans, who have made a strenuous effort to face their history honestly, Japan did not acknowledge its bestial conduct until relatively recently. Even then, the official expressions of regret have not gone far enough to mend relations fully with the Asian countries they devastated. Several other attempts at apology have often sounded insincere. Those scholars who have tried to correct the historical record have been criticized and threatened. Prime Minister Shinzo Abe—assassinated in 2022—even said Japan should stop apologizing. He said, "We must not let our children, grandchildren, and even further generations to come, who have nothing to do with that war, be predestined to apologize." Acknowledging one's own moral failings and moving forward in a spirit of humility requires being open to painful conversations. The previous chapter made clear it is not only the Japanese that need to learn from the Germans, admit their wrongdoing, and make restitution.

As with the Holocaust, however, there are also those who still try to minimize, or even deny entirely, the events that took place in Nanking during the Japanese occupation. To this day, many continue to insist that the practice of forcing women throughout Asia into prostitution to sexually service Japanese soldiers—so-called "comfort women"—was done purely voluntarily by these unfortunate women. Literally, hundreds of thousands of women throughout Asia were compelled to meet the sexual demands of the Japanese soldiers. Today some still assert that these women were "licensed prostitutes." This too, like what happened in Nanking, was rape and was both a war crime and a crime against humanity. Susan Brownmiller, author of the book *Against Our Will: Men, Women, and Rape*, contends that the Rape of Nanking was, outside of the treatment of Bengali women by Pakistani soldiers in 1971—an example of *genocidal* rape we will cover later in this chapter—the single worst instance of wartime rape in history (Brownmiller 1975). This assertion now seems to be inaccurate. Further investigation decades later—after the collapse of Communist regimes in Eastern Europe—showed that the soldiers of the Red Army raped hundreds of thousands, possibly even millions of German women in 1945. Antony Beevor described this as "the greatest phenomenon of mass rape in history" (Beevor 2001, 387). Once again, however, we caution against setting up any kind of hierarchy or competition of suffering. The Rape of Nanking was a monstrous and barbarous crime against humanity and an unmitigated evil, as was the catastrophe perpetrated upon the women of Germany thousands of miles away less than a decade later.

"An Army of Rapists"

The Soviet Red Army entered Berlin in the spring of 1945. This was not the first time that Russians had conquered a European power and entered its capital. In 1812, Napoleon had also made the mistake of invading Russia—the largest country in the world, then and now, by land size—and within a few years Russian soldiers in Paris were demanding fine wines be brought to them *bystro* (in Russian it means "quickly"). The word "bistro" has ever since been associated with a small bar or tavern. In Berlin, the soldiers demanded watches, bicycles, and—especially—women for sexual exploitation. The sexual violence perpetrated upon the women of Germany by the invading Red Army was on a massive scale. They were not the only Allied soldiers to rape, of course, but the Americans, with their unlimited supply of cigarettes—that quickly became a form of currency—did not always have to resort to force (Beevor 2001, 414). Nonetheless, the Americans, British, and French also committed several hundred thousand rapes (Gebhardt 2020, 22). The fact that there were fewer assaults on German women in the

Allied sectors of the front than in the Soviet-controlled areas does nothing to diminish the disgrace of these acts, which are often not even mentioned in the history books.

The numbers of women assaulted by the Soviets are staggering. Norman Naimark, among other experts, put the total figure at over two million (Naimark 1997, 70). Miriam Gebhardt, a historian from Germany, using a perhaps more sophisticated methodological approach thinks this number is "excessive." She puts the figure at 860,000 victims of rape. Naimark, however, points out that a substantial number of these women, perhaps even the majority, were raped multiple times and Gebhardt concedes that because "many women were raped more than once, the total number of cases is much higher" (Gebhardt 2020, 19). She even states flatly that her "estimate is on the low side" (ibid.) Many more women offered themselves to one soldier—preferably an officer—on a transactional basis to spare themselves the trauma of rape, although we must remind readers that there was often a great deal of coercion, as well as unequal power relations, in such "transactions." Untold numbers of German women who were forced into prostitution to survive—a situation the Allied soldiers readily used to their own advantage—are not included in this total. Susan Brownmiller called these incidences "the murky line that divides wartime rape from wartime prostitution" (Brownmiller 1975, 333).

As the war in Europe drew near its end in the spring of 1945, many Germans hoped that the Americans would reach them before the Soviets. Ceaseless Nazi propaganda portrayed the Russians as "barbarians." Depicted as inferior beings whose savagery knew no bounds, the regime warned its people that "the murderous Bolshevist rabble [...] would defile and butcher" German women and girls if the army was unable to stop their advance (Kershaw 2011, 112–15). The citizens of the Third Reich waited for the coming apocalypse. Nazi propaganda undoubtedly had its effect on the populace, as did the rumors of Red Army atrocities that were already filtering back from Eastern Germany. It was, however, the shared knowledge of their own army's unspeakable horrors committed in the East that filled the German people with dread. The revenge that the Red Army would take upon a defeated Germany was too much to bear for many of its people. Hitler Youth members were given cyanide capsules prior to being sent out to fight and many women carried them in their handbags. As the Soviets approached, there was an epidemic of suicides. If no cyanide was available, parents killed their children before killing themselves. Unwilling to accept the defeat of Germany, many hanged or shot themselves. There were even mass suicides "for fear of the monsters from the East" (quoted in Gebhardt 2020, 35). Thousands of Germans took their lives rather than face the consequences of the Nazis' defeat.

The Red Army sexually assaulted women all along the lines of their advance. In the Baltic nations, for example, they raped Estonian, Latvian and Lithuanian women. Monuments in all three countries erected to the Soviet "liberators" during the decades of occupation following the war—often referred to as monuments to, or tombs of, the "Unknown Rapists"—were finally removed after the Russian invasion of Ukraine in 2022. In Poland, Soviet troops raped Polish women. In Hungary, they raped Hungarian women. In Austria, they raped Austrian women. When the Soviet forces crossed the border into Germany after four long years of war, one of their first acts was to relieve themselves ostentatiously (i.e., in a pompous or theatrical manner) on German soil. Then they began their sexual assaults on any women they came across, regardless of age or nationality. They raped Ukrainian, Russian, and other East European women whom they had liberated from work camps just as easily as they assaulted German women. As word of the mass rapes—including gang rapes—spread, parents tried to hide their daughters or mothers offered themselves to the soldiers in order to protect their children. Fathers who protested were shot. Women who resisted were also often killed. Natalia Gesse, a female Soviet war correspondent, witnessed the shocking behavior of the Red Army soldiers. She later reported, "The Russian soldiers were raping every female from eight to eighty. They were an army of rapists" (quoted in *The Guardian*, May 1, 2002).

A common misconception about the mass rape committed by the Soviets is that, like the Japanese rape of Nanking, it was tolerated, even encouraged, by the military commanders on the scene. Stalin himself even supposedly replied to the Yugoslav Communist leader Milovan Djilas, who complained about the Red Army's raping and pillaging their way across Europe, "can't he understand it, if a soldier that has crossed thousands of kilometers through blood and fire and death has fun with a woman or takes some trifle?" (quoted in Naimark 1997, 71). Antony Beevor, who consulted Russian archives for his book—now banned in Russia—insists that the Soviet leadership knew what was happening but did little to stop it (Beevor 2001, 326). Russian historians today deny the scope and scale of the atrocities perpetrated upon German civilians, or that Red Army officers condoned these outrages. Professor Oleg Rzheshevskii, head of war history at the Russian Academy of Sciences in Moscow, also used official documents to assert that 4,418 officers were "punished" for either joining in on or failing to prevent rapes (*BBC NEWS* Online, April 29, 2002). The British historian Richard Overy argues that the Russians are reluctant to acknowledge their war crimes "because they felt that much of it was justified vengeance against an enemy who committed much worse" (ibid.). There was, of course, plenty of Soviet propaganda during the war exhorting the soldiers to kill "the Nazi beast in his lair," but by the spring of 1945 even Stalin, perhaps with an eye on the post-war administration of Germany, said "Hitlers come and go, but the German people and the German state remain" (quoted in Gebhardt, 2020, 73). Gebhardt's new research chronicles the repeated orders issued by the Soviet command to refrain from mistreating German civilians and concludes "the long-held opinion that the military leadership encouraged the violence needs to be revised" (ibid., 75).

We are not excusing the atrocities committed by the Allies in World War II, nor are we suggesting that the suffering unleashed upon the peoples of Europe by the Germans should be forgotten or minimized. We should always recognize victims of violence regardless of their nationality. Scholars such as Miriam Gebhardt hold that the mass rape of German women by Soviet—and other Allied (American and British)—soldiers was "a historically unique phenomenon." We beg to differ. While this mass rape was probably unprecedented in scale, any claim to "uniqueness" would presuppose that these events were not repeatable. The mass rapes in East Pakistan, Yugoslavia, and Rwanda demonstrate otherwise. The mass rape of German women by Soviet Red Army soldiers—as well as the hundreds of thousands of rapes committed by French, British, and American soldiers in their zones of control—and the mass rape of Chinese women by the Japanese were all war crimes and, in both the Soviet and Japanese cases, possibly horrible crimes against humanity under international law. These episodes, however awful and repugnant to humanity's conscience, do not, however, rise to the level of the most heinous, sinister, and irreparable crime of crimes—genocide. This is not to say that mass rape is not one method to commit genocide. The deliberate, forcible impregnation of Muslim women in East Pakistan (now Bangladesh) and the former Yugoslavia were attempts by the genocidists to destroy their social and cultural connections. This most definitely was genocide, as was the Hutu rape of Tutsi women in Rwanda. The idea common to all three of these genocidists, as opposed to the war crimes and crimes against humanity committed by soldiers on both sides in World War II, was to destroy these communities' social cohesion to eliminate them as a people. This, then, was genocide, too.

The Rape of Bengali Women

Among the many examples of the systematic use of rape as a form of genocide are the appalling events of 1971 in southern Asia. Today, Pakistan and Bangladesh are large countries (combined population of more than 400 million in 2023) that appear to have much in common. Muslims are in the large majority in both, and there are many other cultural and historical connections between the two peoples. Great Britain had dominated majority Hindu India since 1757—as well as what is today Burma, or Myanmar, from 1824—and from 1858 ruled the sub-continent directly from London. "British India" was the "jewel in the crown" of its imperial possessions. After World War II the British "quit" India (in reality, they were forced out by the resistance of the Indian people, led by Mohandas K. "Mahatma" Gandhi), proclaiming the completion of their presumed mission to "civilize" the far older Indian society while holding on like grim death to their other colonies and refusing to extend the protection of the 1948 Convention to those possessions. Many Muslims in India desired their own state, and in a process known as Partition, an unprecedented "population transfer" was conducted which involved perhaps the largest-scale expulsions in human history—somewhere between 14 and 18 million people. The communal violence between Hindus and Muslims cost at least one million lives (Dyson 2018, 189). The enmity between these two religious groups in today's India—where two hundred million Muslims still constitute nearly 15 percent of the population—continues to burn fiercely, as President Narendra Modi's Hindu Nationalist Party (the BJP) stokes these fires of hatred for political gain. In 1947, two Muslim-majority areas, West and East, separated by nearly half the width of the United States, became "Pakistan," which means "Land of the Pure" in the Urdu language.

This would prove to be the root of the problems between these two Muslim peoples, as, behind a thin veneer of electoral democracy, Pakistan was in reality ruled by "unelected civil-military bureaucratic elites from West Pakistan" who acted "like colonial masters toward the Bengalis in East Pakistan" (Jahan 2009, 251). General Ayub Khan, military dictator of Pakistan from 1957 to 1968, proclaimed that East Bengalis resemble "downtrodden races," revealed by the darker complexions, "exclusiveness, suspicion" and "defensive aggressiveness," which he believed derived from Indian and

Hindu influence or origins (ibid.). Suffice it to say here that when the Bengali pro-independence party, the Awami League, won nationwide elections in 1970 by a large margin, this was not accepted by the leadership of the western part of the country. They arrested the Awami League leader, Sheikh Mujibur Rahman, on March 25, 1971, and began a military assault on East Pakistan—which then declared its independence, as Bangladesh, on the following day.

Like many, if not most, of the case studies in this book the horrific atrocities perpetrated by the soldiers of West Pakistan against the inhabitants of East Pakistan could be discussed in two, or even three different chapters. The attempt to eliminate Awami League members as part of a "political" group, as well as the unconscionable actions of the United States and China in portraying this conflict as merely a civil war, and thus an entirely internal domestic matter not subject to international intervention, is discussed in the following chapter. The attack on the Bengalis themselves should be understood as the genocide of a Convention-protected "ethnical" group. The "ethnic cleansing" of ten million Hindus is, in our view, also genocide, and thus could have been discussed in the chapter on ethnic cleansing. From the outset the Pakistani leadership called for genocide, with President Khan stating "Kill three million of them, and the rest will eat out of our hands" (Payne 1973, 50).

The subsequent genocide was carefully planned and systematically carried out. As with most genocides, the intellectual class was targeted first. Professors and teachers, as well as ordinary college students, were massacred immediately (Mascarenhas 1972, 116). They were followed by any military-age males, whether they were boys or men. Jahan writes that "All through the liberation war, able-bodied young men were suspected of being actual or potential freedom fighters. Thousands were arrested, tortured, and killed" (Jahan 2009, 298). Hindus were killed as soon as the Pakistani soldiers came across them. The soldiers would "check males for the obligated circumcision among Moslems. If circumcised, they might live; if not, sure death" (Rummel 1997, 323). As Robert Payne writes, "For month after month in all the regions of East Pakistan the massacres went on" (Payne 1973, 29). The US administration of Richard Nixon and his faithful servant Henry Kissinger also played a role, as indeed Kissinger did in many atrocities during the Cold War. According to Payne, the US government supplied almost four million dollars in military equipment *after* the genocide began (ibid., 102). The genocide only ended after nearly nine months when India invaded in December 1971. Somewhere between one and three million Bengalis were killed, making this one of the most murderous genocides of the twentieth century.

While men were specifically targeted for mass murder, women were systematically raped in a deliberate attempt to shatter the social bonds of the Muslim Bengalis. That is not to say that Hindu or Christian women were spared this outrage, as they were not. Susan Brownmiller has compared these events to the episodes of mass rape we have already discussed in this chapter—the Japanese soldiers in Nanking and the Soviet soldiers in Germany after World War II. As in these other episodes, no woman or girl was safe regardless of their age. Brownmiller asserts "Girls of eight and grandmothers of seventy-five had been sexually assaulted [...] Pakistani soldiers had not only violated Bengali women on the spot; they abducted tens of hundreds and held them by force in their military barracks for nightly use" (Brownmiller 1975, 83). The number of East Pakistani women raped during the nine-month campaign of sexual violence encouraged and implemented with full knowledge of the effects it would have on Bengali society has variously been estimated at 200,000, 300,000, and 400,000. These women were subsequently shunned by their partners despite the government's attempt to reintegrate them into society. A program to "marry them off" was started as the government made desperate efforts to encourage husbands to return to their wives or finding men willing to marry single women that had been raped or the hundreds of thousands of widows left husbandless. The sad case of one woman, an officer's wife, is sufficient to illustrate this situation. Her husband had been taken away and brutally tortured; when he returned, she had been gang raped in front of her husband and three children. She was then taken away and raped numerous times. Returning pregnant, her husband refused to have anything to do with her. She kept asking, "But why, why did they do it? It would have been better if we had both died" (quoted in Jahan 2009, 318).

As Lisa Sharlach has noted, there is evidence that "senior officers were aware of, encouraged, or themselves participated in the rape warfare" (quoted in Totten and Parsons 2009, 183). This was not just a war crime, but a calculated effort to destroy the Bengalis as a people, with soldiers telling their victims that they "must carry loyal 'Pakistani' offspring instead of 'bootlickers of India or the Hindus' in their wombs" (quoted in ibid.). One Pakistani major wrote to another that "their [Bengali] next generation must have to be changed/perhaps oneday [*sic*] you or me will be found there" (quoted in ibid.). After India invaded East Pakistan and quickly forced the West Pakistan army to surrender and leave the territory of the now-independent nation of Bangladesh, one of the departing Pakistani soldiers shouted "we are going, But we are leaving our Seed behind" (Malik 1972, 152). Amita Malik rightly contends that this episode "was one of the most savage, organized and indiscriminate orgies of rape in human history: rape by a professional army, backed by local armed collaborators" (ibid.).

The Rape of Bosnian Muslim Women

The dream of creating a "Greater Serbia"—three-quarters of a century after this dream helped spark World War I—led to a campaign of the "ethnic cleansing" of Muslims by Serbs from Bosnia after the dissolution of Yugoslavia. This attempt is fully chronicled in Chapter Seven of this book, "Empire and State-Building through Genocide." Here we are going to focus on the systematic rape of women and girls as a strategy of war, where the intent is to destroy the enemy. In war, however, it is the enemy's military forces that are to be destroyed and not its civilian population. This genocidal destruction was aimed at the entire Bosnian Muslim community as such, and one of the techniques was forcible impregnation. Soldiers detained these Bosnian women until it was too late to procure an abortion—something that in itself would also cause great mental anguish to many Muslim women, who generally do not seek such procedures. The Serbs would then send these unfortunate women back in busses spray-painted with vile comments. "Detention centers" for women only were set up where off-duty Bosnian Serb soldiers would repeatedly victimize these unfortunates for months on end. Some of these "rape camps" were given names such as "Coffeehouse Sonja" and "Fast Food Restaurant." In one "rape camp," there were over 2,000 women and girls detained for several months (Sharlach 183). As in Bangladesh, women and girls were raped in front of family members or even on the street. Gang rape was also common. Beverly Allen has compiled evidence that these rapes were ordered by the Serb leadership with the express purpose of impregnating them (Allen 1996). This sexual violence caused "serious bodily or mental harm to members of the group" and, in addition, imposed "measures intended to prevent births within the group." The latter could be either through impregnation or the subsequent shunning of these women by male members of the group. The intent to destroy the Bosnian Muslim people was plainly evident, and although the International Criminal Tribunal for the former Yugoslavia (ICTY) did not include sexual violence in its deliberations about the crime of genocide, the International Criminal Tribunal for Rwanda (ICTR) did hand down the first conviction for genocidal rape. It is to this mass atrocity, the most concentrated act of human killing in history, to which we now turn (Figure 4.3).

The Rape of Tutsi Women

The collapse of Communism in Yugoslavia left a power vacuum that was eagerly filled by unscrupulous politicians. Inflaming the emotions of their peoples through rhetoric and demagoguery, they used ethno-nationalism to create their own homogenous ethnic states. The violence they incited to achieve their ends led directly to the genocide in the Balkans. The same holds true for Rwanda; after the end of colonial rule, the Hutu

Figure 4.3 Bakira Hasečić is President of the Association of Women Victims of War. She founded the Association after surviving rape during the devastating campaign of ethnic cleansing that took place in Visegrad, Bosnia during the war and genocide of 1992–95.

majority quickly moved to assert its control over the newly independent state and establish their dominance by using myths and appealing to the worst instincts of their ethnic kin. In both these case studies the goal was to establish and maintain a new state dominated by one ethnic group. We will examine this aspect more fully in Chapter Seven, but in this chapter, we are highlighting the deliberate use of genocidal sexual violence to achieve those political goals. As in Bosnia by the Serbs, the Hutu militants and their thuggish compatriots the *Interahamwe*—"those who stand together"—a campaign of rape was used to destroy their enemies. In this case, however, the goal was not forcible impregnation. In Bosnia, the Serbs did not view the Muslim women as physiologically or biologically different from themselves. They were seen only as being "culturally" different and thus the women that were forced to deliver the offspring of their rapists were propagating the Serb "race." In contrast, the Hutu rapists saw the Tutsi as wholly alien, and the goal was "not only to degrade but to socially demote Tutsi women, whom they viewed as haughty and elitist" (Cox 2017, 166).

Up to one million people, the great majority of them Tutsi died in the short span of three months in the spring and early summer of 1994. At least a quarter million women were raped during this time, and possibly as many as twice that number as "victims of rape are stigmatized and made to feel shame for the crime committed against them. As a result, rape is one of the most under-reported crimes" (Nowrojee 1996, 24). Many of these women were raped multiple times. Some scholars believe that these rapes were organized and used systematically as a weapon to destroy the Tutsi community (Bonnet 1995, 19; Royte 1997, 38). Others disagree and assert that these criminals committed rape simply because they could do so without fear of retribution. There is no debate about whether or not there was a concerted effort to impregnate Tutsi women. Hutu men almost always killed the women that they raped. There was, however, a deliberate effort to leave some women alive that had been deliberately infected with the HIV virus; many rapists said they wanted to pass on the virus so that their victims would die slowly and painfully from AIDS. Studies from Amnesty International have concluded that the vast majority—up to two-thirds—of the women that survived the genocide and had been raped were infected with the virus (Bijleveld, *et al.* 2009, 208). As the Human Rights Watch Report *Shattered Lives* noted, the aim of the rapists was to "strip the humanity from the larger group of which she is a part. The rape of one person is translated into an assault upon the community […]" (Nowrojee 1996). Another report from Amnesty International concluded that this trauma was passed down to the next generation, as the children of the rapists face discrimination and are often outcasts in their own community as the mothers "have often been humiliated and marginalized by their communities" (quoted in Cox 2017, 167).

Both of these mass atrocity crimes that occurred at roughly the same time were, in our view, genocides. Since an international criminal court with universal jurisdiction had not been established when the 1948 Convention was instituted, special *ad hoc* tribunals were needed to try the genocidists. We will examine this issue of punishment in the Conclusion to this book. Here we need note that, astonishingly, in the last decade of the twentieth century, there was no clear definition of rape in international law. The ICTY held that rape is the coerced sexual penetration of a victim vaginally, anally, or orally, whether by the perpetrator' penis or by some other object. Although the Court did also concede that not only penetration "but also any serious sexual assault falling short of actual penetration" might also be rape, it coupled that with the idea that there must be "coercion, threat of force, or intimidation." This last was later modified to include situations where the threat of force may not be met, but consent is still not freely given. Genocidal rapists in Bosnia were prosecuted for their criminal acts under the category of Crimes against Humanity, and not under the 1948 Convention on Genocide. In the case of the Rwandan rapists, however, the ICTR *did* not only achieve the first international prosecution's conviction for genocide, it also specifically expanded case law to include rape within the framework of that heinous "crime of crimes." Rape was now more broadly defined as being a "physical invasion of a sexual nature, committed on a person under circumstances which are coercive. Sexual violence is not limited to physical invasion of the human body and may include acts which do not involve penetration or even physical contact." In the case of Jean-Paul Akayesu, the Court ruled that rape was a component of genocide and that the genocidists raped these women because of their ethnicity. Later, a woman, Pauline Nyiramasuhoko, was found guilty of seven charges including genocide and incitement to rape and sentenced to life imprisonment. Nyiramasuhoko had been Rwanda's Minister for Family Welfare and the Advancement of Women.

Questions for Further Discussion

1. While the 1948 Genocide Convention does not explicitly address sexual violence, in your opinion what parts of this legal definition of genocide could be used to secure justice for women subjected to such heinous violations of personal dignity?
2. In some of the case studies of mass rape we have examined, women were deliberately impregnated as part of a campaign to destroy their communities. Is this genocide? Why or why not?
3. In all the cases of mass rape we have examined, victimized women were often left with venereal diseases that rendered them sterile; in addition, all suffered grievous psychological harm that in many cases left them unwilling to engage later in relationships with members of their own group. Is this outcome genocide?
4. Why do this book's authors claim there is a difference between some mass rapes, committed by undisciplined soldiers, and others purposefully designed to destroy a specific community? Do you agree with this distinction? Why or why not?

Chapter Five

GENOCIDES OF POLITICAL GROUPS

> *The organs of state security face the task of carrying out by the most merciless means the destruction of all these bands of anti-Soviet elements [...] and finish at last, once and for all, with their evil under-ground activities.*
> —Stalin's Notorious Order No. 00447, July 31, 1937

"Politicide"

We have explored the outlines of the scholarly disagreement over what the definition of genocide *should* be and how the legal definition crafted by representatives of genocidal governments did not fully align with Raphael Lemkin's concept. In 1946, Lemkin finally gained the support necessary to place before the UN the proposals he had been advocating since 1933. The initial UN Resolution 96 (I) of December 11, 1946, calling for the codification into international law of the crime of genocide, specifically noted that "genocide was the denial of the right of existence of entire human groups" throughout history, and that "many crimes of genocide have occurred when racial, religious, political and other groups have been destroyed, entirely or in part." For Lemkin, the objectives of a genocidal plan of destruction would be "the disintegration of the political and social institutions, of culture, language, national feelings, religion, and the economic existence of national groups" (Lemkin 2008, 79). Genocide is essentially political violence, and the first targets of most genocides are usually the political officials and leaders of the victim group. As Martin Shaw observed, political targeting of these elites is generally a "[...] dimension of genocide, where political elements are targeted alongside, or as the leading elements of, ethnic, class or other social enemies" (Shaw, 2015, 92). Lemkin would agree that attacks on the political representatives of a group would be one method of genocide with the aim being the destruction of a people. Moreover, he clearly spelled out what made a people—their political, social, and cultural institutions and traditions.

Previous chapters have also analyzed debates among scholars and experts who often make distinctions between types of violence—such as "ethnic cleansing" or "ethnocide" as opposed to "genocide"—or have instead focused solely on but one aspect of that violence, such as "gendercide." In this chapter, we will look at another narrowly defined type of violence—"politicide"—an attempt to destroy a group based on its political identity. As Shaw insightfully noted, these designations merely separate "forms of political violence which tend to occur in combinations with each other" (Shaw 2015, 99). He correctly sees this, as with other "cides" as "treating the destruction of one kind of group as different from the destruction of another" (Shaw 2015, 99). Lemkin also believed genocide was a type of conflict, not a type of violence, in which one group embarks on a deliberate, multi-faceted process to destroy another group through a variety of methods—only one of which involves mass killing.

One of the forms or techniques used by genocidists is the destruction of the political institutions of a people. Even if merely targeting a people's political leaders, genocidists are attempting to deprive the group "of leadership and centers of authority," leading to the loss of "its cohesiveness and the ability to sustain its own identity" […] (Bauman 1989, 119). What of attacks by a government on its *own* people's political groups? Murderous attacks on domestic political groups such as opposition parties, movements, or factions have been classified by some observers as being distinct from genocide and they use the term "politicide" to describe them. Shaw again disagrees with this approach and asserts that "only occasionally has the destruction of a political community come to serve as the *defining* aspect" […] of a genocide (Shaw 2015, 92). Genocidists usually designate groups intended for destruction as political enemies, regardless of any other characteristics used to identify them. There are more than just a few cases of so-called political genocides in history, including the crushing of political dissidents now occurring in Burma. Shaw however, does identify two of those episodes that we will examine later in this chapter—the destruction of the Spanish left and working-class movements by General Francisco Franco during and after the Spanish Civil War (1936–39) and the annihilation of the Communist Party by the Indonesian army in 1965–66.

Those who do make this distinction would contend that because the groups targeted for mass murder differ, "politicide" and genocide, though sharing some of the same characteristics such as political violence—usually by governments—are therefore separate phenomena. In their view, in genocides the "victimized groups are defined primarily by their communal characteristics, i.e. ethnicity, religion, or nationality […]" whereas in politicides "the victim groups are defined primarily in terms of their hierarchical position or political opposition to the regime or dominant groups" (Harff and Gurr 1988, 360). We see several different problems in this approach to understanding genocidal violence. In our view, *any group* singled out for destruction amounts to genocide, regardless of the genocidists' motives or the characteristics they ascribe to the group. *Mass killing*, though it usually accompanies genocide, is not necessary to accomplish the destruction of a group. Furthermore, national or state *governments* do not necessarily implement these atrocities, as has been shown in studies of the genocides in Indonesia and Rwanda; sometimes the principal actors are "local political leaders and institutions, paramilitaries and mobs […]" (Shaw 2015, 148). The Ku Klux Klan, for example—though composed of local politicians, judges, civic leaders, and police with close and multiple ties with local or state governments—usually acted independently of any government. The same is also true for "settler" colonial violence against indigenous peoples; it may not have been sanctioned beforehand by a government, but nonetheless is carried out without interference from it.

Those academics that differentiate between genocide and "politicide" seem to be attempting to split the difference between the Convention's definition that included only four protected groups (racial, national, ethnical (*sic*), and religious) and the obvious—that other identifiable human groups can also be marked for destruction. Lemkin specifically addressed both the Nazi and Soviet elimination of political opposition parties and groups in *Axis Rule* as techniques of genocide. Scholars who have reviewed his personal papers also agree that he "explicitly referred to political groups as targets of genocide [...]" (Bachman 2022, 49). When Lemkin assisted in composing the initial resolution on genocide for the United Nations, he included political groups in the proposed definition. As noted, the General Assembly Resolution 96(I) of December 11, 1946, read: "many instances of such crimes of genocide have occurred when racial, religious, political and other groups have been destroyed, entirely or in part" (Bachman 2022, 48). Lemkin also participated in the negotiations over the two drafts of the 1948 Convention and they too included political groups.

As we saw in Chapter One, opposition to including political groups in the Convention came mostly, for obvious reasons, from the Soviet Union. Stalin's execution and exiling of hundreds of thousands of—real or imagined—political opponents and around two million so-called *kulaks*—supposedly "bourgeois capitalist" peasants also classified as being enemies of socialism—are prime examples of the genocide of political groups. Of course, these groups, especially the *kulaks*, did not necessarily see themselves as constituting any kind of formal group but what counted was that the Soviet genocidists believed that they did. The most obvious Soviet example of the wholesale elimination of a political group was the secret police massacre of over 20,000 Polish prisoners at Katyn Forest in April and May of 1940. Captured Polish military and police officers, as well as Polish intellectuals, writers, and poets, were simply shot in the back of the head and buried in mass graves. This obvious war crime, combined later with Soviet deportation policies and the resettling of Russians in the vacated regions certainly suggest the contours of a colonial genocide as defined by Lemkin. Later, the Soviets then tried to blame the Nazis for the murders—admitting their culpability only after the fall of the USSR.

During the negotiations over the Convention, the USSR insisted that political groups, not being stable and permanent and being wholly voluntary associations, unlike being born into the categories of race, nationality, or ethnicity—should not be included among the protected groups. Their opinion was that "political groups were entirely out of place in a scientific definition of genocide, and their inclusion would weaken the convention and hinder the fight against genocide" (Naimark 2010, 21). Research by Anton Weiss-Wendt (2017), Douglas Irvin-Erickson (2017), and Jeffery Bachman (2022), has shown that Lemkin, fearful that the Soviet Union would not vote for the Convention, abruptly switched gears and turned against the inclusion of political groups. In support of the Soviet position, Lemkin echoed their rationale and began calling for the exclusion of political groups "on the grounds that they lacked the permanency and specific characteristics of the other groups" (Schabas 2000, 134). Irvin-Erickson believes Lemkin essentially began misrepresenting his previous position on the matter by contending that in *Axis Rule* he meant that the destruction of political institutions was but one technique of genocide but the destruction of political groups in and of themselves was *not* genocide (Irvin-Erickson 2017, 181). We already saw in Chapter Four how Lemkin would abandon his ideals yet again when, fearing the United States would not ratify the Convention—which it did not until 1988—he suddenly claimed that the treatment of black people in America, including the lynching of thousands, was also not genocide.

The United States initially pushed to include political groups in the definition but to exclude "cultural" genocide or the genocide of "other" groups, such as "social" ones—the specifics of this argument were already briefly touched upon earlier and will be discussed further in Chapter Seven—while the Soviet Union did the exact opposite despite clearly being an imperial power that imposed its own values on myriad peoples. In the end, both were left out. Beth van Schaak flatly asserts that the "exclusion of political groups from the Genocide Convention represents [a] compromise. No legal principle can justify this blind spot" (van Schaak 1997). The United States obviously benefited from the exclusion of cultural genocide but also, ironically, benefited greatly from the exclusion of political groups from the Convention in at least one case covered later in this chapter—the Indonesian army's slaughter of half a million communists. The United States was at least complicit in the Indonesian genocide—if not a co-conspirator. Some scholars have called the Indonesian army's campaign against their own communist nationals in 1965 a "sub-type" of genocide. Leo Kuper, the South African sociologist, proposed that it be placed in a separate category—the "mass killing of political groups" (Kuper 1981). Jeffrey Bachman disagrees, writing that the "genocidal intent of the Indonesian planners and perpetrators is indisputable," moreover, so is "the fact that the United States played a facilitating role" (Bachman 2022, 55).

Other scholars believe the Indonesian case study shows that "political cleansing can also be ethnic cleansing" (Cribb 2001, 221). This is because, like the United States, Indonesia's core national values were devoid of specific ethnic content; Cribb believes that "the political, rather than the ethnic, character of Indonesia" was at the core of Indonesian politics at that time. The victor in the struggle for political power between Islamists, communists, and "developmentalists" would then determine the character of Indonesian identity. Martin Shaw also points out that political associations and parties "often understand themselves as *representing* social groups [...]" and "often become communities, sharing lifestyles and reinforcing political choice with all sorts of communal bonds." He asks, "If a 'political group' is targeted for destruction in the same way as other kinds of groups, then surely this is, likewise, genocide?" (Shaw 2015, 91). In any case, Stalin's murder of the various "political" groups he perceived as being opponents was at the same time also some combination of social (class), cultural (religious or artistic or literary), and ethnic (Ukrainian) elements. Even though the Convention does not protect political—or social groups, the subject of the next chapter—these were at the same time also national, religious, and ethnic groups, which are (Figure 5.1).

When the 1948 Genocide Convention protected only the socially constructed human categories of race, ethnicity, religious affiliation, and nationality, they were then, as Lawrence LeBlanc put it, deemed "more worthy or more fundamental" than other human groups. He states that while "this assumption may have held sway in the pre-1950 era [...] in the 21st century [...] identity is more fragmented" (LeBlanc 1991, 508–9). In addition, as David Nersessian writes in his book *Genocide and Political Groups* "national, racial, ethnic and religious characteristics are often used as a proxy for political identity" and thus "in practice political groups often overlap significantly

Figure 5.1 Statue of Marx and Engels in the former East Berlin. The statue exemplifies the deification of Marx and Engels under the Stalinist regimes of the Soviet Union and, after World War II, eastern Europe—regimes that adopted the banner but little of the content of Marxism or socialism. https://commons.wikimedia.org/wiki/File:Statues_of_Karl_Marx_and_Friedrich_Engels_-_Near_Alexanderplatz_-_Eastern_Berlin_-_Germany.jpg

with the enumerated group categories" (Nersessian 2010, 76). The 1948 Genocide Convention, however, was never meant to be timeless or unchangeable. The beginning of Article II of the Convention plainly states: "In the *present* Convention, genocide means [...]." Articles XXIV and XXV make clear that it would "remain in effect for ten years" and "thereafter remain in force for successive periods of five years" unless a "request for the revision of the present Convention [is] made at any time by any Contracting Party." As Norbert Finzsch has argued, the "framers of the Convention obviously expected political or historical developments that would require altering, in wording or substance, the Convention as it was ratified by the member states of the United Nations" (Finzsch 2008, 123). The continuing Cold War rivalry between the United States and the Soviet Union over the next four decades made such revisions of the Convention impossible, and the prospect of international cooperation to that end in today's world of geopolitical struggles makes it highly unlikely that any more human groups, no matter how deserving, will be protected under the Genocide Convention.

Russia and Ukraine

In 1929, the leader of the Soviet Union, Joseph Stalin, began a ruthless "liquidation" of the Ukrainian "intelligentsia"—a word derived from the Russian word that describes a people's artistic, cultural, or social elite—that was but the first step in a long-term, deliberate Russian process to destroy the Ukrainian people. Vladimir Putin continues to pursue this goal today. The second step was the exile of nearly two million Ukrainian peasants as "enemies of the people." These *"kulaks"*—the word means "fists" as in tight-fisted, implying they were exploitative moneylenders—were simply better off peasants who were often the leaders of their village communities. The *kulaks* were those peasants who had acquired some land, or owned a few horses or hired help for their holdings—thereby supposedly exploiting others' labor, capitalism's "original sin," so to speak, according to Karl Marx. In his *Communist Manifesto*, written with Friedrich Engels in 1848—from which Lenin, the leader of the Communist revolution and founder of the Soviet Union seven decades later, and other Communists and many other leftists drew their inspiration—Marx had England's economic and political development over centuries to predict the future course of history in Europe and the world. English peasants had been violently dispossessed of their land and forced to seek work in the cities, creating a desperately poor urban working class by the late 1700s. The new capitalist class that also arose from industrialization, the "bourgeoisie" or "middle class," profited immensely off their labor. Seeing the revolutions that swept most of Europe in 1848—though none in England—he predicted this class of workers would rise up sooner, rather than later, and throw off their chains. The workers would violently expropriate the bourgeoisie, or capitalist "middle class," and the big industrialists and landlords and establish a classless, egalitarian, socialist state. According to an important argument advanced 30 years later by his patron and collaborator Friedrich Engels, the state would eventually just "wither away" (Marx and Engels 1848; Engels 1878, republished 2016).

Socialism, then, was a political response not only to the exploitation of working people—including children—but to the dangerous workplaces they labored in as well as the dreadful housing and sanitation conditions in Europe's increasingly overcrowded cities. Less radical socialist followers of Marx pushed for social justice and egalitarianism and, allied with various reform movements succeeded in persuading governments to pass acts and laws that led to better working conditions, the expansion of democracy, and, importantly, government support for the disabled, unemployed and retired workers so they could live out their lives in dignity. Marx, however, assumed that, as in England, most peasants would become factory workers in the cities and become increasingly impoverished. Marx had drawn no distinctions between the various strata of the peasantry that remained. To him, peasants were simply *"petit"* (small) bourgeois, attached to their land and ways of life, including their religious superstitions. In his

Development of Capitalism in Russia, however, published in 1899, Vladimir Lenin, the future founder of the world's first socialist state, argued that capitalism had come to Russia and had already destroyed the traditional socialist peasant commune. He arbitrarily divided the peasantry as a whole into the *"kulaks,"* a small class of "bourgeois" peasants, a majority of "middle" peasants, and the "poor" or "worker" ones. This supposedly made it possible to apply the Marxist theory of class struggle and the emergence of an advanced industrial society in a predominantly rural and agricultural one. In trying to do so, Lenin conveniently ignored the obvious fact that these *kulak* "exploiters of the poor peasants" also worked alongside their hired hands as laborers and shared the hardships and uncertainties of rural life with the rest of the peasantry. Lenin used government records of horse holding to divide arbitrarily the peasantry into "rich" and "poor" ones. In most cases, these "rich" peasants were simply more industrious and perhaps less given to drink than their less well-off fellow peasants.

In 1917, Lenin believed the first phase of the Russian Revolution was similar to Marx's "bourgeois" phase of history as the peasantry—again, classified as *petit bourgeois* by Marx—had joined forces with workers and intellectuals to overthrow the tsarist monarchy. The Bolsheviks—renamed the Communist Party in 1918—seized power in November 1917 (this is sometimes termed the "October Revolution" because it took place on October 25 by the Russian calendar then in use but November 7 by the calendar used since 1918 that conforms to common usage) that was supposedly a socialist "revolution" because the workers and the "poor" working-class peasantry joined forces to overthrow the "bourgeois" "Provisional"—temporary—Government of liberals and moderate socialists that had ruled Russia for but eight months. Lenin had promised the peasants "Bread, Land and Peace" in order to come to power in 1917. After a vicious civil war that instead saw the Communists seizing the peasants' grain to feed the Red Army—and the workers in the factories producing arms and munitions for that army—the regime encountered widespread peasant resistance. Lenin tried to justify the requisitioning as necessary to win the war. This so-called "War Communism" was really an effort to bring the communist utopia into reality but basically destroyed the economy. Theoretically, the cooperation between urban and rural "workers," symbolized by the hammer and sickle on the Soviet flag, would usher in the socialist paradise. In fact, this union, or "smychka," was short-lived as the peasants, recognizing the limits of Soviet Power, simply went back to their old ways of life. Their resistance to Soviet rule led to Lenin instituting a "New Economic Policy"—or NEP—that allowed the peasants to keep their grain and sell it on the open market in return for surrendering 10% of their crops in taxes. In other words, a step toward the restoration of capitalism. This policy was quite unpopular with most Bolsheviks but Lenin insisted on its adoption at the 1921 X Party Congress in order for the Bolsheviks to retain state power. Besides adopting the New Economic Policy, however, on the last day of the Congress Lenin also pushed through a plank in the party program that prohibited any factions from forming that advocated any policy that deviated from what had been decided by the Congress. It provided for the disciplining of any party members who engaged in obstruction of any policies once they had been approved by leadership. After Lenin's death in 1924, Stalin would use this to great effect, labeling his opponents "oppositionists" while posing as the only true Leninist. The NEP did pacify the peasantry and small landholders for a while, but soon they realized that their money was worthless as there were few goods to buy and those that were available were expensive and of poor quality. As there was little economic incentive to work hard, they planted fewer crops and grew just enough to sell so they could buy basic necessities they could not produce themselves and saved the rest of the grain for themselves—both to feed their families and to make vodka.

After Lenin's death, Stalin slowly consolidated his power and made sure to present himself as the true heir to Lenin. He wanted to justify completing the socialist revolution by destroying the last vestiges of the "bourgeoisie" in the countryside and achieving the classless society Marx had predicted. Joseph Stalin was born as Joseph Dzhugashvili in 1878 in the Caucuses mountains of Georgia. He took on the name "Stalin" meaning "man of steel" as a young communist revolutionary, though he first operated under the code name "Koba," a heroic Robin Hood-type character in a popular novel of the time. This might have been a more apt name, as Stalin first came to Lenin's attention after a series of spectacular bank and stagecoach robberies. The Tsarist secret police kept close tabs on him and sent him into exile a half-dozen times. Around the turn of the twentieth century, he joined the Russian Social-Democratic Labor Party, and when that party split into two, he aligned himself with Lenin's smaller, more radical faction, the Bolsheviks. Unswervingly loyal to Lenin, Stalin took on numerous organizational and administrative tasks that no one else wanted. Eventually named General Secretary, he controlled the personnel assignments, promotions, and postings of party members and was able to build up a network of supporters. Most important of all, however, was his ability to place subordinates in the lower levels of the party apparatus, which ensured the election of Stalin's loyalists to the Party Congresses. These Party Congresses—suspended once Stalin consolidated his power—in turn elected the Central Committee, which then elected the ruling Political Bureau or "Politburo" in what the American political scientist Robert Tucker described as the "circular flow of power" (Tucker 1990).

To accomplish the "world-historical" task of completing the socialist revolution Stalin needed to undo two different policies instituted under Lenin while convincing party members that he was in fact following the true Leninist path. To socialize agriculture Stalin would have to force the peasantry into giant, state owned collective farms. Then the peasants would become merely workers in the countryside. This would mean ending Lenin's New Economic Policy. By 1927, the result of the peasants cutting back on the acreage they tilled was a severe shortage of food in the cities. There the supposedly favored workers labored in factories and were rationed their food. Stalin faced pressure from these workers to deliver on the promises made at the time of the revolution. Many workers wondered what they had fought for in overthrowing the old regime and fighting in the civil war. Stalin could not afford to lose this base of support for the socialist state so the grain would have to be seized from—and squeezed out of— the peasantry. This would provide food supplies for the working class and the Soviets would sell the "surplus" grain abroad to finance Stalin's plan of rapid industrialization. After the Great Depression began in 1929 world grain prices decreased while that of equipment rose, meaning that the Soviets needed to sell even more grain to finance their industrial development. Much of this grain was in the "breadbasket" of the Soviet

Union—Ukraine. Resistance to "collectivization," there was strong, but Stalin was determined to root out the internal "capitalist" threat that was holding up the revolution by socializing agriculture. To accomplish this he would need to break down peasant cohesion and destroy the traditional village leadership. In so doing, as Lemkin wrote, the Soviets would be pursuing a process "of genocide, of destruction, not of individuals only, but of a culture and a nation" (quoted in Luciuk ed. 2008).

To create this new "Soviet national unity" the "complete destruction of all cultures and of all ideas save one—the Soviet" would be required (ibid.) To accomplish this a brutal assault on *all* the social, political, and cultural institutions of the Ukrainians would be needed. We have already discussed Stalin's later ethnic cleansings of many minority peoples, uprooting them from their homelands and in so doing destroying their social and cultural connections. There were far too many Ukrainians to remove them wholesale, but Stalin could destroy them as a people by first murdering their artists, writers, intellectuals, and priests, and then finishing off the peasantry's former ways of life by forcing them into collective farms. Taken together, his calculated efforts to destroy Ukrainians' social and cultural ties in the name of creating an altogether different society amounted to genocide. In fact, Raphael Lemkin called the destruction of the Ukrainian nation "the classic example of Soviet genocide, its longest and broadest experiment in Russification" (ibid.). As discussed in our Introduction, the current situation in Ukraine is also quite possibly part of an ongoing genocide by the Russians.

Ukrainians, like Russians, are an Eastern Slavic people. They both share a common Orthodox Christian religion and have a similar language. The first Slavic state, with Kyiv ("Kiev" in Russian) as its capital, was located in what is now Ukraine. This impressive and vibrant trading state existed from the ninth through the twelfth centuries CE. Through its broad system of rivers, it connected Europe with Constantinople, the capital of the Byzantine Empire, and a terminal point of trade with Asia. Russians used to claim "Kiev" as the "mother of Russian cities" and pointed to "Kievan" Rus' as the first Russian state; Ukrainians, of course, have always disagreed, although they also trace their lineage as a distinct people back to that time. They are both wrong. What is undisputed is that it was the world's first *Slavic* state. Ukrainians only developed as a people centuries after the dissolution of "Kyivan" Rus.' This mighty state disintegrated because of various factors such as the decline of the Byzantine Empire and subsequent change in trade routes, internal dissension, and, finally, the impact of the Mongols. Being heavily influenced and at times absorbed much later into the Polish-Lithuanian Commonwealth had a huge impact on these Slavs and on the development of a unique Ukrainian culture. They *are* a "people," a "family of mind," separate, unique, and distinct from the Russians.

Russia has, however, dominated Ukraine for centuries. The rise of the Muscovite Grand Dukes saw them proclaim their inheritance of the rich traditions of Rus,' including, most importantly, the Orthodox religion. The Russians controlled Ukraine from the middle of the seventeenth century except for a short-lived independent state that arose after the fall of Imperial Russia in 1917. The Russians then conquered and reabsorbed Ukraine into what would become the Soviet Union in 1921. The collapse of that empire—which is what it really was—in 1991 finally allowed the Ukrainian people the possibility of charting their own future free of Russian interference. If only. Russians have always seen Ukraine as being part of their empire. The very word "Ukraine" means periphery or frontier in the Slavic tongue. Ukrainians rightly bristle when foreigners say "*the* Ukraine"—despite there being no definite article in either Russia or Ukrainian—as it then identifies their land as merely being the outermost appendage of Russia. Russians themselves often contemptuously referred to Ukrainians as "*malorusy,*" or "little Russians." Vladimir Putin went so far as to tell US President George W. Bush that "Ukraine is not a real country." Putin and many other Russians still consider Ukraine part of the "Russian world," an ethno-religious concept based on the idea that Ukraine, Russia, and Belarus all share a common history, religion, and cultural inheritance from Kievan (Kyivan) times. Crucially, Grand Prince Vladimir (Volodymyr in Ukrainian), the ruler of Kyivan Rus' who reigned from 980 to 1015 CE, received his baptism into Orthodox Christianity in Crimea. In 2016, two years after Russia seized Crimea from Ukraine, Putin had a statue of Vladimir erected in front of the Kremlin in Moscow to celebrate the "return" of Crimea to Russia. The Ukrainians had erected their own 50-foot-high monument to Volodomyr in Kyiv in 1853; Putin's statue was, of course, a few feet taller.

In a rambling, paranoid historical treatise released on the Kremlin website in the summer of 2021, Vladimir Putin bemoaned "the wall that emerged in recent years between Russia and Ukraine, between the parts of what is essentially the same historical and spiritual space [...]." He insisted that the "close cultural, spiritual and economic ties" and "commonality of *our* people" had been ruined by Ukraine's "ruling circles" who in Putin's view, began "to rewrite history, edit out everything that united us and refer to the period when Ukraine was part of the Russian Empire and Soviet Union as an occupation." Putin was especially angry that "the common tragedy of collectivization and famine of the early 1930s is portrayed as the genocide of the Ukrainian people." He believes that Ukraine has been reduced to a puppet state "under the power and control of the Western powers" that, as part of an "anti-Russia project," is a "knife at Russia's throat" ("On the Historical Unity of Russians and Ukrainians," July 12, 2021). In February 2022, Putin launched a full-scale invasion of Ukraine and, with the help of the Russian Orthodox Church, convinced most Russians that they were in an existential fight for the traditional values of Russia against the hedonism, materialism, and "gender freedoms" of a decadent West that wishes to destroy Russia. Like Putin, Stalin also saw "the West" as an implacable foe; Stalin's attempt to destroy the Ukrainian people was an integral part of a campaign not only to force all of the Soviet Union's peoples into a common social and cultural straightjacket but also to industrialize a backward Soviet Union which needed to defend itself from the enemies that surrounded it. In his view, very much like Putin's, Russia faced a constant danger of invasion by a hostile West. In 1931, he said that the socialist fatherland must "overtake and outstrip the advanced capitalist countries [...] either we do it, or we shall be crushed" (Stalin 1953, 458).

To seize power in the name of socialism Lenin had made all sorts of promises to exploit the massive unrest created by Russia's participation in World War I. He had not only promised the land to the peasants but "workers' control" of industrial policy and freedom of self-determination to the many nationalities that made up the

Russian Empire, including the Ukrainians. At its inception in 1922, after reabsorbing much of tsarist Russia's earlier conquests, the Union of Soviet Socialist Republics, the USSR—also known as the Soviet Union—was composed of 15 union republics, with each one representing a particular ethnic group. Lenin's policy of *korenizatsiya*—"indigenization"—allowed for the integration of non-Russian nationalities into the governments of "their" union republics and the development of their own cultures, including the use of their native tongue, as long as politically they followed the formula of "nationalist in form, socialist in content." This approach permitted the preservation of the ways of life and culture of a people so long as they supported the new socialist regime's goals. This supposedly would satisfy their longings and aspirations for cultural autonomy. Alongside the NEP, Lenin hoped this would grant the increasingly unpopular Communists a breathing space so they could retain power until the supposed benefits of socialism became more apparent to the masses. Many Ukrainian elites were appointed to government positions and the teaching of the Ukrainian language was permitted, as well as the further development of a Ukrainian culture that was separate and distinct from the Russian or Soviet one (Applebaum 2017, 108).

This policy of "Ukrainization," combined with the brief experience of statehood after the revolution, however, only encouraged longings for an independent Ukraine. Stalin resolved to crush the reviving national feelings of Ukrainians by attacking the intelligentsia, what Lemkin called the "brain" of the Ukrainian people. In 1929, Stalin put an end to Lenin's policy of *korenizatsiya*, and clamped down on the intelligentsia's efforts to pursue "Ukrainization." Tsarist era processes of stamping out Ukraine's independent identity were resumed. The Soviet secret police rounded up anyone who might support the idea of Ukrainian independence (ibid., 117). They arrested tens of thousands of educated elites, including professors, artists, writers, linguists, lawyers, doctors, and so on, as well as engineers, scientists, and technical experts. After a series of "show" trials, in which the outcomes were obviously preordained and all of the defendants were found guilty, these unfortunates were sent into Siberian exile. Later, during the "Purges" discussed below, many of them would be executed. Lemkin asserts that in one year alone—1931—51,713 intellectuals were exiled. A recent careful study holds that most Ukrainian writers and a third of its teachers disappeared into prison camps in Siberia. (Malko 2021). Stalin and his henchmen then moved to destroy what Lemkin termed the "soul" of Ukraine—the clergy of the Ukrainian Orthodox Church. He claims 10,000 priests and bishops were "liquidated" at this time and the church itself was absorbed into the Russian Orthodox Church.

In all the phony trials of the Ukrainian intellectuals, technical specialists, and churchmen, the Soviet press trumpeted the "counter-revolutionary activities" of these "bourgeois-nationalists." To rigid, Stalin-influenced "Marxists," both religion and nationalism were simply tools of the oppressors to hoodwink the laboring masses. These were both dangerous ideologies, and therefore Stalin took an active interest in the trials. He sent detailed instructions to his officials overseeing them. In one memorandum, he claimed that doctors were up to "medical tricks, the goal of which was the murder of responsible workers." (Quoted in Applebaum 2017, 119). Applebaum observes that this pretext would later be used again in the so-called Doctors' Plot, the antisemitic campaign unleashed in Stalin's dying days. What Stalin truly feared, however, was a popular revolt against Soviet power. The Communists, who had themselves come to power as a result of massive popular discontent led by committed idealists, feared that the Ukrainian intelligentsia and the peasantry would join forces and overthrow them in turn. As early as 1925, Stalin had noted that "there is no powerful national army without the peasant army" and the Ukrainian nationalist movement had a "profoundly popular and profoundly revolutionary character" [...] (quoted in ibid., 122). The secret police were acutely aware of the discontent brewing in the countryside ever since the state lowered the price paid to the peasants for their grain, and therefore they kept close watch on them. Their reports back to Moscow "confirmed" what Stalin wanted to hear—the rural bourgeois capitalist kulaks were leading their own "anti-Soviet movements" and trying to link up with the "urban anti-Soviet intelligentsia." To the Soviets, both the "urban bourgeois nationalists" in the cities and the "rural bourgeois peasants," as capitalists, were deadly political enemies of the workers' state.

Dekulakization

The Soviet press described the *"kulaks"* as "swine," "dogs," "vermin," "cockroaches," "filth" and "garbage," calling for the countryside to be "totally cleansed of them." Norman Naimark, who, like the authors of this book, considers the Communist onslaught on the Ukrainian peasantry to be genocide, describes how the regime exiled entire families and that even the children of these *kulaks* would always be marked as such. Because the *kulaks* were "dehumanized and racialized into beings inherently inferior to others [...]," he draws obvious comparisons with other genocides throughout the twentieth century (Naimark 2010, 59). Soviet slogans such as "we will exile the *kulak* by the thousands and when necessary—shoot the *kulak* breed" were translated into practice as some two million peasants were exiled to Siberia, where at least 500,000 would perish, while some 30,000 were "immediately eliminated" (ibid., 57). Those labeled as *kulaks* and thus liable to be subjected to violence, dispossession and deportation could, besides being considered wealthy peasants, simply be outspoken Red Army veterans, priests and other church people, tradesmen, or other village notables (Viola 1996, 6).

The Soviets sent these "special settlers" into the inhospitable wilderness of the northern Russian forests, Siberia and Kazakhstan. Millions of other political "enemies of the people" would follow later. These special settlements marked the beginning of the *Gulag*—a Russian language acronym for "Main Administration of Camps." Stalin's call to "eliminate the *kulaks* as a class," however, did not mean they were to be wholly annihilated. G. Yagoda, the head of the secret police until his own purging and downfall in 1937, ultimately wanted to establish "colonization villages" to "provide a permanent labor force in forestry, mining and other industries in remote territories" [...] in order to ensure the maximum extraction of the Soviet Union's vast mineral and natural resources" (ibid., 4). This "maximum extraction" required forced labor as Stalin wanted to create the same type of modern industrial society as those that flourished in the West. Stalin, however, demanded that this be achieved in the space of a "Five Year

Plan"—that was soon shortened to the "Five Year Plan in Four Years"—whereas in the West it had literally taken centuries.

Stalin knew perfectly well that excessive brutality would be required for this gargantuan undertaking, but he was blithely indifferent to the human misery he would unleash. As with other Russian reformers, from Peter the Great to Alexander II, and, in the 1980s Mikhail Gorbachev, Stalin envied the industrial, technical, and scientific advances made by the West and wanted to catch up and even overtake them. Stalin did, however, correctly identify the sources from which the West had been able to achieve its prosperity and power. He noted, perhaps plagiarizing from Marx or Lenin, as he was wont to do, "In capitalist countries industrialization was usually based not only on internal accumulation but also on the plundering of other countries, the plundering of colonies or vanquished lands [...] for hundreds of years England used to drain all its colonies, from every continent, and in this way injected additional investments into its industry." Although the Soviet Union was in fact an empire and held many peoples in servitude, Stalin flatly declared the Soviet Union "cannot and must not engage in the plundering of colonies or the plundering of other countries in general [...] therefore this path is closed to us." Stalin went on to say that for the capitalist countries, there was also the possibility of substantial loans, "but this path is closed to us as well." The only way forward, which would be "unpleasant," would be to impose a "tribute" on the peasantry (quoted in Viola 1996, 15). In other words, the countryside would become the internal colony of the Soviet Union for the sake of industrial development and the creation of a new "Soviet Man." This obliteration of the Ukrainian peasantry's "ways of life" and imposition of Soviet "patterns" upon them was, along with the Nazis' racial-biological demographic reordering of Europe, Lemkin's classic definition of genocide.

The *kulaks* were the first to feel the blow of the Soviet hammer, but this was not a war between a rural "proletariat" and a rural "bourgeoisie." In Ukraine, it was a war both on the peasantry's way of life and on the aspirations of the Ukrainian people for nationhood. Stalin used the pseudo-Marxism invented by Lenin and others to justify his actions to undermine the Ukrainian people's sense of identity. As late as the end of 1933, after millions had been deliberately starved to death—we will cover this in the next chapter—the head of the Communist Party in Ukraine, Stanislav Kosior, warned, "at the present moment, local Ukrainian nationalism poses the main danger to the revolution" (Luciuk 2008). The Communists had destroyed the Ukrainian intelligentsia and it was now time to strike the "bourgeois" *kulaks*. After confiscating all their possessions and farm animals, Communist officials forced them out of their homes and put them on freight trains to a frozen hell. When they arrived at their destinations weeks later, they were simply dumped in the middle of the wilderness. Told to build their own houses, thousands perished within days from hunger and cold. None of the "special settlements" had the necessary food, supplies, or tools available. Officials and police assigned to oversee these camps often stole anything they could lay their hands on for their own use or profit. As a result, starvation and disease were widespread. Dreadful as it is to contemplate, there were many cases of cannibalism as extreme desperation set in. At least half a million people died setting up what would become Stalin's vast economic empire based on forced labor.

Figure 5.2 Anti-kulak propaganda, 1930, depicting the so-called kulak as an obese exploiter, being driven from the collective farms by the fist of a righteous peasant. In the upper-right corner is a harsh comment made a few years earlier by Lenin, denouncing the kulaks as "brutal" agents of the "landowners, kings, priests, and capitalists." https://en.wikipedia.org/wiki/Dekulakization#/media/File:Away_With_Private_Peasants!_(3273571261).jpg

As we will see in the next chapter, "Genocides of Social Groups," the campaign against the *kulaks* was merely the first phase of an assault on the entire peasantry's way of life wherever they lived in the Soviet Union. This was part of the plan, as Lemkin wrote, "of bringing unity out of the diversity of cultures and nations that constitute the Soviet Empire." This unity was being created "not by a union of ideas and of cultures, but by the complete destruction of all ideas and of all cultures save one—the Soviet" (quoted in Luciuk ed. 2008). The peasantry, considered "backward" with a low level of culture, would have to be "civilized." We see here the essence of Lemkin's concept of genocide—the colonization that is inherent in a process that consists of "two phases: one, the destruction of the national pattern of the oppressed group the other, the imposition of the national pattern of the oppressor" (Lemkin 2008, 79). This was not a "politicide" or—as some have called it in the case of the peasantry as a whole—a "classicide." Better to call it by its correct name: it was genocide, too (Figure 5.2).

Stalin's "Great Purge"

Stalin's determination to crush any resistance to the new regime was similar to that of the French Revolutionaries' attack on the people of the Vendee region. The French Revolution of July 1789 overturned the monarch, Louis XIV, inspired revolutionary-democratic movements throughout the world and gravely rattled the confidence of the ruling aristocracies and monarchs in Europe and beyond. It was perhaps the first truly "modern" revolution in Europe and created a template for other revolutions to follow. The example of the French Revolution loomed large in the minds of the Communists, who were especially haunted by the specter of "counter-revolution." In the conservative Vendee region of western France, the population remained loyal to King Louis XIV and was particularly incensed at the attacks made upon their religious beliefs and institutions by the secular state that had followed the overthrow of the monarchy in 1789. The sparks that set off the violence were the execution of the King in January 1793 and a massive conscription drive by the new Republic to fend off the counter-revolution. The Vendeans quickly put together a Catholic and Royalist army. Trained and put into the field against the revolutionaries, they strung together a series of decisive military victories. This was embarrassing to the ruling body of the Revolution, the Committee of Public Safety, which authorized a vicious and savage retaliation to crush the inhabitants of the region. The Committee authorized the extermination of the entire populace, whether soldiers or civilians, as they were "race of brigands," or bandits. Men, women, and children were all liable to be annihilated, especially the women—whom the Committee blamed for "goading the men [...] into martyrdom"—and the children "who were [just as] dangerous as adults, because they were or were in the process of becoming brigands" (quoted in Jones 2017, 6–7). Approximately 150,000 people perished in the years-long assault, which fits any definition of genocide.

At the same time, the Committee unleashed "the Terror" on its political enemies. Condemned to death, 15,000–20,000 were beheaded by the guillotine, the grisly contraption associated with the worst excesses of the French Revolution that takes its name from Dr. Joseph-Ignace Guillotin, and that supposedly was more humane than hanging. All classes of people could be identified as "enemies of the people" and executed, but of most interest to scholars is how the Revolution began "eating its own children" and sending former leaders off to their deaths. In a shocking development, the Committee of Public Safety first condemned to death the leaders of a faction that had advocated a more radical policy of terror and even more far-reaching changes in French society, and then less than two weeks later ordered the execution of the leaders of a more moderate faction that advocated the opposite. There was only one "correct" policy and any deviation invited the possibility of the death penalty. This would prove to be the case also with Stalin's murder of his own Communist colleagues—and these unpredictable zig-zags in policy would also characterize Stalin's Russia. Here too, there could be only one "correct" party line—even though it might change without warning—and those accused of deviating as being either "Left" Oppositionists or "Right" Oppositionists would pay with their lives. Defense of the Revolution, against its genuine opponents and the monarchists who sought to regain power, quickly degenerated into an unending and indiscriminate search for "counter-revolutionaries" among anybody who criticized the regime, first in revolutionary France and later in Soviet Russia.

When Lenin died in 1924, Stalin had allied himself with two other Politburo members, Grigory Zinoviev and Lev Kamenev, both long-time supporters of Lenin, against Leon Trotsky—a relative newcomer to the Bolshevik faction but a leader in both the revolutionary unrest of 1905 and the 1917 revolution. Trotsky was a man of enormous talents who had commanded the victorious Red Army during the Russian Civil War (1918–21) and many Communists saw him as being on an almost equal footing with Lenin. Popular among the party rank and file, he had also made many enemies, including Stalin. While much more nimble and nuanced in his application of Marxism than Stalin or anyone else in the party leadership, Trotsky could be rigid and doctrinaire, believing that the world was ready for a workers' revolution and calling for a maximum effort to achieve socialism throughout Europe. Trotsky called for a continuation of the policy of "War Communism," that is the seizing of all grain from the peasantry to feed the army and workers who would secure the gains of the revolution. As we have seen, however, Lenin was more politically astute and backed off of this maximalist approach as he recognized the dangers of peasant anger.

In the aftermath of Lenin's death, however, Trotsky's demands simply to once again seize the grain from the peasantry would mean putting an end to the policy instituted at the Congress by the now venerated Lenin. By this time Lenin had been placed in a glass case in a mausoleum on Red Square—where he remains to this day. Although Stalin would eventually adopt Trotsky's tactics to ensure "Socialism in One Country"—which Trotsky thought was theoretical nonsense, as socialism could not possibly exist in a hostile capitalist world—Stalin used the ensuing debate over whether to continue the NEP to identify "oppositionists" to the "party line" decreed by Lenin. Trotsky had missed Lenin's funeral—Stalin deliberately scheduled it so Trotsky could not return in time from a duck-hunting trip—but Stalin delivered a powerful eulogy promising to follow Lenin's path in the future. When Trotsky did return, Stalin allied himself with those members of the leadership who were opposed to Trotsky assuming the leadership of the Party by criticizing him for his continued advocacy of ending Lenin's policy of conciliating the peasantry and instead rapidly industrializing the Soviet Union.

Accused of going against the Party Line and Lenin's wishes, the Politburo removed Trotsky as Commissar of War. Soon thereafter, however, it became clear to some of the other Politburo members that Stalin was simply using this policy as a pretext to consolidate his own personal power and they struck an alliance with their former enemy. Together, they now called for an end to the New Economic Policy. Stalin immediately labeled them as being "Left" Oppositionists. He pointed out that in calling for a full-scale assault on the peasantry not only the "bourgeois" *kulak* peasants would be crushed so would the allies of the workers, the "poor" peasants. This was, of course, unacceptable and supposedly against Lenin's last wishes—and Lenin had in fact called for a long period of patient education and acculturation of the entire peasantry to the ideals of Marxian socialism. Stalin seized on the plank against "Opposition" within the Party ranks after a decision had been reached (the idea of so-called "democratic centralism") and used it to begin eliminating his political opponents.

"Purges" of Party membership had been conducted fairly regularly in the past, where the members were instructed to turn in their Party cards and left to hope they would pass through the somewhat perfunctory "filtration" process and eventually get their Party cards (and their privileges) returned to them. In 1936, however, that process became deadlier. Many "oppositionists" associated with Trotsky's platform were booted from the

Party ranks, though eventually, some were able to crawl back for a time. Others were not so fortunate. Arrested, tortured, and made to confess to obviously absurd and fantastical crimes, those who were exiled to the *GULAG* and not simply shot in the back of the head considered themselves lucky. They were, as we shall see, often only spared for the moment. Trotsky himself fled abroad into exile to Mexico and died there in 1940 from an icepick to the head. In a remarkably cynical political move, Stalin now turned on those who had supported him against the "Left Opposition." These men Stalin now labeled as being the "Right" Opposition. Their "deviation" was that in supporting the NEP they also supported the enrichment of the "bourgeois" *kulaks* at the expense of the "poor" peasants.

Only Stalin followed the true "Leninist" path, the *kulaks* would be destroyed, but the "poor" peasantry would thrive. After first destroying the "Anti-Soviet Trotskyite Bloc" Stalin turned on the "Anti-Soviet Right Trotskyite Bloc" and eliminated them as well. The "purge"—in Russian called *chistka* or "cleansing"—then encompassed other government officials and regional party bosses. Stalin was determined to smash not only the political opposition to his rule within the party but all "Anti-Soviet elements" such as *kulaks* and Ukrainian "nationalists"—most of whom had already been "resettled" in Siberia or sent into the *GULAG*—and other persons deemed as "asocial." Stalin wanted "the direct physical liquidation of the entire counter-revolution" and the elimination of any possible threat to Soviet power "once and for all" (Snyder 2010, 81).

These individuals, often charged with "wrecking," sabotage, or conspiring with foreign powers, represented potential—and sometimes real—threats to Stalin's power. Those "enemies of the people" that had already been tried and sent to Siberia were not safe there as both *kulaks* and political prisoners were taken from the camps and shot in accordance with Stalin's Order no. 00447 of July 31, 1937 (Snyder 2010). The purge widened in scope to include heads of industry, technical specialists, and engineers who failed to meet arbitrary production quotas. The regime even set arrest quotas and the secret police rounded up anyone that was deemed "asocial"—the Nazis had this same category as well—such as petty thieves, prostitutes, drunks, or juvenile delinquents in desperate attempts to meet and even exceed these goals. In the end, the secret police arrested at least another million "enemies of the people" who disappeared into the Gulag's labor camps. Millions more would eventually follow to provide the necessary labor for forced industrialization.

This resulted, at least according to the suspiciously detailed accounting of the Soviet secret police—in the execution of 681,692 people during the years 1937–38 (Haynes 2003, 214). Naimark rightly contends we should not accept these figures at face value. He quotes Alexander Yakovlev—head of a commission set up by Mikhail Gorbachev, the last Soviet leader, to investigate Stalin's crimes—as saying "These [secret police] figures are false. They do not take into account the number of people confined in the internal prisons of the NKVD, and they were jam-packed. They do not break down the mortality rates in camps of political prisoners [...]" (quoted in Naimark, Graziosi and Sysyn, eds. 110). There were undoubtedly many hundreds of thousands more victims of Stalin's terror, and "the number of dead does not in any way capture the bitter suffering and travails of those who survived dekulakization, the famine, the purges, and the terror" (ibid.).

It was Stalin's murderous purge of party members that consolidated his own power as his minions moved up in the party apparatus to replace the victims, thus closing the "circular flow of power." Most of the post-World War II Soviet leadership—down to 1985—consisted of his appointees who had been in the third rank of the regional administrations. Stalin, like Putin, certainly tried to create an image of a state surrounded by enemies without and traitors and saboteurs within, an image that while undoubtedly overdrawn, was not necessarily entirely without merit. This might have served to justify Stalin's harsh policies or excuse the failures of those policies—we see that again with Putin today. Of course, whether or not—or to what extent—the "victory of communism" or the role his own desire for personal power played is open to debate. These are, of course, but motives. The outcome was the wholesale slaughter of his perceived political enemies.

For our purposes, it is difficult to define what a political "group" might be. A party? A faction of a party? Those who come together to oppose a governmental policy or advocate change? It is equally impossible, however, to define precisely what makes up a national, racial, ethnic, or religious group as these are all socially constructed categories that are fluid and not necessarily permanent—in other words, what Lemkin had said when arguing against the inclusion of political groups. Religious groups that are attacked by genocidists can also be subjective—witness the bizarre definition of a Jew in Nazi Germany discussed in Chapter Three. What of non-believers or atheists supposedly lumped into a religious group by genocidists? Even given that any group exists objectively to some extent, the American political scientist Matthew Lippman has argued "Political groups, in particular, historically have been victimized and, like religious groups, are united by a common ideal and vision" (Lippman 1994, 75).

Stalin often referred to the "oppositionists" as "splitters" or "schismatics," in Russian the word *raskolniki*, has a religious connotation and Stalin had studied at a theological seminary. Gustav Wetter adds the idea that "communism incorporates a whole series of particular Christian doctrines in secular form" (Wetter 1958, 559). Religious groups are, of course, one of the four protected by the Convention. We have argued the destruction of *any* human group united as a "family of mind" by virtue of any common ideal or vision—be it religious, nationalist, socialist, communist, or whatever—is genocide. For example, Marxian socialists subscribe to Marx's theory of historical materialism to explain historical change. This theory holds that ideas and social institutions arise from economic relations. Thoughts or ideologies not based on objective material economic conditions are simply reflections of the political interests of those that hold economic power, according to the more simplistic or "vulgar" forms of Marxism, of which Stalinism is the most prominent and influential. Nationalism and religion would be but two examples. Marxian socialists and especially Communist political parties generally believe in the objective "laws of history" discovered by Marx and believe that humankind will continue to make progress toward a more perfect society on earth. Since such a wonderful vision has never yet been realized, it is as much a faith or belief as Christianity where the faithful await the Second Coming.

The exclusion of political parties from the 1948 Convention benefited *all* the victorious powers of World War II, whether it was the determined efforts of Britain and

France to root out resistance to their continued colonial rule, the Soviets' crushing of dissent in Eastern Europe, or the United States' war on the very idea of communism in Indonesia and Vietnam. In fact, according to Jeffrey Bachman, "In the latter case, the lack of protection for political groups [...] served to shield the United States from responsibility for genocide in Vietnam" (Bachman 2022, 55). Left-leaning political parties such as the Loyalists in Franco's Spain, the Communists in Indonesia in 1965, the Awami League separatists in East Pakistan, and the student radicals and organizers in Argentina—the "disappeared"—were all attacked for their beliefs the same as some religious groups and should therefore be, as Lemkin originally intended until political calculations necessitated otherwise, protected from group destruction.

Genocide in Spain

Like all civil wars, the one fought in Spain between 1936 and 1939 was exceptionally violent and brutal. In the early 1930s, Spain was one of the more progressive countries in Europe despite the heavy influence of the Catholic Church. Married couples could get a divorce and women could seek abortions. The Spanish Civil War pitted the left-leaning "Loyalists" who had won power in the recently established Republic's election against the right-wing "Nationalists" who were determined to overthrow this democratically elected government. Both sides were made up of many different political factions. The "Republicans" or "Loyalists" were composed of liberal advocates for democracy, socialists, and more radical leftists such as Communists as well as anarchists, who had a strong movement in Spain. The "Nationalists" included traditional conservatives, monarchists, and fascists. The Nationalist rebels, led by conservative military generals such as Francisco Franco, who would rule Spain until his death in 1975, and the Catholic Church, were adamantly opposed to the social reforms of the "godless Bolsheviks" of the left and openly called for their extermination. They wanted to roll back Spain's liberal social policies. Their vision of Spain's future was a restoration of its past as a traditional, Catholic country. This would include the subordination of women, discrimination against Jews, and the squelching of the Basque and Catalan peoples' yearning for autonomy or even independence from Spain—a desire that is still very strong today.

Mass political violence was carried out by both sides during the war. The more radical factions among the Loyalists killed at least 7,000 Catholic priests and nuns, whom they saw as political enemies and supporters of the rebels, and some historians estimate that they summarily executed between 38,000 (Beevor 2001) and 70,000 (Cueva 1998) persons, though most have settled on approximately 50,000 (Thomas 2012; Payne 2012). The Nationalists, however, led by General Francisco Franco, were far more murderous. According to Antony Beevor, they executed approximately 200,000 persons, including some 50,000 *after* the war was concluded (Beevor 2001; Preston 2012). Special efforts were made to identify and execute schoolteachers who were sympathetic to the Republic's effort to de-emphasize the Catholic Church's influence on educational matters, as well as left-wing political figures—who supposedly carried the "red gene" we discussed earlier. This *limpieza* ("cleansing") was a deliberate murder of the rebels' defeated political opponents, the same sort of political violence Latin

American revolutionary movements sometimes employed against their vanquished enemies that would convince Lemkin to drop "political" groups from the list of those to be protected by the Convention in order to secure its passage. The triumphant Franco regime immediately implemented the Catholic Church's teachings: it criminalized adultery, and outlawed divorce and abortion, as well as contraception. Women, who also lost the right to vote, were forced back into traditional gender roles and were even provided a homemaking schedule to follow.

The last of the acts of genocide that would be listed in the Convention less than a decade later was "forcibly transferring children of the group to another group." Of course, the omission of the important human collectivity of political groups from the protection of the Convention would have made this point moot; however, in Franco's Spain, the children of imprisoned Loyalists or those orphaned through the war's violence were taken away and put up for adoption by supporters of the regime. The idea here was to remove them from the baleful influence of socialism and bring them up as conservative Catholic Spaniards. It is impossible to know for sure how many children were stolen from their parents, but the program continued with the complicity of the Catholic Church for decades, with babies taken from the social group that the political group represented—the working poor. As we will discuss below, this policy was also implemented—again with the connivance of the Catholic Church—in Argentina during its "Dirty War" of 1976–83 when the military junta "disappeared" over 30,000 left-wing opponents of its regime.

Genocide of Indonesian Communists

The massacre of over half a million—and most probably many hundreds of thousands more—members of the Indonesian Communist Party (PKI) in less than six months between October 1965 and March 1966 was the single most concerted murder of a political group in history. The PKI operated openly and peacefully in the Indonesian political system and gained considerable support through its community outreach programs to the impoverished majority of the population. The other major political parties were the Nationalists (PNI) and the Islamists. All three parties had fought together against the Japanese invaders during World War II and then cooperated again against their former colonial overlords, the Dutch. Of course, they all had their own visions of Indonesia's future and they quickly ran into conflict with each other in the chaotic early years of the new nation until the strongman President Sukarno stepped in, suspended parliamentary rule, and imposed his own authoritarian vision of "Guided Democracy." This ideology combined all three of these visions for Indonesia's future into what he called NASOKOM—nationalism, religion (Islam, the religion of 90% of the population), and communism. Robert Cribb, the leading authority on this subject, saw this "as an attempt to construct a political order in which none of the [political] streams would prevail" (Cribb 2001, 226). Unfortunately, two of the three "streams" (the Nationalists and the Islamists) found a common cause in destroying the Communists and joined forces to do so. The Nationalists held sway over the military and the Islamists saw the army as the best hope for stopping the spread of godless communism (Figure 5.3).

GENOCIDES OF POLITICAL GROUPS 143

Figure 5.3 Statue in Jakarta, the capital of Indonesia, celebrating the anti-Communist genocidal massacres. The perpetrators and the Suharto dictatorship went beyond genocide-denial to "genocide-triumphalism": shamelessly celebrating their crimes. https://en.wikipedia.org/wiki/30_September_Movement#/media/File:Monumen_Pancasila_Sakti.jpg

Throughout the Cold War with the Soviet Union the United States backed any government, no matter how authoritarian and undemocratic, that promised to halt the spread of communism—and "communism" was interpreted very loosely. Any nationalistic, independent movement in the colonial or developing world could be deemed "communist" by US policy makers. Contrary to some accounts the United States was fully aware of the bloody massacres taking place throughout Indonesia and provided lists of communists to the genocidists—despite knowing that many of the victims were not necessarily PKI members—and even supplied communications equipment to facilitate those murders. The army provided weapons to paramilitaries and local militias and equipped and trained fundamentalist Muslim youth groups and then set them loose upon the unresisting Communists as well as any Chinese they came across. The victims were often simply hacked to death with swords while others were shot or beaten to death. US authorities kept a running tally of the dead. An Official Action Telegram from the consular official in Surabaya to the US Embassy in Jakarta noted that "we continue to receive reports PKI being slaughtered in many areas [...] [the] largest slaughter had taken place at Tulungagung where reportedly 15,000 Communists killed" and that there was the idea among Muslims that this was a "Holy War" and the " killing of Infidels supposedly gives ticket to heaven and if blood of victim rubbed on their face the path there is even more assured" (Telegram 41 from

Surabaya to State November 27, 1965, RG 59 Central Files). In a telegram to the State Department, the US ambassador to Indonesia approvingly noted how "the main problem being that of what to feed and where to house the prisoners. Many provinces appear to be successfully meeting this problem by executing their PKI prisoners [...] a task in which Moslem youth groups are providing assistance" (Air-gram A—353, No. 45, November 30, 1965).

Incredibly, these horrific atrocities were never discussed by the UN Security Council. Neither the *Index to Proceedings of the Security Council, twentieth year—1965* nor *twenty-first year—1966* show the genocide to be on the agenda. The reason for this glaring omission is that states eradicating their political opponents under the cover of crushing domestic unrest or engaging in civil war does not come under the UN Charter's mandate to "maintain international peace and security." Jeffrey Bachman correctly maintains that the Charter's Articles 2 (4) and 2 (7) prohibit either the threat or the use of force in violation of another state's sovereignty. While Chapters Six and Seven do allow for such intervention in the affairs of another state *if*, in the opinion of the UN Security Council—where the P-5 have the veto—such violence threatens "international peace and security," the cherished principle of state sovereignty, combined with the lack of protection for political groups combine to provide an excuse for the world's powers to abstain from intervening in the internal affairs of another state to prevent genocidal violence as "civil war" does not constitute a "threat to international peace and security." (Bachman 2022). This gap in the Convention was exploited by genocidists to commit appalling violence upon defenseless civilians not only in Indonesia but also in East Pakistan and Argentina.

Genocide in East Pakistan (Now Bangladesh)

The Cold War struggle between the United States and the Soviet Union had a huge impact on the final definition of the 1948 Convention. There were obvious consequences in the application of the Convention as a result. You will recall that the United States wished to keep protection for "political groups" in the Convention's definition in order to charge the Soviets with genocide; Stalin had frequently resorted to political murder and gave every indication he would continue to do so as he brought the recently acquired Eastern European satellite states to heel. Unsurprisingly, the Soviets did not agree. They did, however, see the usefulness of retaining the destruction of a people's culture in the definition as the Americans and their colonialist allies such as Britain and France could then conceivably be charged with genocide for their policies. Both of these aspects of Lemkin's concept were left out of the final definition in what was, at least by outward appearance, a straightforward political compromise. The lack of protection for political groups, combined with the UN's emphasis on maintaining *international* peace and security, allowed for the possibility of genocidists to hide behind the principle of non-intervention in the internal affairs of other countries by claiming they were fighting a civil war. This often gave them a free hand to massacre their political opponents. And, as we saw in the previous section, it also allowed the United States to covertly wage its ideological war against communism by proxy as it fully supported the

Indonesian military's successful campaign to utterly destroy the PKI. In East Pakistan (now Bangladesh) just a half-dozen years later the United States, Russia, and China all supported their allies in the larger geopolitical Cold War and pursued their own political agendas.

When the British finally saw the writing on the wall and "quit India" after World War II—though holding on like grim death in Cyprus and Kenya—the country was partitioned largely along religious lines, with the Muslim-majority areas of India becoming East and West Pakistan. The process of "population transfer" whereby Hindus moved to India and Muslims to Pakistan was a horrific, bloody mess with over a million people dying in communal violence, sparking Muslim-Hindu antipathy which ethno-nationalists such as Narendra Modi, the right-wing prime minister of India since 2014, continue to exploit today to attain their own political ends. "Pakistan," is derived from the Urdu word for "pure" and therefore means "land of the pure," but this emphasis on the Urdu language immediately caused consternation among the Bengali people of East Pakistan and it wasn't until the promulgation of Pakistan's constitution in 1956 that Bengali was elevated to the status of an official language on par with Urdu. Behind the veneer of electoral democracy, however, Pakistan was in reality ruled by "unelected civil-military bureaucratic elites from West Pakistan" who acted "like colonial masters toward the Bengalis in East Pakistan" (Jahan 1972, 251). For over two decades, the Bengalis of East Pakistan felt slighted as their language and culture were looked down upon and, despite comprising the majority of Pakistan's population (54 percent) and contributing heavily to the nation's economy, the Bengalis were effectively denied any real share in political governance (Jahan 2009).

Though both East and West Pakistan were Muslim, the "Pakistani ruling elite looked upon Bengali language and culture as too "Hindu-leaning" and made repeated attempts to "cleanse" it from Hindu influence" (Jahan 2009, 298). These efforts sparked a Bengali nationalist movement that first sought at least a share in Pakistan's governance and when rebuffed, demanded autonomy. A military coup took control of Pakistan in 1958 out of fear that the Bengalis might win in the first national election, which was postponed until the fall of that dictatorship. In 1970, the first truly democratic election in Pakistan was held and the Awami League—the Bengali nationalist party—won an absolute majority. This gave them the right not only to govern East Pakistan but the entire country as well. Once again the military stepped in and postponed the scheduled sitting of the new parliament, throwing the entire country into crisis. The army flew in thousands of troops from West to East Pakistan and began a campaign of murder, rape, and terror supposedly meant to eliminate the Awami League political group, but also to destroy the Bengali's social cohesion through—as we saw in the previous chapter—a systematic policy of rape and murder, as well as driving out of Pakistan ten million Hindu citizens.

The Pakistani military hoped to terrorize the Bengali population into submission and atomize it so it could no longer pose a threat to their vision of what an Islamic state should look like. At a press conference in February 1971, the President of Pakistan, Yahya Khan, called for a genocide when he declared, "Kill three million of them, and the rest will eat out of our hands" (Payne 1973, 50). The general in charge planned on killing up to four million Bengalis and thus achieve—in his words—a "Final Solution" to the Bengali problem (Jahan 1972). The horror unleashed in East Pakistan by their own army over the ensuing eight and one-half months would in fact result in the mass killing of at least two, and possibly up to three million Bengalis—a rate of killing that made it, along with the mass deaths of Soviet POWs, the Holocaust and Rwanda, the most concentrated act of killing in the twentieth century.

The United States, eager for better relations with Communist China in order to play it off against the Soviet Union, supported China's framing of the conflict in East Pakistan as being an internal domestic matter. Archer Blood, the US Consul General in Dacca, stated the obvious when in a cable he called it a "selective genocide" as the Pakistani military was "systematically eliminating" Awami League supporters "by seeking them out in their houses and shooting them down" (quoted in Bachman 2022, 98). He complained that the United States had "chosen not to intervene, even morally, on the grounds that the Awami conflict, in which unfortunately the overworked term genocide is applicable, is purely an internal matter of a sovereign state' (ibid.). Incredibly, the UN Charter's mandate to safeguard *international* peace and security prevented the Security Council from taking any action. As the Pakistani permanent representative to the UN put it "The nature of Pakistan's internal crisis is outside the Security Council's concern [...] The Security Council is concerned with international peace, not with the internal peace and political life of a Member State" (quoted in ibid., 99).

Incredibly, the UN Security Council did not meet to discuss the genocide until fully eight months of rape, murder, and torture had been inflicted on the people of East Pakistan. Even then it only met as a consequence of India's invasion of East Pakistan, thus making it a matter of international peace and security. In a series of meetings, the UN Security Council (UNSC) met to debate what action should be taken to address "the recent deteriorating situation which has led to armed clashes between India and Pakistan" (quoted in ibid., 98). The United States and China called for India to remove its troops from East Pakistan, while the Soviet Union justified its ally's action on the grounds that nearly ten million refugees had spilled over into India, thus making it a matter of international concern. The Soviet Union also correctly identified the source of this conflict as being the refusal of Pakistan to respect the results of the 1970 election. India, for its part, accused the United States and China of attempting to depict the conflict as being one between India and Pakistan when in fact it was a genocide being perpetrated by a state upon its own citizens. The Soviet Union supported India's repeated assertions that genocide was being committed in East Pakistan. Bachman notes that the Soviet Union, during the negotiations over the 1948 Convention, had consistently advocated that *all* possible cases of genocide be referred to the Security Council. He contends that the failure to "internationalize" the language of the Convention, combined both with the UN Charter's mandate that it safeguard *international* peace and security, and the oft-noted omission of protection for political groups, has permitted genocidists to act with what he describes as "impunity" to eliminate its political opponents. The authors agree with this assessment.

The "Disappeared" in Argentina

The United States has a long history of interfering with the internal affairs of the countries of Latin America. During the Cold War, this interference intensified and included not only support for authoritarian regimes but also the overthrowing of democratically elected leaders and replacing them with repressive ones—all in the name of fighting "Communism." In 1954, the Central Intelligence Agency (CIA) organized a coup in Guatemala that overthrew the legitimately elected Jacobo Arbenz Guzman and replaced him with a right-wing government, a genocidal military dictatorship, which remained in power for 35 years. In 1973, just three years after the people of Chile elected the popular, progressive, socialist Salvador Allende as President, the CIA engineered another coup that resulted in his death and the installation of a military junta. During the 1980s, the US under President Ronald Reagan sent hundreds of millions of dollars to support these and other military dictatorships in the region. The death toll during his eight years as US President was well over 100,000 persons, including 70,000 political murders of "leftists" in El Salvador, 20,000 more at the hands of the "contras" (counter-revolutionary terrorist militias) in Nicaragua, and tens of thousands of simple Mayan villagers during General Rios-Montt's murderous campaign against them from 1982 to 1983 in Guatemala. In Argentina, from 1976 to 1983 approximately 30,000 persons designated as state enemies due to their being "leftists," or "socialists," or being members of social justice organizations simply "disappeared"—usually arrested, tortured, and murdered.

The United States funded and supported numerous political coups throughout the region as part of the CIA's "Operation Condor." In 1976, the United States backed the Argentine military's coup against Isabel Peron, the widow of the populist president Juan Peron. Led by General Jorge Rafael Videla, the military declared its intention to stamp out social unrest by any means necessary in a "National Reorganization Process." Over the next half-dozen years the army carried out a war against its own citizens. People were arrested, tortured daily in detention camps with electric shocks and by waterboarding, and then killed. Often they were drugged, flown far out to sea in aircraft on so-called "death flights" and thrown out to drown. Women were routinely raped, and if arrested while pregnant kept alive until they delivered their babies and only then killed. At least 500 babies were taken and given to "deserving" families—that is, conservative and Catholic families, in a practice similar to that in Spain. No records of these "disappeared" were kept, but their mothers began a series of protests that attracted international attention. These "Mothers of the Plaza de Mayo" demonstrated weekly, demanding that their children be returned to them alive. The government stonewalled them, but the official silence about the fate of the "disappeared" only enraged Argentine society. Newspapers published accounts about the torture sessions in the detention camps, and mass graves were unearthed throughout the country. After the military-led government blundered into a war with Great Britain over the Malvinas (also known as the Falkland) Islands in a desperate attempt to use nationalism to gain support for the regime, free elections were finally held again in 1983 and the civilian government of President Raul Alfonsin was sworn in. Eventually, the junta members

Figure 5.4 1982 March organized by the "Madres de Plaza de Mayo" (Mothers of the Plaza de Mayo, a central square in Buenos Aires). "In a time when 'forgetting' was mandated," wrote the great Uruguayan author Eduardo Galeano, "they refused." https://commons.wikimedia.org/wiki/File:2%C2%AA_Marcha_de_la_Resistencia_9_y_10_diciembre_1982.jpg

were put on trial for their crimes, and a commission was established to investigate the details of the "National Reorganization Process" It did not go smoothly as the army refused to cooperate, but eventually a report was published that cataloged 8,960 "disappearances" but the actual figure is much higher, possibly up to 30,000. Today, the mothers of women who disappeared while pregnant and had their babies taken from them are still demonstrating as "Grandmothers of the Plaza de Mayo" (Figure 5.4).

Conclusion

This chapter explored the consequences of leaving out an entire human collectivity from the protection of the 1948 Convention. Not only were political groups physically destroyed, but children of the groups were often forcibly transferred to other groups. In the previous chapter, we examined efforts to destroy groups that *were* protected not only through physical destruction but also through calculated campaigns of forced impregnation designed to destroy the social connections of the targeted community—something not necessarily covered in the Convention. Even if protected, we have learned that the UN Charter has sometimes prevented the rendering of assistance to those groups. We have also seen the large-scale forcible deportations of peoples and the enforced disappearance of persons. None of these crimes are covered by the 1948 Convention. The question therefore must be posed, what good is the Convention on the Prevention and Punishment of the Crime of Genocide if it only rarely does either of those two things? To be sure, all of the offenses listed above are heinous Crimes against Humanity and offenders can be charged under that category. It is our contention that all these crimes are, in fact, also genocidal and should be considered as such.

Questions for Further Discussion

1. Why were "political groups" left out of the 1948 UN Genocide Convention?
2. If "ethnicity" is defined as being the cultural practices, customs, and traditions that are learned and shared by a group of people, might "ethnocide" have been a better term for the destruction of different human groups?
3. Raphael Lemkin originally included political groups in his definition. Since political affiliation is also learned and its adherents are united by common ideals and understandings of human purpose in life, should political groups also be included in *genos* and protected from *cide* by opposing political groups in power?
4. How did Stalin make use of Marxist-Leninist theory (or, his version of it) to justify his genocidal policies?
5. How does the exclusion of political groups from the 1948 Convention combine with the principle of state sovereignty to give cover to genocidists?

Chapter Six

GENOCIDES OF SOCIAL GROUPS

That is why we have recently passed from the policy of **restricting** *the exploiting tendencies of the kulaks to the policy of* **eliminating the kulaks as a class**. *(emphases in the original)*

—Joseph Stalin, 1929

"Classicide"

Readers of this book are by now aware that there are but four protected groups in the 1948 UN Genocide Convention—racial, national, ethnic, and religious. In the previous chapter, we looked at the idea of "politicide" and determined that political groups should also be included as a protected group or identity because of their similarity to religious ones. Both of those human collectivities, cemented by common ideals and visions, have extensive social and cultural connections among their members, and each can change substantially over an individual's lifetime. Individuals in other protected groups—such as the modern nation—also derive their identities from collectivities created by humans. In Benedict Anderson's well-known phrase, nations are socially constructed "imagined communities" in which people perceive themselves as being part of that group (Anderson 1983). In Chapter Four, we discussed the illusory and non-scientific nature of "race"—which, like categories such as ethnicity, are not biological facts but complex socio-cultural constructs that manifest themselves through both the group's agency and its interactions with other groups; they are not genetic or fixed and tend to change over time.

All human groups then, are fluid, ever-changing, and formed by social relations. Social classes are no exception. Like nations and other human collectivities, they too are socially constructed. Persons in the same social class generally have similar social and cultural beliefs. In his classic study of the development of English working-class consciousness, E. P. Thompson asserted that it "made itself as much as it was made" as many workers "came to feel an identity of interests as between themselves, and as against other men whose interests are different from (and usually opposed to) theirs" (Thompson 1963, 958). Social classes, like political groups, are also absent from the Convention's listing of protected groups. The destruction of the social and cultural connections of a human group—a social class—through persecution, violence, and mass murder has been termed "classicide" by the American sociologist Michael Mann. He argues that there are distinctions between "ethnocide," "classicide," and "murderous ethnic cleansing," only the latter of which rises to the level of genocide (Mann 2005). In previous chapters, we have argued it is not necessary to invent different terms such as "gendercide" or "politicide" to describe attacks on specific groups within each type of human collectivity attacked if the aim or result of genocidists is always the same—to destroy the "pattern of the oppressed group." As Lemkin wrote in *Axis Rule*: "many authors, instead of using a generic term use currently terms connoting only some functional aspect of the main generic notion of genocide" (Lemkin 2008, 80). Lemkin also delineated the many "techniques" by which genocidists "employed a coordinated plan of *different actions* [italics ours] aiming at the destruction of foundations of the life of national groups," and therefore also do not think it useful to employ terms such as "ethnocide" to characterize the specific method employed by the genocidists (ibid.,79). We argue instead that deliberate attempts by *any* means to destroy the social cohesion of *any human group*—as it is defined by the genocidists—that results in that group's inability to maintain its own distinct, unique culture should be considered genocide.

Democide and Auto-Genocide

The three case studies in this chapter have much in common. All three were attempts to achieve some form of communism through agricultural reorganization and all three resulted in excess deaths due to terrible famines and diseases brought about by disastrous schemes, driven by unrealistic goals that greatly disrupted agricultural production. The three despots (Stalin, Mao, and Pol Pot) also oversaw the purges of political opponents, the decimation of entire classes of people, and the deliberate internal "colonization" of many ethnic or social groups in their respective societies. As we will see, Stalin's assault on the cultural and social connections of the Ukrainian people, combined with his earlier crushing of its political elite, can arguably fit into the 1948 UN Genocide Convention. What of government murder of its own "ethnic" kin? We have two case studies to examine where this actually occurs—Mao's Great Famine and the horror of Pol Pot's rule in Cambodia. In the former, the American political scientist Rudolph Rummel proposed the explanatory concept of "democide." Rummel suggests the murder by a government of any group *except* those with, in his view, "indelible group membership"—national, ethnic, racial, and religious ones—be classified as democide, with only attacks on the four protected groups in the 1948 UN Genocide Convention being considered genocide. Rummel differentiated between attacks on those protected groups by any of the means delineated in the Convention (killing, serious bodily or mental harm, conditions meant to bring about physical destruction in whole or in part, the prevention of births or transferring children of the group to another group) and government murder of any other group. Mao's famine fits under his rubric of "democide" (Rummel 1997).

One last "cide" for your consideration, then, is the term "auto-genocide" that is sometimes used to describe the case of Pol Pot and the Khmer Rouge (KR) in Cambodia. The word itself, like suicide—from the Latin *"sui"* or self, and *"cide,"* or killing—means self-destruction. Some highly respected legal scholars define "auto-genocide" as the "mass killing of members of the group to which the perpetrators themselves belong." They have concluded that this type of attack— the mass murder of one's own ethnic group—also cannot be considered genocide as it "is inconsistent with the purposes of the Convention, which was to protect national minorities from crimes based on ethnic hatred" (Schabas 2000, 118–19). In the case of Cambodia, there were several different ethnic minorities destroyed by the KR that would fit the UN definition. It was, however, the largest ethnic group—the Khmers—that composed the majority of the KR's victims. Many were marked as social or political enemies, and sometimes not even genuine Khmers, by their murderers. Rummel's concept, then, would contend that the KR committed genocide against ethnic or religious minorities, and democide when it attacked its own ethnic kin. There are also those who would use the term auto-genocide to describe the KR murder of Khmers. In our view, neither democide nor auto-genocide is helpful for an understanding of Lemkin's concept. The same "people" as the genocidists can be the target of destruction if the attempt or outcome is the forcible changing of their ways of life and culture.

In fact, according to Lemkin, even though the human groups most frequently attacked were indeed "religious, racial, national and ethnical" and "political" ones, other groups "selected for destruction according to the criterion of their affiliation with a group which is considered extraneous and dangerous for various reasons" could be victims of genocide (quoted in Irvin-Erickson 2017, 85). According to Irvin-Erickson, Lemkin would even consider criminal gangs, having formed that "family of mind," as such a human group "since states often criminalize certain types of subjectivities and ethnicities" (ibid.). Rodrigo Duterte, the former President of the Philippines, permitted that nation's police forces to assassinate untold thousands of presumed drug dealers, who were actual criminals and not merely designated as such for political purposes—although Duterte certainly used his campaign for political purposes. The International Criminal Court estimates Duterte sanctioned the murder of between 12,000 and 30,000 people involved in the manufacture and sale of illegal drugs over a period of three years, a crusade that also engulfed many completely innocent people (*The Economist* November 22, 2021). This, too, could be genocide according to Lemkin's thinking on the subject.

We certainly do not contend that *any* human group, such as criminal gangs or "people who play at cards"—another group Lemkin specifically mentioned in his papers—should be included as possible victims of genocide. Our concern is with scholarly efforts to categorize genocides by defining victim groups (gendercide, politicide, classicide, and so on) narrowly and in so doing risk not seeing the forest because of all the trees. The human groups attacked need not be minorities, though with but very rare exceptions—the Hutus in Burundi in 1972, the Mayan peoples of Guatemala in the early 1980s, and the peasantry as a whole in the Soviet Union and Communist China—they usually are. The groups attacked also do not need to be broken down into neat categories. In fact, no group *could* be except as one defined by the genocidists; in a "racial" group what of mixed-race children? In a "religious" group what of non-believers or secularists? Political groups can also be amorphous. It is always the genocidists who arbitrarily determine who are the members of any group, and once that is done, as we have seen, the genocide of any "political" group is still a genocide, and the genocide of any "social" group is as well. The same is true with the murder of a human being. It is always a homicide irrespective of any effort to describe further the personal characteristics of the victim. In our view, most of the "cide" theories already put forward in this book have, in Martin Shaw's words, confused rather than clarified "the understanding of violence against civilian social groups" (Shaw 2015,99). Many academics tend to use the 1948 Genocide Convention as a baseline when instead we should be looking at the essence of what Lemkin meant by genocide. Simply put, it is a concerted *colonialist* effort to kill a people by destroying their social and cultural connections by any of a variety of means, thus forever erasing their particular contribution to the world's cultural diversity. And, of course, as we have seen in the case of Native Americans—among others—though violence and killing usually accompany any genocide, it is not necessary to kill people in order to kill a people. As Lemkin said, "mass killing" is but one way to "destroy the essential foundations of the life of national groups," with his idea of "national groups" being any group that considered itself as such through that "family of mind" (Lemkin 2008, 79).

Communist genocidists have often targeted the peasantry as a social class in their countries as domestic political foes that needed to be "acculturated"—colonized—to achieve their revolutionary vision. And, as we have stated, colonialism is the essence of Lemkin's concept of genocide. Stalin's Soviet Union, Mao's China, and the Khmer Rouge (KR) in Cambodia, all sought to destroy the traditional ways of life of the peasantry to "modernize" their lands in keeping with their distorted versions of Marxist theory. In the case of the KR, they also destroyed yet another social class, the "bourgeoisie" or urban middle class. Mao Zedong, the leader of the Chinese Revolution, which took power in 1949, presided over an anti-peasant campaign directed at the entire peasantry as a social class, except in Tibet, where his policy also aimed to destroy that people's national identity. Later, Mao targeted urban intellectuals as political enemies during the so-called Cultural Revolution of 1966–76. Pol Pot—the leader of the KR party, also known as the Communist Party of Kampuchea (Cambodia), which ruled from April 1975 until early 1979—attacked ethnic and national minorities, religious groups, and as we noted, *two* distinct social classes. These three tyrants all directed their attempts at the destruction of different types of human groups, but they were all genocides.

Collectivization

As we saw in the preceding chapter Stalin's assault on the Ukrainian intelligentsia and *kulak* peasant class was part of a process intended to destroy Ukrainians' social, ethnic, cultural, and national identity. By 1930, Stalin had already destroyed one entire arbitrarily designated category of peasants throughout the Soviet Union—the *kulaks*—as well as the Ukrainian intelligentsia. Stalin now attempted to colonize the Soviet Union's entire peasantry but with special emphasis on destroying the social and cultural connections of those in Ukraine. Stalin well knew that it was here, among the common folk that could be found "the repository of the tradition, folklore, and music, the national language and literature, the national spirit of Ukraine" (Lemkin 2008b, 128). This would be the final blow to the idea of a Ukraine separate from Russia. The Soviet collectivization campaign was also designed to forcibly integrate the entire Soviet peasantry as a class into the "worker's state" as being but laborers in the countryside. This last would entail the wholesale imposition of Soviet culture and ideology onto an entire human group—probably 85% of the total population—by attacking their ways of life and traditions. The method Stalin employed to crush peasant resistance, especially in Ukraine, was famine. Stalin's collectivization policy forced the Soviet Union's peasantry off the small plots and farmsteads they had tilled during NEP and into large-scale collective farms. Peasant resistance was, as we will see, fierce.

The resultant famine of 1932–33, however, was not the inevitable result of this struggle between the Soviet state and the peasantry. Nor was it simply a result of bad weather or crop failure. It was, instead, the desired outcome of a genocidal process. The Ukrainian word that perfectly describes this method by which Stalin carried out the last phase of his genocide is *Holodomor*. *Holod* is the Ukrainian word for hunger and *mor* is the word for death. Taken together, *Holodomor* literally means "death by hunger." Stalin ordered tens of thousands of Communist Party officials, supported by 50,000 specially trained demobilized Red Army soldiers, 75,000 "workers" on temporary assignment, and volunteer brigades of urban workers—the so-called 25,000ers—into the countryside not only to force the peasants into collective farms but also as part of a crusade against peasant backwardness, superstition, and ignorance (Conquest 1986). With a zeal and fervor usually found only among religious fanatics or ardent nationalists, many were motivated by a determination to transform the peasantry "into laborers with a social consciousness." These "warriors on an invisible front" were "fanatical believers of a new creed, the only true *religion* of scientific socialism. The party became our church militant, bequeathing to all mankind eternal salvation, eternal peace, and the bliss of an earthly paradise" (Kopelev 1980, 11). Any means to achieve this end were justified. The collectivization of agriculture would transform the peasant economy from a "capitalist" one to a "socialist" one. In accord with their vulgarized form of Marxism—and noting that Marx had written that social being or status determines consciousness (Marx 1859)—the Communists believed that the peasants would thereby lose their "bourgeois" attachments to the land as well as their superstitious religious beliefs and be freed from what Marx once termed "the idiocy of rural life."

Marxian socialism, in its many variants that preceded the Bolshevik revolution, promised a complete change in human nature with the destruction or withering away of class structures. Like its philosophical cousin liberalism, many Marxists held firm to a belief in the inevitability of human progress leading to the perfection of humankind. Like most religions, this too promised a form of paradise, albeit here on earth rather than in heaven. As Lev Kopelev—who worked as a party propagandist among the Ukrainian peasants during the mass collectivization campaign that resulted in the death of millions—later wrote, "Stalin said the struggle for grain was the struggle for socialism. Above all, for the grain, but also for the souls of these peasants who did not understand the great truth of communism" (idem.). Some political theorists also believe that nationalism holds out the same promise of eternal life for its citizens. Indeed, nationalism was readily apparent in Stalin's "socialism in one country"—rejecting the internationalist views of his chief opponent, Leon Trotsky. The "war scare" promoted by Stalin in the late 1920s served to motivate people to achieve the rapid industrialization of the Soviet Union. Stalin asked, "Do you want the socialist fatherland to be beaten and lose its independence? [...] We are fifty or a hundred years behind the advanced countries.

We must make good this distance in ten years. Either we do it, or we shall be crushed" (Stalin 1953, 458).

During the Russian Civil War of 1918–21, state farms had been set up after the confiscation of large noble estates as the ultimate socialist form of agriculture. Peasants labored in these "factories in the field" and were paid a regular wage. In theory, this change in landholding would lead to the conditions for a complete shift to communist agriculture. Lenin believed that this measure—once combined with the production of 100,000 tractors—would turn the peasants into supporters of the Communist state. Instead, they were a colossal failure. Mostly poor and landless peasants signed up for the state farms, and by the early 1930s, the government acknowledged the "wastefulness and complete disorganization of production processes" of the state farms. Most peasants preferred to farm their own small plots. In the winter of 1930, Stalin ordered his party officials and the 25,000ers—named after the number of volunteers, though in fact more than 27,000 signed up—to oversee the "voluntary" merging of the peasants' small farmsteads into supposedly more efficient state-managed collective farms. For him, "unification of small and tiny peasant household farms into large collective farms [...] is the only way" to increase agricultural output and earn enough hard currency to finance industrialization in order to protect the Soviet Union from its enemies (Kotkin 2014, 672).

To join a collective farm, supposedly organized on the cooperative principle where profits would be shared, peasants first had to turn over all their land, tools, and livestock to the collective. They would be expected to labor in the fields much as they did in the past, but instead of sharing in any profits after all the grain quotas and taxes had been met, their meager pay would be calculated in "labor days" which would usually be paid out in goods or food. In a misuse of Karl Marx's dictum "From each according to his ability, to each according to his work," the more skilled workers such as tractor drivers—or the Communist Party members who served as head of the collectives—received a higher valuation of their labor days than, say, a milkmaid. Stalin claimed the virtues of collectivization were so readily apparent that peasants were enthusiastically signing up to join. He called it a "movement [...] that was sweeping the country" (Applebaum 2017, 115). In fact, the vast majority of peasants resisted collectivization and resented this wholesale change in their way of life by any means necessary, including violence. The 25,000ers, who were expected to remain in the villages and serve as administrators after collectivization was completed, did find some willing accomplices among certain elements of peasant society—those regarded as idlers, vagrants, and so on—who were bestowed with the honorary status of "poor peasants" for their collaboration. Soviet secret police reports acknowledge that some even came from "criminal elements" who simply wanted to profit off the misfortune of their neighbors (ibid., 143). There were also more than a few instances in which "poor peasants" participated willingly either in the dekulakization campaign or in the collectivization process, though more often the peasants banded together against the outsiders.

The Soviets, however, took this minimal cooperation of some poor peasants against the so-called middle or "bourgeois" peasants as confirmation of the existence of the class war in the villages—further proof of the correctness of the party line as decreed by the infallible Stalin. The Communist activists flooded the countryside to persuade the peasants to merge their homesteads into collectives. The sudden appearance in the countryside of these culturally—and in Ukraine also linguistically and ethnically—alien city slickers reminded the peasants of the seizures of grain by urban workers and Red Army soldiers during the Civil War only a decade before. Naturally, they were suspicious of the sales pitch made by these interlopers. In Ukraine, the unwelcome visitors were rudely rebuffed, especially the Russian speakers. One peasant later recounted how a Russian activist "came to convince the peasants how wonderful life was under the Soviets [...]. but, who listened? No one. This liar made his way from one end of the village to the other. No one wanted anything to do with him" (ibid., 141).

Although the activists were supposed to enlist the peasants on a voluntary basis through patience and persuasion, the Soviet government did not provide any directives or instructions on how to accomplish this task. They were simply exhorted to achieve "total" collectivization. This would turn out to be quite convenient for Stalin when searching for scapegoats to blame for the ensuing, easily foreseen chaos and violence. The Soviets were determined to observe at least the appearance of a democratic process and have the peasants formally sign up for the collectives. The historians Lynne Viola and Sheila Fitzpatrick, who both contributed insightful and valuable books on the topic of collectivization and peasant resistance, relate hilarious accounts of village meetings called by the activists where someone would burst in shouting that a house was on fire or a horse had gotten loose, whereupon all the men would get up and run off. Meeting over! Sometimes the peasants would pretend to listen during the meeting, nodding their heads as if in agreement, only to decline the "invitation" offered at the end of the meeting to join the collective by saying that, although they agreed in principle, they would like more time to think things over. More often, they simply refused outright. In one village, the poor and middle peasants that remained after "dekulakization" voted unanimously for a resolution that read: "We will not join the kolkhoz, we will not give seed funds, since the grain procurements have crushed us, but we welcome the decision about total collectivization" (Fitzpatrick 1994, 51). In the end, coercion was required.

Peasant Resistance

As peasant resistance continued, the Communist Party activists employed other tactics to force them to surrender everything they owned and join the collective. The collectivizers instructed hospitals to turn away any peasants—and their families—who had refused to enter the collectives and ordered their children expelled from school. The Communist officials also forbade local mills from grinding their corn and watched over blacksmiths to make sure they did not do any work for those peasants who had not joined the collective. The government agents, forced to apply still more pressure, began threatening the peasants with deportation as a *kulak*. These were not idle threats as many peasants were in fact, arrested and deported. In one village, the communist official told the assembled peasants to make a choice "Those who are joining the *kolkhoz* [collective] sign up with me; those who do not want to join sign up with the police chief" (ibid., 53). A dozen peasants refused and the police chief promptly arrested them and they were on the next train to Siberia. In another method that frequently proved effective, the Communist representative simply asked—with armed activists behind him—"who is against joining the collective and against Soviet power?" Official reports note that peasants everywhere complained that the government wanted to take away their freedom and return them to the miserable conditions of serfdom. Throughout the Soviet countryside, the peasants referred to the VKP initials of the All-Russian Communist Party as standing for a "second serfdom"—*vtoroe krepostnoe pravo* (Conquest 1986, 152).

The peasants fought back by assassinating party officials or collectivizers—hundreds in 1930 alone—with the majority of these attacks taking place in Ukraine. The local officials, alarmed at these developments, warned their people to stay away from windows and not to go out alone at night. After the wave of arrests and executions that inevitably followed these brazen attacks, the peasants organized armed bands to drive out the collectivizers and engaged in pitched battles with militias, police units, and even regular units of the Red Army. In Ukraine, a full-scale rebellion broke out in several regions that required army troops to put it down. One Soviet secret police report estimated that in 1930 there were up to 40,000 armed peasant rebels in Ukraine alone (ibid., 155). The violence and reprisals that ravaged the countryside were unrelenting. One secret police officer tasked with putting down these uprisings said: "I am an old Bolshevik. I worked in the underground against the tsar and then I fought in the Civil War. Did I do all that in order that I should now surround villages with machine guns and order my men to fire indiscriminately into crowds of peasants? Oh, no, no, no!" (Deutscher 1949, 325). Exhausted from the struggle, many peasants finally agreed, reluctantly, to sign up for the collectives. According to official figures, by the end of February 1930, 50 percent of peasant households, including 75 percent of all those in Ukraine, had formally enrolled in the collectives. The ink had barely dried on the "agreements" the peasants had been forced to sign when Communist Party activists would arrive to seize all the farm animals and equipment. They were especially keen on seizing horses and cows, but often confiscated the few chickens, pigs, sheep and goats that belonged to individual peasants as well. Absent instructions from Moscow, the collectivization brigades interpreted "total collectivization" to mean just that.

The peasants, however, continued to resist in their own ways. They slaughtered their animals before the activists came to take them away from them. They sold off as many horses and cattle as they could prior to entering the collectives. Obviously, they were reluctant to surrender their cherished property, but they probably also feared that they too could be labeled as *kulaks* if they had too many animals. Socialization was bad enough, but dekulakization would be even worse. One peasant explained "One thing we have now learned [...] and that is not to keep more than one cow or horse and at most only two pigs and a few sheep" (Hindus 1988, 165). If unable to sell their livestock, they simply slaughtered and consumed them. The price of beef and pork dropped considerably. As a result, the peasants feasted as never before. The People's Commissar of Agriculture, revealing the contempt Communist officials had for rural folk, supposedly said, for "the first time in their sordid history, the Russian peasants have eaten their fill of meat" (Conquest 1986, 159). The peasants reasoned that it was better to kill the animals because they "wouldn't taste meat in the collective farm." One peasant remarked, "It's all the same—soon everything we own will be socialized. It's better to slaughter and sell the livestock than to let it remain" (Viola 1996, 75). Most of the horses turned over to the collectives died from mistreatment, neglect, and, as there was no fodder for them, starvation. One regional party official, after inspecting the farms he was responsible for, stated that from two to seven horses died every night in each collective. If the peasants were unable to sell them, they simply released them instead, so that "herds of wild horses ran wild throughout the Ukraine" (Conquest 1986, 179). Between 1929 and 1933, the number of horses in the Soviet Union dropped from 32 million to 17 million (Figure 6.1).

The state desperately tried to stop the wholesale slaughter of farm animals. A decree issued in late 1930 banned the killing of a number of different kinds of livestock (ibid., 73). When this had no effect, the state began classifying those peasants that killed and consumed their animals as being *kulaks* and had them deported. The scale of the widespread slaughter of the peasantry's animals was such that it constituted a national economic disaster. "Official" Soviet statistics released in 1934 admitted that, in addition to half the horses, the number of cattle went down from by almost 27 million, or 43 percent of all cattle in the country. In Ukraine, the percentage was even higher than in the rest of the country—48 percent of the cattle. In addition, 64 million sheep—or 65 percent of the total—were lost. Once again, that figure was higher in Ukraine as there the peasants had killed and eaten 73 percent of both the sheep and goats. Fully 67 percent of all the pigs in the Soviet Union were also

Figure 6.1 A dreadful but typical scene during the *Holodomor*: corpse and passers-by, Kharkiv, Ukraine, 1932. https://commons.wikimedia.org/wiki/File:HolodomorUcrania9.jpg

gone (Conquest 1986, 159). These numbers were quite probably higher. The loss of millions of farm animals would prove disastrous. By March 1930, the regime had forced most peasant households into the collectives. The Soviets did manage to extract more grain, but the *entire* increase in grain seized from the peasants from 1929 to 1933 came from the fact that fodder no longer had to be set aside for animal consumption. The cost was great. Hundreds of thousands of peasants had died in the process of dekulakization and collectivization. Scores more of desperate peasants ran away into the *taiga*—the deep Russian forest—to hide, and many others, in the ultimate protest against collectivization, committed suicide. Even once forced into the collective farms, however, the peasantry continued to resist. The Soviets had to acknowledge that the entire peasantry was in rebellion. The regime, forced to abandon their plan simply to make peasants "workers in the field," would need to make concessions. A compromise would need to be found on the issue of the so-called private plots and, as Stalin put it "a little misunderstanding about the cow."

"Dizzy with Success"

Besides the widespread slaughter of farm animals, the peasants' violent resistance to the state-sponsored assault on their way of life shocked the collectivizers. Physical attacks on them by peasants were common, assassination and murder only somewhat less so. Soviet sources from 1930 document 5,720 assaults on collectivizers—and their collaborators—and 1,197 murders, as well as 6,325 cases of arson (Viola, 1996, 110). There were also 13,794 "terrorist" incidents and another 13,754 "mass protests" (ibid., 103–05). The vast majority of these acts took place in Ukraine, where peasant women played an important role in the opposition to collectivization. Their demonstrations and refusal to cooperate with any state agents completely flummoxed the regime. The Soviets often contemptuously referred to these protests as *bab'i bunty*, or "women's riots." The term *baba*—peasant woman—has the connotation of ignorant, backward, and even hysterical. It plays into long-standing misogynistic stereotypes typical of a traditional, conservative, patriarchal society. A Russian proverb holds that "women's hair is long, but her brains are short." A *bunt* is an unorganized and uncontrolled riot, "senseless and pitiless" as the important Russian poet A.S. Pushkin described them. In fact, these were calculated, rational forms of resistance in response to the threat collectivization posed to the well-being of their families. Their menfolk could stand apart as these "hysterical females" resisted on behalf of the entire village. If the police moved against them, the men could then intervene and take on the outsiders as they were just trying to "protect" these silly, emotional women and of course were certainly not acting against Soviet power.

The state understood perfectly well "that in connection with the excesses in the collective farm movement, women in the countryside played the most "advanced" role in the reaction against the collective farm" (ibid., 18). In the Russian village, the men took care of the horses but the women looked after the cows, which of course provided milk for the children. The socialization of animals directly threatened the economic survival of both the village and their own families. Women fought the collectivizers that came for the cattle tooth and nail. Ultimately, Stalin reversed course and backed off, calling for a cow in every peasant household—about the same time President Franklin Delano Roosevelt was calling for a "a chicken in every pot, and a car in every garage" in the United States and Adolf Hitler was promising new Volkswagens to the German people—to end "the little misunderstanding with collective farm women [...] about cows" (ibid., 183). The scope and scale of peasant resistance—especially in Ukraine—was such that still more concessions needed to be made to quell the violence. In his 1930 article "Dizzy with Success," Stalin blamed his underlings for the "excesses" which had occurred and stressed that the collectivization process was supposed to be purely "on the voluntary principle" and that peasants could leave the collectives if they chose to do so. He also denounced the coercive measures that local officials utilized as being against Lenin's wishes. In effect, he put all the blame on those Soviet agents who carried out the policy for any "excesses." As you will recall, there were—conveniently— no specific instructions ever issued. Stalin simply ordered "total" collectivization as quickly as possible.

Millions of peasants immediately seized what appeared to be the opportunity to leave the collectives and return to their former way of life. They renounced their signatures on the collectivization agreements and demanded the return of their animals and farm equipment. The percentage of collectivized households dropped overall from 57 percent to 28 percent in two months' time; tellingly, in Ukraine, the principal focus of the regime's efforts, the percentage dropped from 83 percent to but 18 percent (Fitzpatrick 1994, 63). It soon became apparent, however, that Stalin was simply posturing. Peasants could not leave until the spring sowing, and even then, could not take any animals with them. In addition, the collectives kept all the best land and only offered plots with poor soil quality to those that wished to withdraw. These measures worked to prevent peasants from actually leaving the collectives and reestablishing their households. Meanwhile, the secret police continued the campaign against the so-called *kulaks* and anyone demanding to leave the collective farm was liable to be labeled as such. In 1931, there was another large wave of arrests followed by deportations. Many peasants feared classification as kulaks and remained in the collectives.

In addition, by this time the economic disruption caused by collectivization was beginning to affect agricultural yields. Even though the state had collected more grain, we have already established this was because there no longer was any need to feed as many farm animals as before. The peasants knew there soon would be shortages and most elected, in the end, to remain in the collectives in hopes of finding food security. By the end of 1931, 60 percent of peasant households were again collectivized. Stalin's did allow one last concession to the peasantry. He intervened in the dispute over whether or not the peasants could retain use of a "private plot" on which to keep the cow, and the few pigs, goats and sheep they were permitted. For some reason, the Soviets absolutely refused to consider allowing the peasants to keep a horse. Most Soviet officials worried about the peasantry devoting more time to "their" plots than to farming the collectives' land. They also objected to the fact that any products from the plots could be sold on the open market—in other words, capitalism would be permitted. Stalin, however, was trying to appear sympathetic to the plight of the peasantry. Saying "the *kolkhozniki* [collective farm workers] just want to live a decent life," he stated that they should be given somewhat larger plots "to plant an orchard, cultivate a vegetable garden, or keep bees" (ibid., 1994, 122). In other words, Stalin gave up on the original plan to force all of the Soviet Union's peasants into gigantic, state-run farms where they would labor like factory workers all day. Although now allowed to have private plots, keep a cow and a few other barnyard animals the peasants—especially those in Ukraine—still saw the communists as colonizers disrupting their lives. There is no evidence that the peasants expressed any gratitude for these concessions from the "Red Tsar."

Stalin's comrades were equally unhappy. Many of the cadres that volunteered to go into the countryside had formerly been supporters of Trotsky. They were ardent communists working toward the world revolution who resented giving in to the class enemy. As a party based on an idea, Stalin had to explain his policies by adjusting Marxist-Leninist theories to fit the situation. In the end, he had adopted Trotsky's plan for the exploitation of the peasantry. Despite the concessions made, Stalin did not waver from the plan and set unbelievably high quotas for grain deliveries. He arrived at these figures simply by calculating the amount of land that supposedly was available for farming and then multiplying that number by the maximum grain yield theoretically possible. Worse, in order to meet his unrealistic goals Stalin ordered that even seed grain used by the peasants for sowing be collected despite knowing perfectly well that the result would be famine. This was clearly premeditated mass murder. Some of his underlings in Ukraine were appalled and lobbied him for reductions. The response came from Stalin's henchman Molotov "There will be no concessions or vacillations in the problem of fulfilment of the task set by the party and the Soviet government" (Conquest 1986, 223). By the summer of 1932, food was already scarce and people were dying of hunger. Stalin issued a decree that anyone caught stealing even a handful of wheat was an "enemy of the people" and theft of "public property" would be punished by ten years in a labor camp—or the death penalty. By the end of 1932, 4,500 people had been executed and another 100,000 sent to the Gulag.

In the fall of 1932, Stalin again sent motivated party activists into the countryside—this time 112,000 of them, known as "100,000ers"—to requisition the crop and deliver it to the state. They did so by terrorizing the peasants, bursting into their huts searching for "hidden" grain. Often they resorted to torturing the peasants to reveal where any grain was stored, beating them, breaking their fingers, dunking their heads under water. The resulting *Holodomor* during the winter of 1932–33 left the peasants desperate for any kind of food. Dogs and cats disappeared. The peasants ate weeds, leaves, tree bark, and any flesh they could get—including human. Children coming home from school disappeared. Mothers faced a choice of which child to feed, or sometimes, since they could always have more children later they chose to save themselves and their husbands instead. The peasants exchanged all their gold and heirlooms for a little flour at special government stores set up for just that purpose. Corpses were everywhere, frozen in the snow. Miron Dolot, who survived the famine, wrote about a neighbor who, after her daughter and husband had perished, dressed up in the Ukrainian national costume and hanged herself (Dolot 1985). By the end of 1934, the number of inmates in the labor camps had nearly doubled from 260,000 to 510,000 and the mortality rate for prisoners had jumped from 4.81 percent to 15.3 percent since so many arrived on the verge of death (Applebaum 2017, 217). Stalin was unconcerned.

What did trouble Stalin was the reluctance—and often the outright refusal—of Ukrainian party officials to follow his orders. Many refused to implement the grain requisition plans and some even resigned from the Party. Stalin wrote another of his underlings, Lazar Kaganovich, that the Communists must close ranks and "make an effort now to improve the situation" for otherwise "we may lose Ukraine" (ibid., 219). The Ukrainian officials' resistance only served to confirm Stalin's belief that Ukrainian nationalism posed a threat to his rule, and by extension, the achievements of the great socialist revolution. By "improving" the situation, Stalin did not mean responding to the dire pleas for help from Ukrainian peasants and officials alike, he meant the purging of unreliable Ukrainian communists from the state machinery. Wholesale arrests followed. The real threat, however, was the mass exodus of peasants from Ukraine in search of food. Between December 1932 and February 1933, at least 100,000 peasants left the collective farms. Most went into Russia, and one Ukrainian noted "interestingly enough, beyond Kharkiv (the correct Ukrainian spelling) where the Russian territory starts there was no hunger" (ibid., 235). Stalin had the borders closed and patrolled by army units. The starving Ukrainians that did make it into the cities outside of Ukraine took to begging in the streets of Russian cities. Stalin's own wife, Nadezhda Alliluyeva, implored him to do something about the peasants' distress. Rudely rebuffed publicly, she shot herself. Altogether at least three and possibly four million Ukrainians starved to death during the *Holodomor* because of Stalin's callous indifference; he would later send in ethnic Russian peasants to repopulate the region.

Collectivization was part of a planned and determined act of state aggression aimed at the internal colonization of the entire Soviet peasantry. At the same time, it was a genocidal assault on Ukrainian culture and national aspirations. Putin claims that Stalin's intent was to terrorize the peasantry as a class and not the Ukrainians as a nation. In 2018, the Russian Foreign Ministry asserted that the Soviet famine "was a common tragedy of Russians, Ukrainians, Kazakhs and many other peoples" while deploring "politicized and anti-scientific" attempts to depict the famine as a genocide of the Ukrainian people (The Bulwark, December 1, 2022). It is true that another one and one half-million Kazakhs also perished in the famine. Between four and one half- and five and one half-million of the approximately seven million excess deaths during this time in the Soviet Union occurred in Ukraine and Kazakhstan. Two million deaths were supposedly "Russian," but as Andrea Graziosi reminds us, "if we count as Ukrainian the Kuban and the southern fringes of the Russian *oblast'* [region or province] bordering Ukraine" that number decreases. He further qualifies that figure of two million "Russian" deaths by urging us to remember that "in 1930–35 Kazakhstan was still an autonomous republic of the Russian federation, so that its victims are often counted as Russian" (Graziosi in Graziosi and Sysyn, eds. 2022, 133).

The total number of both Ukrainians and Kazakhs that died as result of this deliberate state-sponsored process may well be closer to six million, a figure that obviously invites comparison with other genocides. That the entire peasantry was not marked for total annihilation or that up to another few million non-Ukrainian peasants also perished does not change the fact that Stalin deliberately tried to stamp out Ukrainian national consciousness and identity. This calculated effort to destroy that identity reached back into the nineteenth century. In 1876, Tsar Alexander II issued a decree that specified no more materials of any kind—books, newspapers, advertisements, etc.—were to be printed in the Ukrainian language. Putin has done the same in the regions of Ukraine currently occupied by Russian forces. In addition, like Stalin, he is trying to destroy Ukrainian identity in those regions by repopulating them with ethnic Russians brought in from remote parts of that country. Lemkin's classic description of genocide is "the destruction of the national pattern of the oppressed group [and] the imposition of the national pattern of the oppressor." It is an attempt to destroy "the political and social institutions, of culture, language, national feelings religion, and the economic existence of national groups" (Lemkin 2008, 79). Putin's war in Ukraine is but the continuation of Russia's centuries-old attempt to colonize an entire people, and genocide is a colonial crime.

Mao's Great Famine

The Chinese Civil War, fought between the Communists led by Mao Zedong and the Nationalists, led by Chiang Kai-Shek, ranged from 1927 to 1949—with a pause in hostilities to fight the Japanese invaders from 1937 to 1945—and resulted in final victory for the Communists when the Nationalists retreated to the island of Taiwan. Mao's base of support was the peasantry and, after expelling the Japanese from China, in areas that came under communist control the Party pushed for the confiscation and redistribution of the properties held by the landlord class to the peasantry. Many poor peasants received plots of land to till for the first time in their lives. Mao also specified that "middle" peasants were not to be attacked and that "rich" peasants should be considered peasants and not members of the parasitic landlord class (DeMare 2019). As had been the case in the Soviet Union, however, there were fierce debates within the Party over whether or not to expropriate the holdings of these more successful peasants. The official policy directives sent out were contradictory. Despite Mao's initial pronouncement, the Party issued orders calling for the seizure and redistribution of all of the "rich" peasants' land as well, though it then quickly rescinded them. In the ensuing confusion, however, many "rich" peasants perished in the violence sweeping the countryside, as well as not a few "middle" peasants mistakenly reclassified as rich ones. The poor peasants, encouraged by the state, wreaked vengeance on their former betters. Ultimately, however, it was mostly the landlords who were targeted based on their class origins and they suffered enormously. These so-called "class enemies of the revolution," often executed publicly in horrific ways such as dismemberment or being buried or burned alive, were virtually annihilated by the time the Communists achieved full control of the country in 1949. Most estimates of the death toll vary, but most scholars agree that the number is in the millions (Dikotter 2010; Becker 1996). As in the Soviet Union, millions more were sent to labor camps where many of these unfortunates perished. The violence and mayhem unleashed by the Chinese Communist Party, as had been the case also in the Soviet Union, was but the first step in remaking the entire social and cultural structure of the countryside.

As in Soviet Russia, the question of tempo split the Party into two factions. There were those who wanted to move forward toward collectivization at full speed immediately. This group, led by Mao, wanted to emulate Stalin's policies and squeeze as much grain from the peasantry as possible to finance industrialization. The other, more moderate faction, not wanting to risk the peasant support that had put the Communists in power in the first place, advocated following a more deliberate pace. Mao was critical of these comrades, calling them "women with bound feet," but, as he had not yet consolidated his personal political power, he had to fight a protracted battle against those in the Party that thought his plans unrealistic. By 1955, Mao had managed to gain enough support to push through a policy scholars later called the "little leap forward." The government forced peasant families to consolidate into what were termed mutual aid societies and surrender their animals and implements. Party activists, acting similarly as their comrades in Russia, summoned the peasants to meetings and kept them there until they "voluntarily" agreed to join these cooperatives. The policy called for the peasants to work in teams and for the government to take control of the grain market. As had been the case in the Soviet Union, disaster soon followed as the peasants slaughtered their animals rather than turn them over and hid their grain. Famine threatened. Many in the Party advised a change in course, suggesting once again permitting a limited free market to incentivize the peasantry.

Zhou Enlai—who served as premier of the People's Republic of China from its founding in 1949 through his death in 1976—was one of those moderates who came out in opposition to Mao's "rash advance" and stated that the goals set by the Party were unrealistic, if not impossible. Zhou's September 1956 report on the Second Five-Year Plan to the Party Congress, staked out a pragmatic middle position, stating "the party's responsibility is to take pains at all times to prevent and correct any tendency toward right-deviating conservatism or left-leaning risk-taking" (Yang 2008, 92). The Party held off on land reorganization for another year while Mao, not yet the undisputed leader of the Party, bided his time and consolidated his hold on the Party. One year later, he suddenly attacked Zhou and his supporters by condemning those in the Party who had voted to disregard his call for a "greater, faster, better and more economical" tempo, and demanded that the Party "restore it" (ibid.). Zhou continued to advocate his proposal for "opposing conservatism and also opposing rash advance" but Mao had succeeded in quashing any opposition to his undisputed leadership role and Zhou and his faction had been politically isolated. Forced to undergo scathing criticism and denunciations for his heretical ways, Zhou made all the necessary obsequious noises and crawled back into Mao's good graces, where he would remain until his death in 1976. Mao, seeking to flush out any remaining opposition to his rule, suggested that the Party hold a general discussion and allow "a hundred schools of thought to contend." For a few short weeks, officials and intellectuals who had complained about Mao's agricultural policy had the freedom to express their opinions. Then, like a cat pouncing on mice, "at least half a million people were seized in the Anti-Rightist campaign which Deng Xiaoping, then General Secretary of the Communist Party, organized" (Becker 1996, 54). Deng would later succeed Mao after the death of the "Great Helmsman" in 1976 and is largely responsible for the spectacular development of China into the economic power that it is today.

The "Great Leap Forward"

Ever since the death of Stalin in 1953, Mao had been trying to assert his preeminence as the world leader of communism. Like Stalin, he attempted to create a new society by first destroying traditional patterns of life among the single largest social class in any agriculturally based polity—the peasantry. The changes forced through by the communists upended very aspect of the peasants' world. Some of these changes were, in fact, quite progressive even if unwelcome to some in the countryside. Efforts to increase literacy not only made education available to all but also enhanced women's status. The communists also outlawed ancient practices such as foot binding and child marriage and pursued a vigorous campaign against opium use to great effect; however, the rhythms of peasant life and culture were also completely shattered. The communists removed all their traditional spiritual leaders such as astrologers and shamans, as well as Daoist and Buddhist monks and Christian priests from their places in village life. The Party also banned all the customary ceremonies and rituals conducted in conjunction with the agricultural cycle as well as those marking human life celebrations and transitions. The Party outlawed traditional medicine and the healers that practiced these methods. The Party attacked anything traditional or customary, including festivals, songs, and ceremonies, and replaced them with new communist ones. As the American authors of a study on the fate of one Chinese village put it "The Party treated popular mores and peasant norms as enemy forces" (quoted in ibid., 52) (Figure 6.2).

Mao, like Stalin, used the pretext of a possible war against the world's "imperialist" powers to galvanize Party support for his program of rapid industrialization. China

Figure 6.2 "Brave the wind and the waves, everything has remarkable abilities." Chinese propaganda poster during the disastrous "Great Leap Forward." https://commons.wikimedia.org/wiki/File:Brave_the_wind_and_the_waves.jpg

bombarded Nationalist-controlled islands in the Taiwan Strait in 1958 and the United States responded by sending supplies to the Nationalists and reaffirming its commitment to the defense of the Republic of China (Taiwan). Mao used this to create a war scare to promote the need for full-scale collectivization: "A tense situation helps to mobilize people [...] the people's communes should organize militias. Everyone in our country is a soldier" (quoted in Dikotter 2010, 45). Mao announced his "Great Leap Forward" and the Chinese Communist Party sent its cadres out into the countryside to herd all of China's huge peasant population into gigantic "People's Communes." Mao promised China would be the first truly communist society in the world, literally a heaven on earth. Only in China would each receive everything required according to their needs. The Party apparatus, having created a cult of personality surrounding Mao that exceeded even that of Stalin's during his rule, trumpeted propaganda promising each Chinese peasant would soon receive "food, clothing, housing, transportation, cultural entertainment, science institutes, and physical culture" and even asserted that "the time is not remote when each will have an aeroplane" (quoted in Becker 1996, 60). Instead, the Chinese people suffered through the worst famine in history, with official Chinese Communist figures admitting 20 million died and more realistic estimates ranged from 36 million (Yang 2008) to Dikotter's (2010) "minimum" of 45 million peasants dying as a result of Mao's misguided policies.

Those policies included pseudo-scientific approaches to agriculture such as "close-planting" where "with company the crops will grow easily, when they grow together they will be comfortable" (the Soviets had done pretty much the same, misapplying the Marxist dialectic to crop genetics with disastrous results). In addition, Mao ordered that large tracts of farmland be taken out of production altogether in keeping with another one of his slogans "Plant less, produce more, harvest less" (Becker 1996, 68). He promised that the "three years of hard work and suffering" would bring "a thousand years of prosperity." Total grain production dropped precipitously, but the government's demands did not. Convinced the peasants were hiding great quantities of grain from the state, local officials, as they had in Ukraine, carried out searches of peasant homes and often left the peasants beaten senseless in futile efforts to find the "missing" grain. Mao encouraged this approach, and he refused to condemn those who were brutal and violent in their duties, suggesting only that perhaps "we need only criticize them a bit—let them make self-criticism—that's enough" (quoted in Becker 1996, 87). The famine increased in its intensity, but Mao continued exporting grain to other countries to demonstrate China's ascendancy in the communist world. In fact, over the three years of the famine—1958–61—China actually *doubled* its grain exports and cut imports of food. China even provided free grain to other communist countries such as North Korea, North Vietnam, and Albania, leaving millions of Chinese to starve to death.

As in Russia, the brutal exploitation of the peasantry was supposedly a necessary precursor to rapid industrialization. Mao wanted not only to outproduce the Soviet Union in steel production by 1960 but also the United States by 1962. Stalin—whose name meant "man of steel" in Russian—had sold the grain abroad to finance industrialization in the Soviet Union. Mao was determined to go it alone without investment. His solution was to have all of China's rural communes build furnaces where every possible piece of metal—including household cookware and even farming implements such as scythes needed to harvest crops—were melted down into useless lumps of scrap metal. Of course, the villagers needed to collect the wood and coal necessary to fuel these backyard contraptions. They went out into the forest and randomly felled trees, deforesting large parts of the country; according to Dikotter, "we will never know the full extent of the forest coverage lost during the Great Leap Forward, but a prolonged and intense attack on nature claimed up to half of all trees in some provinces" (Dikotter 2010, xi). The peasants also used explosives haphazardly to create mines to dig for coal, killing many people. Millions of Chinese peasants went without food or rest to meet Mao's ridiculous demands, and some even worked themselves to death. Combined with other environmentally damaging "Great Leap Forward" projects such as irrigation and dam building, railroad construction, and the like, most of the men were engaged in efforts other than farming. Since so many men were involved in these projects, according to the British historian of China Frank Dikotter, women had to work in the fields instead, and "many had almost no experience in maintaining complex rice paddies, planting the seedlings unevenly and allowing weeds to invade the fields" (ibid., 62). As a consequence, a fifth of the crop rotted in the fields.

The horrors inflicted upon the Chinese peasantry by their indifferent government led by an egotistical and deluded fanatic are difficult to recount here and will be disturbing to read. Simply put, starvation is a prolonged and horrible way to die. People, literally driven insane by hunger, did things no one would ever do otherwise such as swapping their children for other children—a practice called *yi zi er shi*—to avoid eating their own. All too often, however, parents did eat their own children. There are accounts of older children killing and eating the younger ones. People who died remained unburied and hidden away so that families could still collect their food rations—if they did not eat the corpses first. Strangers passing through towns were murdered and eaten. Young girls sold off by their parents for "marriage" were forced into prostitution. People in the cities were only relatively better off as the Party introduced a rationing system similar to the one Stalin had introduced in the Soviet Union during its famine. In the cities, the government provided clothing and housing and at least a minimum diet while 500 million peasants were left on their own, forbidden to leave their communes, and in effect, became little more than serfs. Of course, Party members did not have to endure such privations, where, as in the Soviet Union, they had access to special, private shops. Mao, who never missed a meal, said "to distribute resources evenly will ruin the Great Leap Forward. When there is not enough to eat, people starve to death. It is better to let half the people die so that the other half can eat their fill" quoted in Yang 2008, 464). The 45 million victims of this manmade tragedy would surely disagree.

Mao, like Stalin, was completely indifferent to the starvation of his own people. Like Stalin, he also used famine to destroy another people. In Stalin's case, the Ukrainians suffered the most, although several million Russian and Kazakh peasants also perished. In Mao's case, the majority of the victims were from his own majority ethnic group— Han Chinese—but he also took advantage to destroy another minority human group, the Tibetans. The Tibetans suffered far more grievously than even the Chinese peasantry, of whom perhaps 10 percent died. At least 20 percent of Tibetans starved to death (Becker 1996). The famine was a deliberate attempt by Mao to erase their cultural heritage and punish them for resisting integration into China. The Tibetans were mostly herders, though some did grow barley. The Party forced the nomads to settle down in collectives and grow wheat, a crop with which they were unfamiliar. Similar to the Irish peasants who were unable to make bread from wheat after their potato crops failed, the Tibetans, being used to barley, had no idea how to prepare wheat for consumption. Fortunately, they learned from Chinese peasants how to eat leaves and grasses, or else they would have all starved to death. Nearly all the Tibetan monasteries were demolished and the monks (lamas) that populated them were lucky if they were only jailed and tortured as thousands were executed. Anyone who resisted was classified as a lama or a landlord. Frequent rebellions were brutally put down. In 1962, the second highest Tibetan religious leader, the Panchen Lama—the Dalai Lama had wisely fled in 1959—wrote a scathing letter to Mao where he "alleged that Buddhism was being virtually annihilated and he warned that, if current policies continued, the Tibetan nationality would either cease to exist or be completely assimilated" (ibid., 175). Today, the Chinese Communist Party under Xi is not only attempting to destroy the Uyghur "family of mind" through forced assimilation (see the Introduction), hundreds of thousands of Tibetan children are also being taken away from their parents and sent to boarding schools where they are subjected to propaganda and completely stripped of their Tibetan culture. For Xi, as it had been for Mao, that is precisely the plan (www.nytimes.com/interactive/2025/01/09/world/asia/tibet-china-boarding-schools.html).

Comparing Stalin's Russia and Mao's China

There are numerous parallels between the famines that took place in the Soviet Union and Communist China. Both communist governments allowed peasants to farm small, privately held plots of land and engage in trade after their victories in vicious civil wars left them weakened. After a decade or so, both then used the threat of further conflict—in the Soviet Union a "war scare" with the West in 1927, and in China, the threat of confrontation with the United States—to justify campaigns collectivizing agriculture and creating huge communes.in order to extract grain deliveries and finance a policy of industrialization. Stalin and Mao both touched off disruptive internal party squabbles and, worse, purposefully ignited "class wars" in the countryside that led to violence, bloodshed, and ultimately famines that cost millions of peasants their lives. Both of these famines were man made, stemming from political considerations. Both regimes pursued policies designed to wipe out national identities—the Soviets tried to crush Ukrainian national aspirations, and the Chinese did the same to Tibetans—by sending their political and cultural leaders to prison camps. Both Stalin and Mao unleashed further chaos and bloodshed in their respective countries a few years after concluding their collectivization campaigns to wreak revenge on those who had opposed their policies. Stalin's "Great Purge," which we examined in the previous chapter, saw the execution of nearly 700,000 of his enemies—real or imagined—and cemented his status as the supreme leader of the Soviet Union. There were no longer any limits on Stalin's power and the Soviet government encouraged a "cult of personality" that portrayed Stalin as the all-knowing and infallible leader of the country. Unlike Stalin's position in Soviet Russia, however, the catastrophe of the Chinese attempt at modernization seriously weakened Mao's control over his Communist Party. Forced to outmaneuver his competitors, he reconsolidated his hold on the Party. In 1966, Mao launched yet another radical movement known as the "Great Proletarian Cultural Revolution." The targets of the "Red Guards"—millions of radicalized youths summoned to finish the revolution—were intellectuals, schoolteachers, and most importantly, party officials opposed to Mao's viewpoints. At least as many people were killed in this turbulent period as died in Stalin's terror and another cult of personality was created around Mao. Finally, both the Soviet and Chinese communists were determined to destroy the traditions and ways of life of their respective peasantries and create an entirely new type of human being who would be a resolute worker for communism. This was also the case with the Khmer Rouge in Cambodia.

The Khmer Rouge in Cambodia

The Khmer Rouge—Khmer being the language and ethnicity of the majority of Cambodians—was another political party motivated by a quasi-religious, pseudo-Marxist political philosophy. They were victorious in a five-year civil war and seized control of Cambodia under their leader Pol Pot in April 1975. For the next nearly four years, until toppled from power by the invading Vietnamese army, the KR plunged Cambodia—renamed Democratic Kampuchea—into an almost indescribable abyss of sheer terror and horror. In their attempt to create a racially pure "communist" society, they implemented a program of social engineering that obliterated entire classes (urban dwellers), ethnicities (Vietnamese, Thai, Laotian, and Cham), religions (Buddhist monks and the Muslim Cham) and political groups (the former regime's intelligentsia and then purges of its own leadership). The party, also known as "Angkar" or the "Organization," wanted to use its ideology of racial nationalism—not unlike the Nazis—to recreate a powerful, ethnically homogeneous state such as had supposedly existed in medieval times. This utopian, racist vision motivated the Khmer Rouge to undertake their multiple genocides of the social and political groups, ethnicities, and religions that made up Cambodian society.

The social transformation envisioned by the KR was designed to skip over the "bourgeois" phase of history and proceed directly to communism. Unlike traditional Marxism, or its perverted form of Stalinism, the Khmer Rouge did not idealize the working class. Instead, the ideology of the KR included "a fervent but formulaic romanticizing of the peasantry" more akin to that of Maoist China (Cox 2017, 134). This idealization of the peasantry was also similar to that of the Nazis, but the KR combined their admiration for the "clean and sound characteristics and essence" of rural folk with an especially virulent anti-urban ideology (Kiernan 1996, 94). Urban dwellers—a large percentage of whom were Vietnamese—were the KR's first victims. The elimination of the urban class was a top priority for their campaign to destroy the foundations of a class society and the influence of the "bourgeoisie," a category that the Khmer applied to any political enemies regardless of their occupation or social status (Cox 2017, 133–34). Despite their celebration of the peasantry's virtues as being the

Figure 6.3 A darkly, perhaps unintentionally humorous sign at Cheung Ek Genocide Center and former genocide site in Phnom Penh, Cambodia. https://www.flickr.com/photos/adam_jones/3773849873/in/album-72157621904944454/

"essence" of the Khmer people, Pol Pot—the leader of the KR—and his comrades, like Stalin and his minions, collectivized farms to destroy individual attachments to private property. They even went so far as to make household items such as pots and pans common property and forced the peasants to eat in communal kitchens. Stalin and Mao had also collectivized agriculture and banned profit-oriented businesses but the goal of the Khmer was the complete obliteration of family life and the creation of a racially pure, classless society (Figure 6.3).

The KR assured the peasants that modern improvements such as electricity and tractors would make possible increased crop yields and a life of plenty. They even promised that one glorious day in the not-too-distant future people would be able to have dessert after a meal (Chandler 1992). Race and nation, however, were far more important considerations than class to the Khmer Rouge. In this respect too, they were more like the Nazis than anything resembling socialism as it had been understood before Stalin. One could separately delineate and address the different collectivities attacked by the KR under most any theme in this book, but we decided to include the horrors of this period in this chapter because the KR considered themselves communists and compared their policies—favorably—with previous Soviet and Maoist models of development. As the American historian Eric Weitz, said, for "all the particularities of Democratic Kampuchea and the Khmer Rouge, its leaders were, first and foremost, twentieth century communists" (Weitz 2003, 149).

Pol Pot

Like many other revolutionaries in history, Pol Pot—born as Saloth Sar in 1925—came from a fairly prosperous family. His family had royal connections—the Cambodian monarchy, although left intact by their French colonial masters, had no real power—and he attended a series of elite Catholic schools. Eventually, due to those connections and his fluency in French, Saloth Sar was one of a very small number of Cambodians invited to continue their education in France—despite the fact that he was not a particularly good student and had never even completed his high school degree. He continued with this indifferent attitude toward his academics during the three years he spent in Paris studying radio technology. Like Ho Chi Minh, the future leader of Vietnam, he became a member of the French Communist Party and supposedly spent most of his time reading the works of Marx, Lenin and Stalin. He later admitted that while he had read "the big, thick works of Marx" but that he "didn't really understand them at all" (quoted in Cox 2017, 133).

After returning to Cambodia, he became a teacher at a private school in the capital of Phnom Penh but devoted most of his energy to the tiny, insignificant underground Communist Party. Forced to flee with his comrades when discovered, he spent two years in exile in Vietnam, where he developed a seething hatred of the Vietnamese. Evidently, the general secretary of the Vietnamese Communist Party informed Saloth Sar that the Vietnamese struggle against the Americans was far more important than his small party's dream of overthrowing the Cambodian monarchy and that he should fall in line and help Vietnam defeat the United States. Saloth Sar was far more impressed with Maoist China, visiting there in 1966 during the "Cultural Revolution." This admiration for the Chinese example would be evident when the KR came to power. Until then, Saloth Sar, by now the undisputed leader of the party, and other top communists such as Ieng Sary hid out in the mountainous jungles of Cambodia, biding their time and waiting for their opportunity. Sometimes referred to as "Brother Number 1," Saloth Sar adopted the pseudonym "Pol Pot," although he was also known as "*Khmaer Daem*" which meant "the original Cambodian." This reflected not only his idealization of the ancient Khmer Empire (ninth through fifteenth centuries CE), but also his obsession with the idea of a racially "pure" Khmer race (Kiernan 2007 xxi). His racist, xenophobic (dislike or prejudice against people from other countries) ideology ultimately created the violent nationalism of the KR (Cox 2017, 127).

Remaking Cambodian Society

By the early 1970s, the indiscriminate and illegal bombing of Cambodia by the United States—in a futile effort to disrupt North Vietnamese supply routes to their forces in South Vietnam—made it easy for the KR to attract at least some popular support in the countryside. With North Vietnamese assistance, the KR made their bid to overthrow the Cambodian government headed by Lon Nol. The bombings only increased after the Americans pulled their ground troops out of Vietnam in early 1973, undermining the Cambodian government still further. On April 17, 1975, two weeks before the North

Vietnamese ended their war of national liberation by capturing the South Vietnamese capital of Saigon, the KR swept into Phnom Penh and declared the establishment of Democratic Kampuchea. The KR immediately set to work to make their feverish, "utopian" dreams a reality. There was no time to waste. In 1931, Stalin had urged his comrades to adopt his radical plan of collectivization and rapid industrialization before Russia was attacked by the enemies that surrounded her, "either we do this, or we go under" he had warned. Pol Pot put forward his own plan and argued that Cambodia would also have to move fast with its own "leap forward" since "outside enemies are waiting to crush us" (Weitz 2003, 150). The use of the term "leap forward" was an obvious reference to Mao's own policy of the "Great Leap Forward" we have already discussed. Pol Pot, wanting to outshine both his communist teachers—Stalin and Mao—went even further with his rhetoric by announcing a "*Super* Great Leap Forward." Pol Pot and his comrades "consciously set out to surpass China and the Soviet Union with the speed and scope with which they implemented communism" (Valentino 2005, 143).

Their very first day in power the KR ordered all urban residents—including the more than two million inhabitants of the capital Phnom Penh—to leave the cities and go into the countryside. The KR regarded the city people as impure and corrupted by Western influence. In the countryside they would be "cleansed" of these foreign influences and "remolded" into the ideal Khmer through hard labor. The forced deportations would help in the process of social leveling, as the social and cultural ties of the urban people would be eliminated. During these brutal evacuations untold numbers of people died. Thousands of captured soldiers, bureaucrats and police were simply shot out of hand, along with their families. The KR also executed anyone who resisted on the spot. The elderly and infirm fared the worst. According to Kiernan, "one order explicitly ordered cadres to kill urban evacuees indiscriminately" (quoted in Kiernan 1996, 165). In just one week the cities of Cambodia were completely emptied of their residents. Labeled as "new people," and forced to work on irrigation systems, canals, roads, and other construction projects or labor in the fields, they toiled for 12- to 16-hour shifts under harsh conditions. The KR considered these "new" people expendable and told them "to kill you is no loss, to spare you no profit." The "pure" Khmer villagers, classified as "old" (or sometimes "base") people, would supposedly be the model citizens for the future egalitarian communist society. The urban dwellers, totally dispersed and atomized, ceased to exist as a social class. In the countryside, the poor peasants, designated as allies of the regime as had been the case in the Soviet Union—unless they caused trouble or spoke out against the KR—also had their traditional way of life disrupted. Of course, those that were better off or resisted collectivization, like the *kulaks* in the Soviet Union, the KR simply executed. The "base" people received better food rations and, when the inevitable food shortages and then famine set in as it had in both Soviet Russia and Communist China, "even slightly more food could mean the difference between life and death" (Weitz, 2003, 160). Nevertheless, the KR completely disrupted their social and cultural ties as well.

The American historian Eric Weitz describes how the KR instituted a system of virtual apartheid (the *Afrikaans* word for the policy of "separateness" between Blacks and Whites in South Africa) between "old" and "new" people. They lived apart, ate in separate communal dining halls, and worked in segregated labor battalions. Not only were they forbidden to marry each other, they were even forbidden to speak to one another (ibid.). There was, however, no family life for anyone under the KR. The Party often forced its members into arranged marriages, and even the weddings for non-party members were communal affairs where officials would sometimes simply pair up men and women. These couples, often assigned to different work brigades, had to live separately in gender-segregated barracks. The KR policed all relationships; they prohibited sex outside of marriage and executed violators. They even removed teens from their families and kept them from their parents by assigning them to different labor gangs. As part of their campaign to refashion society, the KR wanted to eliminate any loyalties other than to "Angkar." In traditional Cambodia, family relationships and ties of kinship were extremely important. Weitz notes that Cambodians addressed each other by these relational ties. The KR purposely disrupted these connections and reoriented them toward "Angkar." Mothers were told they "must not get too entangled with their children [...] there should be time to go and work" (quoted in ibid., 151). The KR intended to cut all emotional ties between couples and between parents and children. Youngsters were told they were the "children of Angkar" and that they should "report all the activities of your parents" (quoted in ibid., 152). He concludes that the KR wanted to "substitute Angkar, the Organization, for the family" (ibid., 163). Pol Pot became "Brother Number One." The KR saw all of Cambodian society as bound together by racial ties, as one party slogan put it, "Do you love your race? Do you love Angkar?" (ibid., 163).

Determined to create a homogeneous communist, "racially pure" Khmer society, the KR began to target any non-Khmer ethnic or religious groups that might try to maintain their identities. The KR slogan "it isn't enough to cut down a bad plant, it must be uprooted" confirmed their intention to destroy at least some of these groups in their entirety. The historian Ben Kiernan, the leading authority on the Cambodian genocide, argues that the conditions imposed upon the "new" people—especially the educated middle class, business elites and civil servants of the old regime that might offer resistance—were specifically intended to bring about their complete destruction (Kiernan 2007). This social group suffered grievously under the reign of terror perpetrated by Pol Pot and his supporters. They were not alone. Up to 20 percent of Cambodia's estimated eight million population, or around one and one half million people, were ethnic minorities. In the future Kampuchea, however, "there are to be no Cham, or Chinese, or Vietnamese. Everybody is to join the same, single, Khmer nationality [...] there is to be only one religion, the Khmer religion" (quoted in Weitz 2003, 162).

The KR, then, were particularly suspicious of any religious groups that might hinder their plans for the future secular "communist" society that they envisioned. Ben Kiernan concludes that virtually all the Buddhist monks in Cambodia—some 68,000 out of 70,000—died during the rule of the KR, with every monastery and temple destroyed (Kiernan in Totten and Parsons eds., 2009, 346). The Muslim Cham people, targeted not only because of their religion but also for their distinct language and culture, suffered cruelly. The Cham, classified as "bourgeois" by the Khmer Rouge even though their men engaged in fishing or individual farming, simply did not fit into their plans. The KR banned the use of the Cham language, closed down their schools, destroyed their religious texts, and compelled them to cut their traditionally long hair and to dress differently than their customs dictated. They forced the Cham to violate their religious beliefs, even compelling them not only to raise pigs, but also to eat them. Some of their temples were turned into pigsties. Those who resisted were killed, and ultimately at least 100,000 Cham died out of a total population of 250,000, though some estimates are considerably higher (Kiernan 1996, 348). Other minorities targeted for forcible integration, or failing that, total destruction, included the Thai population, reduced from 20,000 to 8,000, thousands of Laotians and virtually the entirety of the Kola people (Jones 2011, 299). Despite the assistance given the KR by China, up to several hundred thousand people of Chinese descent in Cambodia also perished. The KR targeted the Chinese and Vietnamese in particular because they were mostly urban dwellers who were involved in commercial or business activities. This made them both "bourgeois" and racially alien.

There had long been hostility between Cambodia and Vietnam, which was one reason why the North Vietnamese were willing to offer sanctuary to their fellow Communists from Cambodia who were seeking to overthrow the government of Lon Nol. Lon Nol, a career military officer and former high-ranking government official, was an ardent anticommunist and despised the Vietnamese. In 1970, he engineered a coup that overthrew the Cambodian monarchy headed by Prince Norodom Sihanouk. After declaring a "Khmer Republic," he immediately unleashed his forces on the large number of Vietnamese people living in Cambodia, killing thousands. David Chandler, an American historian widely regarded as one of the world's foremost scholars of Cambodian history, stated that this assault was a "racially based religious war against unarmed civilians whose families had lived in Cambodia for generations" (Chandler 1992, 203). More than half a million Vietnamese were forced to leave the country. When the Khmer Rouge came to power in 1975, they continued to purge the Vietnamese from Cambodia. Kiernan asserts that within one month of coming to power, Pol Pot ordered the KR to remove the entire Vietnamese population from Cambodia (Kiernan 1996, 107). The KR placed a great emphasis on "cleansing" the Vietnamese from Democratic Kampuchea, saying only when "the Vietnamese are all gone" would their task be complete (quoted in ibid., 366). The regime only became more radicalized as war with Vietnam broke out, and eventually Pol Pot ordered the arrest of all Vietnamese still living in Cambodia.

Pol Pot also sent his troops into the country's Eastern Zone, which bordered Vietnam, and began a horrific assault on the entire population there. Claiming they had "Khmer bodies with Vietnamese minds," the inhabitants were driven out of the region and between 100,000 and 250,000 died either from mass killings or starvation (Kiernan 2007, 59). As had both Stalin and Mao, Pol Pot began a purge of his own party comrades. Unlike those two, however, this was not just about political dissent or questions of loyalty. Instead, like everything else in a party devoted to—in Eric Weitz's words, "racial communism"—it was about suspected connections or ties with Vietnam. The victims included anyone who spoke Vietnamese and especially any of the party cadres that had received training or been sheltered in Vietnam—though of course Pol Pot himself had found refuge there. Many of these party members— who, lest we forget, were themselves complicit in the crimes of the Khmer Rouge—met their fate in the notorious torture chambers of Tuol Sleng. Also known as S-21, an estimated 14,000 people were murdered there. In early 1979, the Vietnamese army, along with thousands of Cambodians, finally put an end to the bloody reign of the Khmer Rouge. Pol Pot fled into the jungle and, incredibly, remained there along with many of his supporters, for another two decades before his death in 1998. While it is impossible to know for sure how many people died from violence, starvation, or disease under the KR, the demographer Patrick Heuveline estimates between 1.17 and 3.42 million excess deaths between 1970 and 1979 (Heuveline 1998, 49–65). Ben Kiernan concludes that as many as 1.7 million people died as result of the extreme nationalism and racism promoted by Pol Pot and the KR. This amounted to nearly 20 percent of the population. Whatever others might call it—ethnocide, classicide, politicide, democide, auto-genocide—it was genocide, too.

Stalin, Mao and Pol Pot

All three of these communist despots were in a hurry to reach their goals. They acted swiftly and brutally in their attempts to achieve them. The cost in human life, numbering in the tens of millions, staggers the mind. Each of the three—supposedly all believers in Karl Marx's ideas about historical development—wanted to give history a "push" and achieve socialism through their own sheer will, regardless of the easily predictable, appalling misery they caused their own, and other, people. Only one of the three, however, followed Marx's thinking that the working class, or proletariat, would be the future beneficiaries of the utopia he envisioned. Stalin applied Marx's theory of historical materialism—one specifically modeled after industrializing England and the growing effect of the Industrial Revolution in Europe on the old regime—to a peasant country. The only base of support for the Soviet regime was, in fact, the working class, but after the "Great October Socialist Revolution," most workers grew weary of food rationing and consumer shortages. Stalin did rule over a police state, but it was not a "totalitarian" one as so often depicted in high school textbooks. Stalin wanted to mobilize the country's resources and industrialize as quickly as possible not only because of his fear of attack from the capitalist powers. He also had to maintain the support of the workers, and the working class benefited the most from collectivization. The peasantry, as we have seen, did fight back and eventually Stalin compromised with them and allowed for the private plots and a cow and a few chickens and pigs. It may not seem like much, but for the peasantry it was a victory of sorts.

Stalin's efforts to harness all the Soviet Union's peoples to the Communist wagon came at a huge cost, both in human lives and in the social and cultural ties that bound peoples such as the Ukrainians and the Kazakhs together. He had warned in 1931 that the Soviet Union only had ten years to make the gigantic leap from being a backward agrarian society to an industrialized and militarized one. He was right. The Nazi invasion in 1941 put the Soviet system to the test, and it passed. If Stalin had not used nationalism—the idea of "socialism in one country" was a thinly veiled appeal to national pride, and during World War II the pretense was dropped altogether—to create the world's first socialist society the Nazis may well have won the war. The ultimate collapse of the Soviet Union in 1991 allowed for its subject peoples—almost half the population left the Soviet Union—to reestablish the national identities Stalin tried so hard to crush. Ukraine, in particular, has risen like a phoenix from the ashes. As much as Lenin and Stalin's "socialism" approximated Marx's version in some ways it also was a product of Russia's own historical development and political culture. Russia today under Putin seems very much like the Soviet Union, but also much like Russia during the tsarist regime. The Russian Revolution's most long-lasting impact on the world might actually be the success of its heir, Communist China.

Mao also pursued communism in an overwhelmingly peasant country. He rode roughshod over the peasantry in the name of creating a future utopia. Unlike in Soviet Russia, which hewed somewhat more closely to Marx's prescriptions, at least in theory, Mao based his power on the peasantry. A true ideologue—he had urged the Soviet Union to attack the United States with nuclear weapons to hasten the victory of world communism—by the time of his death in 1976, Mao had completely wrecked the social and economic systems of his country. It was his far more pragmatic successor, Deng Xiaoping who turned "communist" China into a superpower. He ended Mao's fanatical crusade for communism and—noting "it doesn't matter if a cat is black or white, only that it catches mice"—he unleashed capitalism in China. Pol Pot also wanted to achieve communism and to do so more quickly and successfully than his two older comrades. The racial nationalism of the Khmer Rouge bore more similarities with Western imperialism and the Nazis than with Marxism. All three of these Communist dictators believed that sheer force of will could overcome any obstacles. Stalin proclaimed "there were no fortresses that Bolsheviks cannot storm" and dams were built, villages flooded and the course of rivers reversed—all through forced labor—in massive projects designed to conquer nature. He supported the nonsensical idea of applying the "Marxist dialectic" to crop genetics and the result was the ruin of Soviet agriculture. In China, the environmental damage done by Mao to fulfill his dreams of a communist utopia was incalculable. Forests were cut down, leading to erosion and flooding, poorly conceived irrigation projects resulted in massive flooding, and by the time Mao died in 1976 almost 3,000 shoddily constructed dams had collapsed in Henan Province alone (Dikotter 2010, 183). Pol Pot also thought that communists could achieve remarkable results in agriculture and bend nature to their will. Cambodians would become "masters of the earth and water," "masters of the yearly floods," and "masters of the rice fields and plains, of the forests and of all vegetation" (quoted in Weitz 2003, 152). Perhaps the most disturbing aspect of these attempts at creating socialism, however, was not that these dictators thought they could control Mother Nature, but that they could change *human* nature and create entirely new human beings altogether.

Questions for Further Discussion

1. How did Stalin explain the necessity of his collectivization policy? Who supported this policy and why?
2. Ukrainians today refer to the *Holodomor* as being a genocide while Russians vehemently disagree. Does the famine of 1932–33 meet the criterion under the 1948 UN Genocide Convention of "intent to destroy, a national, ethnic, racial or religious group, in whole or in part?"
3. How does the Chinese famine compare with the *Holodomor*?
4. What ideological motives were used in all three of these case studies (Soviet Russia, Communist China, and the Khmer Rouge in Cambodia) to justify the implementation of their "crash" programs?
5. What "social" groups came under attack by these three communist regimes? Which "religious" groups? "Ethnic or national" ones? Why?

Chapter Seven

EMPIRE AND STATE-BUILDING THROUGH GENOCIDE

Colonialism is the ultimate cancel culture.
—Femi Nylander, British-Nigerian poet-activist, 2020

Colonialism and "Cultural" Genocide

Raphael Lemkin believed that at its core genocide was a colonial undertaking. In *Axis Rule*, he wrote that genocide had two phases: "one, destruction of the national pattern of the oppressed group; the other, the imposition of the national pattern of the oppressor. This imposition, in turn, may be made upon the oppressed population which is allowed to remain, or upon the territory alone, after removal of the population and the colonization of the area by the oppressor's own nationals" (Lemkin 2008, 79). When surveying Nazi occupation practices in the lands that they had overrun, Lemkin explicitly asserted that all the different techniques of administration and control he examined were part of a colonial project. He wrote, "[I]n line with this policy of imposing the German national pattern, particularly in the incorporated territories, the occupant has organized a system of colonization of these areas" (ibid., 83). These methods, or techniques, had as their objective "the disintegration of the political and social institutions, of culture, language, national feelings, religion and the economic existence of national groups [...]" (ibid., 79).

In Lemkin's original concept, there was no separation between physical or biological genocide and cultural genocide. Genocide was the intended destruction of a human group, shattering their social bonds and resulting in the loss of that group's unique culture forever. In other words, because genocide was ultimately about the loss of a particular culture, there was no need to differentiate between "physical" genocide and "cultural" genocide. A people's culture could be attacked as part of a campaign of genocide, but absent the attempt to destroy that human group cultural repression in and of itself was not necessarily genocidal. Of course, he understood that over time the cultures of human groups changed, were assimilated, or even disappeared altogether as a result of contacts with other human groups and cultures. Cultures, along with their peoples, came and went over the long course of history. Though a firm believer in diversity and multi-culturalism, Lemkin nevertheless thought this was a positive feature for the development of world cultures. As Irvin-Erickson put it, "the disintegration of a given group (and, by extension its culture) was not necessarily a bad thing" as "the interactions of groups are what caused groups to change, and that this change was the engine of human progress and creativity" (Irvin-Erickson, 2019, 23).

As we have stated before, central to Lemkin's idea of genocide was the *intended destruction* of human groups with the consequent loss of their unique cultures. We can see this idea in the United Nations General Assembly Resolution 96 (I) of December 11, 1946, which he helped compose. The Resolution requested that the Economic and Social Council (ECOSOC) "undertake the necessary studies, with a view to drawing up a draft convention of the crime of genocide." Genocide was then initially defined as the "destruction of human groups" leading to "great losses in the form of cultural and other contributions."

The General Secretary tasked the UN Division of Human Rights with drawing up an initial draft of the proposed law. Lemkin and two other legal scholars then developed the first "Secretariat" Draft. The definition of genocide there was any act committed against a racial, national, linguistic, religious or political group "with the purpose of destroying it in whole or in part or of preventing its preservation or development." Article II of the draft identified three techniques of genocide: physical, biological, and cultural. This draft was then submitted to the ECOSOC which appointed an *ad hoc* Committee on Genocide to finish the drafting of the Convention. When this committee turned in its revised draft to the ECOSOC committee the definition still included political groups—we have already seen in previous chapters how and why that group was ultimately removed from the Convention's protections—but cultural genocide had been separated from physical or biological genocide and was instead included on its own in Article III. Although Lemkin did not believe that cultural genocide was a "different" form of genocide, he wanted to preserve it from being cut out from the Convention altogether. Sent from there to the Sixth (Legal) Committee, Article III was, despite Lemkin's pleas, removed altogether. Lemkin did, however, understand the political nature of the negotiations over the Convention. It is likely that he agreed to compromises such as the removal of "cultural" genocide and the protection of political groups—on this last point, as we saw earlier, he had completely reversed himself—altogether from the final draft in exchange for the support of otherwise uncommitted delegations. Other considerations, such as the vague promise of the eventual establishment of an international criminal court with universal jurisdiction, also undoubtedly played a role in his thinking. Ultimately, however, neither of these essential features were specifically included in the Convention, although the possibility for such a future court was mentioned in Article VI.

The final resolution was then forwarded to the General Assembly for approval. Leading the way in opposing the inclusion of cultural genocide in the Convention was the United States. In Lemkin's words, the United States had committed "cultural genocide *par excellence*" against Native Americans, in "the most effective and thorough method of destroying a culture, and of de-socializing human beings" (quoted in Decker 2008, 94). Not to be outdone, colonial powers such as France, Great Britain and the Netherlands—who would soon be attempting to brutally crush independence movements in Indochina, Algeria, Kenya, Cyprus, Madagascar and Indonesia—also strenuously objected to the very idea of cultural genocide, recognizing that they could easily be charged with having committed this crime upon the peoples they had long subjugated and exploited. This explains why the post-World War II European empires (the Netherlands, Portugal, Great Britain, Belgium and France) controlling large swathes of Africa and Asia for their own economic benefit, along with those countries descended from "settler" colonies that had pursued genocidal policies against the indigenous peoples of the lands they had colonized (the United States, South Africa, Australia and New Zealand), teamed up to prevent the inclusion of "cultural" genocide in the 1948 Convention. "Cultural" genocide is generally taken to mean an attack on the language, customs and practices of a particular human group; this separation between "cultural" genocide and outright physical elimination was, as Douglas Irvin-Erickson suggests, engineered by the United States during the drafting of the 1948 Convention in order to remove altogether from the final version of the law aspects of Lemkin's original concept that would leave the US—and its allies—open to those accusations of genocide (Irvin-Erickson 2019).

Imperialism was primarily about the extraction of resources and the exploitation of labor, while "settler" colonialism was, as Patrick Wolfe wrote, "first and foremost a territorial project, whose priority is replacing natives on their land rather than extracting an economic surplus from mixing their labor with it" (Wolfe 2008, 103). This obviously involved "ethnic cleansing," and we have already made clear how we fail to see any difference between "genocide" and "ethnic cleansing" as it is the intended destruction of a group through violence in a designated space—the very essence of genocide. As Martin Shaw noted, "genocide always involves territorial displacement" (Shaw 2015, 82). This destruction of the way of life of a community is but one of many different possible methods of genocide. We have already dismissed the popular perception—and the viewpoint of many scholars—that genocide must necessarily involve mass killing. Lemkin knew that there were many other ways to destroy a group and he insisted that "we not describe a crime by one example" (quoted in Lemkin 2013, xvi). By now the reader is also aware that we think that the destruction of the ways of life or the social and cultural bonds that tie a people together constitutes genocide as surely as the deliberate massacring of much, or even most, of a particular human group.

As stated previously, to kill *a* people, then, it is not necessary to *kill* people. Alongside physical violence, genocide can also be accomplished by the imposition of foreign ideologies and belief systems that, over time, undermine the affected human groups and slowly destroys their social and cultural cohesion. Invariably, violence—and killing—is usually resorted to, and often then combined with psychological violence. "Settler" colonists practiced "ethnic cleansing" with physical violence, and then "cultural" genocide with a concerted effort to "remake" a people—both are simply different *methods* of genocide. We discussed this earlier in Chapter Two when we examined the US and Canadian governments' (and settlers') treatment of Native North American peoples. It would be impossible here to discuss in detail the full impact of the imperial policies and colonial practices on indigenous peoples in the Americas, Asia and Africa. The Age of Imperialism saw European powers extend their control over large parts of the Earth and subject many of those captive peoples to "slow-motion" cultural genocides. To be sure, there was also plenty of violence and killing involved. And there was nothing "slow" about the destruction of the Herero and Congolese, our two case studies of the genocidal effects of colonialism and imperialism in this chapter.

We should remind the reader that European settlers had colonized South Africa as early as 1652. The descendants of these Dutch settlers—the Boers, meaning "farmers"—instituted their racist system of *apartheid*, or "separateness" in 1948, the very same year the Genocide Convention was passed. The delegates from the Union of South Africa and the Netherlands disagreed with the idea that "all cultures, even the most barbarous, deserved protection" and were appalled that "assimilation resulting from the civilizing action of a State also constituted genocide" (quoted in Lippman 1985, 45). This restatement of "The White Man's Burden" a half-century after Rudyard Kipling penned the poem well illustrates the mentality of the colonial powers. South Africa, like the Nazi state, had modeled their racial laws after "Jim Crow" in the United States (Fredrickson 2003; Whitman 2017). *Apartheid* was condemned annually between 1952 and 1990 by the UN General Assembly as a violation of the UN Charter; in 1966, the General Assembly also declared it a crime against humanity and in 1973, adopted the Apartheid Convention. The UN Security Council eventually endorsed the Apartheid Convention in 1984. It would be another ten years until the racist, colonial South African regime was abolished—brought down by a powerful domestic resistance combined with a massive global human-rights campaign. This demonstrates that change resulting in a better world is possible. In the 1980s, in South Africa as well as the dictatorial Communist regimes in Eastern Europe, this kind of far-reaching social and political change might have seemed impossible, but all these regimes tumbled by the early 1990s because of small and large acts of resistance.

Despite Lemkin's belief that the forced assimilation of the members of one group into another during the age of imperialism was in fact genocide, the United States and the colonial powers made strenuous, and ultimately successful, efforts to eliminate the links between colonialism and genocide. They not only managed first to remove "cultural" genocide from the definition of the term (though some of Lemkin's thinking on the techniques used by genocidists to commit genocide other than mass killing such as imposing measures intended to prevent births within the group and forcibly transferring children of the group to another group were included in Article II) when finally adopted by the UN they were even able to exclude the application of the Convention itself to their colonial possessions. Article XII allowed these overlords to "at any time [...] extend the application of the present Convention to all or any of the territories for the conduct of whose foreign relations that Contracting Party is responsible." Suffice it to say the "Contracting Parties"—the colonial powers—never had any intentions of doing so. Instead, for the most part they fought tenaciously to hold on to their empires. (Great Britain did recognize the writing on the wall on the sub-continent and they "quit" India while attempting to crush brutally uprisings in Kenya and Cyprus.) As Jeffrey Bachman notes, "at the time the provisions of the UNCG were being negotiated, France had seventeen colonies and two trusteeships in Africa alone. The UK also maintained seventeen African colonies and kept close ties with the apartheid regime in South Africa" (Bachman ed. 2019, 55). No wonder, then, when Lemkin looked for support for the adoption of the Convention, he noticed that it was the delegates from Africa, "on whom genocide was practiced" who were most keen on adopting a law against genocide (quoted in Irvin-Erickson 2017, 152).

The Herero

During the last few decades of the nineteenth century European powers—and eventually the United States and Japan as well—competed with one another in an unprecedented quest for control of still more overseas territories in Africa and Asia. This "new imperialism"—as distinguished from the "old" imperialism of the sixteenth through eighteenth centuries when European states had conquered peoples throughout the world and established colonies and empires—saw the imposition of direct political control of most of Africa. This bloody and violent feat was accomplished largely due to key inventions and innovations such as the machine gun, and, believe it or not, something as seemingly mundane as quinine—which was used to protect European missionaries, settlers, traders, troops, and government officials from malaria, but denied to the indigenous peoples. It is heartening to note that as of 2024, a vaccine has been developed to prevent this terrible disease.

Germany had only become a unified nation under Prussia's leadership in 1871 through Prussian Chancellor Otto Von Bismarck's policy of "blood and iron"—a series of wars engineered by Prussia to consolidate the many German principalities, grand duchies, petty kingdoms, and independent city-states into a single, powerful country. Though Bismarck himself had little interest in imperial expansion, German publicists and propagandists argued that Germany needed colonies to establish itself as a great power. In an 1879 pamphlet, Friedrich Fabri asserted that it was a matter of life and death for the future development of Germany and that "colonies will have a salutary effect on our economic situation as well as on our entire national progress" (quoted in Snyder 1962, 18). Fabri, who had spent time in South West Africa (known today as Namibia), also believed that it was part of Germany's "cultural mission" to rule over the different peoples both of that region and Germany's other new possessions in East Africa. In 1882, just a few years after Fabri's pamphlet calling for Germany to join in with the other European countries in acquiring territories, Bismarck gave a German businessman, Adolf Luderitz, permission to acquire land in South West Africa and assured him of the government's official recognition of those territories as German imperial possessions. As with the other European powers, representatives of the German Empire soon arrived to cajole, trick, or force native chiefs to sign so-called treaties of protection. Settlers quickly followed. Worried about how the British in South Africa would react to the sudden influx of Germans, Bismarck called for an international conference to establish a process for the peaceful division of Africa. At the Berlin Conference of 1884, to which no Africans were invited, Bismarck acted as an "honest broker" to ensure cooperation between the European states as they sought to establish their claims by effectively occupying various parts of the continent. Signed in 1885, the final document set off the "scramble for Africa"—the division of Africa into European colonies and spheres of influence without any consideration of existing cultural, linguistic, and ethnic boundaries and distinctions.

In his draft of a proposed book to be titled *History of Genocide*, Lemkin wrote that the Germans "did not colonize Africa with the intention of ruling the country justly, living in peace with the true owners of the land, and developing its resources for the mutual advantage of both. Their idea was to settle some of the surplus population in Africa and to turn it into a German white empire" (Lemkin 2013, 220). German settlers poured in to take control of fertile lands which greatly reduced the pasture lands available to the native Herero for their livestock. Others came in to explore economic opportunities in diamond or copper mining. One German colonist wrote, "the decision to colonize South West Africa could, after all, mean nothing but this: that the native tribes would have to give up their lands on which they had previously grazed their stock in order that the white man should have the land [...]" (quoted in Lemkin 2013, 268). By the end of 1903, the German farmers had fenced in 3.5 million hectares out of a total available of 13 million hectares; it was apparent to the Herero, a Bantu-speaking people, that their traditional pastoral way of life would soon be lost (Bridgman and Worley in Totten and Parsons eds. 1997, 21). Clashes between the Herero and the German interlopers were frequent, though the Herero chief Samuel Maharero and Theodor Leutwein, German governor of the colony from 1894 to 1905, generally got along well. Lemkin acknowledged that Leutwein tried "to govern the native tribes with some degree of humanity and regard for their rights and native customs." Of course, the settlers saw them as but primitive savages who should provide a ready supply of cheap labor. Some called for their extermination. The settlers treated the Herero badly, calling them "baboons." When the Herero pushed back over the loss of their lands and traditional ways of life it was apparent that their dissatisfaction would lead to further armed conflict.

When German authorities attempted to register all the guns in the natives' possession, however, they rightfully feared this was but a precursor to having them taken away altogether, leaving them defenseless. The last straw for the Herero was in fact an attempt by Leutwein to protect them from being exploited by German traders. Many Herero, lured by the possibility of selling their cattle for cash, had ended up purchasing "all sorts of merchandise and not at all useful and good articles, but often perfectly superfluous [unnecessary] articles of clothing [...]" that left them in debt to the white traders (Lemkin 2013, 268). Some Herero borrowed increasingly large sums at high interest rates to purchase consumer items they had never before seen. In 1903, Leutwein, concerned about the natives being taken advantage of and the mounting debts owed the white traders issued a proclamation that all debts would be voided if not collected within a year. Naturally, the German traders began calling in their loans immediately and pressured the Herero to pay up. Clashes between the German colonizers and the natives increased dramatically and Leutwein was often compelled to take his soldiers into remote parts of the region to quell uprisings. It was during one such campaign when the colonial troops were away that the Herero chief Samuel Maharero determined the time was right to strike a blow against the colonizers.

The German settlers had long thought Leutwein too lenient in dealing with the Herero. They too had seen Leutwein's absence as an opportunity and arrogantly tried to pen in the Herero on reservations, finally destroying completely their pastoralist ways of life. In January 1904, the Herero responded with a full-scale attack on all the German farms in Hereroland. Interestingly, Chief Maharero ordered that only German farms be attacked and not those of the British or Boers. He considered the Herero to be at war only with the Germans and further ordered that only military-age male Germans be killed, sparing the women and children. Missionaries were also to be spared. Bridgman and Worley believed that Maharero had good reasons for conducting his attacks in such a manner. He wanted to ensure other European-descended settlers did not join in with the Germans for a "final solution" to the so-called "black problem," and he also hoped to gain support from missionary associations in Europe (Bridgman and Worley in Totten and Parsons eds. 1997). It is particularly interesting to note that the "savage" African tribe abided by what eventually would become known as the "rules of war" while the German troops freely slaughtered prisoners, massacred women and children, and engaged in mass rape over the course of the nearly four years long war. The attacks on the settlers were depicted in Germany as being "unprovoked," public sentiment called for revenge and Leutwein was replaced as military commander by one General Lothar von Trotha, who was determined to wipe out the Herero.

Additional troops were sent from Germany to aid von Trotha in his campaign of annihilation. In August 1904, the Herero were defeated in a fierce clash at the Battle of Waterberg. Desperately fleeing the marauding German colonial troops, the surviving men, women, and children of the Herero were pursued and slaughtered, with thousands more being driven into the desert to die of thirst. The water holes were patrolled by German soldiers and many were deliberately poisoned (Figure 7.1). On October 2, 1904, von Trotha issued a blood-chilling order:

> All the Hereros [*sic*] must leave the land. If the people do not do this, I will force them to do it with the great guns. Any Herero found within the German borders with or without a gun, with or without cattle, will be shot. I will no longer receive any women or children. I will drive them back to their people or I will shoot them. This is my decision for the Herero people" (quoted in ibid., 28).

Von Trotha saw this as "the beginning of a racial war" (idem.). Though not the official policy of the German government, Bridgman and Worley state "this was genocide because it was an attempt by representatives of the German government to destroy a whole people with the knowledge and the tacit approval of the Kaiser [the German Emperor] and the General Staff [of the German Army]" (ibid., 18). The German troops rounded up the survivors and placed them into "concentration" camps and literally worked them to death. Medical experiments were also conducted on the prisoners. Herero women were sexually abused and exploited.

By the end of the first decade of the twentieth century, of perhaps 100,000 Herero and Nama—another group targeted by the German genocidists—at least three-quarters (75,000) were dead and the survivors had lost their cultural identity and cohesion as a group. Many scholars have drawn a direct line from German colonial policies in Africa to Nazi barbarities in Eastern Europe during World War II. Today, the descendants of these peoples have regained their identity and social cohesion, and like formerly subjugated peoples everywhere, have taken down the statues erected by their former colonial masters and pressed for reparations. In 2021, Germany acknowledged that it had indeed conducted a genocide in South West Africa and apologized, but also asserted that there was no legal basis for either individual or collective reparations. This

Figure 7.1 Samuel Maherero (1856–1923), leader of the Herero people, in 1907. He led a revolt against the German colonizers and is a national hero in today's Namibia. https://commons.wikimedia.org/wiki/File:SamuelMaharero_(cropped).jpg

is in marked contrast to the sincere atonement Germany has made for its genocide of the Jews. Instead, the German government offered $1.3 billion in development aid to the government of Namibia. That government, dominated by persons from the Ovambo tribe who were largely unaffected by the German onslaught of the early 1900s, made virtually no effort to consult with the descendants of the Herero or Nama peoples that had experienced the first genocide of the twentieth century.

The Congolese

By the turn of the twentieth century, almost 90 percent of the world's surface was controlled by Europeans. This included the Congo, the "heart of Africa," which was turned into the "Congo Free State" in 1885 by the Belgian King Leopold II as part of the "scramble for Africa" and exploited by him and his deputies as a virtual slave-holding plantation until 1908. Terrible violence was inflicted upon the Congolese people in Leopold's pursuit of ivory and rubber in the name of a so-called civilizing mission. In fact, many statues of this genocidist are still standing in Belgium, some with the inscription "I have undertaken the work of colonialization for the sake of civilization and for the benefit of Belgium." While Belgium—and certainly King Leopold II himself, who, while eventually forced to sell "his" property to the Belgian state ultimately collected approximately $1 billion in revenues before selling his "property" for another considerable sum—undoubtedly benefited, up to 10 million Congolese died under Belgian rule (Hochschild 1998).

This human-rights scandal was revealed in Joseph Conrad's explosive novel *Heart of Darkness*, based on his decade of work on a ship in the Congo. He had noticed that while tons of rubber were being exported to the world market, nothing was shipped *in* except guns and bullets. He soon realized that he "had stumbled upon a secret society with a king at its head." He was later joined by the British shipping clerk turned human-rights activist E. D. Morel and the Irish humanitarian Roger Casement in making known the criminal abuses of the Congolese people. These reports and exposés shamed even the world's imperialists, and the Belgian government eventually was forced to purchase the "Congo Free State" from Leopold in 1908. The Belgian government also thanked him for "his great sacrifices made for the Congo." The Congo did not rid itself of Belgian rule for another half-century, finally gaining its independence in 1960 under the leadership of the popular, charismatic leader Patrice Lumumba—who would soon be abducted and assassinated (1961) with the complicity of Belgian and US authorities.

During his reign of terror, Leopold commissioned private traders to plunder the Congo's riches on condition they turned over half their profits to him. Initially, ivory was the most sought-after item and Leopold's agents forced the Congolese to hunt elephants for their tusks. Leopold instituted a tax on the Congolese that required local chiefs to supply laborers while their families were held hostage to ensure their "quotas" were met. With the invention of the inflatable tire in the 1890s, a rubber boom resulted, and Leopold's brutal and undisciplined private African army, the *Force Publique*, was tasked with rounding up still more workers to go even deeper into the jungle to tap the rubber trees. The Belgian overseers, who had formerly paid Muslim slave traders for some of the needed workers, now had the *Force Publique* drive them out of the Congo. This was portrayed as a great humanitarian act, but the real reason was simply to acquire more rubber workers by enslaving virtually the entire Congolese population. As before, the men labored away from their families for long stretches of time while their women and children were held hostage. If the quotas were not met, Leopold's henchmen cut off the hands of the men and often those of their children as well.

There was, of course, resistance. The Congolese fought back against the army units. Many fled into the jungle and deliberately set the rubber trees on fire. The *Force Publique* burned down villages and slaughtered the families of any men who refused to work. Soldiers were sent into the jungle to kill anyone hiding there to avoid the labor gangs. Another quota was imposed, this time on the soldiers, as they were ordered to bring back the right hands of anyone they had killed. Sometimes they simply cut off the hands of anyone they met, including children, whether they were resisting Belgian rule or not, to satisfy the quotas set by their officers. King Leopold's rule was an unmitigated disaster for the Congolese people. Millions perished from the violence inflicted upon them as their social and cultural ties were completely destroyed. Though the Belgian government eliminated the worst abuses of Leopold's regime after it took over control from him, the land and its resources of copper, diamonds, oil, uranium, and other important minerals remained in Belgium's hands until 1960. In 2020, 60 years after Belgian rule ended, King Philippe of Belgium issued a statement expressing his "deepest regret" for the "acts of violence and cruelty" committed during Belgian colonial rule (BBC News, June 30, 2020). King Leopold's name was not even mentioned (Figure 7.2).

State-Building Through Genocide

Raphael Lemkin understood genocide to be a type of conflict in which one social group attempts to destroy another social group; he wrote that it is a "crime perpetrated by one *genos* against another" (Lemkin 2013, 182). But the idea that ethnic conflict is simply the result of "ancient hatreds" or of the long-standing animosity of different human groups toward each other obscures the fact that, as Martin Shaw suggests, "Genocide is not ethnic conflict but political and military conflict in which genocidists often mobilize

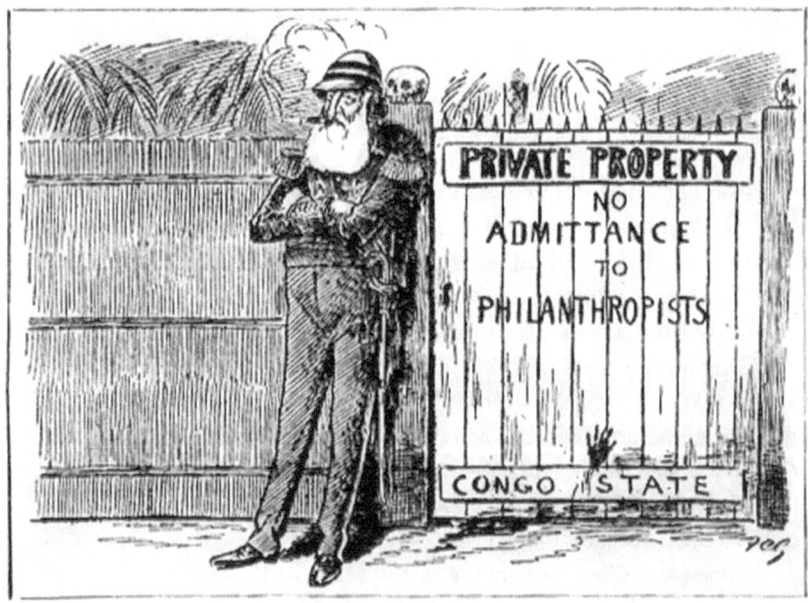

Figure 7.2 Cartoon from 1906 depicting Leopold II leaning against a gate, representing the entrance to Congo—which he treated as his personal property. The cartoonist is drawing attention to Leopold's aversion to the attention his crimes had drawn from humanitarians. https://commons.wikimedia.org/wiki/File:Cartoon_by_British_caricaturist_%27Francis_Carruthers_Gould%27_depicting_King_Leopold_2,_and_Congo_Free_State.jpg

ethnicity [...]" (Shaw 2015, 130). This calls into question the standard view of ethnic conflict being between social groups that are, in and of themselves, political actors. As Jocelyn Alexander, Jo Ann McGregor, and Terence Ranger have written, the idea of ethnic conflict is misleading because it "implies that ethnicity can be seen as the cause of such conflicts, and that ethnic conflicts are apolitical, somehow distinctive from other wars fought over resources or political power" (Alexander *et al.* 2000, 307). In their view, propagandistic "ideas about ethnic antagonism have emerged *during* conflicts rather than themselves *causing* conflict" (ibid., 311 italics in the original). They argue it is the conflict itself that serves to make these ideas about identity, "which were once fluid, inclusive, mutually compatible and weakly ethnicized [...]" into rigid, immutable narratives of "coherent, mutually exclusive peoples with a history of rivalry, persecution and revenge" (ibid., 305).

Of course, genocides also don't simply emerge out of thin air. There is usually a process with many preliminary steps taken before any extreme violence, if deemed necessary to achieve the goals of the perpetrators, is inflicted upon the designated group. And, while the idea of "ancient hatreds" or the long-standing obsession of perpetrators with the elimination of a particular "other" group is undoubtedly overdrawn, there are structural factors such as the collapse of existing political units that leave a power vacuum. This is especially dangerous in culturally plural, diverse societies when one group tries to attain hegemony over another. Genocidists take advantage of such an opportunity to mobilize their own *genos* to attack another *genos* by making use of existing political, social, or cultural differences between groups that can be portrayed as being so "alien" that there is no other solution than to drive out or kill the "other." They take advantage of the fears and insecurity brought on by political and/or economic instability to enlist their "own" in campaigns of terror and elimination. Often these collaborators are simply opportunists seeking their neighbors' property or indulging base passions because the "other" has been removed from what Helen Fein has termed the "universe of obligation" (Fein 1979, 4).

Many scholars agree, then, that ethnic groups are not necessarily "*themselves* political actors" but instead "provide the *social basis* for organized political actors" (Shaw 2015, 129, emphasis in original). Michael Mann, for one, asserts that genocides primarily occur in the context of a struggle for territory and therefore "ethnic conflict concerns primarily *political power relations*" (Mann 2005, 5, emphasis in original). In the modern world of nation-states, ethno-political conflict over which particular group should control a certain territory and wield state power has all too often led to genocide. This was especially true with the collapse of empires and states. The gradual weakening and ultimate collapse of the Ottoman Empire led to the rise of an ethno-national idea embodied by the "Young Turks," who launched a genocidal campaign to eliminate the Armenians. The end of Belgium's colonial rule in Rwanda reversed the social power relations there and ultimately led to the rise of the "Hutu Power" movement that wanted to eliminate any Tutsi influence in that newly independent nation. And the collapse of Yugoslavia sparked still more ethnic conflicts and genocide, with Serbian paramilitaries in particular committing heinous atrocities in an attempt at creating a "Greater Serbia." In each of these case studies the genocidists sought to mobilize their own ethnic group to attain complete political power by ethnically homogenizing their territories.

The Armenians

Twentieth century advances in technology and the development of a virulent strain of racist nationalism made possible the slaughter of entire peoples over the control of territory. While in the popular mind, it is the Holocaust that serves as the prime example of such heinous undertakings, we have seen how decades earlier German forces had already engaged in the wholesale elimination of the Herero people in southwest Africa. We turn now to an examination of another systematic and organized campaign of mass murder in the early part of the twentieth century—that of the Turkish genocidists against their Armenian minority in 1915. It was this horrible crime that sparked Lemkin's determination to incite an international movement and to codify and popularize a term against what, at that time, was still—in Churchill's phrase—"a crime without a name." When Lemkin wrote *Axis Rule* he well understood the connections between the Armenian genocide and Germany's colonization and biological reordering of the demographics of Europe. So too did Adolf Hitler who, in a speech in 1939 describing his murderous plans for a campaign of expansion to the East, called for the removal or extermination of all the people there since, after all, who "speaks of the annihilation of the Armenians today?" Lemkin believed that it was the advent of the modern nation-state, combined with virulent nationalism—often conflated with ethnocentrism and racism—that paved the way for the most dangerous form of genocide in the contemporary world. In many ways, then, it was actually the Armenian genocide that provided the template for the Holocaust.

The Turkish rulers of the decaying Ottoman Empire carried out the deliberate and systematic genocide of the Christian Armenian people under cover of the World War I (1914–18). The "Young Turks," as they became known, a nationalist and racist faction within the Committee of Union and Progress (CUP), which took power in 1908, gained control of the government; they rejected the multi-ethnic Ottoman Empire and sought to forge a homogenous Turkish national state. To do so, the nearly 3,000-year-old Armenian people, who had been a barely tolerated minority under the sultans, would have to be forcibly removed from Asia Minor. Scorned by many Turks for their involvement in commerce and trade, the Armenians had been subjected to periodic brutal state-sponsored massacres by their overlords. Massacres in the mid-1890s had resulted in the deaths of over 200,000 Armenians; in 1909, tens of thousands of Armenians were killed in the city of Adana. These depredations were designed to keep the Armenians subjugated and to forestall the development of a national consciousness among them. These massacres also had the effect of "normalizing" massive violence against the Armenian people, as well as corrupting many Turkish perpetrators and acclimating them to mass murder, thus paving the way for the genocide to soon follow.

The outbreak of the World War I heightened Turkish suspicions of "disloyalty" among their Armenian subjects, as half of the Armenian people were located across the border in the Russian Empire. Now that the Ottoman Empire was at war with Russia, the new Turkish rulers feared that the Orthodox Christian Armenians would make common cause with their co-religionist Orthodox Russians and fellow Armenians across the border to seek their own national state. Like Nazi Germany, the Ottoman

Empire made a deliberate attempt to eliminate an entire ethno-religious community from its territory. Of course, the Jews in Germany were in fact Germans, whereas the Armenians were merely subjects of the Sublime Porte—the central Ottoman government. In the former case, however, eventually all Jews everywhere were marked for extermination, while in the latter, although the Armenian community was to be completely destroyed within the state's borders—as well as neighboring enclaves on the state's borders—the main goal of the CUP was the "Turkification" of Anatolia. Both regime's policies were ideologically driven. The Nazi genocide was a consequence of the idea of a "racial struggle" for primacy and empire and, similarly, for the CUP the goal was a Turkish-only state, and ultimately even a pan-Turkish empire as well. Both genocides were conducted in conjunction with world wars with railroads and forced marches used to move the unfortunate victims to their deaths. Additionally, it was the communication systems and technology of the modern state that made the coordination of the necessary logistics easier. In the Armenian genocide, the orders were all relayed by telegraph. It was no coincidence that Talaat Pasha, the principal mastermind of the Armenian genocide as internal affairs minister, had previously worked in the telegraph and posts ministry. Modern states need bureaucracies to carry out policies, including genocide, and Talaat Pasha installed a telegraph machine in his office in order to personally oversee the conduct of operations.

The Turkish genocidists began their murderous campaign on April 24, 1915, with the arrest of prominent Armenians such as artists, writers, clergymen, and political figures. Armenians who had been conscripted into the Turkish army were disarmed and herded into hastily erected camps. Many of these men were summarily executed, those that were not would be dead anyway within a few weeks from hard labor. Orders then went out to empty all Armenian towns and villages. Some people were deported by trains and others by wagons, but most of the victims were forced to leave for the border on foot. Their homes were looted and ransacked as soon as they left. The roads were clogged with thousands upon thousands of frightened Armenians. As these unfortunates were being driven into the Syrian Desert to perish from thirst and exposure, they were set upon by soldiers of the "Special Organization." The few goods or property they had been able to take with them were now wrested away by force. Women and girls were raped and then killed, others were taken to be forcibly converted to Islam and employed as servants or concubines. Civilians joined in along the way and stole, raped and murdered with impunity. Local Kurdish tribespeople also took advantage of the situation to enrich themselves.

We should pause here to point out to our readers that while Armenians were being denigrated for being Christians—and in a more detailed accounting of this genocide we would learn more about the persecution of other Christian groups, in particular a Greek population—religion or myth was not really a motivating factor. The "Young Turk" rulers sometimes invoked Islam and/or Turkey's Muslim character to generate support for their actions, but Talaat Pasha and the other genocidists were not the least bit religious. Like many other unscrupulous rulers, they simply knew how to exploit religious sentiments among the populace. American Ambassador Henry Morgenthau, who did much to reveal this genocide to the outside world, said as much. At the time he wrote that religion strongly motivated the "Turkish and Kurdish rabble" who carried out massacres, but that "the men who really conceived the crime had no such motive. Practically all of them were atheists, with no more respect for Islam than for Christianity" (Carmichael 2009, 85).

Within a few months one million Armenians were dead. Other deaths would follow, as Turkish soldiers pushed into Russia and massacred more Armenians there. Of a total population of about four million, up to half of the Armenian people perished, either killed outright or dying from a lack of food and water or exposure to the elements. The systematic killing even continued after the war had ended, with Armenians returning to Anatolia being murdered after finding their homes occupied by Turks. In the aftermath of all these massacres, Armenian churches were destroyed and any physical signs of their cultural heritage such as schools, monuments, monasteries, etc. were all obliterated. All that the Armenians could take with them was their language, religion, legends, songs, and the collective memory of their suffering. But these social and cultural connections would be enough for them to reconstitute themselves as a people, both in a national homeland and in the diaspora (a large group of people that share a cultural heritage and have been displaced from their homeland either through either immigration or forced movement) abroad. The Armenians were not destroyed because they are a "family of mind."

Over a century later the Armenians are finally receiving a small measure of justice. The Turkish government has long denied that a genocide even occurred, insisting that the death toll of one and one half to two million people commonly acknowledged by scholars is an exaggeration, and that those that were killed were wartime traitors plotting with the Russians to destroy Turkey. For fear of upsetting a crucial North Atlantic Treaty Organization (NATO) military ally during the Cold War, the United States hesitated to acknowledge the measures taken against the Armenians as being a genocide. During the 2008 US presidential campaign, Barack Obama promised the large Armenian community in California that he would do so. During his eight years in office (2009–17) he did not. The Kurds, however, did apologize for their forbears' complicity in the genocide committed against the Armenian people. Ironically, it was only the Turkish assault on these same Kurds, who had been American allies against the Islamic State until the United States under Donald Trump removed American troops from the region and simply abandoned them, that galvanized the US Congress to vote formally in 2019 to call the Turkish actions in 1915 by their name—genocide. In 2023, Armenians were again driven out of another ancestral homeland—Nagorno-Karabakh—by the armed forces of another Turkic-speaking people, the Azeri, the dominant group in neighboring Azerbaijan.

Bosnian Muslims

The Serbian nationalists were another group that sought to exert their control over more territory in the name of a "greater" homeland by creating or deliberately exacerbating relatively minor enmities between "their" people and two other ethno-national groups of another crumbling, multi-ethnic state—Yugoslavia. This horrific conflict, initially ascribed to "ancient hatreds" as an excuse for world powers to not get involved in a "civil war"—a ploy we will encounter again when discussing the genocide in Rwanda—saw war crimes committed by all three of the paramilitaries of the major belligerents—Serbia, Croatia, and Bosnia-Herzegovina—on innocent civilians. Only the Serb forces in Bosnia, however, committed genocide. The Serbian leadership used myths and the idea of historic grievances to mobilize their populations for the conflict (Karcic 2022). Many scholars agree, however, that for the most part these three ethno-national groups—Croatians, who are mostly Catholic, Serbs, most of whose population are Orthodox Christians, and Bosnians, who were largely Muslim, though there was also a large population of Orthodox Christians and some Catholics—had lived together peacefully for centuries (Cigar 1995). There were also very high rates of intermarriage between all three groups, something we will again see in the case of the Tutsi and Hutu in Rwanda.

None of these three republics were homogeneous—that is, each included large numbers of religious minorities. Many ethnic Serbs lived in Croatia, Croatians lived in Serbia, and so on. And for many years, these distinctions were not overly important: they were all Yugoslavs, or South Slavs. They all speak the same language—a Slavic language, therefore with many similarities to Russian and other Slavic languages—albeit in different dialects. You many know that English is spoken somewhat differently in England than in the United States, and that Mexicans, Argentines, Spaniards, and so on have distinctive dialects, terminology, and slang. This is a reminder that there was really very little separating Bosniaks (Muslims in Bosnia), Croatians, and Serbs, other than religion—religions that happen to have much in common such as the same god and most of the same prophets.

In fact, the soldiers themselves could only be distinguished from each other by the armbands or insignia they were wearing—a green armband representing Islam for the Bosniaks, the Serbian colors of red, blue and white (used also by other Slavic peoples such as the Russians, Czechs, Slovenes and Slovaks) and the Croatian *sahovnica*, or checkerboard, that was also worn by the fascist *Ustashe* during World War II while they were murdering Jews, Serbs and Romani, as we will discuss below. Its use evoked extremely negative reactions from Serbs, much like the Confederate flag in the United States does today for African Americans (and many others as well). Such symbols are often used by politicians to arouse emotions and set people against one another. Before the collapse of Yugoslavia and the rabble-rousing by the ethno-nationalists among these groups, however, the large majority of Serbs, Croats, or Bosniaks, however, were far more concerned with their daily lives than with any historical grievances. You may have noticed that throughout this book we have tried to avoid labeling entire peoples—such as "the Germans," or "the Japanese"—as genocidists. Of course, many did participate in the genocidal violence, and many more profited from it. But the exaggerated differences between these groups were largely invented or manipulated by unscrupulous politicians as part of the process of nation building.

Yugoslavia, roughly meaning "Land of the South Slavs," was created in 1918 from the ashes of the collapsing Ottoman and Austro-Hungarian Empires. The Ottoman Turks had ruled over much of southeastern Europe for centuries, with many Slavs converting to Islam. Often these were the native elites that wanted to retain their privileges under their new ruler, the Ottoman Sultan. We will see this again in our final case study with the Tutsis and their Belgian overlords as some accommodated themselves to the new political reality of European imperialism. But for the necessary historical context to understand what happened in the 1990s we must briefly discuss the impact of World War II on the region. Germany, along with its allies Hungary and Bulgaria, invaded Yugoslavia in April 1941 largely to rescue its fascist ally Italy, which had become bogged down in its own invasion of Greece. The four allies divided up Yugoslavia among themselves except for the Nazi-puppet state of Croatia, led by another fascist, Ante Pavelic, and his ultra-nationalistic and racist *Ustashe* party. Over the next four years a vicious civil war broke out between these Croatian fascists, the Chetniks—Serbian nationalists who wished to restore the pre-war Yugoslav monarchy—and the Communists, led by Joseph Tito.

The *Ustashe* took advantage of this opportunity to establish their own independent state—though in reality they had to accede to any wishes or demands put upon them by the Nazis and Italian fascists—and attempted to ethnically cleanse their country of the supposedly "inferior" Serbs. The Croat politician Mile Budak infamously declared that one-third of Serbs would be killed, one-third would be expelled, and the remaining one-third converted to Catholicism. Not only Serbs, but all Jews and Romani were also to be eliminated. The Serbian nationalists struck back, perpetrating mass killings in Croatian and Bosnian Muslim villages. The Croatian fascists set up a network of concentration camps, where inmates were tortured and killed. The most notorious of these was Jasenovac, where about 80,000 people perished. More than half were Serbs. To this day the estimates as to the total number of victims in Yugoslavia between 1941 and 1945 vary between 200,000 and well over a million, with Croats citing lower figures and Serbs maintaining that the higher figures are more accurate yet probably still too low. The United States Holocaust Memorial Museum puts the number at between 300,000 and 350,000 ethnic Serbs killed with 50,000 of them murdered at Jasenovac.

Tito and the Communists prevailed in the civil war. Marshall Joseph Tito had earned much sympathy and support by leading the powerful partisan resistance to the Nazis and their allies. Although Tito would prove to be a fairly typical Soviet-style "communist"—authoritarian, intolerant of dissent, and the object of a cult of personality—he had some independence from Stalin and Moscow, especially during his first years in power. Tito's state crafted an official ideology of "Brotherhood and Unity" and had some success in forging a Yugoslav national consciousness. In fact, a survey of attitudes toward "national" identity conducted on the eve of the Winter Olympics held in Yugoslavia in 1984 indicated that most citizens saw themselves as Yugoslavs first, and Muslim, Catholic, or Orthodox Christian second. Of course, given that this survey was conducted in a police state, where one's job or personal security was not guaranteed, it is quite likely that many respondents simply repeated the party line. Nonetheless, the celebration and evident pride of all Yugoslavs in hosting the first Olympics ever held in a Communist state was real and not compelled by the state.

But Tito, who was of Slovene (another Slavic ethnic group) and Croat heritage, had died in 1980. By 1987, a long-time Communist official in Serbia, Slobodan Milosevic, dropped any pretense of communist or socialist beliefs and reinvented himself as an ardent Serbian nationalist. Throughout Yugoslavia other bureaucrats also began calling for ethnically based states. These party leaders and state officials who had long called themselves "communist"—which should imply a dedication to internationalism, working-class solidarity, and so on—quickly dropped their facades and re-made themselves as nationalists and even fascists. And why not? In reality, "communism" had been a very thin charade, and these regimes were always authoritarian, nationalist, and antisemitic, relying on police-state methods rather than any connection with the common people. After Slovenia and Croatia declared their independence in June 1991, Milosevic demanded that territories where Serbs resided should be ceded to Serbia. The leader of Croatia, Franjo Tudjman, refused to give in to Milosevic's demands and Croatian Serb military forces wrested one-third of Croatian territory away from the Croats, though Serbs made up only 12 percent of its population. The Croatian forces eventually struck back and recaptured its territory and forced 150,000 Serbs to flee in but the first of many ethnic cleansings.

Meanwhile, Bosnia had also declared its independence in 1992 and was embroiled in a murderous war with Bosnian Serbs, led politically by Radovan Karadzic and militarily by his accomplice Ratko Mladic. Karadzic had threatened that if Bosnia declared independence, "do not think that you will not lead" Bosnia "into hell, and do not think that you will not perhaps make the Muslim people disappear" (Sells 2001, 9). With the assistance of Serbia, the Bosnian Serbs declared their own "Republika Srpska" and began another brutal round of ethnic cleansing that was in fact a genocide perpetrated against Bosnian Muslims, or Bosniaks. General Mladic of the Yugoslav National Army led a well-equipped military force in this campaign against the Bosniak forces. Bosnia was also attacked by Croatia, which, like Serbia, was attempting to bring all its ethnic groups into a single homogeneous state. In fact, Tudjman and Milosevic had already reached an understanding that they would divide Bosnia between them. This is why, as Adam Jones wrote, "Bosnia became the most brutal battlefield of the Balkan wars" (Jones 2017, 45).

Mladic's Yugoslav Army troops, along with Radislav Krstic's Bosnian Serb army and criminal paramilitary cohorts, such as Arkan's Tigers, unleashed a reign of terror on the Bosniaks. The Yugoslav army had a near-monopoly on weapons and the arms embargo imposed on the region by the United Nations left the Bosniaks at a distinct disadvantage. By the middle of 1992, the Serbs controlled two-thirds of Bosnia and had begun the process of clearing that territory of any Muslims. The capital city of Sarajevo was subjected to a siege by Serb forces for well over three years. All the while its residents were subjected to shelling by artillery and worse, multitudes of civilians were shot by snipers as they tried to collect food provided by the United Nations. And this meager supply line was often interdicted by the Serb forces and the residents starved. More than two million Bosniak civilians were forced to flee their homes in Sarajevo and in eastern Bosnia, which was the epicenter of the Serbs' "ethnic cleansing" (Figure 7.3).

Many of those who remained were imprisoned under inhuman conditions in detention camps. The UN attempted to provide "safe havens" for the displaced Bosniaks and set up a half-dozen camps supposedly to be protected by United Nations Protection

Figure 7.3 To the left is Gen. Ratko Mladic, butcher of Srebrenica. Second from right is Col. Thom Karremans, head of the UN force that was presumably safeguarding the Bosnians at Srebrenica, having a toast with the mass murderer on the evening of July 11, 1995. This photo reveals the utterly ineffectual and even collaborationist role of the "international community" during the Bosnian genocide. https://commons.wikimedia.org/wiki/File:Mladic_-_Karremans.jpg

Force (UNPROFOR) troops. One of these was at Srebrenica. It was here that over 8,000 Bosnian Muslim men and boys were rounded up by Serb paramilitaries and butchered in July 1995. The UN troops had been ordered not to intervene and to fight only in self-defense, leaving the civilians utterly defenseless. The women and young children of Srebrenica were bussed out of the territory as the Serb forces continued their ethnic cleansing campaign. As we saw in Chapter Four, many Muslim women were raped and imprisoned in brothels where their bodies were made available to any Serb soldiers. There they were repeatedly raped and often killed. Mosques were destroyed and replaced with Serbian Orthodox churches, an important element of Lemkin's concept of genocide: "the imposition of the national pattern of the oppressor." Such actions are also textbook examples of genocide-denial and of "triumphalism"—to not only deny but to celebrate the cultural and physical genocide of your victims (Karcic in Cox et al., eds. 2022).

During the three years of the conflict—1992 to 1995—over 80,000 civilians were murdered by Serb forces until a UN bombing campaign forced the Serbian politicians to the negotiating table. Of course, by that time they had achieved most of their sinister goals in any case. Later, in 1999, Serb forces would undertake another campaign of ethnic cleansing against Muslims in Kosovo which the Serbians considered a vital part of their historic homeland lost to the Ottoman Turks in 1389 after a major battle. This was a significant and symbolic event for many Serbs, and their leader, Slobodan

Milosevic, used it to great advantage to consolidate in his power in a vitriolic speech in 1989, the 600-year anniversary of the battle. It was used again to justify the continued assault on Muslim peoples in Kosovo in the mid-to-late 1990s, an attack that was only stopped by another bombing campaign, this time by the United States under the aegis of the North Atlantic Treaty Organization (NATO) military alliance. That the UN did not sanction this effort either was due to the veto power of Russia and China on the Security Council. Though legally questionable as a result, NATO could reasonably claim this was a humanitarian intervention that prevented another murderous assault on Muslims.

It cannot be stressed enough that all sides involved in this conflict perpetrated war crimes and other atrocities. The Bosnian and Croatian forces, like the Serbian soldiers, killed civilians, raped women, and looted and burned people's homes. The soldiers of the Kosovo Liberation Army (KLA) were not blameless either; they had conducted their own campaigns to eliminate Serbs from "their" territory. Many were detained and tortured. Worse, it was later ascertained that the KLA had removed organs from Serbian police officers and soldiers before killing them so that they could be sold on the black market. But only the Serbian forces conducted a campaign of genocide. Their "ethnic cleansing" of Bosnia and resettling of the region with Serbians certainly fits into Lemkin's definition of genocide. And, as we discussed earlier, the sexual violence visited upon Bosnian Muslim women was a deliberate attempt to destroy the social fabric of that community. Later, both the International Criminal Tribunal for the Former Yugoslavia (ICTY) and the International Court of Justice (the ICJ or World Court) would find that the massacre and ethnic cleansing at Srebrenica was indeed genocide, but that the majority of the deliberate violence during the war was "ethnic cleansing" rather than genocide. We will discuss these legal findings in the next—and final—chapter, the "Conclusion." William Schabas has written that "this debate is not about whether the crimes […] actually took place; it is only about whether they are most properly described as crimes against humanity, rather than 'genocide'" (Schabas 2001). By now, those of you reading these words know that we unequivocally label these atrocities as genocide.

Rwanda

The Bosnian Genocide can be dated to the attack by Serbian forces on Sarajevo on April 6, 1992. On that very same date two years later, five thousand miles due south, an airplane carrying the presidents of Rwanda and Burundi, neighboring countries in East Africa, was shot down and crashed, killing everyone on board. Within a few hours, a fearsome killing frenzy began—the most intensive mass killing anywhere in the world since World War II. Roughly 800,000 people were killed, more than ten percent of country's population (which numbered seven million at the time). And this unfolded in a mere 100 days. The daily killing rate during the first month of the genocide, when at least a half-million people were killed, "was at least five times that of the Nazi death camps" at the height of the Holocaust, according to one expert (Prunier 1997, 261).

Rwanda is a small country in central-eastern Africa whose population consists primarily of two social or ethnic groups or castes—the Hutu and Tutsi. The Twa people constitute about one percent of the population. As part of the "Scramble for Africa," the Germans established indirect rule over Rwanda and Burundi, but Belgian troops occupied Rwanda in 1916, and after the World War I ended in 1918 Germany was stripped of its African colonies. Belgium became the colonial overlord of "Ruanda and Urundi"—Rwanda and the land to its immediate south, Burundi. The two were administered jointly until they split and gained independence some five decades later. A few points are essential to understand. Hutu and Tutsi originate and live in the same regions and, like the Yugoslavs, share the same language. Unlike the Yugoslavs, however, they also share a common culture and religion. A large majority of Rwandans are western Christians, with Catholics and Protestants in roughly equal proportions. Again, like the Yugoslavs, Hutu and Tutsi clans often intermarried over the decades. You'll recall from the previous section that the supposed differences between Bosniaks, Croatians, and Serbs were similarly thin, but were wildly exaggerated by those with interests in fomenting division. Before European colonization these social identities were not considered permanent or biologically determined. Tutsi tended to own a few heads of cattle, while Hutu usually worked the land—the word *Hutu* means "peasant" or "farmer." A Hutu could become a Tutsi (which was more desirable) by simply acquiring a few cows. The Tutsi, however, had long had a higher social status than the Hutu and held the upper hand politically as well. This, despite their minority status.

In 1932, Belgian authorities required all Rwandans to carry identity cards designating their ethnicity. Because of these ID cards and Belgian records it became much more difficult for Hutu to become Tutsi or vice versa. Additionally, the colonialists imposed strict segregation in religious, educational, and state institutions. European colonialism "racialized" pre-existing ethnic distinctions and social hierarchies, though some peoples in Africa, such as the Igbo, took advantage of the opportunity to do so in order to assert their own identity in British Nigeria. For their part, the Belgians created and then codified a rigid division between Hutu and Tutsi and invested it with European notions of race, that, consistent with European racial obsessions, turned the human race into many dozens of "races." A century earlier, European racial "thinkers" imagined that humanity possessed four or five races, crudely labeled. By 1900, though, race-obsessed European and US elites had invented many, many dozens of races. The quotation marks around "thinkers" are intentional. In reality, scientists and anthropologists and other experts agree that there is only one race, the human race (American Association of Anthropologists 1998).

The Belgian colonizers believed that the Tutsi were destined to dominate—within the constraints of indirect European rule—because of their presumed racial superiority. And, as the Tutsi were dominant in the social hierarchy they adapted themselves to colonial rule in order to maintain that status. The fanciful notion, invented by Europeans that the Tutsi originated in Egypt, Ethiopia, or elsewhere created the image that they were foreign invaders and allies of outsiders. This image would be internalized and then skillfully invoked later by the Hutus—serving as a cornerstone of the genocidal philosophy that was implemented in 1994. The fear and hatred between Tutsi and Hutu did not come easily for everyone, but the Belgians' "divide and conquer" strategy eventually worked. After a few decades of division and differential treatment, many Rwandans came to believe "that the two ethnic groups, distinguished mostly by vocation in prior centuries, were indeed fundamentally dissimilar in nature and irreconcilable in practice" (Caplan, quoted in Totten and Parsons, eds. 2012, 449). Belgium continued to employ this classic divide-and-rule colonialist strategy of favoring the Tutsi minority. This favoritism sowed the seeds for strife and violence in the post-independence era by deepening a sense of grievance and resentment that was keenly felt by many Hutu.

Emergence of Hutu Parties and Independence

After World War II, the "winds of change" swept across Africa and long-time colonies claimed their independence. Rwanda officially became independent in 1962 and the Hutu majority claimed power for itself. The new government purged Tutsis from regional power structures and encouraged anti-Tutsi violence, which broke out in several deadly episodes between 1959 and 1964. Periodic invasions of exile-based militias reinforced the image of Tutsi as foreign invaders and made it easier for the government to conflate Tutsi residing in Rwanda with Tutsi in exile. Ultimately, some 200,000 Tutsi fled or were driven into exile during those first five years of Hutu dominance and at least 50,000 were killed. The refugees settled primarily in Uganda, Burundi, Tanzania, and Zaire, and would provide the manpower for guerilla forces, called *"inyenzi"* ("cockroach" or "cockroaches") by the Hutu government and its propagandists.

Juvénal Habyarimana took power through a coup in 1973. His regime maintained a quota system to preserve Hutu privilege and encouraged an extreme anti-Tutsi faction, the *"akazu,"* which was led by his wife Agathe among others. She would be a key player in the genocide two decades later. By the mid-1980s, Habyarimana's government faced mounting problems, including a severe economic crisis beginning in the mid-1980s that resulted in a marked increase of poverty that only fueled further the discontent among Hutu as well as Tutsi; and, in response, the emergence of a stronger Hutu political opposition, which criticized the government's inept handling of the deepening crisis and also exploited public dismay over the indiscreet displays of wealth by the president and his coterie. On October 1, 1990, the Rwandan Patriotic Front (RPF), an army composed and led largely by Tutsi who were a generation removed from the expulsion of their parents at the dawn of the Rwandan Republic 30 years earlier, invaded Rwanda. The RPF was based in neighboring Uganda, where many Rwandan Tutsi exiles, including future RPF leaders such as Paul Kagame—who is still in power today as president—quickly moved toward the capital, Kigali. The offensive provoked immediate, harsh reprisals against Rwandan Tutsi. The ever-worsening crisis prompted the *akazu* faction and other extremists to strengthen and expand a movement that by late 1993 would be called "Hutu Power" and that included members of assorted Hutu political and paramilitary groups.

This cabal promoted the myth that Tutsi were alien "others," with the popular magazine *Kangura* publishing virulently anti-Tutsi propaganda, often with lurid sexualized content. In December 1990, *Kangura* published "The Hutu Ten Commandments," a revealing document that placed a special emphasis upon the "danger" of Tutsi women. It warned against the Tutsi woman who works "for the interest" of her group and seeks to infiltrate the Hutu populace by marrying, befriending, or being a "concubine" of a Hutu; any Hutu who allows this is a "traitor." In July 1993, seeking to keep the flow of development monies coming from world institutions, Habyarimana's government began negotiations in Tanzania mediated by the Organization of African Unity (OAU, now the African Union (AU)) and diplomats from France and the United States. In August, the parties announced the Arusha Accords, which stipulated power-sharing—something the *akazu* faction did not want as it would also limit their access to development funds that they would now be forced to "share" with the supposedly alien Tutsi—between the Habyarimana government and the RPF and the merger of government and RPF troops into one Rwandan army.

The temporary hope raised by the Arusha Accords was destroyed by the assassination of President Habyarimana on the evening of April 6, 1994. Accompanied by the president of neighboring Burundi, Habyarimana's plane was brought down by a missile outside the Kigali airport. Even now, the culprits have not been clearly established, but it would not be surprising if it was the core group of hardliners within the ruling party who were radicalized in the face of the threat from the RPF as well as from domestic Hutu opposition. To keep power, they formed paramilitaries, funded racist media propaganda, and prepared to do whatever was necessary to retain power—including the murder of their own, which as we will see, they were perfectly willing to do to preserve "Hutu Power." Ultimately, the ruling party elite opted for genocide.

These Hutu hardliners had incentives to get the president out of their way and to create a pretext for the well-planned massacres; yet the plane accident also killed some important figures among the Hutu-power extremists, and occurred at a time that was not propitious for that faction (because some high-ranking government officials were out of the country). So we will probably never know who was behind the assassination. What is known is that it served as a pretext for the genocide. Hutu Power extremists quickly seized power, installing Colonel Théoneste Bagosora, who at the time of the president's death was Cabinet Director in the Ministry of Defense, as head of the government. The Hutu Prime Minister, Agathe Uwilingiyimana, was brutally murdered a few hours after the plane crash, as were ten Belgian peacekeeping soldiers who were supposed to protect her—in violation of United Nations' policy that forbade former colonial powers from sending peacekeepers into their former possessions. The UN had sent a force of several thousand peacekeepers into Rwanda after the Arusha Accords had been signed to help facilitate the organization of a "Broad-Based Transitional Government" incorporating Hutu and Tutsi into one combined government and military. Its commander, General Romeo Dallaire, had known that genocidal plans were being made as early as January of 1994 and had requested permission to seize weapons that were being secretly stored for the planned assault on the Tutsi. That request was denied by the UN General Secretary Boutros Boutros-Ghali. Incredibly, as result of the murder of the Belgian peacekeepers Dallaire was then ordered to withdraw most of his soldiers, an action that undoubtedly costs hundreds of thousands of lives.

On its first full day in power, this new government and allied groups launched the systematic murder of the country's Tutsi population. Much of the killing was done by the *Interahamwe* ("those who stand together"). *Interahamwe* gangs, armed principally with machetes, hunted down and slaughtered Tutsis in their houses; at improvised checkpoints; in large gathering places such as churches and schools; and in the marshes and swamps where survivors had sought refuge, or where some Tutsis had fled immediately upon hearing of the president's death. As we have seen in Chapter Four and again here in the case of the Former Yugoslavia, there was deliberate widespread rape of women. There is no debate over whether or not the mass killing of Tutsi was genocide; significantly, the mass rapes were also eventually designated as genocide by the International Criminal Tribunal for Rwanda (ICTR). We will discuss both the ICTY and the ICTY rulings in the Conclusion to the book under *Prevention and Punishment of Genocide*. Roughly 80 percent of the killings took place in a few weeks' time in April 1994—an unprecedented rate of killing in human history, surpassing the one to two million Soviet POWs who died in the first six months of the Nazi invasion of the Soviet Union in World War II, and even the Holocaust itself. More than 90 percent of the victims were Tutsis, but Hutu who opposed the slaughter, or were misidentified as Tutsi, were also killed. "A remarkable feature of the genocide," noted Adam Jones, "was its routinized character. The killings were 'marked not by a fury of combat'" or outbursts of mob violence, "but by a well-ordered sanity that mirrored the rhythms of ordinary collective life" (Jones 2017, 485; second half of quotation is from Li, quoted in Mills and Brunner 2003, 125).

As in Yugoslavia, the Western news media explicitly described the violence as the result of eternal tribal conflict, exacerbated by the weakness or collapse of the state. The latter point is well taken, as ethno-nationalists after the collapse of Yugoslavia and Hutu ethno-nationalists after the end of Belgian rule rushed in to stake their claims to a pure, homogenized territory. In both cases, however, these different ethnic groups had generally co-existed together for quite some time. It was only the fear and insecurity of economic dislocation, combined with the calculated and deliberate manipulation of minor, and often imagined, differences between the various groups that allowed these power-hungry politicians to magnify these grievances and unleash the genocides that followed. In the former Yugoslavia, these leaders have successfully carved out their ethnic states; however, in Rwanda, the RPF ultimately prevailed and recaptured state power. While the Rwandan national motto today is "Ndi Umunyaranda" or "we are all Rwandan," and their Constitution forbids hate speech of any kind, Paul Kagame and the Tutsi-led RPF have instituted an authoritarian regime that has been in power continuously since 1994.

Questions for Further Discussion

1. Why did the United States, Great Britain, France and the Netherlands oppose the inclusion of "cultural" genocide in the 1948 Convention?
2. How did the "Young Turks" justify their actions? What was their ultimate goal?
3. Why did the Bosnian Serbs, with the help of Serbia, perpetrate genocidal attacks on the Bosnian Muslims?
4. What were the motivations behind the Hutu genocide of the Tutsis in Rwanda?

CONCLUSION

They want non-enforceable laws with many loopholes, so that they can manage life like currency in a bank.

—Raphael Lemkin

The Prevention of the Crime of Genocide

In some limited ways, the 1948 Genocide Convention marked a step forward toward prosecuting individual actors who commit this heinous crime. Yet, it is difficult to rhapsodize over this achievement, as deliberate roadblocks both within the Convention—the high legal bar of intent, political and other human groups left unprotected, and the separation and then exclusion of cultural destruction from the concept—and structural ones embedded in the United Nations Charter itself present obstacles to actually fulfilling the presumed mission of the Convention to prevent genocide and to punish genocidists. Genocide has therefore continued to blight the human race since the passage of the Convention despite that oft-repeated promise of "never again." The UN is but a conglomeration of the world's wholly independent states that each have complete independence and control of domestic affairs within their recognized boundaries. This entrenched legal precept, associated with the Westphalian system devised by Europeans after their ruinous wars of the seventeenth century, is supported by the UN Charter. It guarantees the right of member states to administer their own domestic affairs without the interference of other states and specifically prohibits intervention "in matters which are essentially within the domestic jurisdiction of any state [...]" (*UN Charter, Article 2 (7)*).

Some observers, such as Samantha Power, believe that the 1948 Convention "not only authorized but required [...]" UN member states "to take steps to prevent, suppress, and punish the crime, which no instrument had ever required before" (Power 2002, 58). Unfortunately, as Jeffrey Bachman has argued in his excellent recent book *The Politics of Genocide: From the Genocide Convention to the Responsibility to Protect*, since the UN Charter's mandate is to maintain "international peace and security" the threat or use of force against another member state is forbidden *unless* there *is* such a threat to international peace and security. Genocide is, of course, recognized as a violation of international law. According to Bachman's analysis, however, because genocide was not defined as a threat to international peace and security in the 1948 Convention—though Lemkin had included what Bachman calls "universalizing language" in the initial Secretariat draft—the UN Security Council has no mandate to intervene in the internal matters of individual states in cases of intrastate genocide. The lack of universalizing language in the 1948 Convention as well as the deliberate sabotage of Lemkin's plan for universal jurisdiction—also part of the Secretariat draft—means that, absent the assent of the UN Security Council, not only is the UN unable to intervene when a state conducts a genocide against a group within its own territory, but that state—unless it is a signatory to the International Criminal Court (ICC), established literally a half-century after the 1948 Convention—was solely responsible for prosecuting the genocidists through its own domestic legislation!

Genocides do not simply happen overnight, or *without warning*. There is always a process involved in genocide, and as Gregory Stanton (2023) has usefully pointed out, there are some commonalities that can serve as warnings to the international community. The process tends to move through stages, though not necessarily in a linear or predictable fashion. Stanton identified these stages as classification, symbolization, discrimination, dehumanization, organization, polarization, preparation, persecution, extermination, and denial. So while there is always sufficient warning as to the possibility of a genocide, why then do they still occur, and with greater frequency than ever? Early warnings demand an immediate response, but the lack of such a response due to nations basing their policies on their own narrow and practical concerns rather than moral considerations, again underscores the problem of a static world structure that prioritizes state sovereignty. To be sure, there has been as much discussion about the prevention of genocide as there has been of the many deficiencies of the UN's legal definition of the term and the final Convention itself. There have even been some small steps made. After the failure of the international community to respond effectively to the crises in Yugoslavia and Rwanda in the 1990s—though the United States did prevent the Serbs from "ethnically cleansing" the Kosovars at the end of that decade, an intervention not sanctioned by the UN and that some consider illegal as a result—the Canadian government in 2000 called for the world community to address the problem of intervention to prevent genocides in light of the international legal principle of state sovereignty. This is a complex issue deserving much wider debate among human-rights activists and scholars. Most of us have learned, from history, that outside interventions are rarely "humanitarian" and thus it is not our first instinct to advocate them. Yet, interventions do not have to take the form of great-power invasions of poor countries for obvious illegitimate or imperialistic purposes (Jones, 2011).

In 2001, the *International Commission on Intervention and State Sovereignty* (ICISS) convened and issued a report, *The Responsibility to Protect* (R2P). The report, endorsed by the world's governments at the UN World Summit in 2005, "stressed the need for the General Assembly to continue consideration of the responsibility to protect populations from genocide, war crimes, ethnic cleansing and crimes against humanity" by "helping states to build capacity to protect their populations" from these atrocities "before crises and conflicts break out." More significantly, it stipulated that if a state "manifestly failed" to protect its populations, the international community "*must* [italics ours] be prepared to take appropriate collective action, in a timely and decisive manner and in accordance with the UN Charter." This marked a substantial change to the 1948 Convention, which did not mandate, but only permitted, intervention to protect endangered groups, and even then only if officially designated—in keeping with the UN Charter—as a threat to "international peace and security" by the Security Council, where, of course, the P-5 could always be expected to pursue their own political agendas. It also marked a departure from the notion of the absolute sovereignty of the state. A subsequent 2009 report put out by UN Secretary General Ban Ki Moon, *Implementing the Responsibility to Protect*, made clear however, that any "collective action" could only be authorized by the UN Security Council (UNSC). To ensure the pacific settlement of disputes that "threaten the maintenance of international peace and security," Chapter Six of the UN Charter permits intervention when authorized by the Security Council specifically to facilitate peace-making after an agreement has been reached and the rule of engagement call for any deployed armed units to act only in self-defense. Chapter Seven expressly permits armed intervention or other sanctions to "restore" international peace and security.

Once again, however, as with the codification of the Genocide Convention after World War II, the P-5 nations (the United States, Russia, China, Great Britain, and France) would wield an outsized influence over any decision to intervene, thus maintaining the status quo of power imbalances in the world. The R2P only stipulates that the P-5 "should" abstain from vetoing any resolutions if their own interests are not at stake. Any lawyer will tell you that "should" is not "shall," and these states invariably will take into account their own priorities first and not hesitate to use their veto power to quash any Security Council resolutions they deem contrary or harmful to those interests. One saving grace of R2P, however, is that since it is designed to *prevent* genocide and not to punish it, the high legal bar of proving "intent" to commit genocide need not be met. In addition, "Genocide," a specific law, was placed in the same grouping "with other international criminal acts—specifically, crimes against humanity, war crimes, and ethnic cleansing" thereby "dismantling some elements of the hierarchy of international crimes" (Bachman 2022, 120).

Geopolitical tensions invariably serve to undermine any cooperation between Britain, France, and the United States on the one hand, and Russia and China on the other. While the doctrine proved successful in mediating post-election violence in Kenya, in 2008 (Halakhe), in 2011, when the UNSC again invoked the R2P and authorized a "no fly" zone to protect civilians in Libya under attack by Muammar al-Qaddafi unintended consequences resulted. When the UN action led to the ouster of the long-time dictator, the ever-suspicious Vladimir Putin of Russia came to see R2P as just another instrument in the Western toolkit to effect "regime change," a fairly new term at the time for an old practice—to overthrow a government. Reeling from a series of bombings and other attacks by Uyghur separatists in its Xinjiang province, China, about to intensify its campaign of repression against the Uyghurs, once again publicly embraced the principle of non-interference in the internal affairs of other nations (although China had been practicing settler-colonial strategies, resembling Western imperialism, in places such as Tibet for many years). Another problem is that, even if as in 1999, in the case of Australia's intervention in East Timor during the final phases of Indonesia's genocide there, the UNSC votes in favor of preventing or ending a genocide, there must be countries willing to put their own troops in harm's way for the needs of others.

This UN dependence upon its members to provide troops to prevent genocide and protect civilians—if such a resolution is in fact, authorized by the UNSC—could perhaps be rectified by the creation of a permanent, international rapid deployment force such as the one established by the European Union (EU). This force was modeled after a previous European rapid deployment force that was deployed in Albania in 2000–01 under the auspices of the North Atlantic Treaty Organization (NATO, founded in 1949) and later to Macedonia (2003) and Bosnia and Herzegovina (2007) under a mandate from the EU. The new military unit will be composed of 5,000 troops and is expected to reach full operational readiness in 2025. This new European Union Rapid Deployment Capacity (EU RDC) could potentially be available to implement some UN resolutions, but some human-rights experts and scholars, including ourselves, have in mind the creation of a wholly new volunteer military force as envisioned by the original UN Charter. It could be dispatched within days, not weeks or months, to protect civilians from violence perpetrated by their own governments. Whether to "provide for the Pacific Settlement of Disputes" under Chapter Six after a negotiated halt to violence to foster peace talks, or to "maintain security and public order where the State is unable to do so" under the more robust mandate of Chapter Seven, such an armed force would demonstrate a commitment to the high ideals of the UN and its 1948 Declaration of Human Rights.

Such a force would not be composed of mercenaries or adventurers, but of up to 10,000 highly motivated, educated, trained professionals who would volunteer to serve either fixed terms or, better yet, an entire career, conducting peacekeeping operations and humanitarian interventions—armed, if necessary. These professionals would undergo extensive training not just in military specialties, but also in human-rights law and the noble, if often ignored, ideals of the United Nations. This force would replace the current "voluntary" contributions of troops from member states that often are not only poorly trained and led but sometimes not even maintained properly due to corruption on the part of the contributing states. To deploy such a force under Chapters Six or Seven of the UN Charter, the entire United Nations must be involved—not just the UNSC. This would obviously involve the reworking of the peacekeeping mandates of the Charter to require a more democratic approach, which would be a wonderful development for many reasons. The Charter can be amended by a vote of two-thirds of the members of the General Assembly, but again the P-5 powers have veto power. If this structural impediment can be resolved, the peacekeeping mandates should require two-thirds of the members of the General Assembly to vote in the affirmative to authorize the deployment of this new UN force, as well as the usual supermajority of 9 of the 15 members of the Security Council. Most importantly, however, the veto power of the P-5 should be *suspended* for any resolution to implement action under Chapters Six or Seven of the revised UN Charter. Such important structural changes would demonstrate considerable progress toward a more fair and balanced international order, but we recognize that such modifications would be held hostage, to some degree, to international power relations and the primacy of selfish great power interests deliberately incorporated into the world's current political architecture. We should all aspire to live in a just, democratic, and egalitarian world where such a force would not be needed; sadly, we must live in this one for the foreseeable future.

The Punishment of the Crime of Genocide

Preventing genocide has therefore proven to be quite a difficult task made even more difficult by the structural impediments put in place by the P-5. The world community has not done much better at punishing genocidists. Incredibly, there have been only three cases in which individuals have been prosecuted under the Genocide Convention. These include the Khmer Rouge slaughter of Vietnamese and Cham peoples in Cambodia in the 1970s; the mass killing of Tutsis by Hutus in Rwanda in 1994; and the murder of more than 8,000 men and boys in the village of Srebrenica in Bosnia in 1995. A fourth, against Omar al-Bashir, who ruled Sudan for many years until his ouster in 2019, is pending his extradition (the ICC, established after the atrocities in Bosnia and Rwanda, has jurisdiction here but does not try persons *in absentia*). The United States government has declared seven cases of genocide since the 1990s, although in some cases (e.g., Bosnia and Rwanda), the United States did not make this determination until it was too late to do anything. The others include the genocide in Darfur in western Sudan, the so-called Islamic State's actions against the Yezidi people in northern Iraq in the 2010s, the ethnic cleansing of the Rohingya Muslims by the Myanmar military, and the Chinese government's treatment of the Uyghurs. We agree with this assessment and, as noted in the Introduction, would add to that infamous list the Russian atrocities in Ukraine since 2022 and, as will be discussed below, also the Israeli actions in Gaza since late 2023 after the barbaric attack by *Hamas* on October 7 of that year. In point of fact, the ICC has not only issued arrest warrants for war crimes against Putin but also for Israeli Prime Minister Benjamin Netanyahu and his former defense minister, Yoav Gallant.

That Putin launched a war of aggression resulting in his troops committing war crimes is beyond question. Less certain is whether the charge of genocide can be preferred against him. Israeli military operations have also been assessed as genocidal by many observers, including ourselves. We will point out again: as educated "citizens of the world," for which we hope this book helps prepare you to be, you must employ your own moral and intellectual framework, unconfined by excessively legalistic and narrow concepts, to grapple with today's issues. You may decide for yourself if Russia's war on Ukraine—euphemistically called a "Special Military Operation"—or Israel's depredations upon Gaza are genocides. While there are genocidal aspects being committed in both assaults, at the very least serious war crimes and/or crimes against humanity have undoubtedly been committed.

Importantly, Article IV of the Genocide Convention has made clear that persons engaged in committing genocide shall—the use of the word "shall" leaves no other interpretation open—be punished "whether they are constitutionally responsible rulers, public officials, or private individuals." Lemkin tried, and failed, to get universal jurisdiction inserted into the 1948 Convention. Signatories were instead instructed simply to incorporate a law against genocide in their domestic penal codes. Lemkin's hope for an international court to try genocidists was left unrealized for the time being. Instead, Article VI stated that persons charged with genocide could be tried "by a competent tribunal of the State in the territory of which the act was committed, or by such international penal tribunal as may have jurisdiction with respect to those Contracting Parties which shall have accepted its jurisdiction" (Totten and Parsons 2009, 31). Incredibly, it would be fully half a century after the UN passed the Genocide Convention before the international community adopted the founding treaty—the Rome Statute, adopted in 1998 with sittings of the court beginning after it went into effect in 2002—of this International Criminal Court. Although there are now 124 countries— out of 195 member states of the UN—that are ICC members, three of the P-5 (China, Russia, and the United States) have declined to join the ICC, citing their usual concerns over state sovereignty. To be more honest, they fear legal consequences for their actions. The Court is empowered to investigate and prosecute certain international crimes, including genocide, the crime of aggression, war crimes, and crimes against humanity (the latter two are actually categories of crimes, unlike genocide, which is a specific crime under international law).

The ICC is independent of the UN and cases concerning genocide, war crimes, crimes against humanity and the crime of aggression can be referred for investigation and prosecution by any of its signatories, providing that the aggressor state has signed onto the Rome Statute or accepted its jurisdiction. Cases can also be referred to the UNSC for investigation, but any member of the P-5 can thwart the pursuit of justice through the veto. In the case of Russia's criminal transgressions against the Ukrainian people, neither Russia nor Ukraine are signatories to the ICC, but the latter has accepted its jurisdiction and ICC investigators are on the ground and the first of what will undoubtedly be several charges against Putin has already been lodged. Russia however, will obviously not accept jurisdiction, and, as mentioned, the Court does not try cases *in absentia*. It is therefore highly unlikely that Putin and his accomplices will ever be tried for their crimes. The EU is exploring the possibility of forming another *ad hoc* tribunal such as those formerly used by the United Nations to bring criminals from Serbia and Rwanda to justice. This body, unlike those International Criminal Tribunals for Yugoslavia and Rwanda—discussed in detail below—would not be sanctioned by the UN, and neither Ukraine nor Russia are members of the European Union—although Ukraine is pursuing membership.

For crimes committed before July 1, 2002, the UN had to resort to *ad hoc* tribunals or "special courts." The UNSC established the ICTY in 1993 and the ICTR in 1994. The ICTR was the first international court to deliver a guilty verdict on the charge of genocide and also established that rape could be a means of perpetrating genocide (Akayesu verdict, 1998). In the more than two decades of its existence (1994–2015), the ICTR indicted 93 high-ranking individuals from government and military circles (convicting and sentencing 62, with three still remaining at large). Further, in 2003 the ICTR rendered a landmark verdict, finding members of the Rwandan news media "guilty of genocide" for their inflammatory radio broadcasts inciting Hutus to attack and kill Tutsis. The ICTY (1993–2017) also found several military and political leaders guilty of the crime of genocide for their involvement in the massacre of roughly 8,400 Muslim men and boys at Srebrenica. The former president of Serbia, Slobodan Milosevic, charged with genocide in 1999, was eventually extradited to The Hague, in the Netherlands, where both the International Court of Justice—often referred to as the

Figure C.1 The "Peace Palace" at the Hague. https://commons.wikimedia.org/wiki/File:Zorgvliet,_2517_The_Hague,_Netherlands_-_panoramio_(13).jpg

"World Court," established in 1945 along with the UN itself and to which *all* member states *must* accept jurisdiction, although not necessarily for the crime of genocide—and ICC are located. There, Milosevic he suffered a heart attack and died at the conclusion of his trial in 2006 (Figure C.1).

Other major war criminals, sometimes after "hiding in plain sight" among sympathetic Serbian villagers, were eventually arrested and successfully prosecuted, most notably Radovan Karadzic in 2016 and Ratko Mladic in 2017. Some Croatian and Bosnian Muslim war criminals were also charged and convicted by the ICTY, but the majority, quite fittingly, were Serbian. Although both the ICTR and ICTY have now completed their respective mandates that does not mean any remaining criminals are now safe from prosecution. In 2010, the UN set up the International Residual Mechanism for Criminal Tribunals (IRMCT) to continue investigations into war crimes, crimes against humanity, and genocide committed by individuals not yet brought to justice. In May 2023, the most sought-after fugitive from the Rwanda genocide—Fulgence Kayishima—was captured in South Africa. Accused of orchestrating the murder of over two thousand Tutsi refugees by burning them alive in a Catholic Church, Kayishema will undoubtedly spend the rest of his life in prison. Entering court with a bible and another book emblazoned with the motto "Jesus first," Reuters news service reported "the 62 year old was asked if he had anything to say to [his] victims. 'What can I say,' he responded, 'it was a war at that time.'"

The UN has also sponsored two special courts. In one of these, the Special Court for Sierra Leone (SCSL), Charles Taylor, the former head of Liberia, received a sentence of 50 years in prison in 2012 for war crimes and crimes against humanity during Sierra Leone's civil war of 1991–2002. In the other, the United Nations reached an agreement in 2003 with the Cambodian government to assist and participate in the Extraordinary Chambers of the Courts of Cambodia (ECCC). This body, established by the Cambodian government in 2001, was charged with bringing to justice the senior members of the Khmer Rouge who had terrorized not only Cambodians but other peoples within and without that country during their rule from 1975 to 1979. The leader of the KR, Pol Pot, escaped justice as he continued to lead the remnants of his forces from the jungle until he was overthrown as a result of an internal power struggle. Convicted of "treason" by his former comrades in 1997, he was sentenced to life imprisonment and died under house arrest in 1998 at the age of 72. The ECCC did, however, find two other senior members of the KR guilty of the crime of genocide as well as crimes against humanity. Nuon Chea, the chief ideologist of the KR regime, was convicted in 2018 and sentenced to life in prison (he died the following year at the age of 93), and his co-defendant Khieu Samphan, the Khmer Rouge head of state, had his life sentence confirmed as the last official act of the court in September 2022. A handful of others, including Kaing Guek Eav, aka "Comrade Duch," the notorious head of the Tuol Sleng prison, were convicted of "crimes against humanity" and/or died in custody over the past decade. All told, these were the only three major convictions obtained by the court over its 16 years of existence at a cost of $337 million. At first glance, this might seem woefully insufficient, but at least the regime's crimes were laid bare for all to see and these genocidists were ultimately brought to justice—if genuine justice is truly attainable for such monstrous crimes.

Taken together, these international criminal prosecutions do offer a glimmer of hope. Hope that genocidists cannot act with impunity and that all persons, no matter what their position, will eventually be called to account for their crimes. Even though Milosevic died before being convicted he was subsequently found, like the Nazis at Nuremberg, to be part of a "joint criminal enterprise" that "ethnically cleansed" much of Bosnia of its Muslim population. Later, the ICJ found that Milosevic, as leader of the Serbian nation at the time, was at least complicit in genocide by failing to prevent it in Bosnia as well as for not cooperating with the ICTY in turning over the chief architect of that atrocity, General Ratko Mladic. In its final ruling in 2021, the ICTY made the connection between the Serbian state and the atrocities committed during the war still more explicit when they convicted two Serbian state officials of being in league with the Bosnian Serbs in a "joint criminal enterprise" with "common criminal purpose" in carrying out their war crimes against the Muslims in Bosnia (*New York Times*, June 30, 2021). This last ruling from the ICTY does not mean that those who have not yet been brought to account for their crimes in the conflict will escape prosecution. The former prime minister and President of Kosovo, Hashim Thaci, was indicted on charges of war crimes and crimes against humanity in November 2020 by another *ad hoc* court in The Hague for his role in the war against Serbia in 1998–99. His trial, along with three of his closest associates, began on April 3, 2023.

Omar al-Bashir was the first *sitting* head of state to be indicted for war crimes and crimes against humanity, and in 2010 was also indicted for genocide. Bashir was able to avoid extradition to The Hague, however, by only visiting "friendly" African and Middle Eastern countries such as Egypt, Ethiopia, Qatar, Jordan, and South Africa (despite several of those countries being full members of the ICC). He was tried and convicted of corruption and money laundering after being overthrown by the Sudanese military in

2019. Sentenced to two years' imprisonment, al-Bashir has since been standing trial for his role in the 1989 coup that first brought him to power. In August 2021, the Sudanese government promised to hand him over to the ICC upon the conclusion of that trial. We have noted that while the ICC does not try persons *in absentia*, the Serbs did eventually turn over the indicted war criminal Slobodan Milosevic to the court to stand trial. This fate could also befall Russia's Vladimir Putin. The ICC, having now charged Putin with war crimes, making him the second sitting head of state indicted by that body, will also eventually charge him with the crime of aggression and quite possibly even the crime of genocide. The Serbs handed Milosevic over for trial in order to obtain economic aid and loans from the International Monetary Fund. The Serbian Prime Minister Zoran Djindjic understood that "Any other solution except cooperation [in this matter] would lead the country to disaster" and we can only hope that someday the Russians too may hand over their discredited leader to face judgment for his crimes in order to get the sanctions placed on Russia's economy removed. Unfortunately, like in Serbia in the late 1990s, it might require mass, popular protests and the downfall of his regime to accomplish this—events that are highly unlikely to develop in that rigidly policed state.

The Burmese regime also faces an accounting for the atrocities perpetrated upon the Rohingya. The 2018 UN report on the plight of the Rohingya demanded that the Myanmar military government be held accountable for genocide, crimes against humanity, and war crimes; the International Court of Justice then ordered the Myanmar government to prevent genocidal acts against the Rohingya and preserve all evidence related to the case. Shortly thereafter, the Muslim-majority country of The Gambia formally lodged a complaint with the International Court of Justice, or ICJ— often referred to as the "World Court"—established in 1945 along with the United Nations itself and to which *all* member states *must* accept jurisdiction, although not necessarily for the crime of genocide, as we will discuss below—charging Myanmar with the genocide of the Rohingya. At first represented by Nobel Peace Prize-winning democracy activist Aung San Suu Kyi—ironically defending the same military leaders who had placed her under house arrest for years—in the initial proceedings, Myanmar claimed the Rohingya were involved in terrorism against the state. During these preliminary stages of the trial, in February 2021, the military overthrew the elected civilian government and arrested Aung San Suu Kyi, again placing her under house arrest. She has since been tried numerous times on a variety of bogus charges and has been sentenced to a total of 33 years in prison. Increasingly desperate to put a stop to the ICJ proceedings, the Myanmar government accused The Gambia of not acting as a "nation in its own right" but instead as a proxy for the 57-nation Organization of Islamic Cooperation. They asserted that The Gambia therefore lacked the legal standing to bring these charges.

In July 2022, the ICJ ruled that the case did in fact come under its jurisdiction as any signatory to the Genocide Convention had a duty to punish and prevent genocide and thus The Gambia had acted properly in referring the case to the ICJ. The trial at The Hague (in the Netherlands) is ongoing at the time of this book's publication and will undoubtedly take several years to conclude. Unfortunately, there are also other roadblocks to genocidal states being held to account by the ICJ under the provisions of the Convention. While member states—and only state actors, not individuals—are allowed to file complaints with the ICJ "relating to the interpretation, application or fulfillment of the present Convention, including those relating to the responsibility of a State for genocide [...]" (*Convention*), individual states were permitted to avoid being subject to some aspects of the Convention, such as adjudication by the ICJ, simply by attaching their own reservations or "understandings" of the legal meanings of any of its stipulations. Bachman notes that presently 17 countries do not agree to be bound by the Convention's important Article IX, including the United States and China.

The ICC, for its part, has opened an investigation into the forced deportation of the Rohingya from Myanmar into a member state, Bangladesh, as a crime against humanity in 2019. The investigation is limited to the "cleansing operations" in 2017 and 2018; any other crimes committed against the Rohingya in Myanmar itself would need to be referred to the ICC by the UN Security Council and both Russia and China have indicated they would veto any such resolution. The UN Human Rights Council (UNHRC) has created the *Independent Investigative Mechanism for Myanmar* to build case files against individuals suspected of violating international criminal law and "to facilitate and expedite fair and independent criminal proceedings," in whatever future court they may be held (*Human Rights Watch*, February 14, 2022). Finally, both Argentina and Turkey have begun proceedings against the Myanmar military for genocide, acting in the name of "universal justice" as signatories of the Genocide Convention.

You have already learned that the final text of the 1948 UN Genocide Convention was cynically arrived at by the victors of World War II. The Allied powers agreed to support it only because they were able to write it in such a way that it removed from the definition of genocide atrocities committed by European and European-descended peoples. The treatment of Indigenous peoples in the United States and Canada, racial lynching and Jim Crow oppression and violence in the United States, and the repression of colonial subjects the world over went unmentioned because they did not fit the "prototype" of genocide—the Holocaust. In addition, other acts that should have constituted genocide such as the murder of political opponents, the deliberate mass starvation of social groups, other ethnic cleansings of minority peoples, and sexual violence were also not included. We have now explored these missing topics connected to the world's historical legacy of genocides. We also have called into question the self-congratulatory master narrative presented to students concerning the 1948 Genocide Convention: that it was a great "achievement" resulting from the triumph of the "righteous" Allies over the "evil" Axis in World War II. The mass murder of peoples by the Germans and Japanese is, of course, rightly condemned. The continued mythology of what Eisenhower called the "Great Crusade" or the "good war" against "evil," however, eventually led to the justification of the use of American power to combat "communism" and ultimately to yet another "crusade" against an entirely new "axis of evil" (Samet 2021). Of course, the Europeans had also used violence to subjugate and exploit entire peoples and immediately upon the conclusion of World War II these supposedly "democratic" European states of France (in Indochina and Algeria), Portugal (in Angola and Mozambique), and the Netherlands (Indonesia) scrambled to preserve their colonialist privileges, committing massive and even genocidal crimes in the process. Great Britain, often portrayed as the exception, supposedly "quit" India after instituting a series of reforms during the Raj in the best tradition of the "White Man's Burden."

The historical record does not support this account. Before exiting India, British authorities allowed three million Bengali Indians to perish in a terrible famine. Great Britain, like the other European nations, also had to be forced out of its possessions in India and elsewhere (for example, in Kenya and Cyprus) kicking and screaming after trying to reassert its control over its former empire. At the same time, the Soviet Union was consolidating its control over Eastern Europe while repressing national minorities in the USSR itself. Within this international context, the Genocide Convention was written by the victorious powers while they still held much of the world in bondage. In the United States, after this "good war" concluded, African-American soldiers returning home from their segregated units were once again, as after World War I, subject to racial violence if they wore their uniforms too proudly, and Jim Crow continued unabated (Delmont, 2022). It therefore hardly represented the triumph of democracy over tyranny.

Instead, the Allied victory merely reflected the triumph of the status quo. The imperial states such as Germany, Japan, and Italy—late to the quest for empire and aspiring to catch up to the British and French—had been prevented from acquiring any share of the victors' possessions (Overy, 2022). Despite its laudable intentions, the 1948 Genocide Convention was simply yet another manifestation of the continuing domination of the world by the great powers. The colonial powers such as Great Britain, France, and the Netherlands even thwarted the application of the Convention to their own subject peoples through the "colonial clause." Article XII states "Any Contracting Party may at any time [...] extend the application of the present Convention to all or any of the territories for the conduct of whose foreign relations that Contracting Power is responsible." In other words, the colonial powers such as the French, who were forcing Africans to learn in French about the superior virtues of the Gallic culture, and the British who were busy proselytizing converts to their Anglican religion, and the Dutch, whose citizens didn't need to pay taxes as a result of the riches flowing in from Indonesia, could, if they chose to, extend the protection of the Convention to those they exploited. Needless to say, they did not do so, with the British going so far as to assert that it would be "undemocratic" to force such a law upon its subject peoples! Reading this book you will need to think long and hard about how to effect change in this supposedly "better" world created by and for oppressive regimes of the past, including our own. We are writing this book as a challenge and perhaps an inspiration to think critically about the laws and structures in place in the world today and whom they are really meant to serve.

As we finish this book in late 2024, the debate over what is or is not genocide continues. The brutal and barbaric attack by *Hamas* terrorists on Israel on October 7, 2023, was answered with a disproportionately vicious and inhumane attack by the Israeli Defense Force (IDF) on the Palestinians in Gaza—*Hamas* members and civilians alike. Many scholars, ourselves included, believe that these attacks constitute genocide, or, at the very least, a clear indication of genocidal intent and potential. The acrimonious academic debate over the extent to which the *Nakba* (discussed in Chapter Two) of 1948—the same year the Convention was ratified—was planned or whether or not it constituted genocide as opposed to "ethnic cleansing" is once again being waged between scholars over whether the Israeli claim that its "intent" is to destroy *Hamas* and not Palestinians "as such" is enough to justify the actions of its military forces. According to the Convention, "direct and public incitement to commit genocide" *is* in fact genocide, and there are numerous blood-curdling quotes from Israeli political and military figures that have done just that.

Israeli forces have since visited collective punishment on over two million Palestinians, the entire population of Gaza. They have been "deliberately inflicting on the group conditions of life calculated to bring about its physical destruction in whole or in part," actions that constitute genocide. The forcible relocation of a million people from North Gaza to South Gaza is, of course, ethnic cleansing. Whether or not that too is genocide is yet another hotly contested issue. Both of these actions, however, are most definitely crimes against humanity and war crimes as well. As was discussed in the Introduction, South Africa lodged a complaint against Israel with the ICJ for its response to the *Hamas* attack of October 7, 2023 (as of the end of 2024 fifteen other governments have signed onto this complaint and become parties to it, while another twelve states have requested to "intervene," that is, to present their government's position on the matter without taking sides). In January 2024, the ICJ ordered Israel to ensure that its military actions did not lead to genocide, as legally defined, and to refrain from inciting it. The larger question of whether or not Israel committed genocide in Gaza against the Palestinians will take years to ascertain, but the ICJ found South Africa's claims to be "plausible." Israel did not append "reservations" to the 1948 Genocide Convention and therefore had to appear at the World Court to argue their defense. The irony of a "Jewish" state having to answer for the crime of genocide that was enshrined in international law because of the Holocaust should not be lost on anyone.

In May 2024, investigations by the ICC—and while Israel, like the United States, is not a member and therefore not under its jurisdiction, the territories occupied by Israel since 1967, including Gaza, the West Bank, and Jerusalem, *do* come under the Court's jurisdiction—led to prosecutors asking that criminal arrest warrants for war crimes and crimes against humanity be issued against both Israeli and *Hamas* political leaders. As mentioned earlier, these warrants were ultimately issued against Netanyahu, Gallant, and also Mohammed Deif, the leader of *Hamas's* military wing. As defined in the ICC Rome Statute "Crimes against humanity" include extermination and deportation "as part of a widespread or systematic attack against any civilian population [...]" with extermination being the "intentional infliction of conditions of life, *inter alia* the deprivation of food and medicine, calculated to bring about the destruction of part of a population..." with deportation defined as "forced displacement of the persons concerned by expulsion or other coercive acts from the area in which they are lawfully present" (United Nations: *Report of the International Law Commission*, 2017, 11). As the ICC investigations gathered additional support and momentum, the US Congress responded by passing a bill, in January 2025, that would sanction the International Criminal Court (ICC) in retaliation for its arrest warrants against Netanyahu and Gallant.

As we write this at the end of 2024 the Israeli blockade of food, fuel, and medicine from reaching Gaza has led to a public health crisis, as well as the death of critically ill infants when power to their incubators and resuscitators has been interrupted or cut off—some of the more than 20,000 children that have died as a result of Israeli military actions—with thousands more missing or buried under rubble. Total deaths number well over 45,000. Palestinians are also again being forced off their lands and their homes seized by Israeli settlers in the West Bank, where they live under a system of *apartheid*—yet another crime against humanity. Israeli settlers there have also blocked and then vandalized humanitarian relief convoys carrying food and medical supplies into Gaza and, according to a May 21, 2024 article in *The Guardian*, these right-wing zealots are informed in advance by police and the IDF of the location of these aid trucks.

Both deportation and attacks upon civilians are war crimes as well. Unfortunately, protected places such as hospitals, schools, mosques, and churches often lose that protection if used by combatants. In our view, however, two wrongs do not make a right. IDF attacks on these sites are reprehensible, but *Hamas* militants view Palestinian civilian deaths from a cold, cruel strategic attitude, seeing these deaths as good for propaganda purposes and therefore not adopting tactics that could lessen the calamity that their people are suffering. Incredibly, the Israelis continue to insist that their indiscriminate attacks are *not* a form of collective punishment on an entire people—which is forbidden by international law (in particular, the Fourth Geneva Conventions (1949) that has been incorporated in the Rome Statute—but instead legitimate acts of self-defense against the *Hamas* terrorists; Figure C.2).

But is this genocide? The irresponsible and reprehensible statements of the Israeli political and military leadership evince a clear and convincing intent to destroy a people through extermination, ethnic cleansing, and creating conditions of life leading to physical

Figure C.2 A small child stands amidst the ruins of his town in the Gaza Strip, almost the entirety of which has been destroyed by the Israeli assault since October 2023. https://commons.wikimedia.org/wiki/File:Destruction_of_Gaza_1.jpg

destruction. On the third day of the war, Israeli Minister of Defense Yoav Gallant referred to the Palestinian population in Gaza as "human animals"—terminology employed also by other Israeli leaders—and announced: "I have ordered a complete siege on the Gaza Strip. There will be no electricity, no food, no fuel, everything is closed" (UN Office of the High Commissioner, October 12, 2023). The UN also quoted the Minister as threatening to "bomb those attempting to provide humanitarian aid to the Gaza Strip" (Idem.). The next day, October 10, 2023, IDF spokesperson Daniel Hagari announced that the Israeli military had already dropped "hundreds of tons of bombs [...]" adding that "the emphasis is on damage and not on accuracy" (*The Guardian*, October 10, 2023). Israeli Major General Ghassan Alian, the head of the Coordinator of Government Activities in the Territories ("COGAT") explicitly stated the intention to destroy Palestinian life in Gaza: "Human animals must be treated as such. There will be no electricity and no water [in Gaza], there will only be destruction. You wanted hell, you will get hell" (*The Times of Israel*, 10 October 2023). These are but a few of the incendiary—and revealing—public pronouncements by Israeli leaders during the first month of the war against Gaza. The 1948 Convention delineates different acts that "shall be punishable" such as the act of genocide itself, conspiracy to commit genocide, complicity in genocide, and so on. Most important for our purposes here, however, is that if perpetrators of any of these "crimes against humanity" make "Direct and public incitement to commit the crime of genocide" then they are genocidists.

The case against Israel at the ICJ will take years to adjudicate, as will the many complaints filed at the ICC, also located in The Hague, Netherlands. Israel, like the United States, is not a member of the ICC and therefore does not come under its jurisdiction. While the statements by Israeli leaders and the IDF's actions on the ground make for a compelling case, charges of either incitement to commit genocide or committing the crime itself would still be prosecuted by the ICJ under the high legal bar of "intent" to "destroy, as such" in the 1948 Convention. The Rome Statute, however, does not require this exceedingly difficult legal standard of "intent" to commit international mass atrocity crimes be met for crimes *other than* genocide under its purview, only that there be a "knowledge of the attack." Genocide—along with crimes against humanity, war crimes, and (since 2017) the crime of aggression—is also under the purview of the ICC but as it is a separate and distinct international *law*, as opposed to the other *categories* of crimes, it needs to be applied according to the Convention.

The Rome Statute of the ICC on Crimes against Humanity also offers, unlike the deliberately limited Convention, protection to "any identifiable group or collectivity on political, racial, national, ethnic, cultural, religious, gender [...] or other grounds" and focuses on the outcomes of criminal actions. The ICC, with its international jurisdiction—at least for signatories—established a half-century after the adoption of the Convention was the ultimate goal of Raphael Lemkin. The compromises and concessions he made to get the Convention agreed to by the world's great powers were part of a strategy to outlaw violence that ultimately could kill people. Lemkin understood there were many different means to do just that, and the Rome Statute, delineating myriad crimes against humanity that can result in the destruction of a people, more fully reflects his vision. He understood that law, as a living thing like a people's culture, changes over time. He certainly did not envision that the Convention would be etched in stone for all time like a modern Code of Hammurabi—the famous Babylonian legal text inscribed on a basalt stele some two thousand years before the birth of Jesus of Nazareth—and that this imperfect definition of Genocide would be kept forever. In fact, Article XIV stated that the "present convention" was to remain in force for but ten years and thereafter be renewed for "successive periods of five years." Like Thomas Jefferson's observation that the US Constitution should be rewritten every generation, Lemkin undoubtedly hoped that a more inclusive Convention would someday see the light of day. While it is theoretically possible to amend or revise the Convention under Article XVI, the likelihood of such being done in today's fractured world is next to nil.

Regardless of one's educated opinion on this or that mass atrocity, one thing then is clear: The 1948 Convention, a product of self-serving political compromise by genocidists (be that through "colonizing," "civilizing," "state-building," "resettlement" or some combination of these) is fatally flawed and should be abandoned in its entirety. There is no need to create such a hierarchy of suffering of the different types of heinous violence still being inflicted upon myriad peoples throughout the world. The ICC Rome Statute, as amended in 2017, includes, besides Genocide and War Crimes, these specific Crimes against Humanity: "Attack directed against any civilian population," "Extermination," and "Deportation or Forcible Transfer of Population." Attacks directed against any civilian population include any "course of conduct involving the multiple commission of acts referred to in Paragraph 1, pursuant to or in furtherance of State or organizational policy to commit such act." Extermination "means the intentional infliction of conditions of life, *inter alia*, the deprivation of food or medicine, calculated to bring about the destruction of part of a population" (as do all genocides), and of course these things are genocidal. Deportation or forcible transfer of population "means forced displacement of the persons concerned by expulsion or other coercive acts from the area in which they are lawfully present," in other words, "ethnic cleansing," also genocide. Other Crimes against Humanity include the "Enforced disappearance of persons," such as what happened in Argentina, the genocide of a political group, and "Forced Pregnancy" with "the intent of affecting the ethnic composition of any population." These things are all genocide, too.

These methods employed by perpetrators to destroy human groups have all been included in this book as "genocides," and we believe, no offense intended to Trygve Lie, the first Secretary General of the United Nations, that genocide need not be separated from Crimes against Humanity. We agree that the attempt to destroy a people and in so doing deprive the world of that people's cultural contributions is a uniquely reprehensible crime; but as we have asserted in this book, there are very many ways to accomplish this destruction of a people. The Nazi genocide of the Jews was but the most extreme part of a larger colonizing effort that was intended to destroy other peoples as well. The 1948 Genocide Convention, then, was simply virtue signaling by morally compromised statesmen who essentially snookered Raphael Lemkin into believing his concept could be put into place in the name of justice and not be merely a pious requiem for the Jewish victims of Nazi depravity. Lemkin's vision of international jurisdiction to bring to justice the worst criminals in the world, whether "genocidists" in light of the Convention's flawed legal definition or perpetrators of other mass atrocity crimes that similarly lead to the social destruction of a human group and subsequent loss of their culture—as "genocide" was understood by him—whether in time of war or peace, was, as we have seen, partially realized by the 1998 Rome Statute that established the ICC.

The Rome Statute breaks down international mass atrocities into the categories of genocide, crimes against humanity, war crimes, and crimes of aggression. The Rome Statute's Crimes Against Humanity category has already been used several times as a path forward for the prosecution of genocidists. Though it is true that the ICC is an independent body and therefore free of the constraints of the UNSC in that it can initiate investigations without its consent, the only *enforcement* mechanism for both it and the ICJ is through the use of Chapter Seven of the United Nations Charter. Of course, this requires the consent of the UN Security Council. There, not only are 9 of 15 votes (a super majority) required for passage of sanctions, but any of the P-5's veto power can be used to block such resolutions. In the final analysis, crimes against humanity, a category of crimes, actually encompasses all those actions that can constitute genocide. In the end, after all, this is essentially what the ICTY and the ICTR did with the vast majority of the cases brought before them.

As we have seen, there have been very few convictions for genocide despite the reoccurring instances of this horrific crime and, more often than not, it has simply been easier to get around the high legal bar of proving intent by charging genocidists with crimes against humanity. We should leave the obsession with the wording of the Convention behind and simply charge malefactors with those specific crimes that they have committed. We are left once again, however, with a handful of states that refuse to accede to the Rome Statute out of concern for their national sovereignty. Many of those states are "rogue" nations such as North Korea, Iran, Myanmar, and Syria that refuse to abide by the rules-based international order. Others, that actually created this world order, such as Russia and the United States—as well as China—actively seek to undermine it when it suits their own selfish interests. This is the world you have inherited, and hopefully, this book will help convince you of the need to change it (Figure C.3).

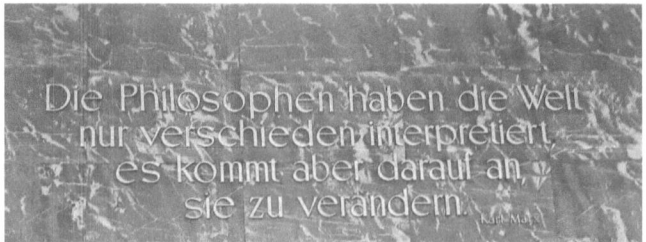

Figure C.3 "The philosophers have only interpreted the world, in various ways" wrote Karl Marx in 1845. "The point, however, is to change it." Inscription in hallway of main building at Humboldt University, former East Berlin. Photo by John Cox, 2012.

BIBLIOGRAPHY

Abdullah, Daud. 2019. "A century of cultural genocide in Palestine." In *Cultural Genocide: Law, Politics, and Global Manifestations*, 227–45. Bachman, Jeffrey S. ed. London and New York: Routledge.
Ainsztein, Reuben. 1974. *Jewish Resistance in Nazi-Occupied Eastern Europe*. New York: Barnes & Noble.
Al Jazeera. 2025. "US House votes to advance bill to sanction ICC over Israel arrest warrants." Accessible at https://www.aljazeera.com/news/2025/1/9/us-house-votes-to-advance-bill-to-sanction-icc-over-israel-arrest-warrants.
Alexander, Jocelyn, McGregor, Jo Ann, and Ranger, Terence. 2000. *Violence and Memory: One Hundred Years in the Dark Forests of Matabeleland*. London: James Currey.
Allen, Beverly. 1996. *Rape Warfare: The Hidden Genocide in Bosnia-Herzegovina and Croatia*. Minneapolis: University of Minnesota Press.
Alliluyeva, Svetlana. 1967. *Twenty Letters to a Friend*. London: Hutchinson.
Alvarez, Alex. 2016. *Native Americans and the Question of Genocide*. Lanham, MD: Rowman & Littlefield.
American Anthropological Association. 1998. "Statement on Race." *Accessible at* https://americananthro.org/about/policies/statement-on-race/#:~:text=%E2%80%9CRace%E2%80%9D%20thus%20evolved%20as%20a,homogenized%20into%20%E2%80%9Cracial%E2%80%9D%20categories.
Anderson, Benedict. 1983. *Imagined Communities: Reflections on the Origin and Spread of Nationalism*. London and New York: Verso.
Anonymous. 2005. *A Woman in Berlin: Eight Weeks in the Conquered City*. New York: Picador.
Applebaum, Anne. 2017. *Red Famine: Stalin's War on Ukraine*. New York: Anchor Books.
Bachman, Jeffrey S. 2022. *The Politics of Genocide: From the Genocide Convention to the Responsibility to Protect*. New Brunswick, NJ: Rutgers University Press.
———. 2019. *The United States and Genocide: (Re) Defining the Relationship*. London and New York: Routledge.
———. ed. 2019. *Cultural Genocide: Law, Politics, and Global Manifestations*. London and New York: Routledge.
———. 2019. "An historical perspective: the exclusion of cultural genocide from the genocide convention." In *Cultural Genocide: Law, Politics, and Global Manifestations*, 45–61. London and New York: Routledge.
Banner, Stuart. 2005. *How the Indians Lost their Land: Land and Power on the Frontier*. Cambridge: Harvard University Press.
Barltrop, Richard. 2011. *Darfur and the International Community: The Challenges of Conflict Resolution in Sudan*. London: I.B. Tauris.
Barta, Tony. 1987. "Relations of genocide: land and lives in the colonization of Australia." In Isidor Walliman and Michael N. Dombowski, eds., *Genocide and the Modern Ag: Etiology and Case Studies of Mass Death*, 237–51. Westport, CT: Greenwood Press.
Bartov, Omer. 1992. *Hitler's Army: Soldiers, Nazis, and War in the Third Reich*. New York and Oxford: Oxford University Press.
Bauman, Zygmunt. 1989. *Modernity and the Holocaust*. Ithaca, NY: Cornell University Press.
Becker, Jasper. 1996. *Hungry Ghosts: China's Secret Famine*. London: John Murray.
Beevor, Antony. 2020. *The Fall of Berlin 1945*. London: Penguin.
———. 2001. *The Spanish Civil War*. London: Cassell Military Paperbacks.

Bell-Fialkoff, Andrew. 1996. *Ethnic Cleansing*. Basingstoke, England: Macmillan.
Bijleveld, Catrien, Morssinkhof, Aafke, and Smeulers Alette. 2009. "Counting the Countless: Rape Victimization During the Rwandan Genocide." *International Criminal Justice Review* 19, no. 2, 208–224.
Biondich, Mark. 2011. *The Balkans: Revolution, War and Political Violence since 1878*. Oxford: Oxford University Press.
Bloxham, Donald. 2008. *Genocide, the World Wars and the Unweaving of Europe*. Ellstree, England: Vallentine Mitchell.
Bonnet, Catherine. 1995. "Le viol des femmes survivantes du genocide au Rwanda." *Rwanda, un genocide du XXe siècle*. R. Verdier, E. Decaux, J. P. Chretien, eds. Paris: L'Harmattan.
Brantlinger, Patrick. 2003. *Dark Vanishings: Discourse on the Extinction of Primitive Races, 1800–1930*. Ithaca, NY: Cornell University Press.
Brown, Haley Marie. 2022. "The forgotten murders: gendercide in the twenty-first century and the destruction of the transgender body." In *Denial: The Final Stage of Genocide*. Cox, et al., eds. London and New York: Routledge.
Brownmiller, Susan. 1975. *Against Our Will: Men, Women and Rape*. New York: Random House.
Brunner, Kira and Mills, Nicolaus. 2003. *The New Killing Fields: Massacre and the Politics of Intervention*. New York: Basic Books.
Bryant, Michael. 2020. "Canaries in the Mineshaft of American Democracy: North American Settler Genocide in the Thought of Raphael Lemkin." *Genocide Studies and Prevention: An International Journal*, 14, no. 1, 21–39.
Burch, Audra D.S. 2024. "Oklahoma Supreme Court Dismisses Tulsa Massacre Lawsuit: The last known remaining survivors of the 1921 attack by a white mob were hoping for their day in court." Accessible at https://www.nytimes.com/2024/06/12/us/oklahoma-supreme-court-tulsa-massacre-lawsuit.html.
Burch, Audra D.S. 2025. *"Tulsa Massacre Was a 'Coordinated, Military-Style Attack,' Federal Report Says." The New York Times*. Accessible at https://www.nytimes.com/2025/01/11/us/tulsa-race-massacre-report.html.
Caplan, Gerard. 2012. "The 1994 genocide of the Tutsi in Rwanda." In *Centuries of Genocide*. Samuel Totten and William S. Parsons, eds. 4th edition. New York: Routledge.
———. 2013. "Kill anything that moves: The real American war in Vietnam." *Journal of Genocide Research*, 15, no. 3, 370–373.
Carmichael, Cathie. 2009. *Genocide Before the Holocaust*. New Haven, CT: Yale University Press.
Cesaire, Aime. 1955. *Discourse on Colonialism*. 1955. Dakar, Senegal and Paris: Presence Africaine.
Chalk, Frank and Jonassohn, Kurt. 1990. *The History and Sociology of Genocide: Analyses and Case Studies*. New Haven, CT: Yale University Press.
Chandler, David. 1992. *A History of Cambodia*. Crow's Nest, Australia: Allen & Unwin.
Chang, Iris. 2011. *The Rape of Nanking: The Forgotten Holocaust of World War II*. New York: Basic Books.
Charny, Israel. 1994. *Toward a Generic Definition of Genocide*. Philadelphia: University of Pennsylvania Press.
Churchill, Ward. 1997. *A Little Matter of Genocide: Holocaust and Denial in the Americas, 1492 to the Present*. San Francisco: City Light Books.
Cigar, Norman. 1995. *Genocide in Bosnia: The Policy of "Ethnic Cleansing."* College Station, TX: Texas A&M University Press.
Coates, Ta-Nehisi. 2014. "The Case for Reparations." *The Atlantic*. Accessible at https://www.theatlantic.com/magazine/archive/2014/06/the-case-for-reparations/361631/.
Cohen, Adam. 2016. *Imbeciles: The Supreme Court, American Eugenics, and the Sterilization of Carrie Buck*. New York: Penguin.
Confino, Alon. 2014. *A World Without Jews: The Nazi Imagination from Persecution to Genocide*. New Haven, CT: Yale University Press.
Conquest, Robert. 1991. *Stalin: Breaker of Nations*. London: Viking.
———. 1990. *The Great Terror: A Reassessment*. London: Hutchinson.

———. 1986. *The Harvest of Sorrow: Soviet Collectivization and the Terror Famine*. London: Hutchinson.
Cox, John. 2024. "It is every individual's obligation to confront the current siege in Gaza." Accessible at https://iccforum.com/israel-and-hamas#Cox.
———, et al., eds 2022. *Denial: The Final Stage of Genocide*. London and New York: Routledge.
———. 2017. *To Kill a People: Genocide in the Twentieth Century*. Oxford: Oxford University Press.
Cribb, Robert. 2009. "The Indonesian massacres." In *Century of Genocide: Critical Essays and Eyewitness Accounts*. Samuel Totten and William S. Parsons, eds. London & New York: Routledge.
———. 2001. "Genocide in Indonesia, 1965–1966." *Journal of Genocide Research* 3, no. 2, 219–37.
Crowe, David M. 2008. *The Holocaust: Roots, History and Aftermath*. Boulder, CO: Westview Press.
Cueva, Julio de la. 1998. "Religious Persecution, Anticlerical Tradition and Revolution: On Atrocities against the Clergy during the Spanish Civil War." *Journal of Contemporary History* 33, no. 3, 355–369.
Davidson, Lawrence. 2012. *Cultural Genocide*. New Brunswick, NJ: Rutgers University Press.
Davis, Mike. 2000. *Late Victorian Holocausts: El Niño Famines and the Making of the Third World*. New York: Verso.
Decker, John. 2008. "Are settler colonies inherently colonial? re-reading Lemkin." *Empire, Colony, Genocide: Conquest, Occupation and Subaltern Resistance in Modern World History*. Dirk Moses, A. ed. Oxford: Berghahn.
Delmont, Matthew. 2022. *Half-American: The Epic Story of African Americans Fighting World War II at Home and Abroad*. London: Viking.
DeMare, Brian. 2019. *Land Wars: The Story of China's Agrarian Revolution*. Stanford, CA: Stanford University Press.
Deutscher, Isaac. 1949. *Stalin: A Political Biography*. London & New York: Oxford University Press.
De Waal, Alex. 2015. *The Real Politics of the Horn of Africa: Money, War and the Business of Power*. New York: Polity.
Dikotter, Frank. 2010. *Mao's Great Famine*. New York: Walker Publishing Company.
Dolot, Miron. 1985. *Execution by Hunger: The Hidden Holocaust*. New York: W.W. Norton.
Douglas, R.M. 2013. *Orderly and Humane: The Expulsion of the Germans after the Second World War*. New Haven, CT: Yale University Press.
Drost, P. N. 1959. *Humanicide*. Vol. I of *The Crime of State*. Leiden: A.W. Sythoff.
Du Bois, W.E.B. 1903. *The Souls of Black Folk*. Chicago: A.C. McClurg.
Dyson, Tim. 2018. *A Population History of India: From the First Modern People to the Present Day*. London & New York: Oxford University Press.
Earl, Hilary. 1992. "A judge, a prosecutor, and a mass murderer. courtroom dynamics in the SS-Einsatzgruppen Trial." Chapter Two. In *Reassessing the Nuremberg Military Tribunals: Transitional Justice, Trial Narratives and Historiography (War and Genocide 16)* Priemel, Kim C., Stiller, Alexa, eds. New York & Oxford: Berghahn Books.
Ellsworth, Scott. 2021. *The Ground Breaking: An American City and its Search for Justice*. London: Dutton Imprint (Penguin Books).
Engels, Friedrich. 2016. *Anti-Duhring*. Create Space Independent Publishing Platform.
Evans, Richard J. 2020. *The Hitler Conspiracies: The Protocols – The Stab in the Back – The Reichstag Fire – Rudolf Hess – The Escape from the Bunker*. New York: Oxford University Press.
Equal Justice Initiative (EJI). 2018. *Lynching in America: Confronting the legacy of racial terror*. Accessible at https://lynchinginamerica.eji.org/report/.
Feierstein, Daniel. 2011. "The Good, the Bad, and the Invisible: A Critical Look at the MARO Report." *Genocide Studies and Prevention: An International Journal*. 6, no. 1, 39–44. https://digitalcommons.usf.edu/gsp/vol6/iss1/5.
Fein, Helen. 1999. "Genocide and Gender: The Uses of Women and Group Destiny." *Journal of Genocide Research* 1, no. 1, 43–63.
———. 1993. *Genocide: A Sociological Perspective*. London: Sage.
———. 1990. "Genocide: A Sociological Perspective." *Current Sociology* 38, no. 1, 43–63.
———. 1979. *Accounting for Genocide*. New York: Free Press.

Finzsch, Norbert, James O. Horton, Lois E. Horton. 1999. *Von Benin nach Baltimore: Die Geschichte der African Americans*. Hamburg: Hamburger Edition.

Fisher, Siobhan K. 1996. "Occupation of the Womb: Forced Impregnation as Genocide." *Duke Law Journal* 46, 91–143.

Fitzpatrick, Sheila. 1994. *Stalin's Peasants: Resistance & Survival in the Russian Village After Collectivization*. New York: Oxford University Press.

Forster, Jurgen. 1986. "The German army and the ideological war against the Soviet Union." In *The Policies of Genocide: Jews and Soviet Prisoners of War*. Hirschfeld, Gerhard ed. London: Allen and Unwin.

Frederickson, George. 2003. *Racism: A Short History*. Princeton, NJ: Princeton University Press.

Friedlander, Henry. 1997. *The Origins of Nazi Genocide: From Euthanasia to the Final Solution*. Chapel Hill, NC: University of North Carolina Press.

Friedländer, Saul. 2008. *The Years of Extermination: Nazi Germany and the Jews, 1939–1945*. New York: Harper.

Gebhardt, Miriam. 2020. *Crimes Unspoken: The Rape of German Women at the End of the Second World War*. Cambridge and Medford: Polity Press.

Gellately, Robert. 2003. "The Third Reich, the Holocaust, and visions of serial genocide." In *The Specter of Genocide: Mass Murder in Historical Perspective*. Robert Gellately and Ben Kiernan, eds. New York: Cambridge University Press.

Ginsburgs, George. 1996. *Moscow's Road to Nuremberg: The Soviet Background to the Trial*. Leiden: Brill.

Grandin, Greg. 2000. *The Blood of Guatemala: A History of Race and Nation*. Durham, NC: Duke University Press.

Graziosi, Andrea. 2022. "The Kazakh famine, the Holodomor, and the Soviet famines of 1930–33: starvation and national UN-building in the Soviet Union." In *Genocide: The Power and Problems of a Concept*, edited by Andrea Graziosi and Frank E. Sysyn, 126–44. Montreal: McGill-Queen's University Press.

Grenier, John. 2005. *The First Way of War: American War Making on the Frontier, 1607–1814*. New York: Cambridge University Press.

Haines, M.R. and Steckel, R.H. eds. 2000. *A Population History of North America*. Cambridge: Cambridge University Press.

Halakhe, Abdullah Boru, 2013. "R2P in Practice": Ethnic Violence, Elections, and Atrocity Prevention in Kenya. *Global Centre for the Responsibility to Protect*. Accessible at www.globalr2p.org/media/files/kenya_occasionalpaper_web.pdf.

Hamburg Institute for Social Research. 1999. *The German Army and Genocide: Crimes Against War Prisoners, Jews and Other Civilians in the East, 1939–1944*. New York: The New Press.

Harff, Barbara and Gurr, Ted R. 1989. "Victims of the State: Genocides, Politicides and Group Repression since 1945." *International Review of Victimology*, 1, no. 1, 23–41.

———. 1988. "Toward Empirical Theory of Genocides and Politicides: Identification and Measurement of Cases since 1945." *International Studies Quarterly*, 32, 359–71.

Haynes, Michael, and Husan, Rumy. 2003. *A Century of State Murder? Death and Policy in Twentieth-Century Russia*. London: Pluto Press.

Heuveline, Patrick. 1998. "'Between One and Three Million': Towards the Demographic Reconstruction of a Decade of Cambodian History (1970-79)." *Population Studies*, 52, no. 1, pp. 49–65.

Hilberg, Raul. 1961. *The Destruction of the European Jews*. London: W. H. Allen.

Hindus, Maurice. 1988. *Red Bread: Collectivization in a Russian Village*. Bloomington, IN: Indiana University Press.

Hirsch, Francine. 2008. "The Soviets at Nuremberg: International Law, Propaganda, and the Making of the Postwar Order." *The American Historical Review* 113, no. 3, 701–30.

Hitler, Adolf. 1971. *Mein Kampf*. Boston: Houghton Mifflin Company.

Hochschild, Adam. 1998. *King Leopold's Ghost: A Story of Greed, Terror, and Heroism in Colonial Africa*. Boston: Mariner Books.

Hull, Isabel V. 2005. *Absolute Destruction: Military Culture and the Practices of War in Imperial Germany.* Ithaca, NY: Cornell University Press.
Iakovlev, Alexander. 1995. *A Century of Violence in Soviet Russia.* New Haven, CT: Yale University Press.
Ibrahim, Azeem. 2018. *The Rohingyas: Inside Myanmar's Genocide.* London: Hurst.
International Commission on Intervention and State Sovereignty (ICISS). 2001. "*The Responsibility to Protect: Report of the International Commission on Intervention and State Sovereignty.*" Ottawa: International Development Research Centre.
International Law Commission to the UN General Assembly. 2017. "Report of the International Law Commission to the UN General Assembly, United Nations Official Records Series. Sixty-Ninth Session."
International Military Tribunal for Germany (IMT). 1946. Judgment of the International Military Tribunal for the Trial of German Major War Criminals: The Nazi Regime in Germany. Accessible at https://avalon.law.yale.edu/imt/judnazi.asp#common.
Irvin-Erickson, Douglas. 2022. "The "Lemkin Turn" in Ukrainian studies: genocide, peoples, nations, and empire." In *Genocide: The Power and Problems of a Concept*, Andrea Graziosi and Frank E. Sysyn, eds. 145–73. Montreal: McGill-Queen's University Press.
———. 2019. "Raphael Lemkin: culture and cultural genocide." In *Cultural Genocide: Law, Politics and Global Manifestations*, Bachman, S. Jeffrey, ed. 21–44. New York: Routledge.
———. 2017. *Raphael Lemkin and the Concept of Genocide.* Philadelphia: University of Pennsylvania Press.
———. 2013. "Genocide, the "Family of Mind" and the Romantic Signature of Raphael Lemkin." *Journal of Genocide Research* 15, no. 3, 273–96.
Jahan, Rounaq. 2009. "Genocide in Bangladesh." *Century of Genocide: Critical Essays and Eyewitness Accounts.* Samuel Totten and William S. Parsons, eds. Routledge: London & New York.
———. 1972. *Pakistan: Failure in National Integration.* Columbia University Press: New York.
Jenne, Erin K. 2012. "The causes and consequences of ethnic cleansing." In *Routledge Handbook of Ethnic Conflict*, Karl Cordell and Stefan Wolff, eds. 112–21. London & New York: Routledge.
Jersild, Austin. 2002. *Orientalism and Empire: North Caucasus Mountain Peoples and the Georgian Frontier, 1845–1917.* Montreal: McGill-Queen's Press.
Jones, Adam. 2024. 4th ed. *Genocide: A Comprehensive Introduction.* London & New York: Routledge.
———. 2017. 3rd ed. *Genocide: A Comprehensive Introduction.* London & New York: Routledge.
———. 2011. "Diffusing Genocide Studies, Defusing Genocides." *Genocide Studies and Prevention: An Interdisciplinary Journal* 6, no. 3, Article 8. Accessible at https://digitalcommons.usf.edu/gsp/vol6/iss3/8.
———. 2004. *Gendercide and Genocide.* Nashville, TN: Vanderbilt University Press.
Kakel, Carroll P. III. 2013. *The American West and the Nazi East: A Comparative and Interpretive Perspective.* New York: Palgrave Macmillan.
Karcic, Hikmet. 2022. *Torture, Humiliate, Kill: Inside the Bosnian Serb Camp System.* Ann Arbor, MI: University of Michigan Press.
———. 2022. "Triumphalism: the final stage of the Bosnian genocide" in Cox, Khoury, Minslow, eds. *Denial: The Final Stage of Genocide.* London and New York: Routledge.
Katz, Steven. 1994. *The Holocaust in Historical Context*, Vol. 1. Oxford: Oxford University Press.
Kendi, Ibram X. 2016. *Stamped from the Beginning: The Definitive History of Racist Ideas in America.* New York: Nation Books.
Kershaw, Ian. 2011. *The End: The Defiance and Destruction of Hitler's Germany, 1944–1945.* London: Penguin.
Khalidi, Rashid. 1997. *Palestinian Identity: The Construction of Modern National Consciousness.* New York: Columbia University Press.
Kiernan, Ben. 2007. *Blood and Soil: A World History of Genocide from Sparta to Darfur.* New Haven, CT: Yale University Press.

———. 1996. *The Pol Pot Regime: Race, Power and Genocide in Cambodia*. New Haven, CT: Yale University Press.

King, Charles. 2008. *The Ghost of Freedom: A History of the Circassians*. New York: Oxford University Press.

King Jr., Martin Luther. 1967. Transcript of speech "The Other America," April 14, 1967. Accessible at https://www.rev.com/blog/transcripts/the-other-america-speech-transcript-martin-luther-king-jr.

Kopelev, Lev. 1980. *The Education of a True Believer*. New York: Harper & Row.

Kotkin, Stephen. 2017. *Stalin: Volume 2: Waiting for Hitler, 1929–1941*. New York: Penguin Press.

———. 2014. *Stalin: Volume 1: Paradoxes of Power, 1878–1928*. London: Penguin Press.

Kreindler, Isabelle. 1986. "The Soviet Deported Nationalities: A Summary and an Update." *Soviet Studies* XXXVIII, no. 3, 387–405.

Kuper, Leo. 1981. *Genocide: Its Political Use in the Twentieth Century*. New Haven, CT: Yale University Press.

LeBlanc, Lawrence. 1991. *The United States and the Genocide Convention*. Durham, NC: Duke University Press.

Lee, Ronan. 2021. *Myanmar's Rohingya Genocide: Identity, History and Hate Speech*. London: I.B. Taurus.

Lemarchand, Rene. 1998. "Genocide in the Great Lakes: Which Genocide? Whose Genocide?" *African Studies Review* 41, no. 1, 3–16.

Lemkin, Raphael. 2014. *Lemkin on Genocide*. Jacobs, Steven Leonard ed. Lanham, MD: Lexington Books.

———. 2013. *Totally Unofficial: The Autobiography of Raphael Lemkin*. Lee-Frieze, Donna ed. New Haven, CT: Yale University Press.

———. 2008. *Axis Rule in Occupied Europe: Laws of Occupation, Analysis of Government, Proposals for Redress*. Clark, NJ: Lawbook Exchange.

———. 2008. "Soviet genocide in the Ukraine." In *Holodomor: Reflections on the Great Famine of 1932–1933 in Soviet Ukraine*. Luciuk, L. Y. ed. Kingston, Ontario: The Kashtan Press.

———. 1945. "Genocide: A Modern Crime." *Free World* Vol. 4, 39–43.

Levene, Mark. 2014. *The Crisis of Genocide, Vol. 2 of Annihilation: The European Rimlands, 1939–1953*. Oxford: Oxford University Press.

Li, Darryl. 2003. "Echoes of Violence in Brunner, Kira and Mills, Nicolaus. 2003." *The New Killing Fields: Massacre and the Politics of Intervention*. New York: Basic Books.

Lippman, Matthew. 1994. "The 1948 Convention on the Prevention and Punishment of the Crime of Genocide: Fifty Years Later." *Arizona Journal of International and Comparative Law* 15, no. 2 415–514.

———. 1985. "The Drafting of the 1948 Convention on the Prevention and Punishment of the Crime of Genocide." *Boston University International Law Journal* 3, no. 1, 1–65.

Lindqvist, Sven. 2003. *A History of Bombing*. New York: The New Press.

———. 1997. *"Exterminate All the Brutes": One Man's Odyssey into the Heart of Darkness and the Origins of European Genocide*. New York: The New Press.

———. 1996. *The Skull Measurer's Mistake: And Other Portraits of Men and Women Who Spoke Out Against Racism*. New York: The New Press.

Lowery, Wesley. 2024. "What We are Owed." *Mother Jones*. Accessible at https://www.motherjones.com/politics/2024/06/40-acres-broken-promise-black-americans-reparations-center-public-integrity/.

MacDonogh, Giles. 2007. *After the Reich: The Brutal History of the Allied Occupation*. New York: Basic Books.

MacKinnon, Catharine. 1994. "Rape, Genocide, and Women's Human Rights." *Harvard Women's Law Journal* 17, 5–16.

Malik, Amita. 1972. *The Year of the Vulture*. New Delhi: Orient Longman.

Malko, Victoria. 2021. *The Ukrainian Intelligentsia and Genocide: The Struggle for History, Language, and Culture in the 1920s and 1930s*. Lanham, MD: Lexington Books.
Mann, Michael. 2005. *The Dark Side of Democracy: Explaining Ethnic Cleansing*. Cambridge: Cambridge University Press.
Marx, Karl. 1859. *A Contribution to the Critique of Political Economy*. Accessible at https://archive.org/details/marxcontributioncritpolecon/page/14/mode/2up.
———. 1847. *The Poverty of Philosophy*. Accessible at https://www.marxists.org/archive/marx/works/1847/poverty-philosophy/.
———, and Frederick Engels. 1848. *The Communist Manifesto*. Accessible at https://www.marxists.org/archive/marx/works/1848/communist-manifesto/.
Mascarenhas, Anthony. 1972. *The Rape of Bangla Desh*. Delhi: Vikas Publications.
Mazower, Mark. 2008. *Hitler's Empire: How the Nazis Ruled Europe*. New York: Penguin.
McWhirter, Cameron. 2012. *Red Summer: The Summer of 1919 and the Awakening of Black America*. New York: St. Martin's Griffin.
Medvedev, Roy. 1972. *Let History Judge: The Origins and Consequences of Stalin*. New York: Vintage Books.
Merten, Ulrich. 2015. *Voices from the Gulag: The Oppression of the German Minority in the Soviet Union*. Lincoln, NE: American Historical Society of Germans from Russia.
Molotov, Viacheslav. 1942. *Nota Narodnogo Komissara Inostranykh Del Tov. V. M. Molotova o Chudovischnykh Zloedeianiiakh Zverstakh i Nasiliiakh Germanskikh Vlastei Za Eti Prestupleniia*. RG-22.009.01.06. United States Holocaust Memorial Museum.
Morris, Benny. 2004. *The Birth of the Palestinian Refugee Problem Revisited*. Cambridge: Cambridge University Press.
———. 1987. *The Birth of the Palestinian Refugee Problem, 1947–1949*. Cambridge: Cambridge University Press.
Moses, A. Dirk. 2010. "Raphael Lemkin, culture, and the concept of genocide." In *The Oxford Handbook of Genocide Studies*, Donald Bloxham and A. Dirk Moses, eds. 19–41. Oxford: Oxford University Press.
———, and Stone, Dan. eds. 2008. *Colonialism and Genocide*. London: Routledge.
Naimark, Norman. 2010. *Stalin's Genocides*. Princeton, NJ: Princeton University Press.
———. 2017. Genocide: A World History. New York: Oxford University Press.
———. 2001. *Fires of Hatred: Ethnic Cleansing in Twentieth-Century Europe*. Cambridge: Harvard University Press.
———. 1997. *The Russians in Germany*. Cambridge: Belknap Press.
Natho, Kadir I. 2009. *Circassian History*. Bloomington, IN: Xlibris.
Nersessian, David. 2010. *Genocide and Political Groups*. Oxford: Oxford University Press.
Nowrojee, Binaifer. 1996. *Shattered Lives: Sexual Violence During the Rwandan Genocide and Its Aftermath*. Human Rights Watch. hrw.org/legacy/reports/Rwanda.htm. Accessed 5 March 2024.
Oppenheim, Lassa. 1955. *International Law, Volume 1-Peace*. 8th ed. Lauterpacht, Hersch ed. London: Longmans, Green & Co.
Overy, Richard. 2022. *Blood and Ruins: The Last Imperial War, 1931–1945*. London: Viking.
Pappe, Ilan. 2017. *The Biggest Prison on Earth*. London: OneWorld.
———. 2007. *The Ethnic Cleansing of Palestine*. London: OneWorld.
Pacchiani, Gianluca. 2023. COGAT chief addresses Gazans: 'You wanted hell, you will get hell', *The Times of Israel*, October 10, 2023, https://www.timesofisrael.com/liveblog_entry/cogat-chief-addresses-gazans-you-wanted-hell-you-will-get-hell/.
Payne, Robert. 1973. *Massacre: The Tragedy at Bangla Desh and the Phenomenon of Mass Slaughter throughout History*. London: Macmillan.
Payne, Stanley. 2012. *The Spanish Civil War*. Cambridge: Cambridge University Press.
Pegorier, Clotilde. 2013. *Ethnic Cleansing: A legal qualification*. London and New York: Routledge.
Pinaud, Clémence. 2021. *War and Genocide in South Sudan*. Ithaca, NY: Cornell University Press.

Pitner, Barrett Holmes. 2021. *The Crime Without a Name: Ethnocide and the Erasure of Culture in America*. Berkeley, CA: Counterpoint.

Powell, Christopher. 2011. *Barbaric Civilization: A Critical Sociology of Genocide*. Montreal: McGill-Queens's University Press.

Power, Samantha. 2002. *"A Problem from Hell:" America and the Age of Genocide*. New York: Basic Books.

Preston, Paul. 2013. *The Spanish Holocaust: Inquisition and Extermination in Twentieth Century Spain*. New York: Norton.

Prunier, Gerard. 2011. *Darfur: A 21st-Century Genocide*. Ithaca, NY: Cornell University Press.

———. 1997. *The Rwanda Crisis: The History of a Genocide*. New York: Columbia University Press.

Putin, Vladimir. 2021. "On the historical unity of Russians and Ukrainians." Accessible at http://en.kremlin.ru/events/president/news/66181.

Randall, Amy. 2015. "Introduction: gender and genocide studies." In *Genocide and Gender in the Twentieth Century: A Comparative Survey*. Randall, A. ed. London: Bloomsbury Academic.

Rapoport, Louis. 1990. *Stalin's War Against the Jews: The Doctors' Plot and the Soviet Solution*. New York: The Free Press.

Redlich, Shimon, ed. 1995. *War, Holocaust and Stalinism: A Documented Study of the Jewish Anti-Fascist Committee in the USSR*. London: Psychology Press.

Reeves, Richard. 2016. *Infamy: The Shocking Story of the Japanese American Internment in World War II*. London: Picador.

Rodinson, Maxine. 1973. *Israel: A Colonial-Settler State?* New York: Pathfinder Books.

Roediger, David. 2018. *Working Toward Whiteness: How America's Immigrants Became White*. New York: Basic Books.

———. 2014. "Historical foundations of race." Accessible at https://nmaahc.si.edu/learn/talking-about-race/topics/historical-foundations-race.

Royte, Elizabeth. 1997. "The Outcasts." *New York Times Magazine*.

Rubenstein, Joshua, and Altman, Ilya. 2008. *The Unknown Black Book: The Holocaust in the German-Occupied Soviet Territories*. Bloomington, IN: Indiana University Press.

Rummel, R. J. 1997. *Death by Government: Genocide and Mass Murder Since 1900*. Brunswick, NJ: Transaction Publishers.

Samet, Elizabeth. 2021. *Looking for the Good War: American Amnesia and the Violent Pursuit of Happiness*. New York: Farrar, Straus and Giroux.

Sanford, Victoria. 2003. *Buried Secrets: Truth and Human Rights in Guatemala*. New York: Macmillan.

Sartre, Jean-Paul. 1968. *On Genocide*. Boston: Beacon Press.

Schell, Jonathan. 2013. "The real American war in Vietnam." The Nation, February 4. Accessible at: http://www.thenation.com/article/archive/real-american-war-vietnam.

Seidman, Derek. 2016. "Vietnam and the Soldiers' Revolt: The Politics of a Forgotten History." *Monthly Review*, 68, no. 2, 45–57. Accessible at https://monthlyreview.org/2016/06/01/vietnam-and-the-soldiers-revolt/.

Sells, Michael A. 2001. "Kosovo mythology and the Bosnian genocide," in Omar Bartov and Mack, Phyllis, eds. *In God's Name: Genocide and Religion in the Twentieth Century*. New York: Berghahn Books.

———. 1996. *The Bridge Betrayed: Religion and Genocide in Bosnia*. Berkeley, CA: University of California Press.

Service, Robert. 2006. *Stalin: A Biography*. New York: Macmillan.

Schabas, William. 2001. "Was Genocide Committed in Bosnia and Herzegovina?" First Judgements of the International Criminal Tribunal for the Former Yugoslavia." *Fordham International Law Journal*, 25, no. 1, 23–53.

———. 2000. *Genocide in International Law: The Crime of Crimes*. Cambridge: Cambridge University Press.

———. 2009. "Crimes Against Humanity." Genocide Studies Reader. Samuel Totten and Paul Bartrop, eds. New York & London: Routledge.

Schaller, Dominik J. and Zimmerer, Jurgen. 2008. "Settlers, Imperialism, Genocide: Introduction." *Journal of Genocide Research* 10, no. 2, 475–477.

Scheck, Raffael. 2008. *Hitler's African Victims: The German Army Massacres of Black French Soldiers in 1940*. New York: Cambridge University Press.

Service, Robert, 2006. *Stalin: A Biography*. Cambridge, MA: Belknap Press of Harvard University.

Sharlach, Lisa. 2009. "State rape: sexual violence as genocide." *Century of Genocide: Critical Essays and Eyewitness Accounts*. Samuel Totten and William S. Parsons, eds. London & New York: Routledge.

Shaw, Martin. 2015. *What is Genocide?* 2nd ed. Malden, MA: Polity Press.

Shaw, Martin and Bartov, Omer. 2010. "The Question of Genocide in Palestine, 1948: an exchange between Martin Shaw and Omer Bartov." *Journal of Genocide Research* 12, no. 3–4, 243–59.

Sierra, Maria. 2024. *The Roma and the Holocaust: The Romani Genocide under Nazism*. New York: Bloomsbury Academic.

Sivakumaran, Sandesh. 2007. "Sexual Violence against Men in Armed Conflict." *European Journal of International Law*, 18, no. 2, 253–276.

Smedley, Audrey. 2003. "Interview with Audrey Smedley: Race—The Power of an Illusion." Accessible at https://www.pbs.org/race/000_About/002_04-background-02-06.htm.

Snyder, Louis L. 1962. *The Imperialism Reader*. New York: D. Van Nostrand.

Snyder, Timothy. 2010. *Bloodlands: Europe Between Hitler and Stalin*. New York: Basic Books.

Stalin, Joseph. 1953. *Collected Works of J. V. Stalin. 13 vols*. Moscow: Foreign Languages Publishing House.

———. 1929. "Speech on agrarian policy." Accessible at https://history.hanover.edu/courses/excerpts/111stalin.html.

Stannard, David E. 1992. *American Holocaust: The Conquest of the New World*: Oxford: Oxford University Press.

Stanton, Gregory. 2023. "The ten stages of genocide." Accessible at https://www.genocidewatch.com/tenstages

Stiller, Alexa. 1992. "Semantics of extermination. The use of the new term of genocide in the Nuremberg trials and the genesis of a master narrative." Chapter Four. In *Reassessing the Nuremberg Military Tribunals: Transitional Justice, Trial Narratives and Historiography (War and Genocide 16)*, Priemel, Kim C., Stiller, Alexa, eds. New York and Oxford: Berghahn Books.

Strauss, Scott. 2006. *The Order of Genocide: Race, Power and War in Rwanda*. Ithaca, NY: Cornell University Press.

Tanaka, Yuki and Marilyn Young, eds. 2009. *Bombing Civilians: A Twentieth-Century History*. New York: The New Press.

Taylor, Mark Lewis. 2024. "How Israel Facilitated the Guatemalan Genocide." *Jacobin.com*, April 2024. Accessible at https://jacobin.com/2024/04/israel-guatemala-genocide-gaza-imperialism.

Taylor, Telford. 1992. *The Anatomy of the Nuremberg Trials*. New York: Alfred A. Knopf, Inc.

Thomas, Hugh. 2012. *The Spanish Civil War*. New York: The Modern Library.

Thompson, E. P. 1963. *The Making of the English Working Class*. London: Victor Gollancz Ltd.

Thornton, Russell. 2000. "Population history of native North Americans." In *A Population History of North America*. Haines, M.R. and Steckel, R.H. eds. Cambridge: Cambridge University Press.

———. 1987. *American Indian Holocaust and Survival: A Population History Since 1492*. Norman, OK: University of Oklahoma Press.

Tocqueville, Alexis. 2003. *Democracy in America*. Chicago: University of Chicago Press.

Tooze, Adam. 2007. *The Wages of Destruction: The Making and Breaking of the Nazi Economy*. New York: Penguin Books.

Totten, Samuel and Parsons, Williams, eds. 2009. *Century of Genocide: Critical Essays and Eyewitness Accounts*. New York & London: Routledge.

———, eds. 2013. *Centuries of Genocide: Essays and Eyewitness Accounts*. New York & London: Routledge.

———., eds. 1997. *Century of Genocide: Essays and Eyewitness Accounts*. New York & London: Routledge.

Traverso, Enzo. 2024. *Revolution: An Intellectual History*. New York: Verso.

———. 2005. "Production line of Murder: Nazism's Roots in European Culture." *Le Monde diplomatique*. Accessible at https://mondediplo.com/2005/02/15civildiso.

———. 2003. *The Origins of Nazi Violence*. New York: The New Press.

Tucker, Robert. 1990. *Stalin in Power: The Revolution from Above, 1928–1941*. New York: W.W. Norton.

Turse, Nick. 2013. *Kill Everything That Moves: The Real American War in Vietnam*. New York: Metropolitan Books.

———. 2008. "A My Lai a Month." *The Nation*, December 1, 2008. Accessible at https://www.thenation.com/article/archive/my-lai-month/.

Tusan, Michelle. 2022. "Is it time to forget genocide? conceptual problems and new directions." In *Genocide: The Power and Problems of a Concept*, Graziosi, Andrea and Sysyn, Frank E. eds. 200–21. Montreal: McGill-Queen's University Press.

Tyson, Timothy. 2006. "The Ghosts of 1898: Wilmington's Race Riot and the Rise of White Supremacy." Accessible at http://media2.newsobserver.com/content/media/2010/5/3/ghostsof1898.pdf.

USHMM (United States Holocaust Memorial Museum). 2022. "The Nazi Persecution of Black People in Germany." Accessible at https://encyclopedia.ushmm.org/content/en/article/afro-germans-during-the-holocaust.

Vaksberg, Arkady. 1994. *Stalin Against the Jews*. New York: Random House.

Valentino, Benjamin A. 2005. *Final Solutions: Mass Killing and Genocide in the 20th Century*. Ithaca, NY: Cornell University Press.

Vanguri, Star. 2016. *Rhetorics of Names and Naming*. London: Routledge.

Van Schaak, Beth. 1997. "The Crime of Political Genocide: Repairing the Genocide Convention's Blind Spot." *The Yale Law Journal*, 106, no. 7, 2259–91.

Viola, Lynne. 1996. *Peasant Rebels under Stalin: Collectivization and Culture of Peasant Resistance*. Oxford: Oxford University Press.

———. 2007. *The Unknown Gulag: The Lost World of Stalin's Special Settlements*. New York & Oxford: Oxford University Press, 2007.

Waller, James. 2007. *Becoming Evil: How Ordinary People Commit Genocide and Mass Killing*. New York & Oxford: Oxford University Press.

Warren, Mary Anne. 1985. *Gendercide*. Totowa, NJ: Rowman & Allanheld.

Weiss-Wendt, Anton. 2017. *The Soviet Union and the Gutting of the UN Genocide Convention*. Madison, WI: University of Wisconsin Press.

Weitz, Eric D. 2003. *A Century of Genocide: Utopias of Race and Nation*. Princeton, NJ: Princeton University Press.

Weiner, Amir. 2001. *Making Sense of War: The Second World War and the Fate of the Bolshevik Revolution*. Princeton, NJ: Princeton University Press.

Westermann, Edward. 2016. *Hitler's Ostkrieg and the Indian Wars*. Norman, OK: University of Oklahoma Press.

Wetter, Gustav. 1958. *Dialectical Materialism: A Historical and Systematic Survey of Philosophy in the Soviet Union*. Westport, CT: Frederick A. Praeger, Inc.

Whitman, James Q. 2017. *Hitler's American Model: The United States and the Making of Nazi Race Law*. Princeton, NJ: Princeton University Press.

Whitt, Laurelyn and Clarke, Allen W. 2017. "Bringing it Home: North American Genocides." *Journal of Gender, Race, and Justice* 20, no. 1, 263–348.

Wolfe, Bertram. 1952. "Operation Rewrite: The Agony of Soviet Historians." *Foreign Affairs* 31, no. 1, 39–57.
Wolfe, Patrick. 2008. "Structure and event: settler colonialism, time, and the question of genocide." *Empire, Colony, Genocide: Conquest, Occupation and Subaltern Resistance in World History*, Dirk Moses, A., ed. Oxford: Oxford University Press.
Worringer, Renee. 2014. *Ottomans Imagining Japan: East, MiddleEast, and Non-Western Modernity at the Turn of the Twentieth Century*. London: Palgrave Macmillan.
Yang, Jisheng. 2008. *Tombstone: The Great Chinese Famine 1958–1962*. New York: Farrar, Straus and Giroux.
Zucchino, David. 2020. *Wilmington's Lie: The Murderous Coup of 1898 and the Rise of White Supremacy*. New York: Atlantic Monthly Press.

INDEX

1948 Convention. *See* Genocide Convention (1948)

A

Abdullah, Daud 66
Abe, Shinzo 113
African Americans
 Daily Record newspaper 78
 Jim Crow laws 76–78, 81, 182
 reparations 81
 Tulsa Race Massacre of 1921 80–81
 We Charge Genocide 95–97
 Wilmington massacre of 1898 78–80
Afro-Germans 93–94
Against Our Will: Men, Women, and Rape (Brownmiller) 113
Akayesu, Jean-Paul 121
Aktion T4, 93
al-Bashir, Omar 99, 101, 207, 210
Aleksandrov, Georgii 62
Alexander, Jocelyn 189
Alexander II, Tsar 164
Allen, Beverly 119
Allende, Salvador 147
Aly, Gotz 45
Anderson, Benedict 151
androcide 109
annihilation 2, 14, 15, 17, 18, 28, 29, 32, 43, 106, 164, 185.
 See also destruction; extermination
 Herero and Nama Genocide 183–86
 of Indonesian Communist Party 126, 142–44
anti-Jewish persecution
 Black Death (1347–51) 83
 the Holocaust. *See* the Holocaust
 Kristallnacht 78, 88
 Law for the Restoration of the Professional Civil Service 87
 Nuremberg Laws (1935) 87–88, 92

 stages in 87–88
 Third Reich, persecution during 87
anti-Jewish prejudice. *See* antisemitism
antisemitism 61, 63, 65, 82–83, 85
 Black Death (1347–51) 83
 during Enlightenment 83
 economic competition 83
 First Crusade (1096–99) 83
 modern 84
 Portuguese Inquisition 83
 Protestant Reformation 83
 racial 82
 Spanish Inquisition 83
anti-slavery abolitionist movement 72
Apartheid Convention 182
Applebaum, Anne 1
Argentina's Dirty War 147–48
Armenian genocide 13–14, 190–92
Aryan supremacy 82
assimilation 182
Aung San Suu Kyi 211
Australia's Stolen Generations 75–76
auto-genocide 152–53
 Cambodian genocide 1, 42, 152, 153, 154, 172–76
Axis Rule in Occupied Europe: Laws of Occupation, Analysis of Government Proposals for Redress (Lemkin) 2, 10, 13, 14, 17, 18, 21, 27, 29, 34, 36, 43, 52, 69, 103, 125, 152, 179, 190
Aycock, Charles 78

B

Bachelet, Michelle 17
Bachman, Jeffrey 23, 30, 125, 126, 141, 144, 182, 203
Bagosora, Théoneste 200
Ban Ki Moon 205
Bangladesh genocide 9, 116–17, 144–47
 sexual violence during 9, 117–18
barbarism 14, 15, 17, 31, 35, 110

Barta, Tony 28
Bartov, Omer 45, 69
Battle of Little Bighorn 49
Beevor, Antony 113, 115, 141
Belgian Congo 74, 186–88
Bell-Fialkoff, Andrew 32, 39
Beveridge, Albert J. 48
Biden, Joe 53
Bismarck, Otto Von 183
Black Death (1347–51) 83
Blinken, Antony 42
Blood, Archer 146
Bolshevik Revolution (1917) 8
Bosnian genocide 39–40, 65, 195–97
  sexual violence during 9, 40, 118–19, 120
Boutros-Ghali, Boutros 200
Brown, Haley Marie 108
Brown, John 72
Brownmiller, Susan 113, 114, 117
Bryant, Michael C. 50
Budak, Mile 194

C

Cambodian genocide, Khmer Rouge and 1, 42, 152, 153, 154
  bourgeoisie class, destruction of 153, 174–75
  collectivities 171
  death rate during 176
  Fall of Phnom Penh 172
  forced deportation of urban residents 173
  forced labor 173
  leap forward 173
  non-Khmer ethnic or religious groups, assault on 174–75
  prosecutions in ECCC 209–10
  segregation 173–74
  Vietnamese in Cambodia and in Khmer Rouge, cleansing of 175
Casement, Roger 187
Césaire, Aimé 102
Chalk, Frank 30
Chamberlain, Kevin 69
Chandler, David 175
Chang, Iris 110, 112
Charny, Israel 30
Chea, Nuon 210
Chechen Republic of Ichkeria 59
Chechen-Ingush Autonomous Soviet Socialist Republic 56
Chechen-Ingush people deportation 57–59
Chiang Kai-shek 110

China
  Great Leap Forward 166–69
  Japanese invasion of
    Manchuria 109–10
    Rape of Nanking (Nanjing) 110–13
  Mao's Great Famine 152, 164–66
Chinese Civil War 164
Chivington, John 50
Churchill, Winston 19, 73
Circassians, ethnic cleansing of 55–57
Civil Rights Congress 95, 96, 97
Civil Rights Movement 77, 95, 96, 97
civil war 98
  Guatemalan 98–99
  in Sudan 99–101
classicide 136, 151–52
  Cambodian genocide 1, 42, 152, 153, 154, 172–76
  in China
    Great Famine, Mao's 164–66
    Great Leap Forward 166–69
  Stalin's collectivization policy in the Soviet Union. *See* collectivization policy
Cold War 12, 75, 96, 97, 117, 127, 144
collectivization policy 154–57
  bab'i bunty (women's protest) 160
  Dizzy with Success (Stalin) 160–64
  economic disruption 161
  party officials or collectivizers, assassinating 158
  peasants' resistance to 157–60
  slaughter of farm animals 158–60
  Stalin's assault on peasants for resisting to join collective 160–64
colonization, genocidal 9, 14, 18, 19, 20, 23, 28, 43, 45, 125, 152
  Congolese genocide 74, 186–88
  Herero and Nama Genocide 75, 183–86
  Native Americans, settler colonialism on 46–53
comfort women 105–6, 113
communism 96, 97, 119, 129, 138, 140, 141, 142, 143, 144, 147, 152, 155, 166, 170, 176, 195
Communist Manifesto (Marx & Engels) 128
Confino, Alon 87
Congo Free State 74, 186, 187
Congolese genocide 74, 186–88
Conrad, Joseph 187
Convention on the Prevention and Punishment of the Crime of Genocide. *See* Genocide Convention (1948)

Cribb, Robert 142
Crimean Tatars 63
   deportation 59–61
Crowe, David 43, 72
cultural genocide 17, 23, 34, 35, 36, 46,
   179–80
   Armenian genocide 13–14, 190–92
   Bosnian genocide 39–40, 195–97
   colonialism and 180–83
   definition
      Chamberlain 69
      Davidson 69
   of First Nations 53–55
   in Genocide Convention, exclusion of 22,
      23–24, 27, 126, 180–81
   of Mayan peoples 98–99
   of Native Americans 52–53
   Rwandan genocide 9, 31, 35,
      199–201, 209
cultural violence 77

D

Dallaire, Romeo 200
Darfur genocide 99–101
Darusman, Marzuki 41
Davidson, Lawrence 69
Dayan, Moshe 67
de Tocqueville, Alexis 55
de Waal, Alex 100
dekulakization 134–36, 138, 139, 154, 156,
   157, 158, 160
democide 152
   Mao's Great Famine 152, 164–66
Deng Xiaoping 165, 177
depopulation 103
deportation 214. *See also* ethnic cleansing
destruction 2, 6, 7, 8, 10, 14, 15, 16, 17, 18, 20,
   23, 25, 26, 27, 28, 29, 30, 32, 33, 34,
   35, 39, 45, 65, 69, 118, 123, 153. *See also*
   annihilation; extermination
   cultural 16, 21, 22, 23, 27, 28, 35, 69
   economic 34
   forcible 8, 14
   group 32, 35, 36, 37, 39, 106
   of Native Americans 46
   physical 24, 27, 32, 39, 67
   social 35
   Stalin's destruction of peoples 57–65
   of Yugoslavia 39
The Destruction of the European Jews
   (Hilberg) 16
Development of Capitalism in Russia (Lenin) 129

Dikotter, Frank 167, 168
Dirty War 147–48
Djilas, Milovan 115
Djindjic, Zoran 211
Doctors' Plot 64, 133
Dolot, Miron 162
Doolittle, James 112
Drost, Pieter 30
DuBois, W. E. B. 71
Duterte, Rodrigo 153

E

ECCC. *See* Extraordinary Chambers of the
   Courts of Cambodia (ECCC)
Ehrenburg, Il'ia 62
Engels, Friedrich 127, 128
ethnic cleansing 3, 9, 16, 26, 31–33, 35–36,
   69, 181, 217
   Bangladesh genocide 9, 117
   Bosnian genocide 39–40, 65, 195–97
   of Circassians 55–57
   definition 32
   during Cambodian genocide 173, 175
   during partition of India 33, 116, 145
   Gaza genocide 6–7, 213–16
   genocide *vs.* 39, 51
   of Native Americans 47–48
   of Kosovo Muslims by Serb forces
      196–97
   of Mayan 98–99
   in Palestine 32–33
   Nakba 65–69
   of Polish Jews during Germany
      invasion 89
   of Rohingya from Myanmar to
      Bangladesh 40–42, 65
   Rwandan genocide 9, 31, 35, 199–201, 209
   of Stalin
      Chechen-Ingush 57–59
      Crimean Tatars 59–61
      and Jews 61–65
      Volga Germans 57
ethnocide 2, 23, 34, 35, 36, 152
European colonialism and imperialism 183
   Congolese genocide 74, 186–88
   Herero and Nama Genocide 75, 183–86
   India's famine relief under British rule 74
   Scramble for Africa 73–74, 183, 187, 198
   in South Africa 182
   South West Africa, German colonization
      of 183–86
   the Holocaust. *See* the Holocaust

European Union Rapid Deployment Capacity (EU RDC) 206
Evans, John 50
extermination 2, 6, 9, 14, 20, 25, 26, 29, 44, 45, 89, 102, 137, 141, 184, 214, 217. *See also* annihilation; destruction
  Armenian genocide 13–14, 190–92
  camps in the Holocaust 16
  of Native Americans 50, 51–52
Extraordinary Chambers of the Courts of Cambodia (ECCC) 209–10

F

Fabri, Friedrich 183
Fein, Helen 28, 31, 105, 189
Finzsch, Norbert 127
First Chechen War 59
First Crusade (1096–99) 83
First Nations, cultural genocide of 53–55
Fisher, Siobhan 104
Fitzpatrick, Sheila 157
Fitzpatrick, Thomas 49
forcible impregnation 103, 104–5, 116, 217
  during Bosnian genocide 118, 119
Franco, Francisco 124, 141
Frank, Hans 90
Friedlander, Henry 92

G

Gallant, Yoav 216
gang rape 101, 119
Gaza genocide 6–7, 213–16
Gebhardt, Miriam 114, 115
gendercide 106, 151
  heteronormative women 108–9
  LGTBQ peoples (homophobia) 107–8
  men 106–7, 117
  transgender women (transphobia) 108
general danger to humanity 13, 14
Geneva Convention (1949) 4, 5
genocidaires 12
genocidal intent 4, 6, 7, 8, 10, 15, 18, 23, 25, 27–29, 46, 104, 106, 205
  characterization of 30–31
genocidal massacres
  Bangladesh genocide 117, 145–46
  of Chechens 59
  Dos Erres massacre 99
  during Armenian genocide 190, 192
  Indonesian genocide 126, 142–44
  Nanjing Massacre 110–13
  of Native Americans 50–51
  of Rohingya 41
  Tulsa Race Massacre of 1921 80–81
  Wilmington massacre of 1898 78–80
genocidal rape 103–4
  forcible impregnation 103, 104–5, 116, 118, 119
  gang rape 101, 119
  mass rape. *See* mass rape
  men 106–7
genocide 181, 189
  in Asia and Europe 1–2
  definition 10, 17, 37, 180
    Drost 30
    in Genocide Convention (legal definition) 21–27, 29–30, 31
  ethnic conflicts 188–89
  euphemisms for 31–36
  group, violence against any 11
  interventions 204
  Lemkin and concept of 2, 13–19, 34–35, 36, 69, 106, 123, 153–54, 164, 179, 188
  Nazis' genocide of Jews. *See* the Holocaust
  neologism of 13
  phases 18–19
  prevention 203–7
  process 15–16, 32
  punishment for 207–18
  The Responsibility to Protect (R2P) 204–5, 205
  victims, people as 10, 11
  war and 10
  warnings 204
Genocide and Political Groups (Nersessian) 126
Genocide Convention (1948) 4, 7, 8, 9, 11, 12, 34, 35, 46, 67, 96, 101, 116, 120, 126–28, 144, 154
  Ad Hoc Committee on Genocide 22, 180
  approval and adoption of 24, 27, 180
  Article I 24–25
  Article II 25, 127, 180, 182
  Article III 5, 25, 180
  Article III (c) 6
  Article IV 207
  Article VI 207
  Article XII 182, 213
  Article XIV 217
  Article XXIV 127
  Article XXV 127
  drafting resolution 21–24
  forcible impregnation in 104–5

genocide prosecution under 207–18
legal definition of genocide 21–27, 29–30
  cultural genocide in, exclusion of 22, 23–24, 27, 126, 180–81
  political groups exclusion from 22–23, 27, 125–26, 140
  limitations of legal definition 27
  destroy, use of ambiguous word 29
  groups, unclear definition of 29
  intent, use of word 27–29
  Naimark on 30
  protected groups of 124, 125, 151
  "Secretariat" Draft 21, 22, 180, 203, 204
  on sexual violence 103–4
  UN Charter and 203–7
  United States, ratification by 26–27, 127
genocidists 8, 9, 11, 28, 29, 30, 32, 36, 41, 103, 104, 106, 108, 124, 140, 143, 144, 152, 153, 185, 187, 189, 191, 218
intention 27
Gesse, Natalia 115
Goebbels, Joseph 85
Gorbachev, Mikhail 135, 139
Graziosi, Andrea 163
Great Famine, Mao's 152, 164–66
Great Purge 8, 34, 138–41, 169
Grossman, Vasilii 62
Guatemala genocide 97–99
Guillotin, Joseph-Ignace 137
Guterres, Antonio 42
Guzman, Jacobo Arbenz 147
gynocide 109

H
Habyarimana, Juvénal 199
Hagari, Daniel 216
Hamas attack on Israelis 6–7, 67–68, 213–16
Harper, Stephen 54
Hasečić, Bakira 119
Haviland, C. Augustus 51
Heart of Darkness (Conrad) 187
Herero and Nama Genocide 75, 183–84, 186
  Battle of Waterberg 185
  black problem 185
  debt collection, restrictions on 184
  Maharero's revolt against German colonizers 184–85
  taking control of fertile lands 184
  von Trotha's annihilation 185–86
Herzl, Theodor 66
Herzog, Isaac 6
Herzog, Yitzhak 67

Heuveline, Patrick 176
Hilberg, Raul 16
Himmler, Heinrich 18, 43
The History and Sociology of Genocide (Jonassohn and Chalk) 30
Hitler, Adolf 9, 84–85, 161, 190
  antisemitism 85
  Beer Hall Putsch 85
  Final Solution 13, 16, 34, 42, 89–90
  the Holocaust. *See* the Holocaust
  Mein Kampf 18, 42, 73, 85
  Nazi Party, birth and elections of 85–87
  Rassenkampf (race war) in the East 42–45
Hitler's Army: Soldiers, Nazis, and War in the Third Reich (Bartov) 45
Hitler's Beneficiaries: Plunder, Racial War, and the Nazi Welfare State (Aly) 45
Holmes, Oliver Wendell 93
the Holocaust 1, 2, 9, 13, 14, 15, 17–18, 25, 27, 29, 32, 33, 45, 66, 82, 113, 190, 212
  Aktion T4, 93
  anti-Jewish persecution, stages in 87–88
  Armenian genocide and 190
  Birkenau 90
  Chelmno 90
  depopulation 103
  ethnic cleansing 18, 34, 43, 51
    vs. Rohingya ethnic cleansing 42
  extermination camps 16, 91
    Auschwitz-Birkenau 90, 92
  Final Solution 13, 16, 34, 42, 89–90
  France, military troops in 44–45
  General Plan for the East 18
  Hunger Plan 43–44
  International Military Tribunal (IMT) 19–21
  Jewish resistance 90–91
  killing centers 90
  Kristallnacht 78, 88
  Law for the Prevention of Hereditarily Diseased Offspring 93
  Law for the Restoration of the Professional Civil Service 94
  mass murder of Jews in 16, 43, 89, 90
  Nuremberg Laws (1935) 87–88, 92
  Nuremberg Trial 19–21
    Jackson opening speech at 23, 26
  Poland, Germany invasion of 16, 20, 88–89
    killing centers in 90
    Warsaw Ghetto Uprising 90–91
  preconditions for 84

the Holocaust (*Continued*)
  Rhineland bastards 93–94
  Roma and Sinti victims (non-Jewish victims) 92
  Soviet Union, invasion of 16, 18, 43
    Operation Barbarossa 89
  SS *Einsatzgruppen* 20
  Third Reich 18, 33, 87, 88, 114
    end of 94–95
  Wehrmacht 44
Holodomor 155, 159, 162
Homestead Act of 1863 48
homophobia 107–8
homosexual activity 107–8
human groups 29
human race. *See* race and racism
Human Rights Council 3
humanity, crimes against 17, 20, 21, 32, 35, 39, 40, 41, 104, 105, 121, 182, 197, 210, 212, 214, 215, 216, 217, 218
  Atlantic slave trade 105
  comfort women 105–6, 113
  criminal activity 105
  rape. *See* gang rape; genocidal rape; mass rape
Hutu and Tutsi genocide. *See* Rwandan genocide

I

Iakovlev, Aleksandr 58
ICC. *See* International Criminal Court (ICC)
ICJ. *See* International Court of Justice (ICJ)
ICTR. *See* International Criminal Tribunal for Rwanda (ICTR)
ICTY. *See* International Criminal Tribunal for the former Yugoslavia (ICTY)
imperialism 181
  Belgian Congo 74, 186–88
  European. *See* European colonialism and imperialism
  experimenting new technologies on colonies during 74–75
  India's famine relief under British rule 74
IMT. *See* International Military Tribunal (IMT)
Independent International Commission of Inquiry on Ukraine 3–4
Independent Investigative Mechanism for Myanmar 212
Indian Act 53
indigenous peoples

Chechen-Ingush people deportation 57–59
Chechens, genocidal massacres of 59
Crimean Tatars deportation 59–61
First Nations, cultural genocide of 53–55
Maya genocide 98–99
Native Americans, cultural genocide of 52–53
Stolen Generations, Australia's 75–76
Indonesian genocide 126, 142–44
International Court of Justice (ICJ) 6, 7, 26, 39, 40, 68, 197, 211–12
  Hamas attack on Israelis prosecution 213–16
International Criminal Court (ICC) 4, 5, 100, 120, 153, 180, 204, 207, 208, 210, 211, 212, 218
  Hamas attack on Israelis prosecution 213–16
  Rome Statute 4, 5, 208, 214, 215, 216–17, 218
International Criminal Tribunal for Rwanda (ICTR) 119, 121, 201, 208, 218
International Criminal Tribunal for the former Yugoslavia (ICTY) 40, 106, 119, 120, 197, 201, 208–9, 218
  Bosnian genocide prosecution 210
International Military Tribunal (IMT) 19–21
International Military Tribunal for the Far East 104, 112
International Residual Mechanism for Criminal Tribunals (IRMCT) 209
IRMCT. *See* International Residual Mechanism for Criminal Tribunals (IRMCT)
Irvin-Erickson, Douglas 15, 16, 17, 36, 96, 125, 153, 179, 181
Israel
  Arab League attack on 7
  Hamas attack on 6–7, 67–68
  Palestinian *Nakba* 65–69
JAC. *See* Jewish Anti-Fascist Committee (JAC)

J

Jackson, Robert 23, 26
Japan
  China, invasion of 110–11, 112–13
  males, violence against 112
  Manchuria 109–10
  Matsui's condemnation on Japanese troops action on Chinese 111, 112
  Nanking Safety Zone 110
  raping of Chinese woman 111–12
  comfort women 105–6, 113

imperialist power 109–10
Korea, invasion of 109–10
Jewish Anti-Fascist Committee (JAC) 62
Jews
  anti-Jewish persecution 87–88
  anti-Jewish prejudice. *See* antisemitism
  Nazis' genocide of. *See* the Holocaust
  Stalin's ethnic cleansing and 61–65
Jim Crow laws 76–78, 81, 182
Jonassohn, Kurt 30, 34
Jones, Adam 195, 201

K
Kadyrov, Ramzan 59, 107
Kagame, Paul 201
Kaganovich, Lazar 163
Kaing Guek Eav 210
Kakel III, Carroll P. 48
Kalinin, Mikhail 62
Kamenev, Lev 137
Karadzic, Radovan 195
Katz, Steven 29
Kayishima, Fulgence 209
Khalidi, Rashid 66
Khan, Ayub 116
Khan, Yahya 145
Khmer Rouge 170
  genocide by. *See* Cambodian genocide, Khmer Rouge and
Kiernan, Ben 173, 174, 176
Kiir, Salva 101
King, Martin Luther, Jr. 19–21, 71, 77, 95
Kipling, Rudyard 48
Kissinger, Henry 117
Kopelev, Lev 155
Kosior, Stanislav 135
Kristallnacht 78, 88
Krstic, Radislav 28, 195
kulaks 129, 139, 157, 158, 161
  collectivization effort against.
    See collectivization policy
  dekulakization 134–36, 138, 139, 154, 156, 157, 158, 160
  exile of 125, 128
Kuper, Leo 30, 126
Kyiv 131

L
Lauterpacht, Elihu 39
Lebensraum (living space) 9, 18, 42, 43, 45, 88, 89
LeBlanc, Lawrence 126

Lemkin, Raphael 2, 13, 46, 103, 179, 188, 203, 216, 217
  about killing 25
  Axis Rule in Occupied Europe: Laws of Occupation, Analysis of Government Proposals for Redress 2, 10, 13, 14, 17, 18, 21, 27, 29, 34, 36, 43, 52, 69, 103, 125, 152, 179, 190
  barbarism 14, 15, 17
  on depopulation 103
  genocide legal definition and. *See* Genocide Convention (1948)
  objectives of destruction 123
  political groups inclusion in Convention genocide definition 124–25
  on racism 76
  vandalism 14, 15
  We Charge Genocide, disagreement about 96–97
Lenin, Vladimir 128, 129
  Bolsheviks 129, 130
  korenizatsiya 133
  kulaks 129
  New Economic Policy (NEP) 129–30, 138
  rich and poor peasants 129
Leopold II, King 74, 186, 187, 188. *See also* Congolese genocide
Leutwein, Theodor 184
Levene, Mark 92
LGTBQ peoples, sexual violence against 107–8
Lie, Trygve 21, 217
Limpieza de sangre 71, 83
Lincoln, Abraham 79
Lindqvist, Sven 45, 74, 102
Lippman, Matthew 30
Lowery, Wesley 81
Luderitz, Adolf 183
Lumumba, Patrice 187
Lvova-Belova, Maria 4

M
Maharero, Samuel 184, 186
Malik, Amita 118
Manifest Destiny 9, 45, 48
Manly, Alexander 79
Mann, Michael 40, 151, 189
Mao Zedong 154
  backyard furnace 167–68
  communism 177
  Cultural Revolution of 1966–7, 154

Mao Zedong (*Continued*)
  exploitation of the peasantry 164–65, 167
  famine during Mao's rule 167, 168–69
  grain exports 167
  Great Famine 152, 164–66
  Great Leap Forward 166–69
  Great Proletarian Cultural Revolution 169
  Stalin's Russia *vs.* Mao's China 169–70
  steel production during Mao's rule 167–68
  Zhou opposition to Mao's "rash advance" 165
Marx, Karl 127, 128, 156, 176
  bourgeoisie as peasantry 128
Marxian socialism 155
mass expulsion 32
mass killing 2, 11, 14, 17, 25, 30, 32, 34, 35, 105, 124, 154, 181. *See also* auto-genocide
  during Guatemala genocide 99
  gender-selective 106
  Indonesian genocide 126, 142–44
mass murder 2, 11, 14, 17, 18, 22, 34, 39, 88, 89, 90, 117. *See also* auto-genocide
  Aktion T4, 93
  during Armenian genocide 190, 192
  of Jews in the Holocaust 16, 43, 89, 90
  Rwandan genocide 9, 31, 35, 199–201
mass rape 104, 105, 106, 113, 115
  during Bangladesh genocide 9, 117–18
  during Bosnian genocide 9, 40, 118–19, 196
  during Herero and Nama Genocide 185
  during Rohingya genocide 41
  during Rwandan genocide 120, 201
  of German women by Soviet Red Army soldiers 113–16
  Rape of Nanking (Nanjing) 110–13
Matsui Iwane 111, 112
Maya genocide 98–99
McGregor, Jo Ann 189
Medvedev, Roy 60
men, sexual violence against 106–7, 117
Mikhoels, Theater Solomon 62
Miliutin, Dmitrii 56
Milosevic, Slobodan 194, 195, 197, 208, 210, 211
Mladic, Ratko 195, 196, 209, 210
modern warfare 10
Molotov, Vyacheslav 61
Morel, E. D., 187
Morgan, Thomas Jefferson 52

Morgenthau, Henry 191
Morris, Benny 67
Mose, Erik 4, 6

N

Naimark, Norman 30, 32, 39, 56, 58, 69, 114, 134, 139
*Nakba, P*alestinian 65–69
Nanjing Massacre 110–13
nation 17, 151
Native Americans
  cultural genocide of 52–53
  decline in population of 49
  extermination of 50, 51–52
  genocidal massacre of 50–51
  Jim Thorpe, false accusation on 53
  population in California 50
  settler colonialism and ethnic cleansing of 46–50
  Wounded Knee massacre of 50–51
Nazis' genocide of Jews. *See* the Holocaust
NEP. *See* New Economic Policy (NEP)
Nersessian, David 126
Netanyahu, Benjamin 6, 68, 214
New Economic Policy (NEP) 129–30, 138
New Imperialism 74
Nixon, Richard 79, 117
Nol, Lon 175
Non-Aggression Pact 57
Nugent, Walter 47
Nuremberg Laws (1935) 87–88, 92
Nuremberg Trial 19–21
  Jackson opening speech at 23, 26
Nyiramasuhuko, Pauline 121
Nylander, Femi 179

O

Obama, Barack 53, 80, 192
Operation Barbarossa 89
O'Sullivan, John 48
Overy, Richard 115

P

Palestine. *See also* Gaza genocide
  ethnic cleansing 32–33
  Nakba 65–69
  Hamas attack on Israelis 6–7, 67–68, 213–16
Pappe, Ilan 65
Patterson, William 95
Payne, Robert 117
peace, crimes against 20

Pegorier, Clotilde 35
Peron, Isabel 147
Peron, Juan 147
perpetrators 2, 8, 10, 11, 28, 32
Perry, Matthew 109
Pfannmüller, Hermann 93
Pinaud, Clémence 101
Poland, Germany invasion of 16, 20, 88–89
    killing centers in 90
    Warsaw Ghetto Uprising 90–91
political groups, genocide of. *See* politicide
politicide 123–24, 151
    Argentina's Dirty War 147–48
    Bangladesh genocide 9, 116–18, 144–47
    genocide *vs.* 124–25
    Indonesian Communist Party, annihilation of 126, 142–44
    political groups exclusion from Genocide Convention 22–23, 27, 125–26, 140
    Soviet Union 125
    Spain, left and working-class movements suppression by Franco in 141–42
    Ukraine, Russia and Soviet Union politicide on 128–34
    Vendee region during French Revolution, counter-revolution in 136–37
The Politics of Genocide: From the Genocide Convention to the Responsibility to Protect (Bachman) 203
population transfers. *See* ethnic cleansing
Portuguese Inquisition 83
Pot, Pol (Saloth Sar) 154, 170, 171–72, 210. *See also* Cambodian genocide, Khmer Rouge and
communism 177
Powell, Christopher 22
Power, Samantha 39, 203
Protestant Reformation 83
Pushkin, A.S. 160
Putin, Vladimir 4, 59, 108, 128, 205, 211
    and Russian invasion of Ukraine 132

R
Rabe, John 110
Rabin, Yitzhak 68
race and racism 71, 151. *See also* cultural genocide; sexual violence
    and Darfur genocide 99–101
    European racism 72, 73, 102
        Congolese genocide 74, 186–88
        Herero and Nama Genocide 75, 183–86
        Scramble for Africa 73–74, 183, 187, 198
    and German Nazism. *See* the Holocaust
    and Guatemala genocide 97–99
    King on 71, 77–78
    overview 71–73
    savage races 73
    Social Darwinism and 73, 92
    Stolen Generations, Australia's 75–76
    in United States
        Jim Crow laws 76–78, 81, 182
        Tulsa Race Massacre of 1921 80–81
        Wilmington massacre of 1898 78–80
    vanishing races 73
racial groups 72
Radovan, Karadzic 209
Ranger, Terence 189
rape. *See also* gang rape; genocidal rape; mass rape
    definition 121
The Rape of Nanking (Chang) 112
Rape of Nanking (Nanjing) 110–13
Razic, Berina Zutic 106
Reagan, Ronald 147
Removal Act of 1830, 47
Rhineland bastards 93–94
Ríos Montt, Efraín 98, 99
Robeson, Paul 95
Roediger, David 71
Rohingya genocide 2
    ethnic cleansing of Rohingya Muslims 40–42, 65
    prosecutions 211, 212
Rome Statute 4, 5, 208, 214, 215, 216–17, 218
Roosevelt, Eleanor 97
Roosevelt, Franklin Delano 19, 161
Rudd, Kevin 76
Rummel, Rudolph 152
Russia 59, 61, 90, 109, 113, 115
    Circassians, ethnic cleansing of 55–57
    Hitler's war against 9, 18, 42, 43, 44, 45
    October Revolution 129
    smychka 129
    Ukraine, politicide on 131, 133–34
        domination by Russia 131–32
        Kyiv 131
    War Communism 129, 138
Russian Civil War 156
Russian invasion of Ukraine 208
    Crimea, annexation of 132
    Donbas, allegations of genocide in 6
    forcible transfers of Ukrainian children to Russia 5

Russian invasion of Ukraine (*Continued*)
  Independent International Commission of Inquiry on Ukraine 3–4
  Mose statement on genocide in Ukraine 4, 6
  Putin and 132
    arrest warrants against 4, 5
  Sergeitsev on 6
  Special Military Operation 207
  violation of human rights 4
  war crimes 4–5
Rwanda 197–99
  akazu 199
  Hutu Parties and independence, emergence of 199–201
  Rwandan Patriotic Front (RPF) 199
Rwandan genocide 9, 31, 35, 119–20, 199–201, 209
  International Criminal Tribunal for Rwanda (ICTR) 119, 121, 201, 208
  sexual violence during 120, 201
Rzheshevskii, Oleg 115

S
Schabas, William 17, 21, 28, 40, 197
Scramble for Africa 73–74, 183, 187, 198
SCSL. *See* Special Court for Sierra Leone (SCSL)
selective genocide 146
settler colonialism 65, 181
  in Canada 53
  European. *See* European colonialism and imperialism
  on Native Americans 46–53
sexual violence 121
  during Argentina's Dirty War 147
  during Bangladesh genocide 9, 117–18
  during Bosnian genocide 9, 40, 118–19, 120, 196
  during Darfur genocide 101
  during Herero and Nama Genocide 185
  during Japanese invasion of China 110–13
  during Rohingya genocide 41
  during Rwandan genocide 120, 201
  during Soviet Union invasion of Germany 113–16
  forcible impregnation 103, 104–5, 116, 118, 119
  gendercide 106
    heteronormative women 108–9
    LGTBQ peoples (homophobia) 107–8
    men 106–7, 117
    transgender women (transphobia) 108
  in Genocide Convention 103–4
Sharlach, Lisa 118
Shaw, Martin 11, 15, 25, 28, 33, 34, 35, 36, 37, 65, 69, 109, 123, 126, 153, 181, 188
Shawcross, Hartley, Sir 20
Sheikh Mansur Battalion 59
Sihanouk, Norodom 175
social class/groups, genocide of. *See* classicide
Soviet Union 8, 131, 133
  Circassians, ethnic cleansing of 55–57
  collectivization policy 154–57
    bab'i bunty (women's protest) 160
    Dizzy with Success (Stalin) 160–64
    economic disruption 161
    party officials or collectivizers, assassinating 158
    peasants' resistance to 157–60
    slaughter of farm animals 158–60
    Stalin's assault on peasants for resisting to join collective 160–64
  Communist Party 63, 129, 156
    Left Opposition 138, 139
    Right Opposition 139
  Doctors' Plot 64, 133
  Great Purge, Stalin's 8, 34, 138–41, 169
  Holodomor 155, 159, 162
  Jewish Anti-Fascist Committee (JAC) 62
  korenizatsiya 133
  kulaks 129, 139, 161
    dekulakization 134–36, 138, 139, 154, 156, 157, 158, 160
    exile of 125, 128
  mass rape of German women by Soviet Red Army soldiers 113–16
  Nazis invasion of 16, 18, 43
    Hunger Plan 43–44
    Operation Barbarossa 89
  New Economic Policy (NEP) 129–30, 138
  politicide 125
  Stalin's ethnic cleansing
    Chechen-Ingush 57–59
    Crimean Tatars 59–61
    Volga Germans 57
Spain, politicide in 141–42
Spanish Inquisition 83
Special Court for Sierra Leone (SCSL) 209

Spencer, Herbert 73
Srebrenica massacre 9, 40, 51, 106, 196, 208
Stalin, Joseph 8, 9, 16, 19, 22, 115, 123, 130, 151, 166
  assault on Ukrainian intelligentsia 128–34, 154, 156, 157, 158, 160
  collectivization policy 154–57
    bab'i bunty (women's protest) 160
    Dizzy with Success 160–64
    economic disruption 161
    party officials or collectivizers, assassinating 158
    peasants' resistance to 157–60
    slaughter of farm animals 158–60
    Stalin's assault on peasants for resisting to join collective 160–64
  communism 176–77
  ethnic cleansing
    Chechen-Ingush 57–59
    Crimean Tatars 59–61
    and Jews 61–65
    Volga Germans 57
  Great Purge 8, 34, 138–41, 169
  kulaks
    dekulakization 134–36, 138, 139
    exile of 125, 128
  social revolution 130–31
  Stalin's Russia *vs.* Mao's China 169–70
  Trotsky, opposition to 138
Stannard, David 46
Stanton, Gregory 204
state-building through genocide 188–90
  Armenian genocide 190–92
  Bosnian genocide 39–40, 195–97
  Rwandan genocide 9, 31, 35, 199–201
Stolen Generations, Australia's 75–76
Strauss, Scott 29
structural violence 77
Sudan People's Liberation Army (SPLA) 101

T
Talaat Pasha 191
Taylor, Charles 209
Temple, Richard, Sir 74
Thaci, Hashim 210
Third Reich 18, 33, 87, 88, 114
  end of 94–95
Thompson, E. P. 151
Tillman, Ben 78
Tito, Joseph 194
Totten, Samuel 100

Trail of Tears 47
transgender women, sexual violence against 108
transgendercide 109
transphobia 108
Traverso, Enzo 102
Treaty of Fort Laramie 48
Treaty of Westphalia 26
Trotsky, Leon 137–38, 155, 162
  Stalin's opposition to 138, 139
Trudeau, Justin 54
Truman, Harry 81
Trump, Donald J. 84, 192
Truth and Reconciliation Commission (TRC) 54
Tucker, Robert 130
Tudjman, Franjo 195
Tulsa Race Massacre of 1921, 80–81
Turkish genocide of Armenians 13–14, 190–92
Tusan, Michelle 36
Tyson, Timothy 80

U
Ukraine
  collectivization policy
    bab'i bunty (women's protest) 160
    party officials or collectivizers, assassinating 158
    peasants' resistance to join collective in 157–60
    slaughter of farm animals 158–60
    Stalin's assault on peasants for resisting to join collective 160–64
  Holodomor 155, 159, 162
  Kyiv 131
  Russia and. *See* Russia, Ukraine, politicide on; Russian invasion of Ukraine
  Soviet Union and. *See* Soviet Union
UN Charter 146, 148, 182, 203, 204
  Article 2, 144
  Chapter VI 205, 206
  Chapter VII 205, 206, 218
  international peace and security under 144, 146, 203
UN Resolution 96 (I), The Crime of Genocide 21, 36, 123, 125
United Nation Protection Force (UNPROFOR) 196
United Nations General Assembly 4, 21, 22, 24, 36, 39, 41, 42, 68, 101, 125, 180, 182, 204, 206

United Nations Security Council (UNSC) 4, 7, 41, 144, 146, 182, 197, 203, 204, 205, 206, 208, 212, 218
  International Criminal Tribunal for Rwanda (ICTR) 119, 121, 201, 208, 218
  International Criminal Tribunal for the former Yugoslavia (ICTY) 40, 106, 119, 120, 197, 201, 208–9, 210, 218
United States
  and Armenian genocide 192
  compulsory sterilization of disabled people 92–93
  racism in
    Jim Crow laws 76–78, 81, 182
    Tulsa Race Massacre of 1921, 80–81
    We Charge Genocide 95–97
    Wilmington massacre of 1898, 78–80
  settler colonialism and Native Americans' ethnic cleansing 46–50
Universal Declaration of Human Rights 4, 101, 206
Uwilingiyimana, Agathe 200
Uyghur Forced Labor Prevention Act 2
Uyghurs in China, genocide of 2, 16–17

V

vandalism 14, 15
Vendee region, counter-revolution in 136–37
victim groups 30, 31
Videla, Jorge Rafael 147
Viola, Lynne 157
virtue signaling 101
Volga Germans deportation 57
von Trotha, Lothar 75, 185

W

Waddell, Alfred Moore 79
War and Genocide in South Sudan (Pinaud) 101

war crimes 4, 5, 6, 10, 19, 20, 104, 105, 107, 111, 115, 118, 193, 197, 207, 210, 214
Warsaw Ghetto Uprising 90–91
We Charge Genocide 26, 95–96
  Lemkin's disagreement about 96–97
Weiss-Wendt, Anton 26, 31, 125
Weitz, Eric D., 34, 171, 173, 174
Weitz, Yosef 66
Wetter, Gustav 140
Wilhelm II, Kaiser 84
Wilmington massacre of 1898, 78–80
Wolfe, Patrick 181
World Court. *See* International Court of Justice (ICJ)
World War I, 73, 75, 84, 93, 190
  aftermath of 84
  Turkish genocide of Armenians during 13–14, 190–92
World War II, 2, 10, 11, 12, 31, 88–89, 92, 94, 101, 110, 115, 142, 194, 197, 212
  and Stalin's destruction of peoples 57–65

X

Xinjiang genocide 2, 16–17, 205

Y

Yakovlev, Alexander 139
Yeltsin, Boris 59
Yugoslavia 192, 193–94, 201
  Germany invasion of 194–95

Z

Zhdanov, Andrei 63, 64
Zhou Enlai 165
  opposition to Mao's "rash advance", 165
Zinoviev, Grigory 137

www.ingramcontent.com/pod-product-compliance
Lightning Source LLC
Chambersburg PA
CBHW021139230426
43667CB00005B/186